Praise for *Spontaneous Evolution*

"Spontaneous Evolution is the life-map we've all been...
With just the right blend of spiritual humor and rock-solid science, Bruce
Lipton and Steve Bhaerman cast a holistic new light on an emerging new
civilization. They lead us beyond collapsing economies and religious extremes
to show us that such chaos is a natural step in an unfolding process, rather
than the tragic end to a broken planet. Once we recognize the big picture, the
choices to a better life and a better world become obvious. The guiding
role of **Spontaneous Evolution** is where our teachings of life,
history, and civilization should begin. I love this book!"*

— **Gregg Braden,** *New York Times* best-selling author of
The Divine Matrix and *Fractal Time*

"The implications of this powerful book have the potential to change the world."

— **Deepak Chopra,** *New York Times* best-selling author of *The Third Jesus*

*"**Spontaneous Evolution** offers an enlightening view of humanity's past,
and an empowering vision of our 'mammalian' destiny. Based on cellular
biologist Bruce Lipton's solid science, informed by Steve Bhaerman's political
insight and wit, this book is a must-read for anyone who seeks to lovingly
transform the world, and fulfill her or his most creative and powerful self."*

— **Marianne Williamson,** author of *The Age of Miracles*

*"**Spontaneous Evolution** is a world-changing book that offers a heartening view
of humanity's destiny. Built on the foundation of the latest discoveries in science,
it points us in the direction of functional politics, sustainable economics, and
individual responsibility in the context of an interdependent community."*

— **Thom Hartmann,** author of *The Last Hours of Ancient Sunlight*

*"This wise and thoughtful book is a powerful antidote for anyone who is pessimistic
and depressed about our future and the challenges we face as humans."*

— **Larry Dossey, M.D.,** author of *The Power of Premonitions*

*"**Spontaneous Evolution** is a brilliant synthesis of science, evolutionary
theory, and spiritual consciousness that provides a unique explanation of our
global situation and how we might move forward to repair the world. It charts
a path for a global 'up-wising' that could save us from planetary disaster,
recognizing that both we as individuals and the global economic/political
systems in which we operate, must evolve quickly to survive."*

— **Rabbi Michael Lerner,** editor of *Tikkun* magazine, chair of the interfaith
Network of Spiritual Progressives, and author of *The Left Hand of God*

*"In **Spontaneous Evolution** the authors redefine our commonly accepted understanding of 'evolutionary destiny,' placing the responsibility right where it belongs: within the mindful awareness of every individual. Their presentation of 'holism' gives us all reason to be optimistic."*

— **Michael Bernard Beckwith,** author of *Spiritual Liberation*

*"**Spontaneous Evolution** is an eye-opening, mind-expanding, and paradigm-shifting journey. The alchemy that happens when Bruce Lipton's cogent articulation of cellular biology and physics joins Steve Bhaerman's lucid explanations of social, political, and economic science produces a coherent depth of 'field' perspective that is both illuminating and inspiring. Bruce and Steve have given us a guidebook for becoming sane in a dysfunctional world."*

— **Nicki Scully,** author of *Alchemical Healing*

*"**Spontaneous Evolution** is a great book, a vital message, and even more, it embodies Causal Evolution. By understanding and incorporating its wise revelation of how nature works, we can cause the future we intend. The future that emerges from this Whole New Story is so attractive that I believe it will encourage us to fulfill our true hearts' desire for more love, more life, more creativity NOW."*

— **Barbara Marx Hubbard,** founder of The Foundation for Conscious Evolution

"An extraordinary and timeless gift to humanity."

— **Leonard Laskow M.D.,** author of *Healing with Love*

*"The future you dream of is as close as your own cells! **Spontaneous Evolution** is a wonderfully exciting, enlightening, and heartening ride! Read it and know exactly where we stand and how we can thrive."*

— **Elisabet Sahtouris, Ph.D.,** evolution biologist,
futurist, professor, speaker, and consultant

*"From imaginal cells to cellular transformation, **Spontaneous Evolution** demonstrates the power of thought and intention in manifesting systemic change in both personal and social consciousness. The mix of leading-edge science and social/political awareness renders this book a must-read for all those working to create a more just, sustainable, and peaceful world."*

— **Georgia Kelly,** director, Praxis Peace Institute

To Rick,

SPONTANEOUS EVOLUTION

Wake up laughing
wise up loving!

ALSO BY BRUCE H. LIPTON, PH.D.

THE BIOLOGY OF BELIEF*

THE WISDOM OF YOUR CELLS (CD)

SPONTANEOUS EVOLUTION (CD)

*Available from Hay House

Please visit Hay House USA: **www.hayhouse.com**®
Hay House Australia: **www.hayhouse.com.au**
Hay House UK: **www.hayhouse.co.uk**
Hay House South Africa: **www.hayhouse.co.za**
Hay House India: **www.hayhouse.co.in**

SPONTANEOUS EVOLUTION

OUR POSITIVE FUTURE
(AND A WAY TO GET THERE FROM HERE)

BRUCE H. LIPTON, Ph.D.

AND

STEVE BHAERMAN

HAY HOUSE, INC.
Carlsbad, California • New York City
London • Sydney • Johannesburg
Vancouver • Hong Kong • New Delhi

Published and distributed in the United States by: Hay House, Inc.: www.hayhouse.com • *Published and distributed in Australia by:* Hay House Australia Pty. Ltd.: www.hayhouse.com.au • *Published and distributed in the United Kingdom by:* Hay House UK, Ltd.: www.hayhouse.co.uk • *Published and distributed in the Republic of South Africa by:* Hay House SA (Pty), Ltd.: www.hayhouse.co.za • *Distributed in Canada by:* Raincoast: www.raincoast.com • *Published in India by:* Hay House Publishers India: www.hayhouse.co.in

Design: Tricia Breidenthal
Indexer: Susan Edwards

Library of Congress Cataloging-in-Publication Data

Lipton, Bruce H.
  Spontaneous evolution : our positive future (and a way to get there from here) / Bruce H. Lipton and Steve Bhaerman.
    p. cm.
  Includes bibliographical references and index.
  ISBN 978-1-4019-2580-2 (hardcover : alk. paper) 1. United States--Social conditions. 2. Human behavior. 3. Social evolution. I. Bhaerman, Steve. II. Title.
  HN55.L57 2009
  306.0973--dc22

                              2009017821

Tradepaper ISBN: 978-1-4019-2631-1

14 13 12 11 8 7 6 5
1st edition, September 2009
5th edition, November 2011

Printed in the United States of America

To Mother Earth, Father Sky,
and All Imaginal Cells

CONTENTS

PREFACE

Why We Wrote this Book

Hello, I'm Bruce Lipton.

And I'm Steve Bhaerman.

Bruce: We welcome you to our new book, *Spontaneous Evolution*.

In my earlier book, *The Biology of Belief,* the emphasis was on how our attitudes and emotions control our physiology, our biology, and our gene expression. The book focused on how personal beliefs affect our personal reality. But there is something more profound to be learned, which is that collective beliefs of a culture or society also affect our personal biology and behavior.

Society is beginning to recognize that our current collective beliefs are detrimental and that our world is in a very precarious position. So, I thought it was time to bring out a message about how the new biology and other insights in the world of science can be applied to our societal beliefs and help us address the threatening situations we currently face.

In this work, I emphasize biology, beliefs, and behavior. However, to fully understand this message, my friend Steve Bhaerman offers information regarding how social structure, politics, and economics also tie into our biology.

Steve: For the past 22 years, I've been doing comedy, disguised as Swami Beyondananda, the cosmic comic. Comedy is a wonderful way to tell the truth and a way to break through the mind's defenses to get new information and perspective in under the radar.

Prior to the Swami, however, my first professional "incarnation" was in political science and social activism during the 1960s. I helped start an alternative high school in Washington, D.C., for students who had grown past traditional schooling. These were exciting times when new ideas were emerging and being tested. As I sadly observed, the most important of those tests—whether we could actually live the lofty principles we espoused—was being flunked left and right. For example, I recall meeting one individual who was a world-renowned expert on communal living. Unfortunately no one could stand to live with him.

Realizing how little I knew about how to turn the ideal into the real deal, I embarked on a 25-year journey into psychology, personal growth, meditation, and spirituality. Over the past seven years, I've had the itch to integrate those ideas in a book I wanted to call *Healing the Body Politic*. After I met Bruce, I thought we could work on the project together, and he agreed.

Bruce: In the medical world, we sometimes have a patient who is declared terminal and everyone counts her out. Then something happens, and this individual has a fundamental change in personal belief through which she expresses a spontaneous remission. One moment, she is terminal and, the next, totally free of disease. This shocks many medical practitioners, but it happens frequently, and most people are aware that the phenomenon exists.

Earth and the biosphere—and that includes us—are an integrated living system. While the system appears to be faltering, the planet itself is capable of expressing a spontaneous remission. What is needed to facilitate that remission is a fundamental change in awareness and beliefs as to who we really are. We used the spontaneous remission concept in the title of this book because we believe that science's new insights will profoundly change civilization's collective beliefs on the nature of life.

We have woven this new science into a hopeful story of humanity's potential future to help promote planetary healing. *Spontaneous Evolution* merges current scientific insights with ancient wisdom to reveal how truly powerful we are and that we can influence our own *evolution.*

According to conventional Darwinian theory, evolution is a very slow and gradual process, requiring millions and millions of years to manifest the evolutionary transformations of species. New scientific insights reveal that evolution actually consists of long periods of stasis, interrupted by sudden, dramatic upheavals. The upheavals are punctuations that change the course of evolution and lead to whole new forms of life.

Our civilization is presently in a state of disorganization and disintegration. We are currently in dire need of evolutionary advancement and don't have time for a slow, gradual evolution. Interestingly, in light of the crises we face, it appears that civilization is already in the throes of a punctuation.

Steve: Perhaps the most burning question now is: Is this punctuation a question mark? An exclamation point? Or, sadly, a period?

People are aware that something is happening. They have been exposed to news of diminishing natural resources, climate change, and population explosion. The doomsday clock is rapidly approaching the midnight hour, when it's going to be more than love that comes tumbling down. Religious people are talking about the end times.

At the same time, we are also coming to realize humanity is connected. The most obvious physical demonstration is the Internet, through which we can send and receive messages around the world at the speed of light. This instantaneous communication ties together the entire global village. Everything is entangled. Everything is related.

As evidence of that, we see science climbing the proverbial mountain of knowledge only to find Buddha sitting on top. In combining Bruce's scientific knowledge of the body with my knowledge of the body politic, we see that science's modern discoveries and the ancient teachings of great spiritual leaders lead to the same conclusion: This is a world of relationship. Nobody gets off the bus. We're all in this together.

Of course, along with this awesome understanding, we realize that the old ways of seeing, believing, and reasoning will not help us alleviate the current situation and step into the new. Our survival is at stake. We need a new paradigm. We need a spontaneous evolution. That is why we have written this book.

INTRODUCTION

A Universal Love Story

This is a love story. A love story for the entire Universe: you, me, and every living organism.

Act I opened billions of years ago when a wave of light from the sun collided with a particle of matter. That spark of love between Father Sun and Mother Earth gave birth to a child on this blue-green spheroid. That precocious child, called *life*, has made Earth its playground ever since, multiplying into an endless array of magnificent forms. Some of those forms are with us today, but many more have become extinct and will never be known.

The curtain rose on Act II of this love story some 700 million years ago when certain *single-celled organisms* decided they'd had it with the single life. Realizing they couldn't live alone, they turned to one another and said (in whatever primal language single cells speak) "Baby, I need your lovin'." And thus, the *multicellular organism* was created.

Act III began over a million years ago when multicellular organisms evolved into the first consciously aware *humans* to arrive on the scene. With consciousness, life was able to observe itself, reflect, and create its own future. Life could experience and appreciate love and joy. Life could even laugh at itself and, eventually, come to write books like the one you hold in your hands.

Act IV traces the evolution of *human clans* who joined forces and carved the globe into nation-states. At the present time, we find ourselves near the closing moments of this act, wondering if the play ends here, like a Greek tragedy that always ends badly. Looking at our chaotic world of human dysfunction and environmental crisis, we seem to be headed for an inevitable train wreck. Fortunately for us, the Greeks also had five-act plays; these were comedies filled with laughter, joy, happiness, and love.

Spontaneous Evolution is a story about how we can safely navigate from Act IV to Act V. The good news is that biology and evolution are on our side.

Inherent within all living organisms is an innate drive to survive, known by science as the *biological imperative*. Contrary to what conventional science and religion have been telling us, evolution is neither random nor predetermined but rather an intelligent dance between organism and environment. When conditions are ripe—either through crisis or opportunity—something unpredictable happens to bring the biosphere into a new balance at a higher level of coherence.

While we often perceive of examples of *spontaneous remission* as miraculous healings that happen by the grace of God, looking a little deeper we see something else at work. Quite often these fortunate individuals actively participate in their own healing by consciously or unconsciously making a key, significant change in their beliefs and behaviors.

So here is the bad news and the good news. The story of human life on Earth is yet to be determined. If there is to be an Act V, it will depend on whether we humans are willing to make changes in our individual and collective beliefs and behaviors and whether we are able to make these changes in time.

For millennia, our spiritual teachers have been pointing us in the direction of love. Now science is confirming that ancient wisdom. We are each and all cells in the body of an evolving giant super-organism we call *humanity*. Because humans have free will, we can choose to either rise to that new level of emergence or, in the manner of dinosaurs, fall by the wayside.

The religions that grew out of the cradle of civilization, the Fertile Crescent that is modern-day Iraq—which, ironically, is now in danger of being the grave of civilization—have all had the notion of redemption through some savior. In that sense, the coming of the Messiah in Act V will turn the play of life into a human comedy.

All good comedies need a joke, so here is the punch line: we are the answer to our own prayers.

THE RISE OF THE PHOENIX

At the current time, many people find themselves transfixed by disturbing symptoms that seem to mark civilization's devolution. However, this myopic focus distracts us from seeing the Light in the darkness.

Whether you call this Light love or knowledge, its flame grows brighter each day. The Light reveals that civilization is in a birthing process as the old way of life falls away and a new one emerges.

This pattern of evolution resembles the phoenix, a sacred firebird in Egyptian mythology. At the end of its life, the phoenix builds a nest of cinnamon twigs that it then ignites. Both nest and bird burn fiercely, but from the ashes arises a new, young phoenix that is fated to experience the same life cycle.

A modern version of the myth is portrayed in the film *The Flight of the Phoenix,* which provides an epic example of conflict resolution, mastering challenges, and transformation. The story begins when an oil exploration team abandons its oil rig in the Sahara Desert. The crew encounters a hitchhiking stranger who joins them, and together they fly off in a twin-engine cargo plane. When the plane crashes in the middle of the desert, the crew and passengers are stranded. Meanwhile, a band of cutthroat nomads follows the trail of jettisoned cargo to the downed plane.

Just like in the real world, a power struggle ensues for control of this small community. Who will prevail: the strongest individual or the one who controls the resources? As it turns out, neither. Faced with infighting that threatens to destroy their community and endanger them all, the group is forced to develop a plan. The hitchhiking stranger, who claims to be an aircraft designer, presents what seems to be an improbable plan to build a viable aircraft from the plane's wreckage. With no other options, the community has no choice but to give this outlandish new idea a chance. Galvanized by this new vision, they band together to create the impossible. In true Hollywood fashion and not a moment too soon, with the nomads firing their guns at the ramshackle aircraft, the untested plane lifts off on its maiden voyage to safety.

The story of a structure failing and something else rising is a familiar one that plays over and over again in the biosphere. Life is in a constant state of perpetual re-creation.

HUMANIFEST DESTINY

If you find it hard to imagine that we can ever get from the crises that we are facing now to a more loving and functional world, consider the tale of another world in transition. Imagine you are a single cell among millions that comprise a growing caterpillar. The structure around you has been operating like a well-oiled machine, and the larva world has been creeping along predictably. Then one day, the machine begins to shudder and shake. The system begins to fail. Cells begin to commit suicide. There is a sense of darkness and impending doom.

From within the dying population, a new breed of cells begins to emerge, called *imaginal cells*. Clustering in community, they devise a plan to create something entirely new from the wreckage. Out of the decay arises a great flying machine—a butterfly—that enables the survivor cells to escape from the ashes and experience a beautiful world, far beyond imagination. Here is the amazing thing: the caterpillar and the butterfly have the exact same DNA. They are the same organism but are receiving and responding to a different organizing signal.

That is where we are today. When we read the newspaper and watch the evening news, we see the media reporting a caterpillar world. And yet everywhere, human imaginal cells are awakening to a new possibility. They are clustering, communicating, and tuning in to a new, coherent signal of love.

Love, we will find, is not some mushy-gushy sentiment but the vibrational glue that will help build this new flying machine and manifest our destiny as humanity—what we call "humanifest destiny."

Chances are you are among the evolutionary imaginal cells who are contributing to the birth of this new version of humanity. Although it may not seem evident now, the future is in our hands. To secure that future, we must first empower ourselves with the knowledge of who we truly are. With a firm understanding of how our programming shapes our lives and the knowledge necessary to change that programming, we can rewrite our destiny.

Spontaneous Evolution introduces the notion that a miraculous healing awaits this planet once we accept our new responsibility to collectively tend the Garden rather than fight over the turf. When a critical mass of people truly own this belief in their hearts and minds and actually begin living from this truth, our world will emerge from the darkness in what will amount to a *spontaneous evolution*.

By the time you finish *Spontaneous Evolution*, we hope you will have a better understanding of past programming, current knowledge, and future possibilities. Most importantly, you will see how all of us can change our programming, our own and civilization's, to create the world we've always dreamed is possible.

Bruce H. Lipton, Ph.D., and Steve Bhaerman

PREAMBLE

Spontaneous Remission

"I have good news. There will, indeed,
be peace on Earth . . . I sure hope we
humans are around to enjoy it."
— **Swami Beyondananda**

To paraphrase American revolutionary Tom Paine, these are soul-trying times. Madness and dysfunction seem inescapable. We used to imagine getting away to a desert island or mountain retreat to live in quiet sanity. But now, the whole concept of away is meaningless. There is no such place as away. National borders, for example, couldn't contain the radioactive fallout from Chernobyl, nor can air pollution from China be stopped from blowing across Asia. Toxic medical debris dumped into the water somewhere washes up and pollutes a beach somewhere else.

The air we breathe and the water we drink are all part of a delicate interrelated ecosystem. Yet, the current system we live by, the human "ego-system" if you will, is simply not equipped to deal with these inconvenient realities.

Albert Einstein stated that a problem couldn't be solved at the same level it was created. Never has that assessment been truer than today when all of our reality checks seem to be bouncing. Clearly, we can no longer solve our problems by doing exactly what we've been doing. More weaponry doesn't bring peace. More prisons don't reduce crime. More expensive health care doesn't make us healthier. Nor does more information make us wiser.

In lieu of focusing on the crises, we are encouraged to escape into addictions and distractions conveniently placed before us to keep us preoccupied and passive. But reality keeps intervening. Everything in the world seems to be rolling toward some inexorable, beyond-our-control crisis. Those of us with children and grandchildren are concerned as to what kind of world we will leave behind for them and their children.

In early 2007, the so-called Doomsday Clock—the marker that the Bulletin of Atomic Scientists has used since the first atomic bomb was dropped in 1945 to measure the danger of nuclear holocaust—was moved up to 11:55 P.M., a mere five minutes before midnight. This is the closest it's been to the doomsday hour since 1953 when the Soviets exploded their first hydrogen bomb.

The latest movement of the doomsday marker reflects not only the increased threat of nuclear war but also threats to our survival from deterioration of the biosphere, oceans, and climate—what Lord Martin Rees, president of the Royal Society, has called "threats without enemies."[1] Actually, there are enemies, but these enemies are in the form of false, self-perpetuating mindsets and the obsolete institutions based upon them.

In the face of disturbing news reports that the impact of global warming is coming sooner than expected, combined with intransigence by a system that doesn't want to change, it looks more and more like the world needs a miracle. This miracle would be something akin to the spontaneous remission of an advanced terminal condition.

After assessing civilization's plight using insights offered by cutting-edge scientists, we are happy to report that there are, indeed, golden opportunities hidden in the dark clouds of crisis. Those willing to face the music and dance together will be the ones who will help transform the threatening crises we face into awesome opportunities.

The spontaneous remission we seek appears to be contingent upon a spontaneous re-missioning of civilization through which we change our mission from one based on survival of the individual to one that encompasses survival of the species. This is our fundamental evolutionary mission, our biological imperative. Achieving this remission necessitates that we individually and collectively reexamine many of the fundamental assumptions our civilization accepts as true. Those beliefs we find inadequate or incomplete must be revised so that the new awareness is incorporated into civilization and becomes our new way of life.

Once we understand what science is now revealing about who we truly are, the structures that have kept us from that truth will crumble and a new path will present itself.

It is our intention that *Spontaneous Evolution* bridge the gap between what we now know and what we will need to know in order to manifest a spontaneous remission. Ironically, some of the new insights offered by science are so far outside of what we've accepted as conventional wisdom that science itself is having a hard time coming to grips with the implications. In other words, if you suspect that reality isn't what it used to be, you're in good company.

So strap yourself in, keep your eyes open, and hold on tight because we are about to experience the adventure of a lifetime. When we realize our role as awakened and aware cells in the body of humanity, when we all participate in and fully experience what may be the most profound and pivotal moment in the history of the planet, then we will witness a new order spontaneously emerge out of chaos. How do we know? The science tells us so.

Oh, really?

If this new reality is truly upon us, why do things seem to be getting more chaotic and disconnected? The answer is that these crises are simply symptoms, which is Nature's way of informing us that our civilization has pushed the biosphere to its limits and must now consider a new way of life in order to sustain our existence.

We know things cannot continue in the same way, and we are frustrated because there appears to be no pathway to lead us anywhere else. Interestingly, the way out isn't a linear path. If anything, it is likely represented by a higher level of consciousness that must be attained by a critical mass of the population. Maybe, when the real rapture comes, we won't have to fly into the sky and leave our clothes behind. Maybe we can stay right here on Earth, fully dressed . . . or not. Rather than being beamed up by Scottie, perhaps all we need to do is beam Buddha down.

Now at this point, if we were you, we'd be saying, "Boy, this spontaneous evolution stuff sure sounds good. But how can we know that this is not merely some wishful pie-in-the-sky thinking and that it actually represents a real possibility?" That is exactly the question the rest of *Spontaneous Evolution* addresses. And the place to begin is with evolution itself.

IT'S TIME TO EVOLVE EVOLUTION

The fundamental argument about evolution is, excuse the expression, a bunch of BS. Belief Systems, that is. We have two opposing belief systems that are like two barking dogmas making so much noise the rest of us can't hear ourselves think.

On one side, we have scientific materialists who insist we got here by random chance. Their argument is akin to the belief that an infinite number of monkeys pecking away on an infinite number of typewriters would in infinite time produce the works of Shakespeare.

On the other side, we have religious fundamentalists who insist that God created the world just like the Bible said He did. Some of these believers have even calculated that God initiated Creation at precisely 9 A.M. on October 23, 4004 B.C.E.

While these points of view, respectively, are in all probability wrong, when taken together they paradoxically point us in the right direction. The latest science is telling us that, while Creation didn't happen in seven days, it was not the result of random evolution, either. Thanks to the new science of *fractal mathematics,* we are aware that self-similar intelligent patterns recur throughout Nature. As we will see, when these universal patterns are used to assess the state of human civilization, they reveal the evolution of our human species is on the path toward a hopeful and positive future.

Of course at this point, you might be thinking, "If things are so hopeful, why do we have such a mess right now?" In our discussion of evolution, we will describe the nature of *punctuated equilibrium,* in which crises drive evolution. Accordingly, there are vastly long periods of stability that are punctuated by radical and unpredictable changes. In the wake of such upheavals, which are frequently marked by mass extinctions, evolution rapidly provides a profusion of new species.

Crisis ignites evolution. The challenges and crises we face today are actually signs that spontaneous change is imminent. We are about to face our evolution.

How will our evolutionary advancement come about? Our path is similar to that of cells in the metamorphosing butterfly larva. When provided with a new awareness, the cellular population that comprises the deteriorating larva collaborates to restructure their society in order to experience the next highest level of their evolution.

We use the caterpillar-to-butterfly pattern to illuminate our current situation, and yet there is one significant difference. While caterpillars inevitably become butterflies, the success of our evolution is not inevitable. Even though Nature is nudging us toward this exciting possibility, it cannot happen without our participation. We are conscious co-creators in the evolution of life. We have free will. And we have choices. Consequently our success is based on our choices, which are, in turn, totally dependent on our awareness.

The good news is that we are already well on our way to the next level of human evolution. We believe this leap in evolution was inaugurated by an event that changed civilization's perceptions forever. The first pictures of Earth beamed back from space in 1969 offer photographic evidence of what spiritual seers have proclaimed for centuries: the world is one.

A picture may be worth a thousand words, but the value of the picture of Earth that appeared on the January 10, 1969, cover of *LIFE* magazine was incalculable. Etched into the imagination of the world's citizens was not only the beauty of our precious blue-green planet but also its smallness and fragility. Anthropologist Margaret Mead called that image "the most sobering photograph ever made. Our lovely, lonely planet afloat in a vast black sea of space. So beautiful yet so tragically fragile. So dependent on so many people in all countries."[2]

That image of Earth from space inspired American visionary John McConnell to create the Earth Flag in 1969. And this greater concern for Earth also stoked the first environmental legislation in the United States in the 1970s.

So what happened? Why does it seem we've been moving backward since then?

Even though the world's imaginal cells were activated by their new awareness, the global body of humanity is still a caterpillar that, naturally, feels threatened by and is resistant to the upstart imaginal cells. And it is that paradigm of struggle that continues to shape the world's energy field.

In order to secure our future, we must empower ourselves with the knowledge of who we truly are. With an understanding of how our programming shapes our lives and with the knowledge of how we can change that programming, we can rewrite our destiny.

Spontaneous Evolution is designed to be a primer for that transformation. We hope it provides information, inspiration, and encouragement for those readers seeking a healthful, peaceful, sustainable world.

PART I

WHAT IF EVERYTHING YOU KNOW IS WRONG!

"The best way to face the unknown is by not knowing."
— **Swami Beyondananda**

Gaze into the sky on a clear, dark, moonless night, and you will see thousands of pinholes of light—each one a massive, magnificent star in a Universe too large to imagine. Focus on one star and realize that it might no longer exist but may have burned out and collapsed into space rubble eons ago. But because the star was light-years away, illumination from its former existence is still visible, serving as a navigational guide for mariners.

Now, turn your gaze from the heavens to our less-than-heavenly Earth and ask: "Is it possible that we have been charting our course by a burned-out philosophical star? What if our belief system about life is wrong?"

On the surface, that contention seems odd. After all, we now generate, share, and absorb more scientific information than ever through books, CDs, DVDs, radio, television, and the Internet. But information alone is not enough. Right content in a wrong context is really misinformation that will lead us either off course or on a dangerous course.

Consider the story of the captain of a ship who demanded that the light he saw on a dark horizon change course. When a voice from that other light radioed back, suggesting that the ship change course instead, the captain bellowed his authority to hold his course. The voice from the distant light replied, "Captain, we are a lighthouse."

So you see, the course we choose depends on our perspective.

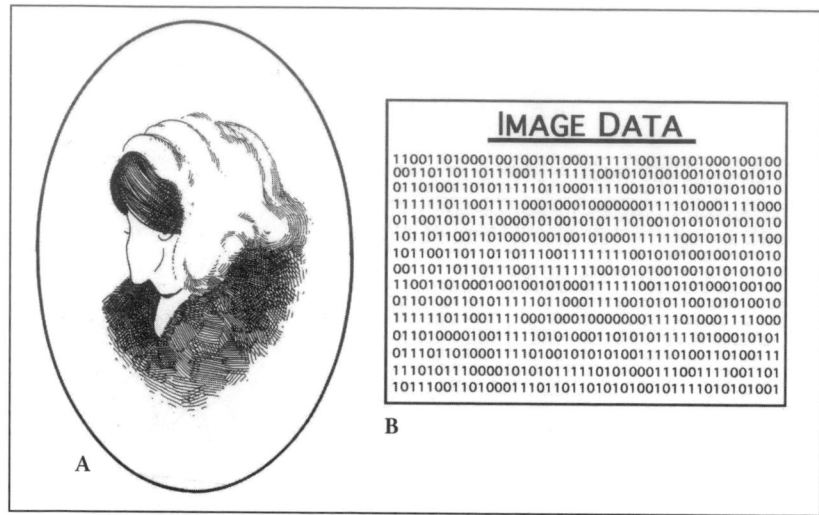

This simple example emphasizes our point.

In image A, you might see either a hag or a young woman (you may have to study the image for a while to see them both). Image B is binary code of image A. While the image data in B can scientifically define the content of A, the determination about which image you see at any given moment does not reside in the data code but in your interpretation and perception as the observer.

The message is simple and insightful: *one piece of scientific data* can describe *two entirely different perceptions*. And when we truly believe in a perception, we see it as the one and only reality and ignore all other possible realities.

In fact, as individuals and society, we are navigating by old, scientifically disproved philosophical perceptions. But, like those burned-out stars light-years away, the news of their deaths hasn't yet reached us. Like the light on the lighthouse, beacons are shining forth to guide us in a new direction—if we perceive them correctly.

Today, human evolution is at a turning point where an old paradigm and a challenging new awareness are uneasily trying to coexist. We are wedded by habit and tradition to an outmoded view of the Universe and yet civilization is pregnant with a new, exciting, and optimistic understanding of life.

To understand our predicament, let's travel back in time 500 years when astronomer Nicolas Copernicus, looking at the sky from a cathedral turret, made a world-shattering astronomical observation. Contrary to popular belief that Earth was the center of the Universe, Copernicus realized that Earth rotated on its axis daily as it orbited the sun annually.

Church leaders considered Copernicus' idea blasphemy and clung to old beliefs, even to the point of forcing Galileo, at the point of a sword 90 years later, to renounce his support of Copernican theory and spend the rest of his life in prison. Yet, ironically, those same Church leaders adopted Copernicus' mathematical formulas to reconcile discrepancies in their religious calendar. The point is, as Galileo experienced, it takes time for human consciousness to accept major changes.

A century has elapsed since Einstein mathematically proved that everything in the Universe is made out of energy and intertwined. Yet a vast majority of humanity still lives by the outdated principles of *Newtonian physics,* which say the world is a physical mechanism engaged in a series of cause and effect actions and reactions. While those in power used Einstein's theory of relativity to build atomic weaponry—just as the Church employed Copernicus' calculations to reconcile their calendar— they ignored the immense implications of bombing even a small part of the planet we share.

Meanwhile, our adherence to misunderstandings and "myth-perceptions" has so disconnected humanity from Nature that human activity has become "web of life–threatening." While headlines bear alarms about suicide bombers in the Middle East, too many people fail to realize that our entire species has become a ticking time bomb for the planet. Scientific studies have incontrovertibly established that human gluttony and pollution are causing the greatest mass extinction since dinosaurs disappeared 65 million years ago. If present trends continue, half of all species will be extinct within this century.[1]

While our daily routines will continue without lions roaming the Serengeti (hey, we can always visit them at the zoo, right?) there is no life outside the web of life. Unspoken, but definitely implied among warnings of animal and plant extinction, is our own imminent human extinction.

Modern humanity has taken a great deal of pride in the knowledge we have amassed about the Universe and life. As the most highly educated and information-laden population in history, we collectively know a lot. But what do we really know about what we know? True, we have lots of data, but, as the crises before us reveal, we are apparently a little short of knowledge.

Our problems are not with the data, itself, but arise from our interpretation of the data. As the illustration of the hag/young woman demonstrates, the same data can be used to interpret two completely different images. When it comes to understanding the nature of life, the image we assemble from the data can mean the difference between the life and death of civilization. Fortunately, the radical science discussed in *Spontaneous Evolution* offers a new interpretation of scientific data, one that casts doubt on our conventional perception of life.

René Descartes advised us to doubt everything. And now is the time for us to begin. Not everything we know is wrong, but everything we think we know is up for examination, reflection, and reconsideration.

In Part I of *Spontaneous Evolution*, we begin with a biological view of how we've come to believe what we believe. In doing so, we firmly establish the relationship between beliefs and biology, and how the interaction of these two, in fact, creates our reality.

In Chapter 1, *Believing Is Seeing*, we turn the cliché "seeing is believing" on its head. Starting with how cells process information, we trace biological pathways that convert perceptions into beliefs and what might appear to be reality. We offer irrefutable evidence that the mind is, indeed, the master over matter, and then we get right down to the cellular level to show how and why this is how life really works.

In Chapter 2, *Act Locally . . . Evolve Globally*, we explain how subconscious programming unconsciously thwarts our best intentions. When tracing the evolutionary history of the mind, we show how each of us is, at once, blameless and yet completely responsible for our actions!

In Chapter 3, *A New Look at the Old Story*, we move from biology to philosophy and describe how the story we use to explain reality controls our perceptions and, inevitably, our behavior. We explain how civilizations evolved over millennia and how each new paradigm greatly influenced the world our ancestors and parents saw and created as well as the world we see and create today.

Most importantly, by stepping outside our *stories*, we can see that stories are, well, merely stories, no more real than words on a restaurant menu are edible. However, the meaning we bring to those words ultimately determines our choices of what we end up eating. By lifting ourselves outside the matrix of unquestioned beliefs, we allow new stories to emerge that will take us from the tragedy of Act IV to a lighter and brighter Act V.

In Chapter 4, *Rediscovering America*, we relate the principles and practices that influenced the creation of the Declaration of Independence and still apply to the evolution now at hand. This is not a patriotic paean to glorify America, rather it is an acknowledgment of the revolutionary, visionary truths that "all men [and women] are created equal . . . endowed by their Creator with certain unalienable Rights . . . Life, Liberty and the pursuit of Happiness." These truths, which have yet to be fully realized in the United States, were actually a gift to the whole world, a gift that originated with Native indigenous tribes.

Reading Part I should provide some relief because its message explains what is wrong with the world and helps generate a new life-sustaining story. When we understand that cultural philosophy and individual perceptions are actually *acquired beliefs* that determine not only our biology but also the world we live in, we gain personal and world-changing insight. We cease to be dazed accident victims and claim our right to become personally empowered co-creators and architects of a brave and loving new world.

CHAPTER 1

BELIEVING IS SEEING

"We don't need to save the world, just spend it more wisely."
— **Swami Beyondananda**

We all want to fix the world, whether we realize it or not. On a conscious level, many of us feel inspired to save the planet for altruistic or ethical reasons. On an unconscious level, our efforts to serve as Earth stewards are driven by a deeper, more fundamental behavioral programming known as the *biological imperative*—the drive to survive. We inherently sense that if the planet goes down, so do we. So, armed with good intentions, we survey the world and wonder, "Where do we begin?"

Terrorism, genocide, poverty, global warming, diseases, famine . . . *stop already*! Each new crisis adds to a looming mountain of despair, and we can be easily overwhelmed by the urgency and magnitude of the threats before us. We think, "I am just one person—one out of billions. What can *I* do about this mess?" Combine the enormity of the mission with how small and helpless we imagine we are, and our good intentions soon fly out the window.

Consciously or unconsciously, most of us accept our own powerlessness and frailty in a seemingly out-of-control world. We perceive ourselves as mere mortals, just trying to make it through the day. People, on presuming helplessness, frequently beseech God to solve their problems.

The image of a caring God deafened by a never-ending cacophony of pleas emanating from this ailing planet was amusingly portrayed in the movie *Bruce Almighty*, in which Jim Carrey's character, Bruce, took over God's job. Paralyzed by the din of prayers playing endlessly in his mind, Bruce transformed the prayers into Post-It notes only to become buried under a blizzard of sticky paper.

While many profess to live their lives by the Bible, the perception of powerlessness is so pervasive that even the most faithful seem blind to the frequent references in the scriptures that extol our powers. For example, the Bible offers specific instructions in regard to that looming mountain of despair: "If you have faith as small as a mustard seed, you can say to this mountain, 'Move from here to there' and it will move. Nothing will be impossible for you."[1] That's a hard mustard seed to swallow. All we need is faith, and nothing will be impossible for us? Yeah . . . right!

But, seriously, with these divine instructions at hand, we ask ourselves, "Is our presumed powerlessness and frailty a true reflection of human abilities?" Advances in biology and physics offer an amazing alternative—one that suggests our sense of disempowerment is the result of *learned limitations*. Therefore, when we inquire, "What do we truly know about ourselves?" we are really asking, "What have we learned about ourselves?"

ARE WE AS FRAIL AS WE HAVE LEARNED?

In terms of our human evolution, civilization's current "official" truth provider is materialistic science. And according to the popular *medical model*, the human body is a biochemical machine controlled by genes; whereas the human mind is an elusive "epiphenomenon," that is, a secondary, incidental condition derived from the mechanical functioning of the brain. That's a fancy way of saying that the physical body is real and the mind is a figment of the brain's imagination.

Until recently, conventional medicine dismissed the role of the mind in the functioning of the body, except for one pesky exception—the *placebo effect*, which demonstrates that the mind has the power to heal the body when people hold a belief that a particular drug or procedure will effect a cure, even if the remedy is actually a sugar pill with no known pharmaceutical value. Medical students learn that one third of all illnesses heal via the magic of the placebo effect.[2]

With further education, these same students will come to dismiss the value of the mind in healing because it doesn't fit into the flow charts of the Newtonian paradigm. Unfortunately, as doctors, they will unwittingly disempower their patients by not encouraging the healing power inherent in the mind.

We are further disempowered by our tacit acceptance of a major premise of Darwinian theory: the notion that evolution is driven by an eternal *struggle for survival*. Programmed with this perception, humanity finds itself locked in an ongoing battle to stay alive in a dog-eat-dog world. Tennyson poetically described the reality of this bloody Darwinian nightmare as being a world "red in tooth and claw."[3]

Awash in a sea of stress hormones derived from our fear-activated adrenal glands, our internal cellular community is unconsciously driven to continuously employ fight-or-flight behavior in order to survive in a hostile environment. By day, we fight to make a living, and by night, we take flight from our struggles via television, alcohol, drugs, or other forms of mass distraction.

But all the while, nagging questions lurk in the back of our minds: "Is there hope or relief? Will our plight be better next week, next year or ever?"

Not likely. According to Darwinists, life and evolution are an eternal "struggle for survival."

As if that were not enough, defending ourselves against the bigger dogs in the world is only half the battle. Internal enemies also threaten our survival. Germs, viruses, parasites, and, yes, even foods with such sparkly names as Twinkies can easily foul our fragile bodies and sabotage our biology. Parents, teachers, and doctors programmed us with the belief that our cells and organs are frail and vulnerable. Bodies readily breakdown and are susceptible to sickness, disease, and genetic dysfunction. Consequently, we anxiously anticipate the probability of disease and vigilantly search our bodies for a lump here, a discoloration there, or any other abnormality that signals our impending doom.

DO ORDINARY HUMANS POSSESS SUPERHUMAN POWERS?

In the face of heroic efforts needed to save our own lives, what chance do we have to save the world? Confronted with current global crises, we understandably shrink back, overwhelmed with a feeling of insignificance and paralysis—unable to influence the affairs of the world. It is far easier to be entertained by reality TV than to participate in our own reality.

But consider the following:

Fire walking: For thousands of years, people of many different cultures and religions from all parts of the world have practiced fire walking. A recent Guinness World Record for longest fire walk was set by 23-year-old Canadian Amanda Dennison in June 2005. Amanda walked 220 feet over coals that measured 1,600 to 1,800 degrees Fahrenheit.[4] Amanda didn't jump or fly, which means her feet were in direct contact with the glowing coals for the full 30 seconds it took her to complete the walk.

Many people attribute the ability to remain burn-free during such a walk to paranormal phenomena. In contrast, physicists suggest that the presumed danger is an illusion, claiming the embers are not great conductors of heat and that the walker's feet have limited contact with the coals. Yet, very few scoffers have actually removed their shoes and socks and traversed the glowing coals, and none have matched the feat of Amanda's feet. Besides, if the coals are really as benign as the physicists suggest, how do they account for severe burns experienced by large numbers of "accidental tourists" on their fire walks?

Our friend, author, and psychologist Dr. Lee Pulos has invested considerable time studying the fire-walking phenomenon. One day, he bravely faced the fire himself. With his pants rolled up and his mind clear, Lee walked the gauntlet of burning embers. Upon reaching the other side, he was delighted and empowered to realize that his feet showed no sign of trauma. He was also totally surprised to discover upon unrolling his pants, his cuffs detached along a scorch mark that encircled each leg.

Whether or not the mechanisms that allow fire walking are physical or metaphysical, one outcome is consistent: those who expect the coals to burn them, get burned, and those who don't, don't. The belief of the walker is the most important determinant. Those who successfully complete the fire walk experience, firsthand, a key principle of *quantum physics*: *the observer*, in this case, the walker, creates the reality.

Meanwhile, on the extreme opposite of the climate spectrum, the Bakhtiari tribe of Persia walk barefoot for days in snow and ice over a 15,000-foot mountain pass. In the 1920s, explorers Ernest Schoedsack and Merian Cooper created the first feature-length documentary, a brilliant award-winning movie titled *Grass: A Nation's Battle for Life*. This historic film captured the annual migration of the Bakhtiari, a race of nomads who had no prior contact with the modern world. Twice a year, as they have done for a millennium, more than 50,000 people and a herd of half a million sheep, cows, and goats cross rivers and glacier-covered mountains to reach green pastures.

To get their traveling city over the mountain pass, these hardy, barefooted people dig a roadway through the towering ice and snow that blankets the 14,000-foot-high peak of Zard-Kuh (Yellow Mountain). Good thing these people didn't know they could catch a death of cold by being shoeless in the snow for days!

The point is, whether the challenge is cold feet or "coaled feet," we humans are really not as frail as we think we are.

Heavy Lifting: We are all familiar with weightlifting, in which muscled men and women pump iron. Such efforts require intense bodybuilding and, perhaps, some steroids on the side. In one form of the sport called total weightlifting, male world-record holders lift in the range of 700 to 800 pounds and female titlists average around 450 to 500 pounds.

While these accomplishments are phenomenal, many other reports exist of untrained, unathletic people showing even more amazing feats of strength. To save her trapped son, Angela Cavallo lifted a 1964 Chevrolet and held it up for five minutes while neighbors arrived, reset a jack, and rescued her unconscious boy.[5] Similarly, a construction worker lifted a 3,000-pound helicopter that had crashed into a drainage ditch, trapping his buddy under water. In this feat captured on video, the man held the aircraft aloft while others pulled his friend from beneath the wreckage.

To dismiss these feats as the consequence of an adrenaline rush misses the point. Adrenaline or not, how can an untrained average man or woman lift and hold a half ton or more for an extended duration?

These stories are remarkable because neither Ms. Cavallo nor the construction worker could have performed such acts of superhuman strength under normal circumstances. The idea of lifting a car or helicopter is unimaginable. But with the life of their child or friend hanging in the balance, these people unconsciously suspended their limiting beliefs and focused their intention on the foremost belief at that moment: *I must save this life!*

Drinking Poison: Every day we bathe our bodies with antibacterial soaps and scrub our homes with potent antibiotic cleansers. Thus, we protect ourselves from ever-present deadly germs in our environment. To remind us how susceptible we are to invasive organisms, television ads exhort that we cleanse our world with Lysol and rinse our mouths with Listerine . . . or is it the other way around? The Centers for Disease Control and Prevention along with the media continuously inform us of the impending dangers of the latest flu, HIV, and plagues transported by mosquitoes, birds, and swine.

Why do these prognostications worry us? Because we have been programmed to believe our body's defenses are weak, ripe for invasion by foreign substances.

If Nature's threats weren't bad enough, we must also protect ourselves from by-products of human civilization. Manufactured poisons and massive amounts of excreted pharmaceuticals are toxifying the environment.

Of course poisons, toxins, and germs can kill us—we all know that. But then there are those who don't believe in this reality—and live to tell about it.

In an article integrating genetics and epidemiology in *Science* magazine, microbiologist V.J. DiRita wrote: "Modern epidemiology is rooted in the work of John Snow, an English physician whose careful study of cholera victims led him to discover the waterborne nature of this disease. Cholera also played a part in the foundation of modern bacteriology—40 years after Snow's seminal discovery, Robert Koch developed the germ theory of disease following his identification of the comma-shaped bacterium *Vibrio cholerae* as the agent that causes cholera. Koch's theory was not without its detractors, one of whom was so convinced that *V. cholerae* was not the cause of cholera that he drank a glass of it to prove that it was harmless. For unexplained reasons he remained symptom-free, but nevertheless incorrect."[6]

Here's a man who, in 1884, so challenged the accepted medical opinion that, to prove his point, he drank a glass of cholera, yet remained symptom-free. Not to be outdone, the professionals claimed he was the one who was wrong!

We love this story because the most telling part is that science dismissed this man's daring experiment without bothering to investigate the reason for his apparent immunity, which was very likely his unshakable belief that he was right. It was far easier for the scientists to treat him as an irksome exception than to change the rules they created. In science, however, an exception simply represents something that is not yet known or understood. In fact, some of the most important advances in the history of science were directly derived from studies on anomalous exceptions.

Now take the insight from the cholera story and integrate it with this amazing report: Rural eastern Kentucky, Tennessee, and parts of Virginia and North Carolina are home to devout fundamentalists known as the Free Pentecostal Holiness Church. In a state of religious ecstasy, congregants demonstrate God's protection through their ability to safely handle poisonous rattlesnakes and copperheads. Even though many of these individuals get bitten, they do not show expected symptoms of toxic poisoning. The snake routine is only the opening act. Really devout congregants take the notion of Divine protection one giant step further. In testifying that God protects them, they drink toxic doses of strychnine without exhibiting harmful effects.[7] Now, there's a tough mystery for science to stomach!

Spontaneous remission: Every day, thousands of patients are told, "All the tests are back and the scans concur . . . I am sorry; there is nothing else we can do. It is time for you to go home and get your affairs in order because the end is near." For most patients with terminal diseases, such as cancer, this is how their final act plays out. However, there are those with terminal illnesses who express a more unusual and happier option—spontaneous remission. One day they are terminally ill, the next day they are not. Unable to explain this puzzling yet recurrent reality, conventional doctors in such cases prefer to conclude that their diagnoses were simply incorrect—in spite of what the tests and scans revealed.

According to Dr. Lewis Mehl-Madrona, author of *Coyote Medicine*, spontaneous remission is often accompanied by a "change of story."[8] Many empower themselves with the intention that they—against all odds—are able to choose a different fate. Others simply let go of their old way of life with its inherent stresses, figuring they may as well relax and enjoy what time they have left. Somewhere in the act of fully living out their lives, their unattended diseases vanish. This is the ultimate example of the power of the placebo effect, where taking a sugar pill is not even needed!

Now here's an utterly crazy idea. Instead of investing all of our money into the search for elusive cancer-prevention genes and what are perceived to be magic bullets that cure without the downside of harmful side effects, wouldn't it make sense to also dedicate serious energy to research the phenomenon of spontaneous remission and other dramatic, noninvasive medical reversals associated with the placebo effect? But because pharmaceutical companies haven't come up with a way to package or affix a price tag to placebo-mediated healing, they have no motivation to study this innate healing mechanism.

DO WE NEED SURGERY? OR JUST A "FAITH-LIFT?"

All who participate in walking across coals, drinking poison, lifting cars, or expressing spontaneous remissions share one trait—an unshakable *belief* they will succeed in their mission.

We do not use the word *belief* lightly. In this book, belief is not a trait that can be measured on a scale from 0 to 100 percent. For example, drinking strychnine is not a game for the "I *think* I believe" crowd. Belief resembles pregnancy; you're either pregnant or you're not. The hardest part about the belief game is that you either believe something or you don't—there is no middle ground.

Even though many physicists might say they believe lit coals are not really hot, they are not apt to shovel the briquettes out of their Weber grill and practice fire walking on them. While you may hold a belief in God, is it powerful enough to believe God will protect you if you drink poison? Put another way, how would you like your strychnine—stirred or shaken? We suggest before you answer that question you have zero percent doubt. Even if you have up to a whopping 99.9 percent belief in God, you might want to forego the strychnine and settle for iced tea.

If you consider the extraordinary examples cited above as exceptions, we agree. However, even if they are exceptions that cannot be explained by conventional science, people experience them all of the time. Even if we don't have the science to explain what they did, theirs are experiences of conventional human beings. As a human being yourself, you could likely do the same things as well as, or even better, if only you had belief. Sound familiar?

And, while these stories are exceptional, remember that the exception of today can easily become the accepted science of tomorrow.

One final compelling example of the mind's power over biology can be gleaned from the mysterious dysfunction commonly referred to as *multiple personality disorder*, more officiously known as Dissociative Identity Disorder (DID). A person with DID actually loses his or her own ego identity and takes on the unique personality and behavioral traits of a completely different person.

How could this be? Well, it's like listening to a radio station in your car and, as you travel, the station becomes staticky and fades out as a different station on the same frequency grows stronger. This can be jarring if, for example, you are cruising with The Beach Boys and, a couple of choppy moments later, you find yourself in the midst of a fire-and-brimstone, Bible-thumpin' revival. Or, for that matter, what if you're enjoying Mozart and the Stones suddenly roll in?

Neurologically, multiple personalities resemble radio-controlled biological robots whose "station identification" uncontrollably fades from one ego identity to another. The unique behavior and personality expressed by each ego can be as vastly different as folk music is from acid rock.

While almost all attention has been placed on the psychiatric characteristics of persons affected with DID, there are also some surprising physiological consequences that accompany ego change.[9] Each of the alternate personalities has a unique electroencephalogram (EEG) profile, which is a biomarker equivalent to a neurological fingerprint. Simply put, each individual persona comes with its own unique brain programming. Incredible as that may seem, many persons with multiple personalities change eye color in the short interval it takes to transition from one ego to the next. Some have scars in one personality that inexplicably disappear as another personality emerges. Many exhibit allergies and sensitivities in one personality but not in another. How is this possible?

DID individuals might help us answer that question because they are the poster children for a burgeoning new field of science called *psychoneuroimmunology*, which, in people-speak, means the science (*—ology*) of how the mind (*psycho—*) controls the brain (*—neuro—*), which in turn controls the immune system (*—immun—*).[10]

The paradigm-shattering implications of this new science are simply this: while the immune system is the guardian of our internal environment, the mind controls the immune system, which means the mind shapes the character of our health. While DID represents a dysfunction, it undeniably reveals the fact that programs in our mind control our health and well-being as well as our diseases and our ability to overcome those diseases.

Now you might be saying, "What? Beliefs control our biology? Mind over matter? Think positive thoughts? Is this more of that New Age fluff?" Certainly not! As we launch into a discussion of new-edge science you will see that the fluff stops here.

THE WORLD ACCORDING TO NEW-EDGE SCIENCE

What does science say about this mind-over-matter stuff? The answer depends upon which science you ask.

The science of conventional medicine tries to reassure us that none of the phenomena we just described actually exist. That's because today's biology textbooks and mass media describe the body and its component cells as machines made of biochemical building blocks.

This perception has programmed the general public to accept the belief in genetic determinism, which is the notion that genes control physical and behavioral traits. This sad interpretation is that our fate is inextricably linked to ancestral characteristics determined by genetic blueprints derived from our parents and their parents and their parents' parents, *ad infinitum*. This causes people to believe that they are victims of heredity.

Fortunately, the Human Genome Project (HGP) has pulled the rug out from under conventional science's beliefs concerning genetic control. This is ironic because it set out to prove the opposite. According to conventional belief, the complexity of a human should require vastly more genes than are found in a simple organism. Surprisingly, the HGP discovered that humans have nearly the same number of genes as lowly animals, a finding that inadvertently reveals a fundamental myth-perception underlying genetic determinism.[11] Science's pet dogma has long outlived its usefulness and needs to be mercifully put to sleep.

So, if genes do not control life . . . (pause to formulate a mind-blowing question) . . . *what does?*

The answer is: we do!

Evolving new-edge science reveals that our power to control our lives originates from our minds and is not preprogrammed in our genes.[12]

This is great news. The power for change is within us! However, to activate the amazing power of mind over genes we must reconsider our fundamental beliefs—our perceptions and misperceptions—of life.

Our first serious misperception occurs when we gaze into the mirror and see ourselves as singular, individual entities. In reality, each of us is a community of 50 trillion cells. While this number is easy to say, it is almost unfathomable. The total number of cells in a human body is greater than the total number of humans on 7,000 Earths!

Nearly every cell in your body has all of the functions present in the entire human body, which means that every cell has its own nervous, digestive, respiratory, musculoskeletal, reproductive, and even immune systems. Because these cells represent the equivalent of a miniature human, conversely, every human is the equivalent of a colossal cell!

As we will come to see, our mind represents a government that coordinates and integrates the functions of the body's massive cellular civilization. In the same manner that decisions by a human government regulate its citizens, our mind shapes the character of our cellular community.

Insights into the nature of the mind, how it influences us, and where it lives, offer an opportunity for us to fully realize our true powers. An awareness of this knowledge allows us to actively participate in the unfolding of our individual lives as well as contribute to the evolution of our collective world.

AND NOW . . . THE *REAL* SECRET OF LIFE

Both conventional science and new-edge science agree that, at its basic level, life derives from molecular movements within a biochemical mechanism. To uncover the real secret of life that lies beyond mere mechanics, we are obliged to first examine the mechanical nature of our cells. This information is relevant to our survival, which is more of a question now than ever before.

To make it easier to understand life according to new-edge science, we've created an illustration of a cell with metaphorical parts: a set of gears, driven by a motor, controlled by a switch, and monitored by a gauge. (For readers not mechanically inclined, we ask for your patience. There is a payoff.)

A switch controls the function by turning the mechanism on and off. The gauge is a feedback device that reports on how the mechanism is functioning. Turn the switch on, the gears move, and the function can be observed by monitoring the gauge.

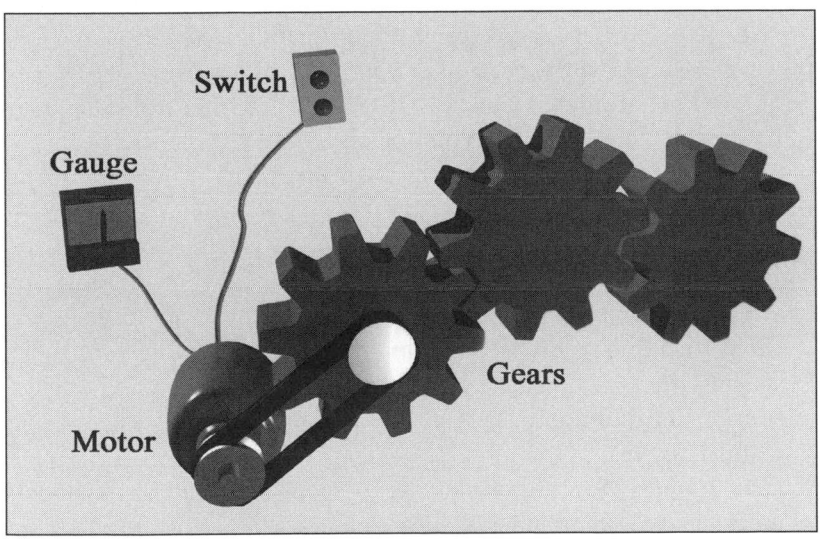

The mechanics of how cells work can be represented by an assembly of gears driven by a motor and regulated by a switch and a gauge.

The Gears: The gears are the moving parts.

In a cell, these moving parts are molecules called *proteins*. Proteins are physical building blocks that assemble themselves and interact to generate the cell's behaviors and functions. Each protein has a unique structure and size; in fact, there are over 150,000 different protein parts. While man-made machines can be quite complex, human mechanical technologies pale in comparison to the sophisticated technology within our cells.

Assemblies of protein gears that provide specific biological functions are collectively called *pathways*. A respiratory pathway represents an assembly of protein gears responsible for breathing. Similarly, a digestive pathway is a group of protein molecules that interact to digest food. A muscle contraction pathway consists of proteins whose interactions produce the body's movements.

> ### New-Edge Biology Conclusion #1
> *Proteins provide the structure and function*
> *of biological organisms.*

The Motor: The motor represents the force that puts the protein gears in motion.

The motor is necessary because the primary characteristic of life is movement. In fact, if the proteins in your body stop moving, you're well on the way to becoming a cadaver. Therefore, life derives from the forces that put protein molecules into motion and, thus, generate behavior.

The Switch: The switch is the mechanism that tells the motor to put the protein gears into motion.

The switch is necessary because life requires precise integration and coordination of cellular behaviors. Think of the cell's functions—respiration, digestion, excretion, and so on—as instruments in an orchestra. Without a conductor, orchestras would produce a cacophony. In living organisms, the switches that reside in the cell's membrane represent a conductor that harmoniously controls and regulates the cell's various functional systems.

The Gauge: The gauge represents the body's method for accurately monitoring the system's physiological functions.

Biological gauges are essential to maintain life. Think of the gauges in your body as being like the gauges in your automobile. Even though gauges reside on the dashboard, which is your driving command center, the gauges monitor functions in the engine as well as throughout the vehicle. Just as your automobile's gauges report oil and fuel levels, battery amperage, and speed, so the body also gives you feedback to regulate behavior and sustain your life. But unlike mechanical gauges with pointing needles or LED readouts, biological gauges convey information via *sensation.*

These sensations originate from *by-product chemicals* that cells create in the process of carrying out normal functions. These chemicals are released into the environment within our bodies. Specialized cells in the nervous system use membrane switches, equipped to recognize these chemical markers, to monitor the concentration of specific by-products. When these nerve cells are activated, they translate the by-product's signal into sensations that our consciousness experiences as feelings, emotions, or symptoms. To fight an infection, for example, activated immune cells release chemical messengers, such as interleukin 1, into the blood. When interleukin 1 molecules are recognized by specific membrane receptors on blood vessel cells in the brain, these cells forward the signal molecule prostaglandin E2 into the brain. Prostaglandin E2 activates the fever pathway and simultaneously produces symptoms we sense as elevated temperature and shivering.

One of the basic problems with our health-care system today is that the medical industry gauges success by how well it relieves symptoms. Doctors prescribe pills to eliminate pain, reduce swelling, or lower fever. However, drugging our symptoms can be as destructive as putting masking tape over our car's gauges. It does not solve the problem; it helps us ignore it—until the vehicle breaks down.

Likewise, drugging the cells and masking symptoms ignores signals bombarding our bodies from the external environment.

THE FINGER ON THE SWITCH

We have revealed that molecular switches activate protein gears, which, in turn, move and generate behavior. Now the big question concerning the secret of life is, "Who or what turns on the switch?" To turn the switch, we introduce . . . the signal.

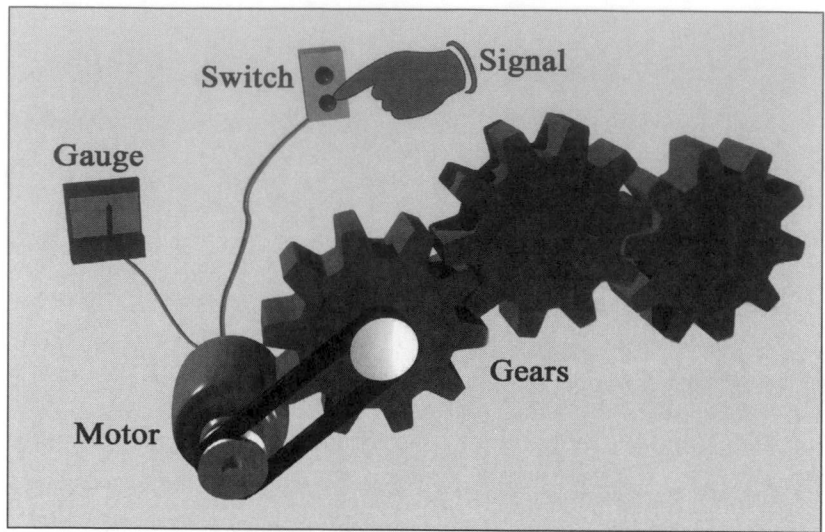

A signal from the cell's environment puts the gears, motor, switch, and gauge into motion.

The Signal: Signals represent environmental forces that switch on the motor within a cell and cause protein gears to move.

Signals represent both physical and energetic information that comprise the world in which we live. The air we breathe, the food we eat, the people we touch, even the news we hear—all represent environmental signals that activate protein movement and generate behavior. Consequently, when we use the term *environment* in our discussion, we mean everything from the edge of our own skin to the edge of the Universe. This is environment in the truly large sense.

Each protein responds to a specific environmental signal with the intimacy and accuracy of a key fitting into its matching lock.

The coupling of a protein molecule with a complementary environmental signal causes the protein molecule to change its shape, which, by its nature, is expressed as movement. The cell harnesses these molecular movements to drive its life-providing protein pathways, such as respiration, digestion, and muscle contractions. Protein movement animates the cell, bringing it to life.

> **New-Edge Biology Conclusion #2**
> *Environmental signals cause*
> *proteins to change shape; the resulting*
> *movements create the functions of life.*

BRAIN VERSUS GONADS

We must emphasize that even though the vast variety of protein pathways in the cell provides for the *functions of life*, merely having those pathways does not *generate life*. Life is dependent upon the precise coordination and regulation of the cell's protein pathways. The brain and supporting nervous system represent the regulatory mechanism that coordinate all of these many pathways that provide for life.

So . . . where is the cell's brain? Well, contrary to what you probably know, it's not in the genes. If you think back to high school or college biology, you probably remember that the cell's largest organelle, the nucleus, is described as the control center, or brain, of the cell. Because genes are housed within the nucleus and it was presumed that genes control life, it was a no-brainer to assume that this organelle represented the cell's brain. However, in light of the infamous nature of assumptions, we must question the accuracy of this belief.

Observations from experiments published 80 years ago challenge the assumption that the genes are the brains of the operation. When one removes the brain from a living individual—chicken with its head cut off notwithstanding—that individual dies. But if a nucleus is removed from a cell, a process called *enucleation*, the cell survives, and many can live for two or more months without their genes![13] In fact, enucleated cells will continue to function normally until they need to replace protein parts vital to their survival.

Genes are simply blueprints used to make protein parts. Enucleated cells eventually die, not due to an immediate absence of genes, but because they cannot replace their worn-out protein parts and, as a result, they inevitably begin to decay. While traditional thinking has taught us to believe that the nucleus is the cell's brain, in truth, the nucleus is the functional equivalent of the cell's gonads, its reproductive system.

This misrepresentation is understandable. Throughout history, science has predominantly been an "old boy's club." Because males reputedly think with their gonads, confusing the cell's nucleus with its brain is, in the light of that bias, an understandable error.

So, if the genes are not the brain, what is? The brain is actually the *cell membrane*, the equivalent of the cell's skin. Built into the membrane are protein switches that respond to the environmental signals by relaying their information to internal protein pathways. A different membrane switch exists for almost every environmental signal recognized by a cell. Some switches respond to estrogen, some to adrenaline, some to calcium, some to light waves, and so on.

Although there may be one hundred thousand switches in a cell's membrane, we don't have to study each one of them individually, because they all share the same basic structure and function. Following is a conceptual illustration of a genetic membrane switch.

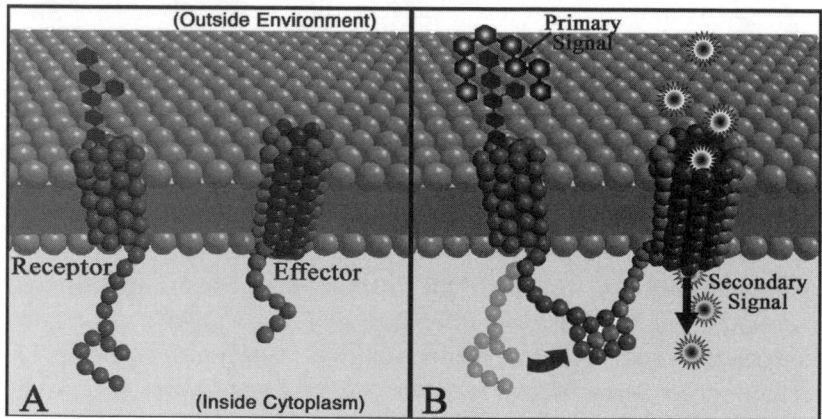

Figure A: Each cell has receptor proteins and effector proteins that extend through the cell's membrane, connecting its cytoplasm with the surrounding environment. Metaphorically, these proteins serve as switches that put the cell's motor and gears into motion. *Figure B:* When the receptor protein receives a signal from the environment, it modifies its shape and connects with the effector protein.

Each membrane switch is a unit of perception, comprised of two fundamental parts, a *receptor protein* and an *effector protein*. The receptor protein, as its name implies, receives, or senses, signals from the environment. Upon receiving its primary complementary signal (Primary Signal in Figure B), the now activated receptor moves to and is, thus, able to bind to the switch's effector protein.

In the illustration on the right, it appears as if the receptor protein and the effector protein are shaking hands (arrow in Figure B). It is this connection that allows information from outside the cell to be transmitted into the cell where it is used to engage behavior.

When activated by a receptor, the effector protein sends a secondary signal (Secondary Signal in figure B) through the cytoplasm inside of the cell that controls specific protein functions and pathways. The coordinated activity of membrane switches enables the cell to sustain its life by orchestrating metabolism and physiology in response to an ever-changing environment.

Receptor proteins provide the cell with an awareness of the elements of the environment, while the switch's effector proteins generate signals, which are physical sensations that regulate specific cell functions. Together, these switches, located in the cell membrane, provide "an awareness of the elements of the environment through a physical sensation."[14]

That very phrase offers the key to unlocking the secret of life. Are you ready?

Those words are the dictionary definition of *perception*, a word that's Latin roots mean "comprehension" or, literally, "a taking in." Consequently, the protein switches in the cell membrane represent fundamental molecular units of perception. Because these switches control the cell's molecular pathways and specific biological functions, we can confidently conclude that *perceptions control behavior!*

Also, dear readers—the fact that perceptions control behavior at both the cellular and the human level—is the *real* secret to life!

> **New-Edge Biology Conclusion #3**
> *Protein perception switches in the cell*
> *membrane respond to environmental signals*
> *by regulating cell functions and behavior.*

THE NATURE OF DIS-EASE

Sometimes, the body's natural harmony breaks down, and we experience *dis-ease*, which is a reflection of the body's inability to maintain normal control of its function-providing systems. Because behavior is created through the interaction of proteins with their complementary signals, there are really only two sources of dis-ease: either the proteins are defective or the signals are distorted.

About 5 percent of the world's population is born with birth defects, which means they have mutated genes that code for dysfunctional proteins.[15] Structurally deformed or defective proteins can "jam the machine," disturb normal pathway functions, and impair the character and quality of lives. However, 95 percent of the human population arrives on this planet with a perfectly functional set of gene blueprints.

Because the majority of us have a perfectly healthy genome and produce functional proteins, illness in this group can likely be attributed to the nature of the signal. There are three primary situations in which signals contribute to dysfunction and dis-ease.

The first is trauma. If you twist or misalign your spine and physically impede the transmission of the nervous system's signals, it may result in a distortion of the information being exchanged between the brain and the body's cells, tissues, and organs.

The second is toxicity. Toxins and poisons in our system represent inappropriate chemistry that can distort the signal's information on its path between the nervous system and the targeted cells and tissues. Altered signals, derived from either of these causes, can inhibit or modify normal behaviors and lead to the expression of dis-ease.

The third and most important influence of signals on the dis-ease process is *thought*, the action of the mind. Mind-related illnesses do not require that there be anything physically wrong with the body at the outset of the dis-ease. Health is predicated upon the nervous system's ability to accurately perceive environmental information and selectively engage appropriate, life-sustaining behaviors. If a mind misinterprets environmental signals and generates an inappropriate response, survival is threatened because the body's behaviors become out of synch with the environment. We may not think that a thought could be enough to undermine an entire system, but, in fact, misperceptions can be lethal.

Consider the situation of a person with anorexia. While relatives and friends clearly perceive that this skin-and-bones individual is near death, the anorexic looks in a mirror and sees a fat person. Using this distorted view, which resembles an image in a funhouse mirror, the anorexic's brain attempts to control a misperceived runaway weight gain, by—oops!— inhibiting the system's metabolic functions.

The brain, like any governing entity, seeks harmony. Neural harmony is expressed as a measure of congruency between the mind's perceptions and the life we experience.

An interesting insight into how the mind creates harmony between its perceptions and the real world is frequently illustrated in stage hypnosis shows. A volunteer from the audience is invited onstage, hypnotized, and asked to pick up a glass of water, which the volunteer is told weighs one thousand pounds. With that misinformation, the volunteer struggles unsuccessfully with straining muscles, bulging veins, and perspiration. How can that be? Obviously the glass doesn't weigh one thousand pounds even though the mind of the subject firmly believes that it does.

To manifest the perceived reality of a thousand-pound glass of water, something that cannot be lifted, the hypnotized subject's mind fires a signal to the muscles used to lift the glass at the same time it fires contradictory signals to the muscles used to set the glass down! This results in an isometric exercise wherein two groups of muscles work to oppose each other, which results in no net movement—but a lot of strain and sweat.

Cells, tissues, and organs do not question information sent by the nervous system. Rather, they respond with equal fervor to accurate life-affirming perceptions and to self-destructive misperceptions. Consequently, the nature of our perceptions greatly influences the fate of our lives.

While most of us are aware of the healing influences of the placebo effect, few are aware of its evil twin, the nocebo effect. Just as surely as positive thoughts can heal, negative ones—including the belief we are susceptible to an illness or have been exposed to a toxic condition—can actually manifest the undesired realities of those thoughts.

Japanese children allergic to a poison-ivy-like plant took part in an experiment where a leaf of the poisonous plant was rubbed onto one forearm.[16] As a control, a nonpoisonous leaf resembling the toxic plant was rubbed on the other forearm. As expected almost all of the children broke out in a rash on the arm rubbed with the toxic leaf and had no response to the imposter leaf.

What the children did not know was that the leaves were purposefully mislabeled. The negative thought of being touched by the poisonous plant led to the rash produced by the nontoxic leaf! In the majority of cases, no rash resulted from contact with the toxic leaf that was thought to be the harmless control. The conclusion is simple: positive perceptions enhance health, and negative perceptions precipitate dis-ease. This mind-bending example of the power of belief was one of the founding experiments that led to the science of psychoneuroimmunology.

Considering that a minimum of one third of all medical healings are attributed to the placebo effect, what percentage of illness and dis-ease might be the result of negative thought in the nocebo effect? Perhaps more than we think, especially since psychologists estimate that 70 percent of our thoughts are negative and redundant.[17]

Perceptions have a tremendous influence in shaping the character and experiences of our lives. They're the reason why those faith-filled folks can swig poison and joyously play with deadly snakes. Perceptions shape the placebo and nocebo effects. They are more influential than positive thinking because they are more than mere thoughts in your mind. Perceptions are beliefs that permeate every cell. Simply, the expression of the body is a complement to the mind's perceptions, or, in simpler terms, *believing is seeing*!

> **New-Edge Biology Conclusion #4**
> *Accurate perceptions encourage success;*
> *misperceptions threaten survival.*

Almost all of us have unknowingly acquired limiting, self-sabotaging *misperceptions* that undermine our strength, health, and desires.

As we will show in the next chapter, our most influential perceptual programs have mainly been acquired from others and do not necessarily support our own personal goals and aspirations. In fact, many of our strengths and weaknesses, the parts of ourselves we own as who we are, are directly attributable to familial and cultural perceptions downloaded into our minds before we were six years old. Programmed perceptions acquired in these developmental years are primarily responsible for health and behavioral issues experienced in our adult lives. Consider how many children never realize their full potential or dreams because of limiting programming.[18]

Not surprisingly, these self-sabotaging programs also thwart us as we try to change conditions in the world. This insight tells us that before we go out to change the world, we must first look inward to change ourselves. Then, by changing our beliefs, we do change the world.

As with changing the world, changing ourselves sometimes requires more than good intentions. We must understand the nature of the mind and how the brain's divine dualities, the conscious and subconscious minds, control the expression of our perceptions. In the next chapter, we will see how what we perceive locally is a gateway to global evolution.

CHAPTER 2

ACT LOCALLY . . .
EVOLVE GLOBALLY

"In a shrinking world that can use a good shrink,
we don't need another theory of evolution.
What we need is a practice of evolution."
— Swami Beyondananda

The promise of spontaneous evolution signifies nothing less than a global transformation. But before we can reshape our outer environment, we must first be fully aware of the world within.

Beneath our skin is a bustling metropolis of 50 trillion cells, each of which is biologically and functionally equivalent to a miniature human. This is not a hyperbolic claim made merely for impact. No, indeed, because once we see the remarkable similarity between our cells and ourselves, we will begin to learn some of the processes and practices cells have refined over the course of billions of years. We will also gain insight into how our cells created consciousness. And, by becoming more aware about how that consciousness operates within the cells, we can learn to rewrite our limiting beliefs at this pivotal time in our human evolution.

Conventional wisdom holds that the fate and behavior of our internal cellular citizens are preprogrammed in their genes. Since molecular biologists James Watson and Francis Crick discovered the genetic code in 1953, the public has been imbued with the perception that deoxyribonucleic acid, or DNA, acquired from our parents at the moment of conception determines our traits and characteristics. The conventional view of genetics further has us believe that our inherited gene programs are fixed and as unchangeable as a computer's read-only program.

The notion that our fate is indelibly inscribed in our genes was directly derived from the now outdated scientific concept known as *genetic determinism*, which would have us believe that we are victims of genetic forces outside of our control. Unfortunately, the assumption of powerlessness is a one-way street to personal irresponsibility. Too many of us have said, "Hey, I can't do anything about it anyway, so why should I care? Overweight? It runs in my family. Pass me the bonbons."

SOMEWHERE BEYOND THE GENES

By the 1980s, genetic scientists were convinced that genes controlled life. They thus set out to map the human genome, intending to identify the complete set of genes that define all of the heritable traits of the human organism. They hoped that, by revealing that code, they would find the key to finally preventing and curing human illness.

We will read more about the fate of the Human Genome Project later, but, for now, let's just say a surprising thing happened on the way to genetic engineering. Scientists began to uncover a revolutionary new view of how life really works and, in doing so, founded a new branch of science known as *epigenetics*.[1] Epigenetics has shaken the foundations of biology and medicine to their core because it reveals that we are not victims but masters of our genes.

For those who don't know Greek, the prefix *epi-* means "over or above." Students in high school and basic college biology courses are still learning about *genetic control,* which is the notion that genes primarily control the traits of life; however, the new science of *epigenetic control* reveals that life is controlled by something above the genes. Exciting new insights concerning what that something above the genes is provides a gateway to understanding our proper role as co-creators of our reality.

As we learned in the previous chapter, environmental signals acting through membrane switches control cell functions. It turns out that environmental signals, using the same mechanisms, also regulate gene activity. In the case of epigenetics, environmentally derived signals activate membrane switches that send secondary signals into the cell's nucleus. Within the nucleus, these signals select gene blueprints and control the manufacture of specific proteins.

This is far different than the conventional belief that genes turn themselves on and off. Genes are not *emergent entities*, meaning they do not control their own activity. Genes are simply molecular blueprints. And blueprints are design drawings; they are not the contractors that actually construct the building. Epigenetics functionally represents the mechanism by which the contractor selects appropriate gene blueprints and controls the construction and maintenance of the body. Genes do not *control* biology; they are *used by* biology.

The conventional belief that the genome represents read-only programs that cannot be influenced by the environment has now been proven to be one of those things we thought we knew, but we were wrong. Epigenetic mechanisms actually modify the readout of the genetic code. The creative power of epigenetics is revealed in this fact: epigenetic mechanisms can edit the readout of a gene so as to create over 30,000 different variations of proteins from the same gene blueprint![2]

Depending on the nature of the environmental signals, the contractor characteristic of the epigenetic mechanism can modify a gene to produce either healthy or dysfunctional protein products. In other words, a person can be born with healthy genes but, through a distortion in epigenetic signaling, can develop a mutant condition such as cancer. On the positive side, the same epigenetic mechanism can enable individuals born with potentially debilitating mutations to create normal, healthy proteins and functions from their inherited defective genes.[3]

Epigenetic mechanisms modify the readout of the genetic code so that genes represent read-write programs, not read-only programs. This means that life experiences can actively redefine our genetic traits.

This is a truly radical discovery. Where we once were certain that our genes marked our destiny, new-edge science now tells us Nature is smarter than that. As organisms interact with the environment, their perceptions engage epigenetic mechanisms that fine-tune genetic expression in order to enhance the opportunities for survival.

This environmental influence is dramatically revealed in studies of identical twins. At birth and shortly thereafter, twin siblings express almost the same gene activity from their identical genomes. However, as they age, their personal individualized experiences and perceptions lead to activation of significantly different sets of genes.[4] News media delight in stories about the amazingly similar parallel lives led by twins separated at birth, to the extent that they may even end up with the same job or marry partners with the same name. Although these stories are perceived as generalizations, they are extremely rare exceptions, and, more importantly, they fail to consider the important period of prenatal behavioral programming that profoundly shapes the life and behavior of those twins when grown.[5]

Take a moment to fully comprehend what new-edge biology is revealing.

Perceptions not only control behavior, they control gene activity as well. This revised version of science emphasizes the reality that we actively control our genetic expression moment by moment, throughout our lives. We are learning organisms that can incorporate life experiences into our genomes and pass them on to our offspring, who will then incorporate their life experiences into the genome to further human evolution.

Therefore, rather than perceiving ourselves as helpless victims of our genes, we must now accept and own the empowering truth that our perceptions and responses to life dynamically shape our biology and behavior.

Now let's take a look at how those all-powerful perceptions are actually shaped.

FROM THE MICROCOSM OF THE CELL
TO THE MACROCOSM OF THE MIND

For the first 3.8 billion years of life on this planet, the biosphere consisted of a massive population of individual single-celled organisms, such as bacteria, yeast, algae, and protozoa like the familiar amoeba and paramecium. About 700 million years ago, individual cells started to assemble into multicellular colonies. The collective awareness afforded in a community of cells was far greater than that of an individual cell. Because awareness is a primary factor in an organism's survival, the communal experience enhanced the opportunity for its citizens to stay alive and reproduce.

The first cellular communities, like the earliest human communities, were hunter-gatherer clans wherein each member offered the same services to support survival. However, as population densities of both cellular and human communities reached greater numbers, it became neither efficient nor effective for all individuals to do the same job. Evolution eventually led to specialized functions. For example, in human communities, some members focused on hunting, others on domestic chores, and some on child rearing. In cellular communities, specialization meant that some cells began to differentiate as digestive cells, others as heart cells, and still others as muscle cells.

Most cells in human and animal bodies have no direct perception of the environment beyond the skin. Liver cells, for example, see what's going on in the liver but don't directly know what's going on in the world. Therefore, the brain and nervous system must interpret environmental stimuli and send signals to the cells, which then integrate and regulate life-sustaining functions of the body's organ systems to support survival in that perceived environment.

The successful nature of multicellular communities allowed evolving brains to dedicate vast numbers of cells to catalog, memorize, and integrate complex perceptions. Through evolutionary advances, the brain's cellular population acquired the ability to remember millions of experienced perceptions and integrate them into a powerful database. Complex behavioral programs created from this database endow the organism with the characteristic trait of *consciousness,* a term we use in its most fundamental context to mean "the state of being awake and aware."

Many scientists prefer to think of consciousness as something an organism either has or doesn't have. However, the study of evolution suggests that consciousness mechanisms evolved over time. Consequently, the character of consciousness would likely express itself as a gradient of awareness from less-conscious in primitive organisms to the unique character of *self-consciousness* manifest in humans and other higher vertebrates. What we mean by self-consciousness isn't "I hope my hair looks okay," but, rather, a quality of being both a participant in life and an observer of life at the same time.

The expression of self-consciousness is specifically associated with a small evolutionary adaptation in the brain known as the *prefrontal cortex.* The prefrontal cortex is the neurological platform that enables humans to realize their personal identity and experience the quality of thinking. Monkeys and other animals that do not express self-awareness will look in a mirror and always perceive the image to be that of another creature. In contrast, neurologically advanced chimps looking in a mirror recognize the image as their own reflection.[6]

An important difference between the brain's consciousness and the prefrontal cortex's self-consciousness is that conventional consciousness enables an organism to assess and respond to conditions in the environment that are relevant at that moment. In contrast, self-consciousness enables the individual to factor in the consequences of his or her actions, not only in the present moment but also in the future.

Self-consciousness is what enables us to be co-creators, not merely responders to stimuli, meaning we can engage a *self* in the decision-making process. While conventional consciousness enables organisms to participate in the dynamics of life's theater, the quality of self-consciousness offers an opportunity to be not only an actor but also a member of the audience and even a director. Self-consciousness provides the option for self-reflection and the ability to review and edit the performance.

As significant as self-consciousness is to our own identity, it is actually a small part of what we call the *mind*. While the self-conscious mind is engaged in self-reflection, another mind is monitoring the world and controlling everything from our breathing to our driving—enter, from behind the curtain on center stage, the *subconscious mind*.

In conventional parlance, the brain's mechanism associated with automated stimulus-response behaviors is referred to as the subconscious mind, or *unconscious mind*, because this function requires neither conscious observation nor attention. Functions of the subconscious mind evolved long before the prefrontal cortex. Consequently, organisms unable to express self-consciousness are fully able to operate a body and navigate the challenges of a dynamic environment. In a manner similar to lower organisms, humans, too, can cruise on automatic pilot with self-regulating systems that manage themselves without need for advice or input from the self-conscious mind.

The subconscious mind is an astonishingly powerful information processor that can record perceptual experiences and forever play them back at the push of a button. Interestingly, we sometimes only become aware of our subconscious mind's push-button programs when *someone else* pushes our buttons.

Actually, the entire image of pushing buttons is far too slow and linear to describe the awesome data-processing capacity of the subconscious mind. It has been estimated that the disproportionately larger brain mass devoted to the subconscious mind can interpret and respond to over 40 million nerve impulses per second. In contrast, the diminutive self-conscious mind's prefrontal cortex only processes about 40 nerve impulses per second. This means that, as an information processor, the subconscious mind is one million times more powerful than the self-conscious mind.[7]

In contrast to its computational wizardry, the subconscious mind has only a marginal aptitude for creativity, best compared to that of a precocious five-year-old. While the self-conscious mind can express free will, the subconscious mind primarily expresses prerecorded stimulus-response habits. Once we learn a behavior pattern—such as walking, getting dressed, or driving a car—we relegate those programs to the subconscious mind, which means that we can carry out complex functions without paying attention.

While the subconscious mind can run all internal systems and chew gum at the same time, the much smaller prefrontal cortex responsible for self-consciousness can juggle only a small number of tasks simultaneously. Although its ability to multitask is physically constrained, the trained self-conscious mind is quite adept at single-tasking. It is the organ of focus and concentration.

It was once thought that some of the body's so-called involuntary functions, like the control of heartbeat, blood pressure, and body temperature, were beyond the control of the self-conscious mind; however, we now know that persons with higher mental evolution, such as yogis and other advanced meditators, can, indeed, control involuntary functions.

This tells us that the subconscious and self-conscious components of the mind work as a marvelous tag team. The subconscious mind controls every behavior that is not attended to by the self-conscious mind. This, it turns out, is just about everything happening in present time! For most of us, the self-conscious mind is so preoccupied with thoughts about the past, the future, or some imaginary problem that we leave the day-to-day, moment-to-moment tasks to the subconscious. Cognitive neuroscientists conclude that the self-conscious mind contributes only about 5 percent of our cognitive activity. That means that 95 percent of our decisions, actions, emotions, and behaviors are derived from the unobserved processing of the subconscious mind.[8]

WHO'S DRIVING OUR KARMA, ANYWAY?

If you've ever said you're of two minds about something, you were right. The mind that had that idea was your self-conscious mind, that small 40-bit processor that is the seat of cognitive thinking, personal identity, and free will. It is the part of the mind that proclaims wants, desires, and intentions, and consequently the part that makes God laugh. The joke is that that part of the mind imagines who we think we are, but it controls only 5 percent or less of our lives.

The data reveals what those of us who tried positive thinking but got negative results sadly came to realize: that our lives are not controlled by our conscious wishes or intentions. If you disbelieve, do the math.

Our subconscious is running the show 95 percent of the time. Therefore, our fate is actually under the control of *recorded programs*, or habits, that have been derived from instincts and the perceptions acquired in our life experiences.

The most powerful and influential programs in the subconscious mind are the ones that were recorded first. During the extremely important formative period between gestation and six years of age, our fundamental life-shaping programs were acquired by observing and listening to our primary teachers—our parents, siblings, and local community. Unfortunately, as psychiatrists, psychologists, and counselors are keenly aware, much of what we learned was based on misperceptions that are now expressed as limiting and self-sabotaging beliefs.

Most parents don't realize their words and actions are continuously recorded by their child's subconscious mind, which compiles an imprint of early life experiences. When a young child is frequently scolded as being bad, the child does not comprehend the nuance that this is a temporary condition associated with a recent deed. Instead, their young mind registers this declaration as a permanent condition that defines who they are. The same is true with transmitted beliefs, spoken or unspoken, that a child is undeserving, not good enough or smart enough, or that they are sickly or weak.

These unwitting parental pronouncements directly download into the child's subconscious. Because the role of the mind is to create coherence between its programs and real life, the brain unconsciously generates appropriate (or inappropriate) behavioral responses that assure the truth of its programmed perceptions. Once acquired, subconscious programs automatically manifest their perceptions as false realities that shape an individual's life.

Let's apply this to an unfortunate real-life experience. Imagine you are a five-year-old child throwing a tantrum at the mall because you want a certain toy. To silence your outburst in a public place, your father—upset himself—blurts out something his parents said to him when he threw a tantrum: "You don't deserve it!" Fast-forward 20 or 30 years, and now you are an adult on the threshold of a new job that will offer fantastic financial reward. You've been entertaining wonderful thoughts about your future prospects. Then all of a sudden, glitches and setbacks arise. The road to wealth that once seemed clear now seems blocked. You know you have the ability to succeed, but all of a sudden things go wrong, your new behavior becomes erratic and unprofessional—and your prospective employer notices.

"What's happening?" you ask. The problem is that your subconscious mind's programs are conflicting with your conscious mind's desire. While your self-conscious mind is positive and hopeful about the opportunities, the recorded message from your dad—"You don't deserve it!"—is subversively programming your subconscious mind's behavior. As with the hypnotized individual trying to lift a glass of water that weighs a misperceived one thousand pounds, your subconscious mind is dutifully engaging in self-sabotaging behaviors to assure your reality matches your program—and chances are you don't even know this is happening.

Why? Because the automated programs are running the show while your conscious mind is preoccupied with other thoughts, such as how you are going to spend the extra salary. Consequently, when the self-conscious mind is engaged, it usually does not observe the automatic behaviors being generated by the subconscious mind. And because subconscious programs encompass 95 percent of what we do, most of our own behavior is invisible to us!

For example, let's say you have a friend, Bill, whom you've known since childhood. Being familiar with him and his family, you recognize that Bill's behavior closely resembles that of his father. Then one day you casually remark, "You know, Bill, you're just like your dad." Bill backs away in shock, indignant that you could even suggest such a thing. "How can you say something so ridiculous?" he demands.

The cosmic joke is that everyone *except Bill* can see that his behavior resembles his dad's. Why? Because when Bill engages in subconscious behavioral programs downloaded in his youth as a result of observing his dad, his self-conscious mind is, at the same time, busy in thought. At those moments, his automatic subconscious programs operate without observation; hence they are *unconscious.*

As another familiar example of how invisible behavior operates, imagine that you are driving your car while having an intense conversation with a friend in the passenger's seat. You become so involved in the discussion that only later, when your gaze returns to the road, do you realize that you haven't paid attention to driving for the last several minutes. Because the self-conscious mind was preoccupied with the conversation, the car was being driven by the subconscious mind's autopilot. If you were asked to describe your driving during that hiatus, you would say, "I don't know. I wasn't paying attention."

Aha! That's the point. When the conscious mind is busy, we do not observe our own programmed subconscious behaviors. We aren't paying attention! Consequently, when life does not work out as planned, we rarely recognize that we very likely contributed to our own disappointments. Since we are generally unaware of the influence of our own subconscious behaviors, we naturally perceive ourselves as victims of external forces.

Unfortunately, victimhood becomes a self-fulfilling condition. If we perceive ourselves as victims, the brain's function is to manifest that truth within our reality. As victims, we perceive that we are powerless to manifest our intentions. Nothing could be further from the truth.

As we will see, the database of perceptions and beliefs programmed in our minds is a primary factor in shaping our lives. The good news is that we actually wield power over the contents of that database. Becoming conscious of our subconscious beliefs and programming is the gateway to spontaneous evolution.

TRANSFORMING THE TRANCE

Because our programmed perceptions directly shape the biology, behavior, and character of our lives, it is important that we know the three primary sources of our perceptions.

Our first programmed perceptions are acquired through inheritance. Our genomes contain behavioral programs that provide fundamental reflex behaviors referred to as *instincts*. Pulling your hand out of an open flame is a genetically derived behavior. More complex instincts include the ability of newborn babies to swim like dolphins or the activation of innate healing mechanisms to eliminate a cancerous growth. Genetically inherited instincts are perceptions acquired from *Nature*.

The second source of life-controlling perceptions comes from experiential memories downloaded into the subconscious mind. These powerful learned perceptions represent the contribution from *nurture*. Among the earliest perceptions of life to be downloaded into the subconscious mind were our mother's emotional patterns while we were in the womb.

Nutrition isn't the only thing a mother provides for her fetus. A complex chemistry of maternal emotional signals, hormones, and stress factors also cross the placental barrier and influence fetal physiology and development. When the mother is happy, so is the fetus. When the mother is in fear, so is the fetus. When the mother thinks thoughts of rejection toward her fetus, the fetal nervous system programs itself with the emotion of rejection.

Sue Gerhardt's valuable book *Why Love Matters* emphasizes that the fetal nervous system records womb experiences.[9] By the time the baby is born, emotional information downloaded from the mother's experiences has already shaped half of that individual's personality!

However, the most influential perceptual programming of the subconscious mind occurs from birth through age six. During that time, the child's brain is recording all sensory experiences as well as learning complex motor programs for speech, crawling, standing, and advanced activities like running and jumping. Simultaneously, the child's sensory systems are fully engaged, downloading massive amounts of information about the world and how it works.

By observing the behavioral patterns of people in their immediate environment—primarily parents, siblings, and relatives—children learn to distinguish acceptable and unacceptable social behaviors. It's important to realize that perceptions acquired before the age of six become the fundamental subconscious programs that shape the character of an individual's life.

During this time of accelerated learning, Nature facilitates the enculturation process by developmentally enhancing the subconscious mind's ability to download massive amounts of information. We know this thanks to our study of brainwaves in adults and children. Electroencephalogram (EEG) readings from adult brains reveal that neural electrical activity is correlated with different states of awareness. Adult EEG readings show that the human brain operates on at least five different frequency levels, each associated with a different brain state:

Brain Activity	Frequency Range	Adult State Associated with Frequency Range
Delta	0.5–4 Hz	Sleeping/Unconscious
Theta	4–8 Hz	Imagination/Reverie
Alpha	8–12 Hz	Calm consciousness
Beta	12–35 Hz	Focused consciousness
Gamma	>35 Hz	Peak performance

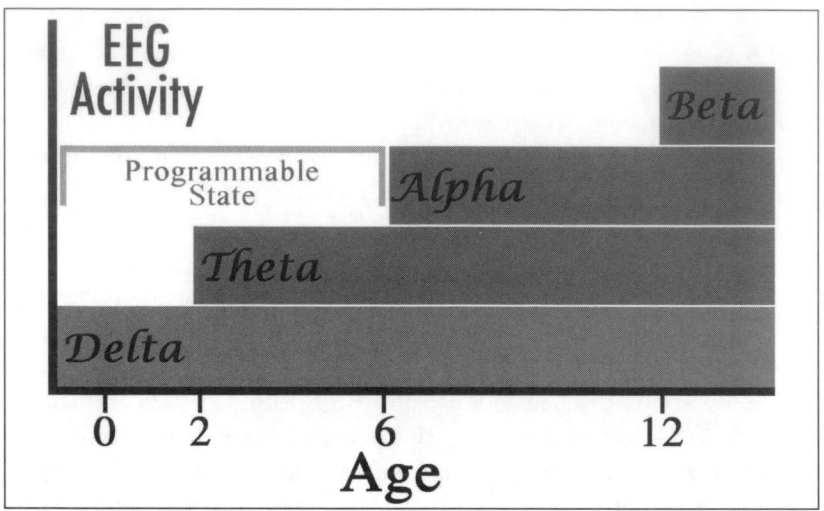

Chart revealing predominant EEG activity state during stages of child development

EEG vibrations continuously shift from state to state over the whole range of frequencies during normal brain processing in adults. However, brain frequencies in developing children display a radically different behavior. EEG vibration rates and their corresponding states evolve in incremental stages over time.[10]

The predominant brain activity during the child's first two years of life is *delta*, the lowest EEG frequency range.

Between two and six years of age, the child's brain activity ramps up and operates primarily in the range of *theta*. While in the *theta* state, children spend much of their time mixing the imaginary world with the real world.

The calm consciousness associated with emerging *alpha* activity only becomes a predominant brain state after age six.

By twelve years, the brain expresses all frequency ranges, although its primary activity is in the *beta* state of focused consciousness. Children leave elementary education behind at this age and enter into the more intense academic programs of middle school.

In case you missed it, here is a very important fact: children do not express the *alpha* EEG frequencies of conscious processing as a predominant brain state until after they are six years old. The predominant *delta* and *theta* activity expressed by children younger than six signifies that their brains are operating at levels below consciousness. *Delta* and *theta* brain frequencies define a brain state known as a hypnagogic trance—the same neural state that hypnotherapists use to directly download new behaviors into the subconscious minds of their clients.

In other words, the first six years of a child's life are spent in a hypnotic trance!

A child's perceptions of the world are directly downloaded into the subconscious during this time, without discrimination and without filters of the analytical self-conscious mind, which doesn't fully exist. Consequently, our fundamental perceptions about life and our role in it are learned without our having the capacity to choose or reject those beliefs. We were simply programmed.

The Jesuits were aware of this programmable state and proudly boasted, "Give me the child until it is seven years old and I will give you the man." They knew the child's trance state facilitated a direct implanting of Church dogma into the subconscious mind. Once programmed, that information would inevitably influence 95 percent of that individual's behavior for the rest of his or her life.

The absence of conscious processing, that is the *alpha* EEG activity, as well as the simultaneous engagement of a hypnagogic trance during the formative stages of a child's life, are a logical necessity. First of all, the thinking processes associated with the self-conscious mind's functions cannot operate from a blank slate. Self-conscious information processing requires a working database of learned perceptions. Consequently, before a person can express self-consciousness, the brain must go about its primary task of acquiring a working awareness of the world by directly downloading experiences and observations into the subconscious mind.

However, there is a very serious downside to acquiring awareness by this method. The consequence is so profound that it not only impacts the life of the individual, it can also alter an entire civilization. The problem is that we download our perceptions and beliefs about life years before we acquire the ability for critical thinking. When, as young children, we download limiting or sabotaging beliefs, those perceptions or misperceptions become our truths. If our platform is one of misperception, our subconscious mind will dutifully generate behaviors that are coherent with those programmed truths.

Perceptions acquired during this pivotal developmental period can actually override genetically endowed instincts. Consider, for example, that every one of us can instinctually swim like a dolphin the moment we emerge from the birth canal. "Why then," you might ask, "do we have to teach children to swim? Why are so many afraid of the water?"

If you are a parent, think about your likely reaction when your toddler gets anywhere near open water. Concerned for the safety of your child, you rush to pull him or her away. However, in the baby's mind, your frantic behavior is taken to mean that water is life-threatening. Fear, acquired from the perception that water is dangerous, overrides the instinctual ability to swim and makes the formerly proficient child susceptible to drowning.

By now you may be thinking, "Gee, this is great. I'm so relieved to find I am not a victim of my genetics. However, I now appear to be a victim of my programming. What chance does my little 40-bit conscious processor have against the subconscious mega-computer of doom? Where's the good news?" The good news is, whatever has been programmed can be deprogrammed and reprogrammed.

That brings us to a third source of perceptions that shape our lives and which also derive from the actions of the self-conscious mind. Unlike the push-button reflexive programming of the subconscious mind, the self-conscious mind is a creative platform capable of mixing and morphing perceptions with an infusion of imagination in a process that generates an unlimited number of beliefs and behavioral variations. The quality of the self-conscious mind endows organisms with one of the most powerful forces in the Universe—the opportunity to express free will.

> **Sources of Life-Shaping Perceptions**
> 1. Genome Programming (Instincts)
> 2. Memories in the Subconscious Mind
> 3. Actions of the Self-conscious Mind

FROM THE BLAME GAME TO RESPONSE-ABILITY

Most of our personal and cultural problems arise from the fact that our own subconscious behaviors are largely invisible to us. These behaviors, as we've learned, were recorded indiscriminately, derived from the words and actions of others, themselves no doubt programmed with many of the same limiting beliefs. While our conscious mind is trying to move us toward our dreams, unbeknownst to us, our invisible subconscious programs may be sabotaging us and impeding our progress.

Fortunately, the subconscious is not an ominous Freudian pit of evil and darkness. It's simply a record-and-playback mechanism that downloads life experiences onto behavioral tapes. While the self-conscious mind is creative, the subconscious mind engages previously recorded programs. Unlike self-consciousness that is overseen by an entity (you), the subconscious mind is more closely related to a machine, which means there is no conscious entity to control your subconscious programs.

However, the next time you are talking to yourself with the hope of changing sabotaging subconscious programs, remember this: using reason to communicate with and change your subconscious has the same effect as trying to change a program on a cassette tape by talking to the tape player. In neither case is there an entity or component within the mechanism that will respond to your dialogue.

The good news is that subconscious programs are not fixed and unchangeable. We do have the ability to rewrite our limiting beliefs and, in the process, take control of our lives. However, changing the programs requires that we activate a process other than engaging in a futile, one-sided dialogue with the subconscious mind. A resource list of techniques that have been shown to facilitate the rewriting of disempowering, limiting, and self-sabotaging beliefs in the subconscious mind is provided in the endnotes of this book.

Once we realize that our past behaviors were predicated on the invisible operation of the subconscious mind, we afford ourselves the opportunity to forgive ourselves. It helps to know that our invisible behaviors are programs primarily derived from the beliefs of other people, who, in turn, were programmed by others, backward through time. Perhaps instead of original sin, we should be talking about original misperception.

In any case, neither our parents nor their parents were aware they were acting out a pre-written script. In this regard, it is important to remember that all the people with whom we have ever interacted were also engaging in invisible behaviors derived from programs downloaded into their infant subconscious minds. Consequently, they, too, were unaware of how their invisible participation and contributions impacted our lives.

These insights are extremely important in trying to bring peace to a world where most citizens are unconsciously responding to cultural wrongs perpetrated generations ago by and to their ancestors. From this perspective, it behooves us to step back and reconsider our emotionally charged notions regarding blame, guilt, victims, and perpetrators. As confirmed by recent scientific discoveries, the Biblical injunction, "Forgive them; they know not what they do," makes perfect sense.

By studying the life and teachings of Jesus, we can see that he employed this new science of consciousness in his biology and behavior.

This is why Jesus emphasized that, were it not for our limiting beliefs, all of us could perform the miracles he did. He was on target when he declared that we could renew our lives with our beliefs. Most importantly, he saw the reality of forgiveness as the most important path toward peace. If enough of us perform this simple local act, we would, indeed, advance our global evolution.

Based on the scientific insights regarding how our mind works, the new-edge biology implores us to heed the advice of all the great prophets: to forgive the transgressions of others. We have been shackled with emotional chains wrought by dysfunctional behaviors, programmed by the stories of the past. Through forgiveness, we unshackle ourselves and others, allowing all of us to let go of the old story. Then, and only then, will we be free to create our positive future.

As Dr. Fred Luskin, an expert in counseling, health psychology, and forgiveness, says in his book *Forgive for Good,* "Forgiveness allows us not to stay stuck in the past."[11] Colin Tipping, another forgiveness guru and author of *Radical Forgiveness*, goes even further in suggesting that forgiveness "transforms the victim archetype" once and for all.[12]

In addition to our individual subconscious programming, society also holds invisible collective beliefs. Remember Bill who couldn't see that he was acting just like his father? Consider that our individual subconscious cultural perceptions are really shared beliefs and are, therefore, invisible to others as well. Consider how that situation makes those beliefs that much more damaging.

Indeed, philosophy ultimately determines biology because our brain's function is to create coherence between our collective subconscious beliefs and the reality we experience in our world. The next step in our journey is to see how our cultural storylines have evolved and how the story is likely to unfold next.

CHAPTER 3

A NEW LOOK AT
THE OLD STORY

"Stick to your story and you're stuck with it."
— Swami Beyondananda

A STORY ABOUT A STORY

A friend of ours, a psychologist in his mid-50s, found himself in the midst of a family crisis concerning his aging parents. The situation had nothing to do with illness or infirmity. The tumultuous issue was far more unusual. After having been divorced for 50 years, remarried and then widowed, our friend's parents decided to reconcile their differences. In their mid-80s and in reasonably good health, they reunited and chose to spend whatever time they had left together.

What a great story! So what's the problem? Simply this: the children from the original family and from the two new families the parents had started were being asked to make a great adjustment. After having heard about acrimony and betrayal all their lives and having made this story their own—and having spent thousands of dollars and years in therapy talking about it—they now had to adjust to their parents' sudden reversal! The children had to come to grips with the fact that their parents, at a point in their lives when every moment is precious, decided it was more important to share a few years of happiness than to hold on to an old story that no longer served them.

We humans live and die by our stories. We are a meaning-making species, and the meaning we make becomes as important as life itself. Consider what happened back in the late 1930s when Orson Welles broadcast his famed radio program "War of the Worlds." Those who tuned in a few minutes late thought the fictional broadcast was an actual news report informing them that Martians had invaded Earth. The result was mass hysteria and panicky evacuation of neighborhoods. Some people even considered suicide because this change in story was too devastating to handle.[1]

We build our lives on the foundation of our stories. And the more we invest in a story, the more important it becomes to continue investing in that story, even after it's clear the story no longer works. Consider the Palestinians and Israelis in the Middle East or, until recently, the Catholics and Protestants in Northern Ireland. Animosity continues because each death or indignity builds the story one story higher.

Many of our stories have been with us for millennia. But what if those supposed truths we learned about the world were wrong? What if we have it backward? What if the struggle we've been taught is natural turns out to be the most unnatural thing we could be doing? What if the social Darwinists were mistaken? What if cooperation, not competition, is the key to survival?

Today, as the Doomsday Clock creeps inexorably toward the Midnight Hour, might it be that our collective story has delivered us to this dangerous precipice? Might we learn something from our friend's elderly parents who decided their old story could no longer serve them in their remaining precious days?

Now our entire species faces the same choice: your story or your life? Our storied history is filled with familiar tales of war, feuding, exploitation, and mistrust. In front of us, however, is a new story that holds the key to our survival as a species. Do we go down with our old story, or do we wise up and rise up with a new one?

Insanity has been defined as "doing the same thing over and over while expecting different results." Therefore, we pose a provocative question: what would happen if our insane world went sane?

HOW TO CHOOSE AN "OFFICIAL" TRUTH PROVIDER

To fully understand our current story, how to change it, and why we must change it, we must first look at the history of stories.

Since the dawn of human consciousness, we have sought to answer three perennial questions:

1. How did we get here?
2. Why are we here?
3. Now that we're here, how do we make the best of it?

Whoever or whatever entity provides the most satisfactory answers to these questions becomes society's "official" truth provider. But from time to time, the privilege of holding that title has changed hands. At certain pivotal points, civilization has faced challenges for which old answers no longer sufficed. At such times, humans reached out for new and more functional explanations of life. Society seems to be at such a time now, on the threshold of adopting a new worldview and yet still stuck in old metaphors and explanations.

Throughout history, people have applied two different descriptors on the nature of human existence: static and dynamic. Static stories show the world as unchanging and cyclical. Often these stories are based on predictable, repeating patterns of Nature and the stars, along with the belief that whatever happened last year or over the last ten thousand years will likely happen again. An icon that best represents the character of a static civilization would be a circle or, better yet, a snake circling back to bite its own tail.

Dynamic stories demonstrate progress, based on evolution and learning. History clearly reveals that humans profoundly changed behavior when they encountered new information and experiences. Our ancestors discovered fire, made tools, invented the wheel, learned to hunt and plant seeds, created weapons, and built dwellings. In the past one hundred years, technological innovations have not only changed our lives, they've impacted every species on the planet. An iconic image for a dynamic human existence would be a moving arrow as a vector of progress or, better yet, a zooming rocket.

So which story is true? Do we live in a cyclical, ever-repeating pattern? Or do we evolve and grow? The answer is yes. And yes. Both situations occur simultaneously.

Aboriginal people and those who live close to the land survive by maintaining harmony with the cycles of Nature. Living in balance provides for survival but does not encourage or, for that matter, require technological progress.

However, Western civilization and a growing number of Asian nations have been preoccupied with the arrow of progress. Unfortunately, the glamour of technology has eclipsed humanity's connection with Nature, and the pursuit of technological advancement has contributed to disharmony, imbalance, and global crises. Our arrow of progress has become an out-of-control rocket careening from one catastrophe to the next.

To survive—and thrive—must we make a choice between static and dynamic, between wheatgrass and cell phones? Fortunately, we need not answer with an either-or response. Rather, we can choose a both-and solution.

For one thing, life wouldn't exist without technology. As cellular communities evolved from free-living individual cells to form closely packed, social, multicellular organisms, technology became an evolutionary mandate. To build and operate these massive bodies, cells developed the necessary technology to create lightweight structural supports (bones), cables of steel-like collagen (connective tissue), malleable reinforcement materials (fibrocartilage), and hundreds of other biological innovations.

What makes those technological structures so amazing is that they are not found *in* the cells, but were created *by* cells and assembled in their environment through purposeful cellular interactions. So let's show some respect for technology! Without it, we might not be here.

Clearly, the nature of Nature is twofold—to simultaneously change while staying the same. So, what happens when we combine static patterns with dynamic evolution? Simply morph a circle, representing cyclical existence, with a vector, symbolizing directional progress, and voilà: we end up with a universe-friendly *spiral of evolution*. Uniting the principles of harmony and balance with the principles of technological evolution leads to a self-sustaining and thriving civilization.

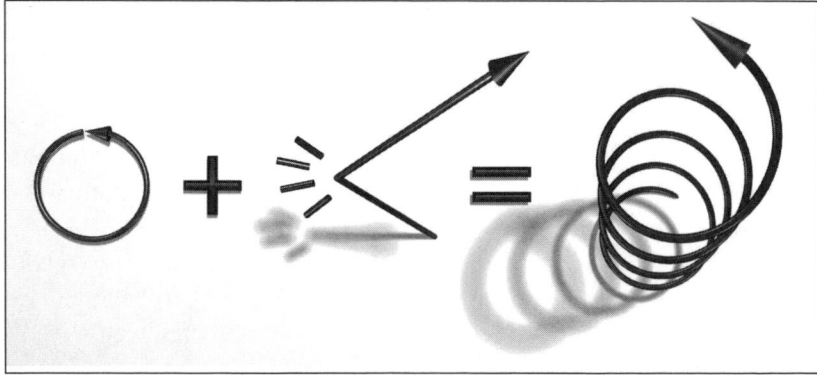

The circle represents cyclical existence, harmony, and balance. The vector symbolizes directional progress and technological evolution. Combined, they create a universe-friendly spiral of evolution toward a self-sustaining and thriving civilization.

However, be forewarned; such a solution requires rewriting basic beliefs that underlie our present culture. Fortunately, we have precedent to aid us; this will not be the first time that new thought has changed the course of humanity. In the last 8,000 years, Western civilization has rewritten its mission statement four times, each time precipitating a historic social upheaval.

BASAL PARADIGMS: A SHORT HISTORY OF STORY

Archaeologists and historians reveal that civilizations around the world have experienced four *basal paradigms,* that is, agreed-upon explanations for existence: *animism, polytheism, monotheism,* and *materialism.* As each stage reached the limits of its understanding and influence, an evolution occurred in which a new stage emerged that both refuted the previous paradigm and also retained vestiges either as an integrated understanding or as an isolated holdout.

The character and fate of each version of civilization is predicated on how people perceive their existence in relationship with the cosmos. From the dawn of civilization, humans have subdivided the Universe into two polarized domains—the material realm and the nonmaterial realm. The material realm represents the physical universe and is comprised of matter. The nonmaterial realm represents invisible forces that the ancients referred to as spirit and today's scientists call *energy fields.* Both modern scientists and the ancient mystics agree that nonmaterial forces greatly influence our human experience. Our discussion treats energy fields and spirits as interchangeable terms.

The four basal paradigms that shape each phase of civilization define that culture's relationship with the material and nonmaterial realms. Some cultures recognize the spiritual realm as the most important factor controlling the character of life on Earth, while others emphasize the material realm as primal in shaping the Universe. Some civilizations believe that both realms are causative factors in determining life's experiences. Plotting a timeline of Western civilization's evolution on a chart to measure society's perceived relationship with the cosmos offers amazing insight into the evolution and future of humanity.

We use the following illustration to trace a civilization's beliefs in regard to their perceived relationship with the spiritual and material realms. In Figure A, the realms are designated as separate elements. Figure B is a more realistic expression in which beliefs that emphasize the material or spiritual realms are presented as overlapping gradients that range from 100 percent belief in the primacy of spirituality to 100 percent belief in the primacy of material reality. The horizontal midline represents a balance of 50 percent emphasis on the material and 50 percent emphasis on the spiritual.

Figure A: Spirit represents the nonmaterial spiritual realm. Matter represents the material physical realm.

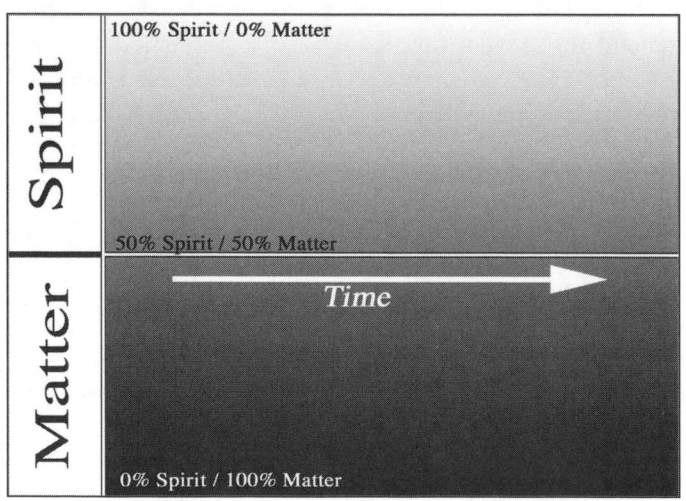

Figure B: In reality, Spirit and Matter overlap, creating a continuum between 100% Spirit / 0% Matter and 0% Spirit / 100% Matter.

The midline in Figure B represents the arrow of advancing time along which we will plot the path of civilization's evolution. An accelerating succession from one basal paradigm to the next through history reveals that humanity is evolving at an exponential rate. Passage through one level of awareness provides a deeper understanding that facilitates a more rapid evolution into and through the next level of awareness. As we shall see by adding dates to this timeline, time is truly speeding up.

All indications are that civilization is now on the brink of evolving into its fifth basal paradigm. But before we go there, let's take a look at where we've been.

ANIMISM: MAKE ME ONE WITH EVERYTHING

Animism is, perhaps, the most ancient religious practice and is believed to have had its origins among primitive cultures in the Neolithic, or Stone Age, around 8000 B.C.E. It is founded on the belief that the spirit is universal, existing in all things—animate or inanimate. Because animism represents a culture based upon a perfect balance between the material and spiritual realms, we have placed it on the figure's midline.

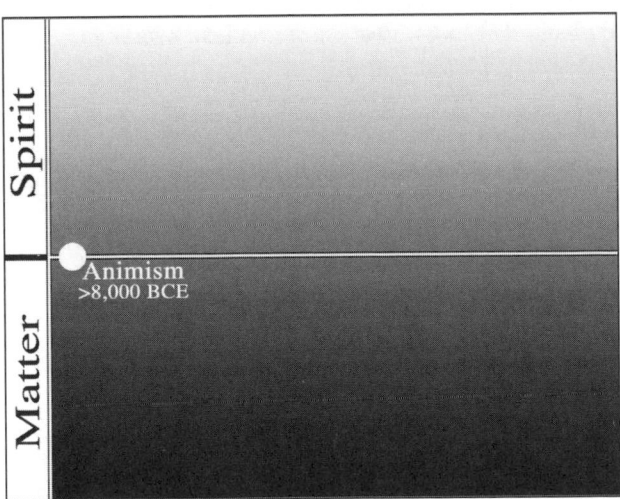

During the Animism period, the prevailing paradigm was the inherent balance between Spirit and Matter.

Derived from the word *anima*, which is Latin for "breath" or "soul," animism is the spiritual experience of the Garden of Eden wherein there is no distinction between the self and the environment. Everything—rain, sky, rocks, trees, animals, and, of course, humans—possesses an intangible spirit. And, while every piece of Nature experiences a single spirit, all of the world's spirits are collectively part of a whole.

Lest we imagine that the Garden of Eden is an invention of the Judeo-Christian religious tradition, mythologist Joseph Campbell observes that some version of this story is universal to all human cultures.[2] The universality of this myth indicates a commonly held primal memory of our connection with all that is.

Animism still exists in a few places among indigenous people. For Australian Aborigine, the spiritual realm is their true reality. What appears to be life in the physical realm is, quite literally, perceived as a waking dream state. Thus, the veil between this world and the next, between matter in the material realm and invisible forces in the spiritual realm, is indeed thin. To some ancient peoples, time itself doesn't really exist and every moment is just another now.

Animism offers these answers to the perennial questions:

1. How did we get here?
   We are children of Mother Earth (material realm) and
   Father Sky (spiritual realm).

2. Why are we here?
   To tend the Garden and thrive.

3. Now that we are here, how do we make the best of it?
   By living in balance with Nature.

Animism is, perhaps, the closest that humankind has come to balancing its emphasis on spirit and matter since the Garden of Eden. During the paradigm of animism, harmony prevailed between the invisible spiritual realm and the visible material realm. Everything was one with the same One. If life were only static and cyclical in nature, we would still be in the Garden, fully integrated in and virtually indistinguishable from our surroundings, wearing a fig leaf or less. People would be like all of the other animals in what would amount to a great global petting zoo.

But some power or incentive, perhaps innate human curiosity, sent our ancient ancestors on a path outside the idyllic Garden so that we, as a species, could observe, evolve, and become knowledgeable in the world. What theology subsequently ascribed as our downfall from the grace of innocence or our separation from God was, in reality, an "up-wising" that has motivated humanity's evolution through our quest for understanding and awareness.

With one bite of the Apple of Knowledge, Earth shook, the unity of the Garden was fractured, and civilization set out on a path to experience the separate realms of spirit and matter. However, there was a significant fly in the ointment: in order to act as observers of the world, our ancestors had to stand outside and look in. This perspective significantly changed their relationship with Nature. All of a sudden, the Universe was subdivided into *me* and *not me*. And somehow, all those forces that had become part of *not me* had to be mollified lest *me* and *others like me* be victimized by the very forces *me and we* once saw as being in balanced harmony; that is, *one*, with all.

POLYTHEISM: THE FIRST SPIRITUAL SUBDIVISION

As humans began to emphasize the difference between me and not me, the unity of the Garden's oneness gave way to "spiritual subdivision." Untethered from the physical world, the spiritual realm took on an energy of its own.

Polytheism came into prominence around 2000 B.C.E. when society disconnected from the oneness of animism through the introduction of a multitude of spiritual deities. In separating spirit from matter, polytheists coalesced the spiritual realm into a variety of iconic gods representing Nature's elements. And wouldn't you know, each of those deities demanded that they be honored with special rituals and ceremonies in order to ensure humankind's continued health and well-being. In seeking the answers to life's mysteries in the spiritual realm, polytheists began to disconnect from Nature.

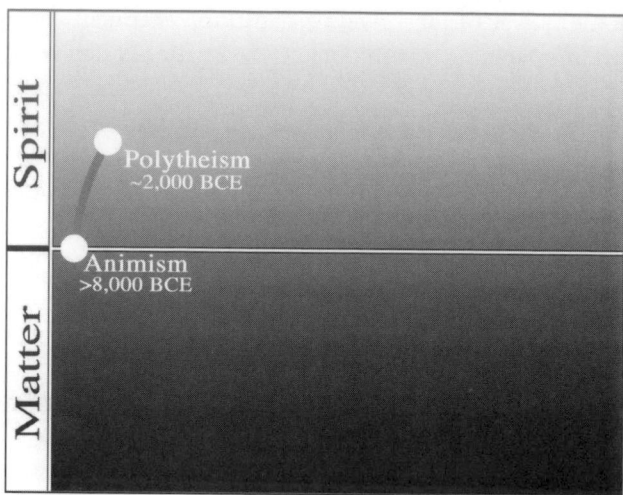

With the advent of polytheism, the prevailing paradigm began to shift into the Spirit realm.

The culmination of the polytheistic epoch came when the Greek gods and goddesses, who exhibited human and superhuman qualities, decided to live in crystal mansions atop Mount Olympus, from which they "commuted," often masquerading in various disguises. As a result, real people never knew if some person or creature was, in reality, a god.

The implications were weighty: fooling around with fickle gods could lead to disaster. Therefore, the message was simple: live in harmony as if everyone and everything were god because the last thing you'd ever want to do was get on the wrong side of an entity who would later get the last laugh by making you roll a boulder uphill every day for eternity.

Polytheists offered new answers to the perennial questions:

1. How did we get here?
   We came from chaos.

2. Why are we here?
   To please the whims of mischievous gods.

3. Now that we are here, how do we make the best of it?
   Don't anger the gods.

Seeking explanations for what primitive people took for granted, persons living during the paradigm of polytheism birthed the first philosophers. Greek thought evolved into two distinct and mutually exclusive points of view.

The first, popularized by Democritus (460–370 B.C.E.), suggested the primacy of matter. Democritus coined the word *atom,* which means "uncuttable." He surmised that invisible and irreducible atoms, the smallest bits of material reality, were at the core of every physical structure and that the Universe consisted of atoms suspended in a void. To Democritus and his followers, the only thing that mattered was *matter.* In other words, what you see is all there is.

In contrast, Socrates (470–399 B.C.E.) offered a philosophy with a vastly different point of view. He perceived the nature of the Universe as a duality. On one hand, there was a nonmaterial realm in which thoughts take on *form.* The more common term for form, as used by Socrates, was *soul.* He also said that forms in the non-physical world were perfect, while the tangible material realm represented an approximation or a "crude shadow" of perfect forms. For example, a person could imagine a perfect chair, but the constructed chair would, at best, only approximate the perfection of the original thought.

As polytheism matured, the Greeks allowed both Democritic and Socratic points of view to coexist.

MONOTHEISM: GOD DOESN'T LIVE HERE ANYMORE

After watching the gods cavort and wreak havoc for a few millennia, it was time to once again move the story along the path of evolution and deeper into the spiritual realm.

Just as children of a certain age begin to sense a need for order and discipline, the search for spiritual understanding led to monotheism and belief in an omniscient, omnipotent, and omnipresent One God who dictates the rules for all. Not only was this God completely out of this world, but He promised us a cushy place out of this world as well, so long as we lived according to His rules—at least those presented by His holy missionaries here on Earth.

While the minority population of Hebrews in the Middle East had been worshipping one God for 2,000 years, Christianity advanced monotheism, with its belief in a single, all-encompassing God as the dominant theological paradigm of the Western world.

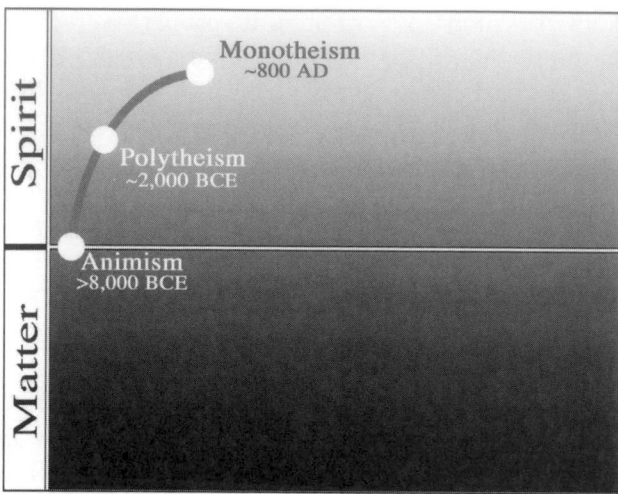

Monotheism took the prevailing paradigm deep into the Spirit realm.

In the first millennium after Christ, the rise of the Church of Rome provided a wonderful example of how a new stage of civilization can subsume and restructure vestiges held over from a former society. Many idols and feasts from the preceding pagan Roman civilization experienced extreme makeovers and returned as Christian icons and festivals.

Under the auspices of Albertus Magnus and his student Thomas Aquinas, the Church revamped the 1,500-year-old version of science and philosophy handed down from the Golden Age of Greece. They winnowed out objectionable polytheistic rhetoric and modified the contents so as to reconcile them with the Old and New Testaments. Through his synthesis of Christian and Aristotelian philosophy, Aquinas created *Natural Theology,* a belief system that strove to understand God through a study of Nature.

The Judeo-Christian Church was particularly drawn to Socrates' notion of a dualistic universe and his concept of a perfect form or soul. The Church taught that the imperfect life in this crude shadow of the material realm, Earth, represents what modern visionary activist Caroline Casey called a "spiritual hardship post."[3] The planet is merely a stage to live out morality plays, a way station on the path to perfection in the invisible Kingdom of Heaven. This last-shall-be-first, suffer-now-and-party-later selling point made an otherwise intolerable *this life*—in the service of opulent higher-ups—a stepping-stone to a blissful *afterlife* for the soul.

Simply stated, monotheism represented a full emphasis on the spiritual realm while the material world was linked with damnation. Therefore, while living in the monotheistic paradigm, civilization became solely invested in the spiritual realm and soared to its maximum deviation from the balance point at the midline of the timeline. Humankind became so focused on the promised life out of this world that life became out of balance in this world.

A philosophical difference between polytheism and the new monotheistic paradigm was the location and accessibility of the Divine Powers. While the Greek gods lived on Mount Olympus, the new Christian God had an unpublished address somewhere in the High Heavens.

Being above it all, this One God naturally needed a chain of command, from the hierarchy all the way to the "lowerarchy." Now that we humans were fully separated from the Creator, mere mortals needed priests to serve as intermediaries. Missionaries enhanced the Church's power and their personal prowess by traveling the world converting animistic primitives who were already communing with their creator with their every breath and doing it very well, thank you.

Monotheists answered the three perennial questions this way:

1. How did we get here?
   Divine intervention.

2. Why are we here?
   To live out morality plays.

3. Now that we are here, how do we make the best of it?
   Obey the Scriptures—or else.

While asserting that life was short and brutal, the Church was making a very compelling offer: do as we say and you, too, will be able to enter the Pearly Gates to an afterlife with the one and only God. Their marketing plan was direct and highly effective: Buy our product; get to Heaven. Don't buy our product; go straight to Hell.

But along with the religious hierarchy came lots of rules, not to mention torture and repression in the name of Father God. And with self-proclaimed infallibility came absolute knowledge. Given that knowledge is power, absolute knowledge is absolute power. Therefore, questioning the Church's claim of infallibility was deemed to be heresy, punishable by death, which gave incredible power to the Church's unchallengeable authority.

The Church became so preoccupied with its absolute knowledge, so corrupted by its absolute power that it began to unravel itself, and the Church eventually fell from its lofty position as civilization's prime arbiter of truth.

A key event in the fall of the Church's dominion occurred in 1517 when Martin Luther, a German monk and teacher, protested the Church's sale of indulgences, which were get-out-of-Hell-free passes for the more well-to-do sinners. Luther's challenge precipitated the Protestant Reformation, and, in its wake, the reach of the infallible Church began to recede. Bolstered by the contributions of Descartes, Bacon, and Newton, among others, humankind's evolutionary path began to move away from its preoccupation with the spiritual realm as science began to unveil the mysteries of the physical Universe.

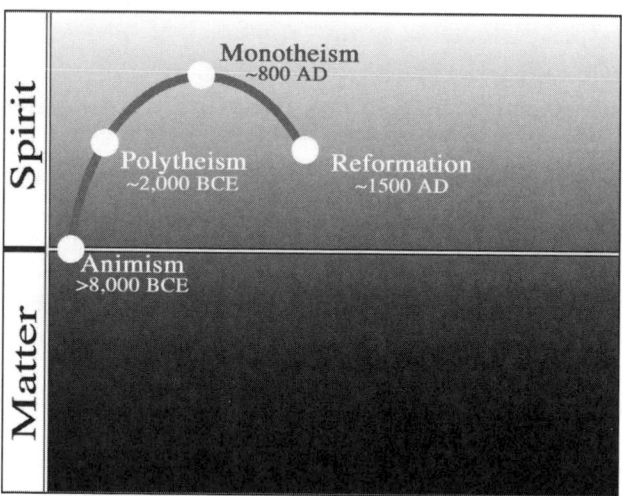

The Reformation marked the first change in direction as the prevailing paradigm began to shift back toward the balance point between Spirit and Matter.

DEISM: A FLASH OF LIGHT

By the late 17th and 18th centuries, humanity's evolutionary path was leading civilization toward the powerful midpoint where it would reflect a balance between spirit and matter. Western civilization was, at the time, experiencing the Age of Enlightenment, a European intellectual movement that emphasizes reason and individualism rather than monotheistic religious tradition. Enlightenment philosophy acknowledged that God and Nature were one and the same and that, through a scientific understanding of Nature, people would learn to live in harmony with God.

Interestingly, the balancing of spirit and matter that marked Enlightenment philosophy was actually derived from studies of the animistic culture of the American Indians by French philosopher Jean-Jacques Rousseau. Rousseau's idealized description of the Native Americans as noble savages who symbolized the innate goodness of humanity, free from the corrupting influence of civilization, launched a wave of European immigration to the newly formed American colonies.

Many of the Founding Fathers were deists, practitioners of Enlightenment philosophy who accepted the existence of a Supreme Being but rejected belief in a supernatural deity who interacts with humankind. They based their beliefs on what they called "natural law and reason." Like the animists 8,000 years prior, deists honored their relationship with both the material and nonmaterial realms of Nature.

Steeped in deist philosophy with elements directly derived from Native American society, the U.S. Declaration of Independence and Constitution represented an exquisite balance between deep spiritual truth and the physical principles of an elegant material Universe. The auspicious event that marked civilization's return to spiritual-material balance was the founding of the United States of America.

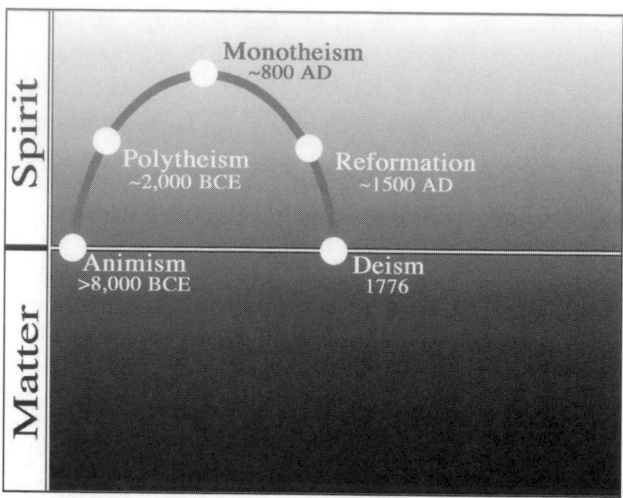

The Deistic period marked a brief moment when Spirit and Matter were again in balanced harmony. This balance didn't last long, but it did foreshadow that it is possible to reattain evolutionary balance.

However, the arrow of time never stands still, so the path of evolution continued, passing through the midpoint as it progressed into the uncharted realm of matter—away from otherworldliness to this worldliness.

As civilization transitioned deeper into the physical realm, science's intensified exploration of the material Universe resulted in awareness and technologies that provided a better physical life than anyone up until that time could imagine. How does one compare the reported miracle of Jesus turning water into wine to the marvels of a steam engine trip to the Orient or a vaccine to prevent the ravages of smallpox? And yet, in spite of all of its technological miracles, modern science during the Age of Enlightenment was not yet in position to vie for the title of civilization's "official" truth provider.

Simply, science was unable to offer a better truth for our origins than provided by the Bible, which meant that the truths of science played second fiddle to the accepted truths of the Church.

SCIENTIFIC MATERIALISM: MATTER MATTERS

Monotheism was based solely on faith. But philosophers and scientists, such as Sir Francis Bacon and Sir Isaac Newton, offered humans an opportunity to question dogma and seek answers for themselves. For people of that era, scientific truths were predicated on mathematical certainty and predictability, and technological miracles would become the foundation of the new industrial revolution.

Meanwhile, the Church desperately tried to retain control of knowledge, suppressing creative thinkers with the threat of an invitation to the Holy Office of Inquisition, the consequences of which were an unusually effective incentive to help people "think correctly."

The Church also limited the quest for knowledge by making many topics off limits, discouraging curious budding scientists who wanted to know more about the world. For example, the Church claimed that the human body was a restricted domain, a "Mystery of God" for His eyes only and to peer inside was a sin. Christians were not allowed to be physicians because of the intellectual prohibition against studying the body's internal workings. The practice of medicine was, therefore, a trade restricted to Jews, Muslims, and those the Church considered to be nonbelievers. But, in spite of the Church's decrees regarding human biology, scientists forged ahead in other fields.

Philosopher and mathematician Rene Descartes, then later Isaac Newton, postulated that the Universe was a machine. Newton's principles of mathematics extrapolated the precision of gears in a clock onto the solar system. While the new science did not deny that God might have been the original watchmaker, once the "world watch" was wound up, it was running pretty well solely on mathematics.

In a world where science ruled, God was so far off the planet that His work operated without him. The subsequent industrial revolution and technological inventions further nudged God out of the picture. Who needs God when we humans can make our own technological miracles?

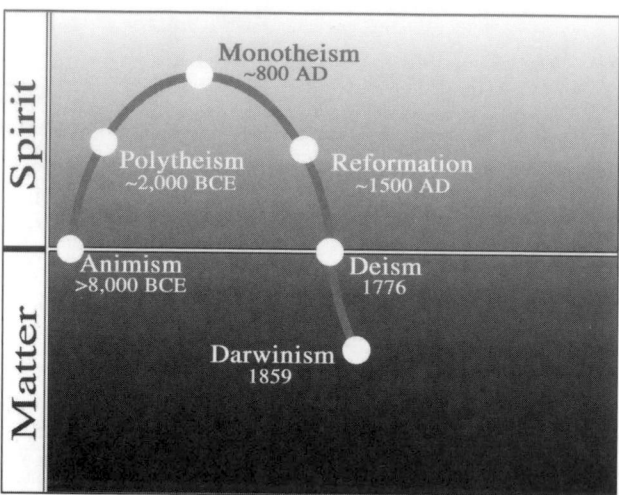

Darwinism marked the prevailing paradigm's shift into the realm of Matter.

It wasn't until English naturalist Charles Darwin arrived on the scene in the mid-19th century that scientific materialism became civilization's dominant paradigm. Remember, a basal paradigm story has to answer all three perennial questions. Until Darwin postulated his *The Origin of Species*, science wasn't able to offer an adequate explanation for the question, "How did we get here?" Darwin's theory of origins proposed that humans were derived from a primitive life form through millions of years of hereditary variations shaped by a never-ending struggle to survive. The people of the 19th century readily accepted Darwinian theory because they were quite familiar with the consequences of plant and animal breeding

Once the theory of evolution was accepted as a scientific fact, civilization quickly dropped the Church as its supreme authority and adopted scientific materialism, with its materialist worldview of science, as the "official" truth provider.

Materialists answered the three perennial questions this way:

1. How did we get here?
   Random acts of heredity.

2. Why are we here?
   To go forth and multiply.

3. Now that we are here, how do we make the best of it?
   To live by the law of the jungle.

And there we have it—a rapid descent from the laws of Scripture to the law of the jungle. With honing, the double-edged sword of materialism has provided us with comforts of technology that would have been unimaginable to our ancestors; simply put, civilization traded one absolute authority for another. In light of science's perceived miracles, the dogmatic religion of monotheism gave way to the dogmatic religion of scientific materialism, or scientism. For science, the material world is all there is and anything that doesn't fit into that ideological package is branded as heresy.

Like an adolescent asserting independence for the first time, we humans even began to imagine that we could understand the mechanics of a matter-based Universe and, hence, unlock all the secrets of life. Civilization's path hit the extreme deviation toward the material realm in 1953 when molecular biologists James Watson and Francis Crick declared they had uncovered the ultimate secret of biology with their discovery of the DNA double helix. In defining the nature of the cell's genesis elements, Watson and Crick identified the material origins of life.

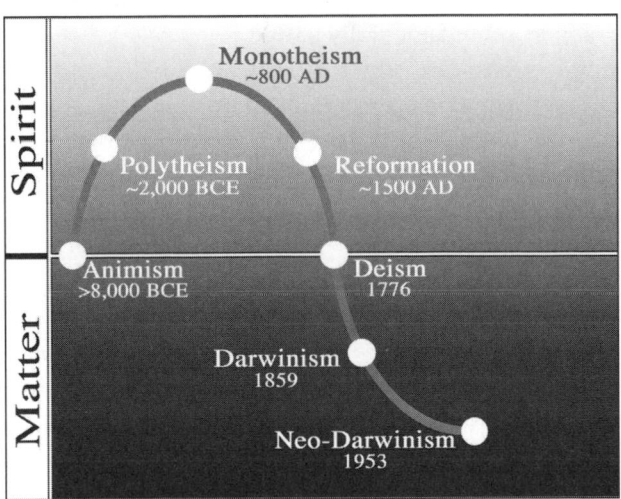

Neo-Darwinism took the prevailing paradigm deep into the realm of Matter.

THE TIDE HAS TURNED

Well, what goes up must come down, and we humans have been suffering a "come-downance" ever since. Over the past 50 years, deified technology has generated unimaginable negative reverberations.

In Walt Disney's *Fantasia*, Mickey Mouse plays the role of the Sorcerer's Apprentice who attempts to re-create the sorcerer's magic with neither the knowledge nor the wisdom his master possesses. The result is disastrous, as Mickey is unable to control the power he has unleashed. Similarly, modern civilization has activated the power of technology while operating from a limited Mickey Mouse consciousness. Consequently, the same matter-based medicine that gave us penicillin, the polio vaccine, and open-heart surgery—without the countervailing understanding of the invisible realm—has become a leading cause of death in Western societies.

In a last ditch effort to capitalize on the culture of scientific materialism, venture capitalists convinced scientists and the public to invest in the Human Genome Project (HGP). This project was designed to identify and patent each of the 150,000 genes that neo-Darwinian molecular biologists theorized were necessary to create a human being.

However, the completion of the HGP in 2001 revealed the human genome consists of only approximately 23,000 genes. The missing 125,000 genes glaringly reveal that the neo-Darwinian belief in a genetically programmed biology is fundamentally flawed.[4]

Creating a health-care system based on this flaw, in conjunction with other fundamental misperceptions to be described later, has limited advances in health care and is directly responsible for allopathic medicine's decreased effectiveness and increased costs. The public's dissatisfaction with the current state of allopathic care is reflected in the fact that nearly half the population of the United States has sought relief through complementary medicine modalities.

Interestingly, most alternative healing practices emphasize the role of invisible energy fields in shaping the character of human life. The figure on the next page shows civilization's trend away from materialism and toward balance with the realm of invisible sources, the realm of spirit.

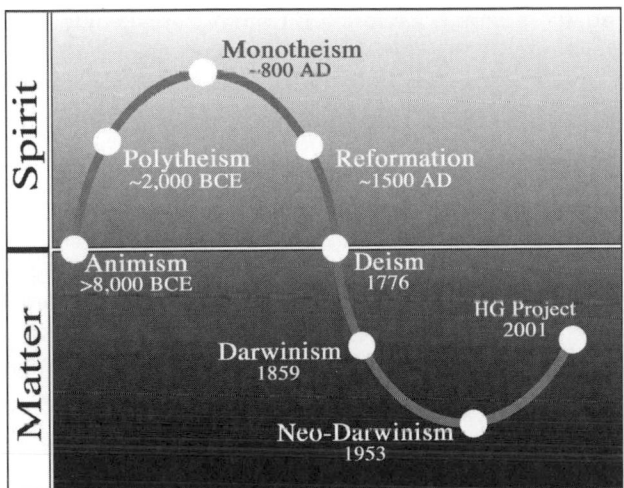

The Human Genome Project, while still an endeavor of Matter, was a key point in the prevailing paradigm's shift back toward the balance point.

A new science has arisen to replace the erroneous belief that genes are masters of our fate. The new-edge science of epigenetics recognizes that an organism's biology and genetic activity are directly influenced by their interaction with the environment. Rather than being victims of our genes, epigenetic science reveals, that by controlling our environment, we have the power to control our biology and become masters of our fate.

The good news in the bad news is that society's evolutionary path is rapidly returning to the powerful midpoint and not a moment too soon. Each day reveals a new lesson about how our unbalanced preoccupation with materialism is threatening life on this planet. Thankfully, we seem to be on a quickening learning curve. But if we are to move beyond the unconscious rollercoaster ride of the sine wave, we must become fully conscious and aware that what we need now is not more spiritual-material polarization, but instead harmonizing integration.

The resurgence of religious fundamentalism, particularly the obsession with the rapture and other off-planet rewards, seems to indicate there is a collective knowing that we humans are cruising "fool speed ahead" down the road to destruction. Neither the black-cloaked priests nor the white-coated scientists can help us right now—at least not within the confines of existing belief systems. Both monotheism and scientism have essentially disconnected humans from Nature. Religious fundamentalism holds humans above the rest of creation, instead of being part of it. Scientific materialism tells us that the miracle of life was merely an accident that resulted from a random roll of genetic dice.

THE STORY BEHIND THE STORY

Are you beginning to see why we need a new story? The old stories keep us powerless, at the mercy of either a distant God or random genetic events. They steal our attention and energy by polarizing the population to adopt untenable positions rather than enabling us to move forward. Must we deviate once again? Or will we cultivate unity and coherence that will allow us to take an emergent step forward when, in the near future, the path of evolution once again brings civilization to the powerful midpoint of balanced spirituality and materiality?

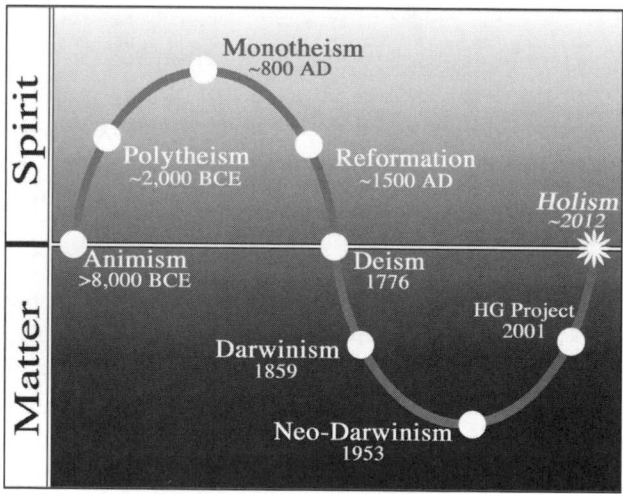

With holism, which is the forecasted result of the pending spontaneous evolution, the prevailing paradigm will, once again, be balanced between Spirit and Matter, drawing upon the best and most powerful attributes of each.

At a time when persistent archaic patterns are fueling the dueling dualities, it would be wise to remember what quantum physicists tell us about the nature of physical existence: behind every particle, there's a wave telling the particle what to do. Just as animists and deists understood that spirit and matter must fully coexist, we are being challenged to move past either-or and to recognize both-and. It's like those beer commercials: Great taste *and* less filling. Spirit *and* matter. Wave *and* particle. You *and* me *and* all the others, too.

Consider the story of life itself. Life came into existence at the midpoint, or zero-point, where both waves of energy and particulate matter were fully present. For billions of years, energy from the sun hit the particles of matter that comprise *Mater*, our Mother Earth. The energy from those light waves merged with Earth's inorganic chemistry through a process called photosynthesis. The composite of light waves and chemical particles generated *organic chemistry*, the chemistry of living organisms. Through *photosynthesis*, the energy of sunlight enlivened inert matter. So life, indeed, began with light from the sky fusing with the physical matter of Earth! Can you see where Native American animists generated the concept of Father Sky and Mother Earth?

In a similar fashion, the sperm cell, which is essentially designed as a means of delivering genes, carries only information. In that capacity, sperm function is the equivalent of the wave that fuses with the physical matter in the mother's egg. Once again, in the Universe's amazing web of integrated self-similar patterns, life is created. From information and matter emerges a new life, something that cannot be predicted by studying the egg and the sperm as separate entities. Is it possible that by integrating the opposites of spirit and matter, energy and particle, masculine and feminine, we can create an emergent human society, one never before seen, whose expression is completely unpredictable by studying what we have and who we are now?

The notion of an emergent humanity may seem like a pie-in-the-sky ideal, but consider the alternative. We are being forced into a situation wherein we either evolve or die. Which would you prefer? And, as we will see in Part II, *Four Myth-Perceptions of the Apocalypse*, our personal preferences exert a lot more control over our reality than we have, so far, imagined. Consequently, what we choose to prefer might actually make a difference in the fate of humanity.

Unlike our deistic forebears, the battle we face now is not against some external king, but rather against our own internal conscious and unconscious limitations, against our distorted misperception of human nature and human potential. We are at war with the out-picturing of our own fears and habitual defenses against things that might not even exist anymore. The sad joke is that most of us are "remotely controlled" by the beliefs and limitations of people who have lived in the past, and we don't even know it!

When a baby elephant is being trained, its leg is tied to a post with a strong rope. No matter how hard and how long the baby elephant pulls, there is no budging the post. The elephant ultimately comes to associate the rope with an all-powerful, immovable force. When the elephant becomes an adult, simply placing a rope around its leg causes it to stay put because it has already resigned itself to the all-powerfulness of the rope. Even though the adult elephant has the strength to break any rope or uproot nearly any post, the belief of limitation it acquired from past programming in its youth keeps the elephant immobile and docile.

In that light, we might ask: "Which stories and beliefs are keeping us unconsciously tethered, disempowered, and thwarted from expressing our true abilities? Are we limited by unquestioned beliefs about original sin or the meaninglessness of the Universe? Despite our moral guidance, are we secretly afraid that maybe might does make right? Have we resigned ourselves to the pervasive belief that there will always be warfare and poverty, and that's just the way the world is?"

Well, tell that to Mahatma Gandhi. Or Martin Luther King, Jr. Or, better yet, to Washington, Jefferson, and Franklin. Because, as we will see in the next chapter, the unfinished business of America's Founding Fathers may very well hold the key to our next evolutionary stage.

Just as they founded the United States of America on what they called "natural law," perhaps what is needed now is an updated natural law through which we live by our higher nature as cells in the body of Mother Earth *and* in the spirit energy of the eternal Universe.

That new direction may be our return ticket to the Garden, but this time, we will return as conscious gardeners, co-creating ever more beautiful, functional, and loving expressions of life.

CHAPTER 4

REDISCOVERING AMERICA

*"We don't need a revolution in the United States.
We already had one, thank you. What we need
now is an American Evolution, where We the People
evolve into the citizens the country's founders dreamed of."*
— **Swami Beyondananda**

EVOLUTION IN THE PETRI DISH

When we began to write this book, our original working title was "The American Evolution." Because we, Bruce and Steve, came from the vastly different domains of biological science and political science, we each recognized the evolutionary potential in the political science experiment called the United States of America. Our nation's founding slogan *e pluribus unum*, "out of many, one," reflects evolutionary science's new understanding that each of us is a conscious, aware, participating cell in the body of humanity. The science experiment notion makes even more sense when we look at America as a human culture dish, a macrocosmic science project from which people throughout the world can learn.

From a biological perspective, Earth represents a giant petri dish that supports the growth and survival of all the organisms in the biosphere. Oceans, rivers, mountains, and deserts create natural geological boundaries that carve the terrain into specific habitats that are populated with unique and diverse communities of flora and fauna. The characteristics that define each environment shape the evolutionary traits of their resident species.

The same is true for Earth's human inhabitants. With the rise of civilization, the environment was further subdivided by geopolitical boundaries that delineated states and nations. Citizens contained within national countries or states were, until recently, walled off from the influence of surrounding tribes. Therefore, each political territory provided a defined environment that shaped the traits and character of its human inhabitants.

Separated by political boundaries, walled-off nations represent the biological equivalent of a culture dish that supports the growth and development of its citizens. Over time, the cultural environments within sovereign petri dishes shape the distinctive customs and traits that define each population's national character.

As is evident in any husbandry program, inbreeding can capture and enhance an organism's special traits. We see the upside of inbreeding in the amazing number and variety of cat and dog species that have been created. Unfortunately, the same breeding practices that create national champions can also create hereditary defects. Inbred genetic disorders can produce degenerative diseases such as malformed bones and joints, hemophilia, mental retardation, and a vast array of other dysfunctions.

By the 18th century, cultural inbreeding had defined the unique positive and negative traits that characterize each of the petri dish nations that comprise Western civilization. Just as collies and pit bulls express different traits, humans bred in relatively isolated cultures develop cultural personalities. These tendencies have been represented humorously in the joke about Heaven and Hell as it relates to the countries in Europe. In Heaven, the police are English, the mechanics are German, the cooks are French, the lovers are Italian, and it's all run by the Swiss. In Hell, the police are German, the cooks are English, the mechanics are French, the lovers are Swiss, and it's all run by the Italians. We laugh in recognition of the differences in these "human breeds."

Something else was true about the human breeding grounds of Europe in the 18th century. Citizens within each country were eventually molded into a stratified, caste-like hierarchy of power and position predicated by their family lineage. The rigid nature of a stratified social class essentially defined a citizen's future prospects before they were even born.

Consequently, when deistic Enlightenment philosophy swept through Western civilization in the 1700s, Jean-Jacques Rousseau's accounting of the noble savages' freedom in the New World inspired visions of unlimited possibilities. Fueled by the dream of unbridled opportunity in the casteless New World, people around the globe sought a better life by immigrating to the fertile environment offered in the American colonies.

The founding of the United States of America was a grand experiment in the evolution of human civilization. The American colonies were seeded with a widely diverse population that represented numerous races, creeds, and nationalities. Contained within its geopolitical borders and isolated from Europe and Asia by great oceans, the U.S. provided a cultural petri dish to test the dynamics and potential of a global civilization.

Farmers, geneticists, and pet lovers have historically been aware that there is a tendency of crossbred individuals to express qualities superior to those of their purebred parents. Scientists refer to this phenomenon as *hybrid vigor*. In terms of intercultural breeding, the meteoric success of the U.S. to global supremacy was a testament to the powers of hybrid vigor.

In addition to cultural crossbreeding, the founding of the United States also contributed to humankind's further recognition of the need to balance the spiritual and material realms. The amazing success of the U.S. was due, at least in part, to the incorporation of these advanced evolutionary principles of an egalitarian civilization, fostered by Enlightenment philosophy, directly into the Declaration of Independence and the Constitution. In doing so, the Founding Fathers put their lives on the line, not for themselves or even the citizens of the American colonies. No, they demanded recognition for the value of human life in a declaration dedicated to all of humanity.

Unfortunately, as illustrated by our evolutionary timeline in the previous chapter, the harmony of civilization's deistic phase represented only a short transitional period in humanity's march into the material realm. In the 1860s, Darwinian theory introduced the world to the notion of a godless, matter-based existence. At the same time, the American Civil War and the subsequent industrial boom ushered in a new, materialist philosophy—one that would lead the United States to trade in its deistic spiritual roots and adopt the gold standard. Along with the worship of money came the rule by the machine. America's enormous financial success during this period was facilitated by the empowerment of a nonliving entity to make a profit at any cost. In the 1880s, this entity, the corporation, was given the rights of persons but without the moral conscience of a human heart. As is often the case in Nature, an organism, such as an invasive species, arises in the environment in response to an imbalance and then becomes the imbalance.

Given the corporations' imperative to grow at any cost, we could argue that these once beneficial organisms have become parasites on the body politic, that they have over-mined America's material assets and undermined the moral and spiritual ideals introduced by the Founding Fathers. As we will show in this chapter, the founding vision of the United

States was a significant step in the evolution of humanity and has stood as a beacon for the rest of the world—in spite of all the ways the United States has fallen short of that vision.

Nonetheless, this grand experiment is far from over. Some would say that in the awakening following the Bush years, there is a rededication to live up to the Founders' vision. As we emerge from an era of cynicism to one of evolutionary possibility, we can see how the original intention for the United States has been lost . . . and how it can be discovered once again.

AMERICA: REVOLUTION TO DEVOLUTION

As we explore the rise and fall of paradigms along the path of human evolution, it's important to remember that history ultimately belongs to those who write and interpret it and that interpretations tend to correspond with the notions of those doing the interpreting. Consequently, we must be aware that, in addition to parts of the story being incorrectly recorded, many interesting and accurate events are often conveniently omitted because their truth didn't fit with the story line that the current "official" truth provider was presenting.

Those of us who grew up in the United States probably remember stories of the Declaration of Independence, the Bill of Rights, and the idealistic principles the country was built upon. Stories in elementary school gave the Founding Fathers a supernatural aura, as exemplified by the iconic painting by Emanuel Leutze, *Washington Crossing the Delaware*, which depicts General George Washington standing near the bow of a boat while his men row through the icy waters of the Delaware River during the Revolutionary War.

As befitting their historical contributions, the Founders were initially placed on an iconic pedestal. But within 100 years of putting quill to parchment, their halos were tarnished by political strife of the greatest magnitude; the rise of American industry with its machine mentality; and scathing attacks by investigative journalists, writers, and scholarly skeptics who clearly demonstrated that all cherished icons and ideals were ripe for deconstruction.

Certainly, the Civil War severely eroded America's innocence. Then, following that war, the U.S. economy transformed from agriculture to manufacturing, primarily within the industries of coal, steel, and railroads—all of which served to feed the machine. Even urban political organizations, which gave away Thanksgiving turkeys in exchange for votes in the November elections, were called machines.

In the late 1800s, people enjoyed the simplistic rags-to-riches stories written by American author Horatio Alger, which celebrated individuals plucking the plums of success in a competitive world. By the early 1900s, optimism gave way to books revealing harsh realities; these included *The Jungle* by Upton Sinclair, an exposé on the horrible conditions in America's meat packing plants. Muckraking journalists Ida Tarbell, Lincoln Steffens, and others exposed the darker side of the machine age, including the destructive abuses by corporate giants such as Standard Oil Company. Perhaps the most influential American historian of the first half of the 20th century was Charles Beard, who, literally and figuratively, came of age during America's machine age. Writing at that time of unenlightened self-interest, it's understandable that Beard would look beneath the halos of the Founding Fathers and find ordinary human beings with selfish interests much like those of Beard's contemporaries, the businessmen and politicians of the early industrial age.[1]

Reinforced by the increasing cynicism of the postmodern paradigm, Beard's disparaging view of the Founding Fathers took hold and permeated conventional wisdom. As a result, over the past 50 years, the Founding Fathers have come to be associated with archconservative Jeffersonian patriots, longing for a less meddlesome federal government.

At the same time, leftist scholars operating in their own paradigm of *political correctness,* saw the Founding Fathers as privileged white men, many of whom were slaveholders, who sanctioned expropriating the lands of Native peoples. These scholarly critics chastised: If the writers of the Bill of Rights were so enlightened, why did they say all men—and not women—were created equal? And why was the only woman they ever talked about, Betsy Ross, relegated to sewing the flag?

Today, we can only imagine Washington, Jefferson, Adams, Franklin, Hancock, and the rest of the 56 delegates who signed the Declaration of Independence—many of whom were ostracized and suffered financial hardship after assuming their heroic position—wondering how the ideas for which they risked life and fortune could have fallen by the wayside and how their contributions could be dismissed as mere selfishness.

THE AMERICAN REVOLUTION WAS NO TEA PARTY

Thom Hartmann, a contemporary American radio "uncommon-tator" and author of *What Would Jefferson Do?*, offers a more integrated view and challenges the "elitist white guys" label applied to the Founding Fathers by both conservatives and liberals. Hartmann, who called his political perspective "the radical middle," discovered in his research that the wealthiest of the American revolutionaries, John Hancock, would, at his wealthiest, be worth about $750,000 in today's dollars. Another of the wealthier signers, Thomas Nelson of Virginia, had his lands and home seized by the British and died penniless at the age of 50.[2]

And, while educators today would have American youngsters believe that throwing the British out of the colonies was the thing to do, the revolutionaries were, in actuality, a minority of colonists. As Hartmann wrote: "These men [who signed the Declaration] were the most idealistic and determined among the colonists. While the conservatives of the day argued that America should remain a colony of England forever, these liberal radicals believed in both individual liberty and societal obligations."[3]

When they signed the Declaration of Independence, the Founding Fathers were totally aware that they were signing their own death warrants. When they wrote, "We mutually pledge to each other our Lives, our Fortunes, our Sacred Honor," they understood they were legally marking themselves as traitors—and the penalty for treason was death. When Patrick Henry declared, "Give me liberty, or give me death!" this was no oratorical hyperbole. And when Ben Franklin told his fellow revolutionaries, "We must all hang together or we shall most assuredly hang separately," he, too, was speaking literally.

John Hancock, the first to sign the Declaration of Independence and whose signature looms as the largest by far—"so King George can read it without his spectacles"—already had a price on his head for sedition. When he and his wife were forced to flee the British army, their baby died in childbirth.[4]

According to Hartmann, 9 of the 56 signers lost their lives in the war and 17 lost their homes and fortunes. He concluded: "While many of the conservative Tory families still have considerable wealth and power (in Canada and England), not a single Founder's family persists today as a wealthy or politically dominant entity."[5]

With cynicism still the currency of the current political conversation, it's easy to accept the tired, persistent belief that nothing ever really changes as true. Yet consider this: a band of mostly young men (Franklin was, by far, the oldest at 72, and Jefferson, at 33, was closer to the average age) stood up to what was then the greatest power in the world, the British Empire. In addition to his military clout, King George III wielded phenomenal economic power over these revolutionaries because he was also an owner of the largest multinational corporation of that time, the East India Company, which was the target of the celebrated Boston Tea Party.

SOVEREIGN EQUALS UNDER NO KING

Even more remarkable than the rebellion—for rebellions had occurred before—were the evolutionary ideals upon which this revolution was based: "We hold these truths to be self-evident, that all men are created equal, that they are endowed by their Creator with certain unalienable Rights, that among these are Life, Liberty and the Pursuit of Happiness." This statement flew in the face of European law, even at its most enlightened.

According to the law of England, God granted kingship to the king who then may, as documented in the Magna Carta, bestow rights on his subjects. This doctrine is classic hierarchy, which places ordinary, non-royal humans squarely at the bottom of the "lowerarchy." The entire notion that ordinary humans could be equal sovereign citizens who endow government with authority—instead of the other way around—was unheard of. Where did those ideas come from?

As we may vaguely remember from high school or college history, those ideas came from the Age of Enlightenment in Europe, from philosophers such as John Locke and Jean-Jacques Rousseau and something called natural law. Under natural law, all human laws are to be judged on the basis of how closely they conform to the laws of God and Nature.

This might seem like something up for interpretation, and it was. Initially, the idea was this: God, and God's agent, the state, intends for human happiness. Natural law most insures the happiness of most.

In his classic work, *Leviathan*, published in 1651, English philosopher Thomas Hobbes attempted to codify this natural law in nine precepts, roughly summarized here:[6]

1. Seek peace first, use war as a last resort.

2. Be willing to offer the same freedom to others as to oneself.

3. Keep your agreements.

4. Practice gratitude.

5. Accommodate your own needs to the laws of the community.

6. As appropriate, forgive those who repent.

7. In the case of revenge, focus not on the great evil of the past but the greater good to follow.

8. Never declare hatred of another.

9. Acknowledge the equality of others.

John Locke, for his part, sought to hold governments accountable to these principles. In his *Two Treatises of Government*, which he initially published anonymously in 1689, Locke suggested that if a ruler went against these natural laws and failed to protect "life, liberty and property," the populace could justifiably overthrow the government.[7] Sound familiar? This is the very argument Thomas Jefferson used when he crafted the Declaration of Independence.

GRASSROOTS DEMOCRACY ROOTED IN SACRED GROUND

If we stopped with the philosophers of the Age of Enlightenment, however, we would be missing, perhaps, the most important influence on our Founders and the government they created. From where did the European philosophers such as Locke and Rousseau get their ideas? The answer: from Jefferson's, Washington's, and Franklin's backyard—the New World.

While high-minded philosophies of human perfection existed in Europe since the Golden Age of Greece, the idea of life, liberty, and the pursuit of happiness remained an abstract ideal in Socrates' perfect world of form and never made it into the crude shadow of reality. Until, that is, the first reports from the Americas described the ways and customs of its native peoples.

While Rousseau's depiction of the "noble savage" of North America might have been over-idealized, it had its basis in reality. As a matter of fact, the concepts of democracy and balance of powers were alive and well-established at least 300 or 400 years before the signers of the Declaration lifted a quill! Perhaps as early as 1100 c.e. or, according to some accounts, in the 1400s or 1500s, six tribes that populated what is now the northeastern United States, southern Ontario, and Québec, came together and formed the Iroquois Confederacy.[8]

The story of the Iroquois Confederacy begins with a seer and great teacher of mysterious origin, a Native American whose name was The Confluence of Two-Rivers. Two-Rivers proposed a League of Peace and Power as a way to establish tranquility between warring tribes in what is now upstate New York. He chose a negotiator, Hiawatha, to bring the tribes together. The result was the League of *Haudenosaunee*, the Onondaga word for "People of the Long House." The confederacy was comprised of the Mohawk, Oneida, Onondaga, Cayuga, and Seneca tribes, and, later, the Tuscaroras, who migrated from the Carolinas. Through this confederacy, six diverse nations found a way to live in relative peace and harmony through a political system that remarkably presaged the United States Constitution.[9]

Other similarities between the Iroquois Confederacy and the United States government are also apparent. As with America's subsequent federal system, the tribes retained autonomy in regard to local issues. The confederacy was a mutual-defense pact, which provided a strong multi-tribe nation to protect against outside enemies. It conserved lives, resources, and energies that would have been spent on waging war with each other. Plus, the confederacy employed a sophisticated system of checks and balances between three governmental branches.

In the Iroquois Nation of colonial America, the Age of Enlightenment philosophers of Europe found a real-world object lesson in freedom. As noted historian of the Iroquois Nation Donald A. Grinde, a professor of American Studies and a Yamasee Indian, points out, the Iroquois believed in freedom of expression, provided that expression caused no harm. Unlike European society, which Grinde called "guilt-oriented" and riddled with copious "thou shalt nots," tribal culture was "shame-oriented." That is, a strong identification with the community motivated individuals to avoid transgressions that could bring shame to the clan and to themselves.[10]

THE "AMERICANIZATION" OF THE WHITE MAN

The similarities between Indian governance and the structure of the United States, no doubt, originated from the profound influence that Native Americans had on the everyday life of the colonists. This was particularly true for those who grew up in the New World rather than England.

More so than in Europe, wild nature was everywhere in America and the customs of down-to-earth informality and equality naturally pervaded the colonies. As Indian law scholar Felix Cohen put it, "The real epic of America is the yet unfinished story of the Americanization of the white man."[11]

For example, settlers just off the boat from the Old World were surprised to find colonists dressed in Indian buckskins and shocked to learn that some had even adopted indigenous customs—such as bathing! In European society at the time, bathing was thought to be detrimental to health, so imagine their reaction seeing European-looking folks actually skinny-dipping with the natives.

In his boyhood, Thomas Jefferson was deeply influenced by Native American culture. His father, Peter Jefferson, was a cartographer who took young Tom on numerous excursions. A frequent visitor to Jefferson's childhood home in Shadwell, Virginia, was the Cherokee chief Ontasseté. There, young Tom joined his father and the chief as they held conversations long into the night.[12]

A Native American from the Iroquois Nation was the first to actually propose the creation of the United States—on the Fourth of July no less! On July 4, 1744, at a meeting designed to forge an alliance between the Iroquois and the English colonists against the French, a charismatic chief named Canassatego spoke to the colonists. He said, "Our wise forefathers established union and amity between the Five Nations. This has made us formidable. This has given us great weight and authority with our neighboring nations. We are a powerful Confederacy and, by your observing the same methods our wise forefathers have taken, you will acquire much strength and power; therefore, whatever befalls you, don't fall out with one another."[13]

According to Benjamin Franklin, who was present at the meeting, Canassatego also offered a powerful demonstration to the colonists. The chief held up an arrow and easily snapped it in two. But when he lashed together twelve arrows—one for every one of the colonies represented— not even the strongest man in the room could break them.[14] Interestingly, the Great Seal of the United States, designed in 1782 by Charles Thomson, the secretary of the Continental Congress, and attorney William Barton, shows an eagle clutching thirteen arrows in his claws.

Shortly after the meeting with Canassatego, Franklin began his campaign for a federal union. In 1751, he wrote: "It would be a very strange thing if six nations of ignorant savages should be capable of forming a scheme for such a union and be able to execute it in such a manner as that it has subsisted ages, and yet a like union should be impractical for ten or a dozen English colonies."[15]

Aside from the slam at "ignorant savages," Franklin deeply respected the Iroquois' political wisdom. Franklin's Albany Plan of Union, which he presented to the Albany, New York, Congress in 1754, adopted many features from the Iroquois Confederacy, including the principal position of a President-General who would be appointed by the British Crown and colonial delegates.[16]

The Albany Plan didn't pass, but it did serve as a model for the U.S. Articles of Confederation, which, in 1781, became the first governing document of the new United States of America. As a result, the Iroquois Nation was represented by delegates to the Constitutional Convention, as they well deserved to be.

While the Constitutional Convention was convening in Philadelphia, another revolution against a monarchy had erupted in Europe. Using the United States Declaration of Independence as its model, the National Assembly in France drew up its own Declaration of the Rights of Man and of the Citizen. Like the U.S. Declaration, the French document included a statement that underscored basic human rights.

But the French version didn't take. Perhaps the energy field of European monarchies was so present and pervasive that even a riled citizenry couldn't overcome it. However, on the New World side of the Atlantic, where the voice and reach of the British monarchy was fainter and weaker, the revolutionary and evolutionary colonialists established a new republic.

AMERICA'S EVOLUTIONARY TRADITION

In addition to the Native American impact on the formation of the U.S. government, there is another largely untold story about America's Founders, a story that relates to the very evolutionary threshold we stand upon today.

Depending on which axes were being ground, the Founders of the country have been described as scientists or religious men or deists, while, in fact, they were all three. In his book, *America's Secret Destiny*, author Robert Hieronimus probes deeply into the spiritual lives of Benjamin Franklin, George Washington, and Thomas Jefferson. All three of these American founders were influenced both by Native Americans who invoked spirit without establishing religion and by the moral and metaphysical ideals of Freemasonry.[17]

Many of the nation's founders were fraternal Freemasons. While the word *mason* in the name relates to artisans who craft buildings with stone, the word *free* is a direct reference to that organization's ancient founders who were granted freedom to travel across national boundaries to build cathedrals and other buildings. The Freemasons, whose origins are traced to the secret societies of the Knights Templar, are dedicated to the worldly expression of the ideals of "moral renewal and perfection of mankind."[18]

Through harmonious development of their minds and their hearts, Freemasons pledge to dedicate their lives to unselfish service to mankind. There is no doubt that our Founding Fathers were affected by special Masonic rituals, which historian Charles Leadbeater described as influencing the energies of the body "so that evolution may be quickened."[19]

Benjamin Franklin was so taken with Freemasonry that, rather than wait until the required age of 21 to join, he founded his own secret society at age 20. He called his society The Leather Apron Club in reference to the leather aprons worn by masons. He later changed the name to the Junto Club and, finally, the American Philosophical Society. And their credo? Quite simply: "To build a Universe of peace, devoid of fear and based on love."[20]

Franklin also founded another secret organization in France, the Apollonian Society, to further his lifelong dream of uniting science with religion. As a Mason, he found Masonic doctrine to be virtually indistinguishable from deism, which is the belief in God based on evidence of reason and Nature. He, therefore, referred to God as "the Supreme Architect."[21]

The nature of George Washington's religious devotion is the subject of conflicting stories. That's because Washington was a bridge between deistic practices of secret societies and religious practices of mainstream religions. As such, he was able to communicate with all his brethren. This is why some religious sources quote his most pious statements, while freethinker sources declare he was never baptized and left churchgoing to his wife, Martha.

Nevertheless, Washington gave command only to generals who were Freemasons, and he adopted the fundamental principles of "the brotherhood of man, and the Fatherhood of God." He spent time in prayer and meditation every day and ordered that his soldiers say prayers every morning. When no minister was present, he would often lead Bible readings himself.[22]

Thomas Jefferson, while not as overtly religious, wrote the Jefferson Bible and once said, "I am a real Christian, that is to say, a disciple of the doctrines of Jesus." Jefferson saw equality as a Biblical and scientific fact, suggesting that these evolutionary principles be extended to a brotherhood of humanity where all humans are created equal.[23] In his inaugural address in 1801, Jefferson declared America as "enlightened by a benign religion, professed in deed, and practiced in various forms, yet all of them, including honesty, truth, temperance, and the love of man acknowledging and adoring an overruling Providence . . ."[24]

Even more interesting and pertinent to our time and place today, according to Heironimus, is the theosophical "ye are brethren" traditions of Franklin, Washington, and Jefferson, which hold ". . . that every nation has a spiritual destiny—using all ethical means of manifesting the divine plan through the will of the nation's leaders."[25]

Perhaps the destiny of the United States, in regard to living in deistic balance between spirit and matter, is to challenge, by example, all nations to find their own sacred mission. Doing so involves not only boldly moving forward with new action but also going back to acknowledge the unacknowledged past.

Related to our Native American roots, there are two pieces of unfinished and largely unacknowledged business. The first is the sad truth of what became of our spiritual benefactors. The other has to do with a central and key aspect of Native American culture that even the most enlightened of our Founders could even dream of adopting.

REPAYING OUR BENEFACTORS: FROM SQUANTO TO TONTO

Here is a startling and sobering statistic. According to Donald Grinde, when Christopher Columbus thought he was the first to discover the New World in 1492, there were at least six million Native Americans living in the territory that is now the United States. That's the conservative estimate. Others say there were 15 to 20 million. By 1900, the Native American population was only 250,000.[26]

Much of this attrition can be attributed to Europeans bringing diseases such as smallpox, measles, and syphilis from crowded European cities—diseases to which Native Americans had no immunity. However, warfare, forced migration, outright slaughter, and all of the other fallout of manifest destiny—a.k.a. manifested land grab—finished off what the diseases merely began.

Grinde points out an obvious relationship between the decimation of the Native population and the repression of information regarding their contribution to the founding of the United States. "You can't justify the whole conquest and subjugation and destruction of Indian populations if there are things of value in the people you are destroying," he wrote.[27]

Until 1970, the only things the general population knew about Native Americans were fables of Squanto, the Patuxet Indian who helped the pilgrims survive their first difficult years, and the depiction they acquired from radio and TV shows like *The Lone Ranger.* In other words, awareness ran the gamut from Squanto to Tonto.

But, in 1970, novelist and historian Dee Brown published *Bury My Heart at Wounded Knee,* an eye-opening history of Native Americans in the west. With this outstanding book and a later television film adapted by scriptwriter Daniel Giat, American society could no longer deny the genocide and ethnocide wrought upon the indigenous people by European invaders—er, settlers. In addition, the lid was also lifted on the denial of the contributions Native Americans made. And as we will see shortly, their full contribution has yet to be received.

HONORING OUR FOUNDING MOTHERS

To reiterate, perhaps the most important lesson from Iroquois tribal society is the notion that authority comes from the ground up, not from the top down. Remember, European law, even at its most enlightened, maintained that God delegated power to the King who delegated power at his discretion to the nobility, and there it ended. The most radical evolutionary notion of our Founders—a notion that came directly from Native American culture—is that the need for government arises from equally sovereign citizens who enter into a compact to ensure a mutually beneficial and thriving community. Again Grinde on Native American society: "Power is breathed into leaders by the people, and those leaders then exist on that support. When that support no longer exists, then their power ceases to exist."[28]

Although Franklin and others acknowledged the contributions of the Iroquois Nation, the one thing they failed to mention—and conspicuously failed to include in America's constitutional system—was the role of women in the tribe. There was a reason why Native American society had neither kings nor nobility; the culture was roughly egalitarian; and resources in the tribe were distributed according to need, not social class. And that reason is what came to be called The Council of Grandmothers.

Native American culture perceived Earth, plants, and land as feminine in character. Because older women were closest to the basics of life, which had to do with growing and preparing food, birthing and caring for children, and the domestic work of the community, it was a no-brainer for the men to acknowledge women's fundamental power.

The basic unit of government for the Native Americans was the clan, usually headed by an older woman.[29] Clans owned property collectively and used it to grow enough to feed all of their members. Politically, the Iroquois understood the need for women and men to achieve unity and work together in balance and harmony. The older women, the Council of Grandmothers, assumed the true political power, possessing sole authority to choose the chief or impeach a chief for incompetence or wrongdoing. Women even made the final decision regarding whether or not to go to war.

Lest we over-glorify the influence of women, Iroquois men sometimes had a problem with giving women the right to decide when to go to war. Men complained that women wanted to take them to war too frequently! Keep in mind that, while the Iroquois Confederacy prevented warfare among its confederates, there were conflicts with tribes outside their nation that often involved abduction of children. Thus, women were eager to avenge those kidnappings. In addition, women felt and expressed greater grief over lost husbands and sons, which also translated into calls for vengeance and warfare.[30]

When women were past childbearing age, they would become clan mothers; some became warriors as well. They would often accompany war parties to make sure the men were doing the proper amount of killing and not shirking their duties. Some reports state that war parties took captives and turned them over to the women to torture. One chief was asked why that was done and he answered, "I do that so they will grow tired of war."[31]

Interestingly, but not surprisingly, contact with Native cultures actually may have sparked the women's movement in America. Researcher

Sally Roesch Wagner, one of the first women to receive a doctorate in women's studies, reports that the founders of the women's rights movement in the late 19th century, Susan B. Anthony and Elizabeth Cady Stanton, among others, had early and influential contact with Iroquois women.[32]

Stanton reported that, as a young girl of 12 or 13, she visited an Iroquois reservation. She was surprised to see the mother of her Indian playmate selling a horse and accepting cash from a man. Young Elizabeth asked, "What will your husband say when he gets home?" The woman replied that the horse was hers, and she could do with it as she pleased.[33]

At a time when women—in what was then known as "civilized culture"—could not own property, this was an eye-opener. In Native American culture, equal rights to property for both genders and all classes enhanced freedom and democracy because it made it more difficult to bend the will of others through use of economic leverage.

As we read these tales of history, as often about ignorance and cruelty as about kindness and wisdom, it's important to step up and view these situations objectively from a higher perspective. Instead of blaming dysfunctional or evil traits on particular peoples, that is, *others*, it is far more useful and transformational to recognize these traits as universal human tendencies kept in place by largely invisible beliefs.

As we will see, we hold on to evils in our society by projecting them onto others. When we acknowledge and own those evils within ourselves and within our culture—not out of hatred for our culture but out of love—we stop projecting evil and, in this way, disempower it. This awareness and recognition is the first step in awakening consciousness within ourselves and others.

UNITING BOTH HEMISPHERES: THE CONDOR AND THE EAGLE

The Native Americans bring us one more gift—this, in the form of a heartening prophesy from the natives of the Andes. According to their tradition, centuries ago, humans took two diverging paths: the path of the condor and the path of the eagle.

The condor path, which has come to represent the peoples of the Southern Hemisphere, is associated with the heart, the intuitive, and the spiritual. The eagle path, which represents the peoples of the Northern Hemisphere, is associated with the brain, the rational, and the material.

For the past 500 years, the power of the eagle—mental and materialistic—has dominated that of the condor's spirituality and heart-centeredness. But according to the prophecy, this is about to change.

The indigenous tradition among the peoples of the South has divided time into epochs called *pachacutis*, each spanning roughly 500 years. According to the Aztec Calendar—a.k.a. *The Sacred Stone Calendar of the Mexican People*—the Fourth Pachacuti that began in 1492 was characterized by the prophecies as a time of turmoil, struggle, and conflict. Since October 12, 1992, we've been in the Fifth Pachacuti, which is said to be a time of partnership and union, where eagle and condor "fly together in the sky as equals."[34]

And not a moment too soon. In our evolutionary journey through basal paradigms that have taken us deep into the realms of spirituality and materialism over these many centuries, the one thing these paradigms had in common was their disconnection from the sacred feminine and, consequently, from Earth itself. As we will expand upon later, the very detachment and denial of the feminine in Western society has put us out of touch with the natural world. For centuries, the powers of unbalanced domination, empowered first by a He-God then by a He-Science, have forced our world further and further out of kilter to where we are on the brink of destroying the very ground upon which we stand.

Now, in its infinite sense of humor, the Universe is finally asking us to reconcile the hemispheres, left and right, north and south. This time of spiritual reunion, when we will link the sacred masculine and sacred feminine, is not merely the province of indigenous spirituality or reconstituted goddess worship.

The Dalai Lama has also spoken of it. He says he will be the last Dalai Lama from the Himalayas, and the next one will likely be from the other high mountains, the Andes. Meanwhile, many international organizations have banded together under the banner of the Pachamama Alliance to foster this emergent human culture by helping the people of the condor and the people of the eagle share their gifts with one another.

While the people of the condor live simply, with relatively small means, their lives are rich in joyful relationships and wisdom that comes from connecting with Nature. Confronted by the forces of development and civilization, the people of the condor must learn to choose carefully which of these gifts they accept and which they turn down.

The people of the eagle are often materially rich yet spiritually impoverished. Wealth and possessions seem to have distorted life and diminished community. This imbalance is particularly intense in the United States where citizens fail to notice a gluttonous absurdity. With a mere 5 percent of the world's population, the U.S. consumes a whopping 30 percent of the world's resources and then spends $35 billion a year trying to lose weight.[35]

In order to confront the serious insanity in which we currently reside, we must examine and reconsider the invisible beliefs with which we have been programmed. Psychologist James Hillman suggests "northern thinkers" who value the linear and the intellectual must "go south" and release themselves from the confinement of familiar "psychological territory."[36]

In Part II, *Four Myth-Perceptions of the Apocalypse,* we will see how Western Civilization has paradoxically gone south by adhering to the northern values of scientific materialism. We will examine the consequences of four myth-perceptions that challenge civilization's survival and are forcing humankind to evolve through a reconciliation of the hemispheres. In the words of activist and author John Perkins, "If the condor and eagle accept this opportunity, they will create a most remarkable offspring, unlike any seen before."[37]

FOUR MYTH-PERCEPTIONS OF THE APOCALYPSE

*"When you find yourself on a vicious cycle,
for goodness sakes, stop pedaling!"*
— Swami Beyondananda

We have seen how perceptions impact our biology and, in turn, help create our reality. We have also seen that our story—the philosophical lens of perception through which we see and understand the world—largely determines the parameters of our collective reality. Our review of history reveals that civilizations continuously evolve as one basal paradigm story gives way to another in a dynamic, spiral dance.

Civilization is, indeed, in a spiral dance, but we seem to be spiraling out of control. Global crises and mounting chaos signal an impending evolutionary turning point, a sign that we are close to the next paradigmatic hand-off. Now that we have fully experienced the polarity of scientific materialism, our path is rapidly approaching its return to the powerful midpoint—the most powerful point in the chart.

Twice before, we have been at the midpoint where the spiritual and material worlds are one. The first time was in the Garden when our animistic worldview made no distinction between spirit and matter. That was before we left on our great learning adventure.

On the first leg of our evolutionary journey, civilization traversed a path that went deep into the nonmaterial domain of an off-planet God. After completing our exploration of the spiritual realm, humanity's path momentarily passed through the midpoint again as its journey proceeded into the domain of materialism. That was the time when people of the Age of Enlightenment and deistic philosophy embraced both spiritual and material philosophy. The Declaration of Independence is a perfect example of blending spiritual idealism and practical realism. However, civilization's flirtation with balance was fleeting because humanity was rushing headlong into the polar realm of scientific materialism.

Civilization's forays into the polarities of spiritualism and materialism have provided us with deep insights into the nature of reality. And, now, as our evolutionary path is once again returning us to the midpoint, humanity is at a crossroads, confronted with two fundamental paths. We can either unite as a global community to assimilate and integrate our polarized insights, thus making a quantum evolutionary jump, or we can continue the bipolar insanity as religious and scientific materialist fundamentalists duke it out to be the last paradigm standing on a dying planet.

Whether or not we make this quantum leap depends upon how well we learn the lessons of the current and the previous paradigms. If we understand that evolution is the progression of accumulated awareness, then, perhaps, if we focus our collective awareness, we might just speed up the evolutionary process.

UNVEILING THE OLD, REVEALING THE NEW

In Part II, we take a close-up view of the life-threatening consequences of scientific materialism, our current basal paradigm. We specifically focus on four cultural beliefs that form the cornerstones of our current reality even though contemporary science has found each of them to be flawed, if not downright false. We present these beliefs as the Four Myth-Perceptions of the Apocalypse in reference to where we are likely headed if we keep going where we are going.

Modern society's faith in or worship of the material realm has us hurtling down the track to a train wreck of Earth-shattering proportions. Continued economic growth from accelerated extraction of natural wealth is not sustainable. Treating the land as landfill and our air, water, and soil as final resting places for pollutants is suicidal. Warfare, as a method of problem solving, has actually taken us to the brink of the ultimate solution to the human problem: no humans, no problem.

Clearly, the current paradigm of scientific materialism is not up to the evolutionary task at hand. Nor can going back to religious monotheism, the prior paradigm, take us forward, either. We seem to be at a life-threatening impasse in the face of ominous apocalyptic predictions. The key to avoiding apocalyptic collapse, however, lies in appreciating the meaning of the word *apocalypse*—*before* it became a code word for "the end of the world."

Originally, apocalypse meant a prophetic revelation, "a lifting of the veils." It represented the exposure of something hidden and has, since the time of the Greeks, been associated with revelations that would occur at the end of time. A new—or, actually, old—interpretation of the word suggests that, by lifting the veil on our own invisible programming, we might yet avoid the inevitable train wreck that awaits us if we stay on the current track.

Scientific materialism has offered four tenets in the dominant basal paradigm that, until recently, have been accepted and regarded as indisputable scientific fact:

1. Only Matter Matters—the physical world we see is all there is.

2. Survival of the Fittest—Nature favors the strongest individuals, and the Law of the Jungle is the only real natural law.

3. It's in Your Genes—we are victims of our biological inheritance and the best we can hope is that science finds ways to compensate for our inherent flaws and frailties.

4. Evolution Is Random—life is basically random and purposeless, and we got here pretty much the same way as an infinite number of monkeys pecking on an infinite number of typewriters over an infinite amount of time might produce the works of Shakespeare.

In the next four chapters, we trace the development of each of these tenets from their origins as myth-perceptions through the profound revisions offered by current science.

In Chapter 9, *Dysfunction at the Junction,* we will examine the consequences of taking each of these beliefs to its logical illogical conclusion.

The institutions we examine—economics, politics, health care, and communications—all suffer from the same fatal affliction: they have pursued scientific materialism to the point of distortion and made money, materialism, and machinery more important and more valuable than human life.

Then in Chapter 10, *Going Sane,* we explore how we can make sane choices that will transform us from our current role as children of God to adults of God. We'll see how we can synergistically learn from where we've been on this evolutionary path and, thus, become willing participants in our reconnection with each other, with Nature, and with the divine in all. We'll learn how to embrace our untapped power—and to do so with kind, benign humility.

This examination of current situations and future possibilities is necessary because, if we look at the world with clarity, loving compassion, and even humor, we stand a chance of breaking free from this trance and achieving spontaneous evolution. Perhaps the most appropriate lens to use when looking at where civilization now stands is an entertainment genre that wouldn't exist were it not for our worship of all things scientific: science fiction. As an example, consider the movie *The Matrix.*

In a scenario set in the near future, a young computer hacker named Neo finds himself in two parallel worlds. One world, the Matrix, seems to be the reality-as-usual world of everyday life in the Cyber Age. The other world is the world-behind-the-world where he discovers machine-like humanoids that keep living and breathing humans happily distracted while exploiting them as power-sources for the humanoids' machinery. The vast majority of humans in Neo's world, knowingly or unknowingly, have taken the *blue pill* of blissful or, at least, passive ignorance. Neo and his compatriots, Morpheus and Trinity, have taken the *red pill,* which is the much more dangerous path of awakening through which they step outside the Matrix.

Awakening to what? As Morpheus told Neo, "The Matrix is a computer-generated dream world built to keep us under control in order to change a human being into this." And Morpheus shows him a copper-topped battery. Considering that science fiction is often a predecessor for science fact—think of submarines in Jules Verne's *Twenty Thousand Leagues under the Sea*—we might do well to step outside the matrix of life and be curious about the world that has been spun out before us.

As we will see in our discussion of "weapons of mass-distraction," most people have chosen the blue pill and have signed off on reality in favor of reality TV. However, every day, increasing numbers are opting for the red pill and are awakening to a world of awesome wonder and overwhelming confusion.

The confusion is clarified the moment we realize that much of what we perceive as natural human behavior is actually the consequence of developmental programming. In Part II, we describe how we came to accept beliefs that made sense once upon a time but are now contributing to the destruction of our world. With nobody telling us what else to do in the face of these crises, our programming has us feeling helpless in a situation that seems hopeless.

The real issue we must come to terms with is that, for millennia, we have been programmed to be powerless and, consequently, dependent upon others for our survival, especially in the areas of spirituality and health. Of course, fees were involved, and this exchange has significantly contributed to our current global crises. Yet there is an easy way out of our self-imposed matrix: we can simply reprogram our lives. By acquiring and acting upon new awareness, we afford ourselves an opportunity to rewrite the programs of cultural limitations.

The first step in reprogramming is deprogramming. We do this by examining the program from *outside* the matrix. How? In his book, *The Power of Now,* Eckhart Tolle describes a time in his life when he was going through such despair and torment that he considered suicide. Then, a wild thought came to him: "Exactly who is the 'who' who wants to do away with whom?" With this epiphany, Tolle realized that *he* was also the observer outside the matrix, beyond the world of circumstance; this liberated him from attachment to the *who* whom he thought he was.[1]

Quantum physicists tell us that our observations change reality. If this is indeed the case, the insights we offer regarding the four apocalyptic myth-perceptions and the human and societal dysfunctions they spawn should help you, and all of us, change the way we observe the world. Hopefully, that will enable us to awaken our collective consciousness and change our collective reality, as well.

CHAPTER 5

MYTH-PERCEPTION ONE: ONLY MATTER MATTERS

"It is said that invisible forces control our world,
but personally I just can't see it."
— Swami Beyondananda

IS SCIENCE A RELIGION?

Monotheism became Western civilization's basal paradigm during the Dark Ages when it offered the best and most acceptable answers to the three perennial questions.

1. How did we get here?
2. Why are we here?
3. Now that we're here, how do we make the best of it?

By replacing the former paradigm of polytheism, the Church positioned itself as the sole fount of civilization's knowledge. As the primary provider of mass education, the Church used its power of controlling knowledge to amass vast wealth and great influence. Meanwhile, as the self-proclaimed intercessor between God and king, it enlisted the mighty arm of the law to forcibly secure its dominion.

Over time and intoxicated with authority, the Church's original mission of helping humanity took a backseat to the more pressing mission of helping itself. Yet its power rested precariously upon the fragile foundation that its knowledge represented absolute truth.

But let's be realistic. No authority, especially one predicated on static ancient knowledge, can support that claim. So, in time, Church theologians faced the inevitable likelihood that others would arrive at truths that differed from their own.

Enter the Inquisition, through which the Church's mafia made challengers of the faith an offer they couldn't refuse: lose that thought or lose your life. Those whose views conflicted with Church dogma were subject to imprisonment and torture with the sentence dutifully executed—pun intended—by civil authorities.

The oppressive leadership of the Church was finally challenged by Renaissance scientists who came on the scene like a breath of fresh air. With a liberating and more humane, sane view of knowledge, scientists promised to keep an open mind and apply an apparently unbiased eye regarding truths.

However, over time, after science had solidified its position as civilization's "official" truth provider, practitioners of that paradigm also began to oppressively profess and defend its truths as absolute and infallible. Subsequently, in the modern world, the term *scientific* is synonymous with *true*. In contrast, a belief designated as unscientific becomes, at best, questionable and, at worst, illegal and punishable, again, by civil law.

Cloaking its authority in the guise of "We know what's best for *you*," scientific authorities have carried out their own witch-hunts of those deemed guilty of scientific heresy. Chiropractors, energy healers, midwives, and others whose modalities often fall outside of and challenge mainstream scientific thinking have been hounded, abused, and jailed for their "unscientific" beliefs and practices.

Even civilians who decide not to follow scientific norms are subject to arrest and conviction. For example, the courts have taken custody of children with cancer and other diseases after their parents refused to follow traditional therapies, even though the medical therapies offered no better resolutions than alternative methods of treatment.

In 2004, doctors determined that Amber Marlowe's baby was too large to deliver by natural childbirth and that she would be required to have a caesarian birth. When she balked, medical authorities at Wilkes-Barre General Hospital obtained a court order to force Marlowe into surgery under threat of arrest for "endangering the life of a child." Fortunately, this story had a happy ending. According to a news article, "Marlowe escaped from the hospital and had a quick, natural birth at a different facility."[1]

Is modern science the infallible source of absolute knowledge it now claims to be? Absolutely not!

But here's the good news. The spirit of science is alive and well. Pioneers thinking outside the box are now precipitating upheavals at the leading edge of science, and their new thoughts are radically rewriting the way we see life. With the revolution underway, the old guard, defending the institution of old science, has dug in to defend its territory. By preserving and protecting its cherished, yet obsolete dogma, the scientific establishment—or, more accurately, those that profit from science, for example, the pharmaceutical industry—have slipped into the realm of religion by touting the dogma: "It's true because we say it is!"

As we will see, however, when we follow Newtonian linear logic to its illogical conclusion and declare that only matter matters, we end up excluding the entire dimension of the unseen realm. And that's the reality we are beginning to realize may be of greatest importance in regard to the nature and mechanics of the Universe. Meanwhile, leaders of the new science have nailed their theses to the door of the Church of Scientific Materialism. Let the reformation begin!

A FUNNY THING HAPPENED ON
THE WAY TO ABSOLUTE CERTAINTY

The film *Quest for Fire* provides a keen insight into the world of prehistoric human civilizations. By using fire as a tool for survival, ancient humans were able to protect themselves from carnivorous predators and, in the process, take a huge step toward mastering their environment. While early humans could manage fire, they were unable to create it. These tribes spent a great deal of collective energy maintaining their flame even as they traveled. If a tribe lost its fire, it would quickly devolve to the status of prey, ever vigilant of the circling predators in the dark.

In the movie's final scene, our prehistoric hero learns how to make fire. The film's portrayal of this emotionally charged event brilliantly captures one of the pivotal moments in our evolution. Up to that point, human awareness was preoccupied with immediate survival in a world dominated by voracious predators. By mastering fire, humans were no longer just another animal; they were on their way to becoming the dominant force in the biosphere. The film ends with the tribe safely sitting around the fire pit and our protagonist gazing skyward, contemplating the full moon. With primary survival assured, humankind was free to reflect on the nature of the world.

From these humble beginnings, the endeavor of science ultimately evolved to formally explore, classify, and understand how our world works. In Western civilization, conventional science officially arose in the Golden Age of Greece when philosophers, such as Aristotle, collected observations and insights about their world and integrated them with conclusions derived from simple experiments.

As Christian monotheism took hold of Western civilization's basal paradigm, it carried forth and incorporated ancient Greek science into its mix of world knowledge. Thomas Aquinas and Albertus Magnus modified and adapted Grecian scientific philosophy to accommodate and support the tenets of Christian scripture. The new Church-based science, known as Natural Theology, formalized the way that science would perceive and study God's creation. In this supportive capacity, science obediently took its place as the Church's handmaiden.

As described earlier, when science was called in to resolve the Church's calendar conundrum, the seeds of a paradigmatic revolution were set. Copernicus' discovery that the solar system is heliocentric was the birth of modern science as a formal institution, separate and distinct from the Church. And pronouncement of that discovery marked a turning point that would lead to more challenges regarding the Church's infallibility and, ultimately, to the collapse of the monotheistic paradigm.

The year 1543 is considered to be the advent of the modern scientific revolution. It was the year that Copernicus, at the end of his life, published his book *De Revolutionibus Orbium Coelestium* (*On the Revolutions of the Heavenly Spheres*) and successfully challenged the Church's claim of infallibility.

One of the first issues that modern science had to wrestle with was simply, "What is a truth?" Remember, the science of the 16th century was a collection of ancient speculations that had been passed down from the Greeks and modified by Christian theologians. Science was confounded by the fact that there was no way to distinguish or validate a real *truth* from a fervently held *belief.*

Consequently, the first task of modern science was to create a scientific method for assessing data. Essentially, the scientific method involves making observations and measurements, creating explanatory hypotheses, and conducting experiments designed to test the hypotheses. The results of the experiments are then used to refine the hypotheses so they become more predictive of the experimental results. In the end, predictability is the primary hallmark of a scientific truth.

Rene Descartes further advanced the new paradigm by calling for complete scientific reform. He boldly suggested throwing out the existing ancient Greek beliefs and replacing them with verifiable truths, subjected to Francis Bacon's analytical scientific methodology. "Doubt everything," said Descartes, and, indeed, the only thing he knew that was undoubtedly true was his own existence. "I think, therefore I am," Descartes said famously. Perhaps, as we will see shortly, the Universe is capable of making the same claim.

The scientific method requires that direct observations and measurements be made on the subject of study. In the absence of today's technology, early scientists were restricted to studying only things they could see, touch, and measure. The concept of an invisible energy matrix—which modern quantum physicists named "the field" and which Einstein later attributed as "the sole governing agency of matter"—was clearly not accessible to scientific observation at the time of Newton and Descartes.

Consequently, the parameters of the scientific method unavoidably limited science to studies of the physical, material world. By narrowing its focus of study and determining that nonmaterial concepts, such as spirit and mind, were outside the box of analytical science, science officially acquired the status of scientific materialism. As a result, science considered such elements of the invisible realm to be metaphysical notions, which were happily left to the Church and were not subjected to the rigid laws of physical science.

By detaching from the beliefs of the Church and narrowing their observations to the physical, tangible Universe, scientists initiated a new philosophy. Rather than viewing the Universe as controlled by spiritual forces, scientists pursued the notion that the Universe was a physical machine. To them, the planets, stars, plants, and animals were merely mechanical gears in a giant clockwork mechanism.

While scientists supported the notion that God created the machine, they also believed that once the machine was set in motion, God was no longer personally involved in its day-to-day operation. Rather than imagining God hovering above the world and controlling it like a marionette with spiritual strings, science perceived the Universe as a perpetual motion machine that reflected the behavior of its mechanical parts.

Sir Isaac Newton used mathematics to scientifically verify and solidify Descartes' premise that the Universe is a machine. By observing and measuring planetary bodies, Newton generated a new philosophy regarding how the Universe—and life in general—works. Newton officially founded the science of mechanics, also known as physics, which is the discipline that studies the mechanisms that underlie the operation of the Universe.

Newton's science was based upon two absolutes: absolute space and absolute time. In a quantifiable Universe, as he defined it, objects move through these absolutes because of gravity. While gravity is an invisible force, Newton recognized it by its fruits, specifically, a falling apple. As materialists, Newtonian followers were undaunted by gravity's invisible character. They simply ascribed gravity as being caused by a combination of matter and a gaseous substance they called "ether." They, therefore, perceived gravity as an attribute of the mass of the object.

Since the 1700s, three main tenets of Newtonian philosophy have shaped how scientists approach their study of the Universe:

1. Materialism—Physical matter is the only fundamental reality. The Universe can be understood through knowledge of its visible physical parts. Rather than invoking unseen vital forces or spirits, life is derived from self-reactive chemistry that comprises the body. Simply stated: "All that matters is matter."

2. Reductionism—No matter how complex something appears, it can always be dissected and understood by studying its individual components. Simply stated: "To understand something, take it apart and study its pieces."

3. Determinism—Occurrences in Nature are causally determined, a consequence of the concept that every action produces a reaction. An outcome can be predicted by the linear progression of discrete events. Simply stated: "We can predict and control the outcome of natural processes."

Newtonian materialism, reductionism, and determinism offered not merely an analysis of the Universe but also the promise of a controllable utopia. The price? The thinking world would have to sacrifice its preoccupation with God, spirits, and invisible forces.

Somewhere between the time of Newton in the early 1700s and the Age of Enlightenment in the late 1700s, tensions eased between the upstart paradigm of modern science and the still-dominant, Church-controlled monotheistic paradigm. By conveniently dividing the Universe into a material realm and a spiritual realm, science ruled the physical world and religion took dominion over the metaphysical world.

Therefore, science was free to pursue its proof of the material nature of the Universe, and religion still guided the course of transcendent souls. While that was a convenient truce between two intellectual superpowers, the resulting separation of spirit from matter has led to an imbalance that continues to endanger our world today.

As the 19th century neared a close, the entire material Universe rested comfortably on a foundation of irrefutable Newtonian truth. Science had presumably proved that the Universe was a physical machine made out of elemental particles called atoms and that universal dynamics could be understood and determined by studying billiard-ball-like atomic actions and reactions. In fact, by the end of the 19th century, physicists were so pleased with themselves, they publicly acknowledged that the science of physics was complete and there was nothing more to learn.

William Thomson, renowned as Lord Kelvin, was an Irish mathematical physicist and engineer who addressed an assemblage of physicists at the British Association for the Advancement of Science in 1900 and stated, "There is nothing new to be discovered in physics now. All that remains is more and more precise measurement."[2] A similar statement is attributed to Albert Michelson, the first American physicist to receive a Nobel Prize. Newtonian science had appeared to be so complete that, as chairman of physics at the University of Chicago, Michelson quipped that no more physics graduate students were necessary because, as he said, "the grand underlying principles have been firmly established . . . further truths of physics are to be looked for in the sixth place of decimals."[3]

But a funny thing happened on the way to absolute certainty. Demonstrating once again that pride goeth before the fall, unanticipated anomalies began to turn the world of *Newtonian physics* upside down. The first crack in the mechanical worldview came in 1895 with investigations by German physicist Wilhelm Conrad Roentgen of x-rays, which demonstrated the existence of a mysterious force that emanates from matter and penetrates other matter. Subsequently, French physicists Antoine-Henri Becquerel and then Marie and Pierre Curie discovered the phenomenon of radioactivity, which revealed that atomic elements are not immutable as presumed but that fundamental elements could, in fact, transmute into other elements.

Two years later, British physicist Sir Joseph John Thomson detected electrons, which demonstrated that the atom isn't the Universe's smallest particle, as Newtonian physics had claimed, but is comprised of even smaller subunits.

While studying the spectrum of light emitted by heated elements, German physicist Max Planck discovered that electrons could jump from one energy shell of the atom to another shell, going instantaneously from one energy level to another without expressing intermediate energy values. Consequently, Planck recognized that the electrons were made up of discrete units of radiant energy, which he described as *quanta*. His work revealed that as electrons jump between energy shells they either gain or lose a quantum of energy, hence the origins of the science of *quantum physics*.

In 1905, studies on the photoelectric effect by German physicist Albert Einstein showed that nonmaterial light waves expressed physical characteristics that were formerly attributed only to matter. Based on his observations, Einstein postulated the existence of *photons,* which are quanta of radiant light energy expressing particulate qualities. With matter behaving as light and light behaving as matter, the certainties of Newtonian physics suddenly seemed uncertain.

In 1926, French physicist Louis-Victor de Broglie predicted that all particles of matter should also behave as nonmaterial waves, and his de Broglie Hypothesis was confirmed three years later in studies on electrons. These experiments showed that electrons have both wavelike properties and particle properties; that is, they are simultaneously material and nonmaterial.

With these discoveries, within a mere quarter century after Thomson's and Michelson's statements about the definitive end of physics, the solid foundation of Newtonian physics had seemingly dissolved into a Zen-like paradox.

The particle-versus-wave confusion was eventually resolved with the advent and establishment of quantum mechanics. The wave-particle duality, a hallmark of quantum physics, provided a single unified theoretical framework for understanding that all matter has characteristics associated with both particles and waves. Welcome to the world of quantum weirdness!

Einstein's mass-energy equation (often symbolized with the equation $E=mc^2$) acknowledges the unification of energy and matter, wherein energy (E) equals mass (m) times the speed of light (c), squared. With this, Einstein showed that atoms are actually not made out of matter, but consist of nonmaterial energy! Today, it is fully established that physical atoms are comprised of a menagerie of subatomic units such as *quarks, bosons,* and *fermions.* Interestingly, particle physicists perceive of these fundamental atomic units as vortices of energy resembling nano-tornados.

In other words, the long-held perception of a Newtonian Universe, made exclusively of physical objects, turns out to be an elaborate illusion! In contrast, Einstein's unified theory, which attempts to explain the nature and behavior of all matter and energy, proposed that the Universe is one indivisible dynamic whole wherein all physical parts and energy fields are entangled and interdependent.

While quantum mechanics undermined science's preoccupation with materialism, Planck's work also questioned the emphasis on reductionism, which focuses on individual parts rather than the whole. While reductionism appears to explain simple mechanical processes, Planck demonstrated that some events cannot be predicted by linear cause-and-effect reactions but seem to occur simultaneously as part of an interacting energy matrix called *the field.* Planck's insights emphasized that, in order to understand the nature of the Universe, we must abandon reductionism and, instead, turn to holism, wherein everything interacts with everything else.

Interestingly, the classic analogy used to describe reductionism involved taking apart a wind-up watch to see what makes it tick. By observing the interaction of mechanical gears and springs, one would presumably be able to repair or alter the mechanism of any other watch. Similarly, scientists presumed that, in order to determine what makes a living organism tick, they could simply take a body apart and study its pieces.

Fortunately for us, both reductionism and the watch analogy are now completely out of vogue. Consider the digital watch. Take it apart, examine its components, and . . . what?

Digital watches involve technology derived from quantum mechanics and operate by energy movement, not through interaction of physical gears. Disassembling a digital watch and examining the organization of its bits and pieces will never reveal the nature of its operation. The pursuit of reductionism, with its focus on individual material parts, simply does not offer insight into the integrated mechanics of an entangled quantum Universe.

In addition to challenging our fixation on materialism and reductionism, the science of quantum physics also dispenses with the notion of determinism, which is the doctrine that all events, including human choices and decisions, are predicated on a specific sequence of causal reactions that adhere to natural law. Simply stated, determinism proposed that, with enough data, we can predict the future.

However, Werner Heisenberg, a German physicist and one of the founders of quantum mechanics, discovered that it was not possible to simultaneously map both the position and the velocity of an atom's electron. The more accurately its position is measured, the more uncertain the value of its velocity becomes, and vice versa.

Heisenberg's theory of uncertainty applies to any two conjugate variables, such as position and velocity, time and energy, or angle of rotation and angular momentum. The theory implies that the measurement of one variable results in the disturbance of its conjugate partner, so that both variables can never be accurately predicted at the same time. Not only is Heisenberg's theory a direct affront to determinism, it also suggests that the existence of matter is, itself, an uncertainty.

Please note that the adoption of quantum mechanics does not negate Newtonian physics, but, rather, subsumes it. In other words, quantum physics is a larger realm of awareness that includes and substantially adds to the information provided by Newtonian physics. Consequently, quantum mechanics accounts for what was already known plus a whole new realm of heretofore-unrecognized forces that control the unfolding of our Universe.

Quantum mechanics emphasizes that the material Universe—with all of its atoms, particles, and matter—is actually a component of, and controlled by, the invisible universal matrix of energy forces that collectively comprise the field.

Perhaps you recall an elementary school experiment that involves a magnet, a piece of paper, and iron filings. When you sprinkled iron filings onto a piece of paper, the particles distributed themselves in a random manner. However, if you placed a magnet beneath the paper, the sprinkled filings always arranged themselves in a defined pattern that reflected the shape of the invisible magnetic field; the filings did this every time, regardless of how many times you repeated the process.

Now, imagine trying to explain the phenomenon of how the pattern is formed without knowledge of the magnet or the role of invisible fields. What kind of conclusion would you draw if you could see *only* the iron filings? You could easily conclude that those iron filings, those physical objects, are truly amazing—they filed themselves!

This is the predicament we find ourselves in if we try to make sense of our world by only focusing on the material realm. It is a particularly egregious error in the Universe where we now understand that the invisible field is the agency that governs matter. Or, as Einstein stated with inimitable simplicity: "The field is the sole governing agency of the particle." What Einstein meant was that the field is the Universe's energy matrix that governs all matter, including those mysterious iron filings.[4] Einstein further emphasized the field's role in shaping the Universe when he said, "There is no place in this new kind of physics both for the field and matter, for the field is the only reality."[5]

A century after Einstein presented his mass-energy equation $E=mc^2$, and the belief that matter and energy are inherently interrelated and entangled, many people tenaciously hang onto the illusion of a material-based reality. The insanity we see around us, provided we're not so caught up in it ourselves that we don't notice, is a by-product of trying to live a Newtonian existence in an Einsteinian world.

Interestingly, the invisible energy field that shapes matter, as defined by quantum physicists, has the same characteristics as the invisible shaping fields that metaphysicians define as "spirit."

WHAT IF JESUS AND EINSTEIN WERE *BOTH* RIGHT?

If you're puzzled by the fact that science has ignored Einstein for one hundred years, it should be even more puzzling that society has ignored Jesus for two millennia.

When we consider the messages of both Jesus and Einstein together, we can assign a possible scientific basis for the Golden Rule. Along the same line, Jesus' prescription to "love thy neighbor as thyself" makes perfect sense in an Einsteinian world where thy neighbor is thy self. The bottom-line implication of the theory of relativity is . . . we're all related.

While scientifically advanced nations have had no problem using quantum physics to develop atomic power and nuclear destruction, when it comes to understanding the everyday world, many are still blind to the invisible realm. For example, in the domain of politics and diplomacy, governments still operate in a Newtonian world comprised of individualized interacting parts and pieces, labeled as nations, governments, departments, or territories.

Instead of focusing on the cooperative nature of the energy field and natural resources that we all share, the emphasis is on a competitive war-based political system that intensifies separation and divisiveness, borders and barriers, us and them. The same Newtonian action-reaction mechanics uphold a justice system that emphasizes punishment. "An eye for an eye" is clearly a very Newtonian principle that will make the whole world blind.

We hold nothing personal against Isaac Newton, whose genius will be rightly celebrated as long as there is human history. Newton's science provided humanity with a technical foundation that enabled civilization to gain some control over its external environment. And much of the improvement in the physical conditions of humankind must be attributed to Newtonian science staking its own claim outside of religious dogma. However, society must now deal with the horrors and insanities wrought by a physical science that is unglued from the invisible world.

To see what happens when only matter matters, all we have to do is look at Western society and the monster stepchild it spawned: globalization. In a Frankensteinian sense, humanity has created and released into the world a purely materialistic, mechanical, and nonliving entity known as the corporation. Not only have we given life to the nonliving, we have given it statutory primacy over humanity. In the industrialized world, the wishes and desires of corporations generally hold more power than the wants and needs of the public.

The modern corporation is an entity endowed with one purpose only: to make money. True, a growing number of corporations are managed by executives with conscience and consciousness. These are the heartening seeds of a future world in which corporations serve people, but that is a far cry from today's world in which people serve corporations. A further discussion of how the Rule of Gold has overruled the Golden Rule will be found in Chapter 9, *Dysfunction at the Junction*.

A world-threatening implication of the Newtonian preoccupation with matter involves the desire to accumulate matter. Never has the world seen a society so possessed by material possessions and so consumed by consumerism.

Those born into Western society since the end of World War II, and particularly those in the United States, have been influenced and programmed by television to such an extent that they hardly grasp the power that media has over their lives. From the early days when Howdy Doody exhorted kids to tell their moms to buy Wonder Bread to the present time when the Baby Channel enables young consumers to develop brand-name recognition while still in diapers, humans have been reduced to the status of consumers and customers.

Conscious of the life-threatening consequences of corporate commoditization of global resources, more and more individuals and organizations are seeking to introduce human values into the economy. The forces that promote human evolution and sanity are often perceived as defensive fringe groups fighting a losing battle in spite of the fact that the majority of humans truly value life above money. The harbingers of the new humanity are, indeed, up against a mighty adversary—perhaps the world's most powerful force and a largely invisible one at that—because they are challenging civilization's basal paradigm, the fundamental beliefs that shape our way of life.

The conventional paradigm of Newtonian materialism, reductionism, and determinism also has provided the fundamental structure of our academic institutions. Students, the products of schools, are graded and rated by *measuring* their achievements. What better way to know who is better than by measuring? And how better to distribute the financial rewards of materialism than by rewarding those who prove they can produce? Of course, the questions "Produce what?" and "For what purpose?" remain largely unanswered, not to mention unasked.

The realm of medicine, which is the voice of materialistic science, has saved many lives. However, the primarily Newtonian treatments have continuously proven to be costly, often ineffective, and, at times, life threatening. In alignment with the philosophy of materialism, conventional medicine only focuses on the physical character of the body through efforts designed to adjust and manipulate the body's chemistry, even though working with the body's energy fields has proven to be far more efficient and effective.

We must fully acknowledge that modern science has created outright miracles, especially in trauma medicine, by using a Newtonian approach that perceives the body as a machine. Medical marvels include the ability to take the body apart and put it back together, transplant organs, and even create spare parts. But in spite of all the technical knowledge, we are still outmaneuvered by and live in fear of the lowly bacteria and viruses that continually threaten our existence.

Those who go outside mainstream medicine and experience anomalous healings and spontaneous remissions often find a startling lack of curiosity on the part of traditional medical authorities. This is especially true if the physician cannot invoke a conventionally accepted physical, material explanation to account for the healing. In such situations, doctors often tell their patients they really did not have the disease in the first place—in spite of what the x-rays and CAT scans showed, it was simply a misdiagnosis. In far too many cases, physicians not only dismiss miraculous cures, they actually turn a deaf ear to their healed patients by responding, "Whatever you did, I don't want to hear about it."

Fortunately, the acceptance of holistic medicine is doing much to dispel materialistic medical dogma. There's nothing like a friend's successful treatment to motivate a visit to some complementary health-care practitioner. We still have far to go to dismantle the limitations imposed by Newtonian thought, but as we will soon see, the important field of study is the field itself.

IT'S IN THE FIELD

So . . . the first key myth-perception of the apocalypse, only matter matters, is wrong.

Science, itself, through its own courageous quest for the truth, has disproved its own pet dogma. But if matter doesn't matter as much as we once believed, what does? To quote Einstein: "The field is the only reality."

But if matter is so nonmaterial, why does it seem so real? And if that brick wall is, indeed, an illusion, why can't I put my hand through it? As physicists have discovered, it isn't the density of matter that stops us, it's the density of energy.

At the subatomic level, *vortices of energy* are constantly spinning and vibrating. If the notion of energy vortex seems too abstract, visualize a mini-tornado, which is a whirling vortex of wind energy. When we observe a tornado, what we actually see are the swirling particles and debris—dirt, shingles, tree limbs, Mrs. O'Grady's cat—swept up in a field powerful enough to implode buildings and hurl vehicles. You cannot put your hand through a solid wall for the same reason you cannot drive your car through a tornado; invisible energy forces are palpable.

And lest we be fooled into thinking empty space is actually empty, the invisible is abuzz with more energy than we can imagine. What Aristotle referred to as "the plenum" and physicists named the "zero-point field" is a "quantum sea of light." According to American physicist Richard Feynman, the energy in a single cubic foot of perceived empty space is enough to boil all the oceans in the world.[6] So, paradoxically, nothing—no thing—is more powerful than any thing! Perhaps zero-point energy is the energy of the future, which is great incentive to actually have a future!

Another marvelously puzzling paradox about physical reality is that it technically doesn't exist. According to journalist Lynne McTaggart, author of *The Field: The Quest for the Secret Force of the Universe,* this zero-point field is "an ocean of microscopic vibrations in the space between things—a state of pure potential and infinite possibility." McTaggart wrote: "Particles exist in all possible states until disturbed by us—by observing or measuring—at which point, they settle down, at long last into something real." In other words, reality exists on a need-to-exist basis.[7]

Although physicists find it hard to reach a consensus on something so vast and mind-boggling, the current unconventional wisdom indicates that everything is everywhere all the time and our minds pluck things out of the cosmic soup and sort them into time and space, thus creating what we assume to be reality. By playing in the field's cosmic soup, scientists have been able to send signals great distances instantaneously and have even found ways to affect events that already happened! But more about that later.

For now, let's consider a simple experiment based on observations familiar to many people described in *Dogs That Know When Their Owners Are Coming Home,* a book and video by British biologist Rupert Sheldrake. An article in *Journal for the Society of Psychical Research* reports that 45 percent of the dog owners surveyed claimed their animal knew in advance when a household member was returning home.[8]

In Sheldrake's experiment, which was videotaped for Austrian TV, video cameras with time codes were simultaneously trained on dog owner Pam Smart, who was out of her home, and her homebound dog, Jaytee. At a random time, unbeknownst to either Pam or her dog, she received a call on her cell phone telling her to return home. At that very instant, Jaytee ran to the door to await his owner. Similar results were confirmed in over one hundred videotaped experiments.[9]

So why is this important? Most of us know there is a special and, perhaps, psychic connection between pets and their owners, just as many of us have had the experience of knowing when a loved one was in trouble. The significance is not that Sheldrake proved something we already know, but that the experiment evoked little curiosity in the scientific community. Just imagine: dogs receiving instant messages at speeds faster than the speed of light, and scientists are not even curious about how they do it?

The problem is that materialistic science cannot come up with an explanation for this phenomenon, nor does it care to. Just as the Church refused to acknowledge the implications of Copernicus' conclusion about Earth's position in our heliocentric solar system, orthodox science must ignore the demonstrated fact of canine instant messaging because it flat out contradicts their belief that only matter matters. There is an unexplainable invisible field at work that can provide us with telepathic communications, but because science doesn't believe in the invisible, well, they just can't see it.

Sheldrake suggested there is a *morphic field,* which he described as "memory inherent in nature," wherein communications we would call psychic can be sent at the speed of thought.[10] He would be the first to admit that his morphic field concept is merely a speculative explanation that doesn't prove how it works. But, fortunately, that lack of a scientific explanation has spurred him toward further experimentation with the field.

The importance of Sheldrake's experiment is that it demonstrates that the phenomenon is real and that an influential invisible field does, indeed, exist. And the implications are far more significant than being able to call your dog by whistling in your head. As we will see, carefully constructed double-blind experiments have shown that prayer and healing intentions have had a measurable positive effect on AIDS patients and those recovering from surgery. Similarly, studies also indicate that when the number of people practicing transcendental meditation reaches the square root of one percent of the population in a given city, the crime rate falls precipitously.[11]

Clearly, it is foolish for us to ignore the power of the field simply because we can't explain it. And fortunately, more scientists are becoming curious. Physicists are already there, in a sense, as evidenced by their use of the phrase "invisible moving force" to describe these fields. Interestingly, that is the same definition of the traditional Shaper of Fields—God, Creator, Spirit, or whatever term you choose to describe the unifying force in the Universe. The cosmic joke is this: science and religion are essentially each describing the same thing.

So why is understanding the field important? And how can that understanding help us? The answer is threefold: First, we can end, once and for all, the useless argument between science and religion. Instead of fighting over the existence of an off-planet God, we can work together for on-planet good. Second, by acknowledging the power of invisible fields—even if we don't understand them—we open up an entirely new field of inquiry and challenge science to explore what it has previously ignored. Finally, we can realize that humanity is operating on a unified field of dreams, and we can rejoice that the field is a playing field, not a battlefield.

CHAPTER 6

MYTH-PERCEPTION TWO: SURVIVAL OF THE FITTEST

"When your only intention is looking out for number one, everyone and everything else gets treated like number two."
— **Swami Beyondananda**

"It's a dog-eat-dog world." "It's a jungle out there." "Every man for himself." We've heard these catchphrases so many times that we've embedded them into what we call reality.

But what if the Darwinian philosophy about the competitive nature of life is all wrong? What if cooperation and sharing are the entire reason for our evolution? What if survival is really dependent on how well we communicate with each other and how quickly we share and process information? And what if there is a world condition much better than mere survival? What if there's also a state of *thrival?*

WHICH CAME FIRST, DARWIN OR DARWINISM?

Charles Darwin, who was also a child of his times, played one of the most important roles in establishing the paradigm of scientific materialism, especially as it applies to human health and the evolution of humanity. Evolutionary thought had been ripening for nearly a century and even his own grandfather Erasmus Darwin had studied and written about the subject.

In fact, the first scientific paper on evolution, *Philosophie Zoologique*, was published by French biologist Jean-Baptiste de Lamarck in 1809, the year Darwin was born.[1] And phrases that we have attributed to

Darwinism—the law of the jungle and survival of the fittest—were also well-established before Charles Darwin's birth.

The opening act for Charles Darwin's opus was performed by Thomas Robert Malthus. Malthus was an economic philosopher whose beliefs and writings provided the theoretical foundation for Darwinian theory. He was also the son of a leading light of the Age of Enlightenment who counted as his friends Jean-Jacques Rousseau and philosopher and economist David Hume. Yet young Malthus took a deeper, darker view of the world than his mentors. Perhaps in rebellion against his father, Malthus championed a pessimistic position in regard to world affairs. He set out not only to prove the glass was half empty but also that it would soon be three-quarters empty, then seven-eighths empty, and on and on subtractum infinitum.

Using logical constructs and linear projections popular at the time, Malthus concluded and subsequently wrote that vegetation reproduced at an arithmetic progression rate:

$$1 \Rightarrow 2 \Rightarrow 3 \Rightarrow 4 \Rightarrow 5 \Rightarrow \text{etc.}$$

In contrast, he suggested that animal life reproduced at a geometric progression rate:

$$2 \Rightarrow 4 \Rightarrow 8 \Rightarrow 16 \Rightarrow 32 \Rightarrow \text{etc.}$$

Malthus's logic went thusly: a farmer managing his land could, with effort and luck, possibly raise an extra bushel of feed in each succeeding year. However, his animal population would double as offspring continued to spring off with each generation and would rapidly diminish the farmer's ability to produce feed for them. Thus, animal life, which, of course, includes humans, would reproduce to the point that we exceed our food supply. In such a reality, life would truly become an ongoing struggle for existence in which only the strongest and most ruthless survive.

Malthus described the consequences of his vision of reality in his 1798 work titled *An Essay on the Principle of Population*: "The power of population is so superior to the power of the earth to produce subsistence for man that premature death must in some shape or other visit the human race. The vices of mankind are active and able ministers of depopulation. They are the precursors in the great army of destruction and often finish the dreadful work themselves. But should they fail in this war of extermination, sickly seasons, epidemics, pestilence, and plague advance in terrific array and sweep off their thousands and tens of thousands. Should success be still incomplete, gigantic inevitable famine stalks in the rear and with one mighty blow levels the population with the food of the world."[2]

Well, at least, the upside of pessimism is that you can never be disappointed. But the essence of Malthus's concern didn't have to do with things getting worse, but with them actually getting better. What if nations curtailed warfare? What if poverty was eliminated and disease cured? Then, according to Malthus, we would *really* have a mess on our hands! The more successful we became at saving lives, the sooner we would run out of food. Malthusiasts of the 19th century engaged all kinds of social programs to forestall this inevitability, including discouraging the poor from breeding and the creation of slums in swamps where disease would cull the poor from the herd.

However, there is a minor problem with Malthus's gloomy projections—they happen to be false! Seeing the world from a strictly materialist, linear point of view, Malthus was blind to the dynamic complexities inherent within the web of life and to Nature's tendency toward balance and harmony. Furthermore, animal populations simply do not double every year, and their rate of increase is, again, a total variable based upon prevailing environmental conditions. Malthus's linear mathematical conclusions, currently defined as "static projection," would only be reasonable in a linear, mechanistic Newtonian Universe.

Fortunately, the Universe we live in is a probability-based quantum reality that is greatly affected by chaos, which is, in the world of mathematics and physics, defined as a system that outwardly appears random but is, in reality, quite ordered and deterministic. In a chaotic Universe, static projections are useless because they fail to factor in the dynamic and unpredictable processes of living systems. The whole Malthusian notion that evolution is driven by a bloody and brutal battle for survival actually has no scientific merit.

THE EVOLUTION OF DARWIN

Darwin, whose life spanned three quarters of the 19th century, came into a world when many views shared an uneasy coexistence. The bright shaft of light called the Age of Enlightenment, which was the philosophy that bred the American and French revolutions a generation earlier, was still shining, although dimmed by the darkness of creeping Malthusianism. The return of the monarchy in France had recently revitalized the Church, breathing life into its quest to retain its powerful paradigmatic crown. And, in the background, the progress of materialist science was steadily moving forward through the work of English chemist John Dalton and his atomic theory, published in 1805, which brought Newtonian physics down to earth by employing its principles to define the mechanics of the newly minted science of chemistry.

Although Charles Darwin was born into an upper-class family of Unitarians and freethinkers, his father, in deference to convention, had young Charles baptized in the Anglican Church. As a child, Darwin attended Unitarian Church with his mother. He later enrolled at the University of Edinburgh, where he eagerly studied science and attended lectures on Jean-Baptiste de Lamarck's radical theories of evolution.

Apparently, pre-med wasn't Charles's calling—his poor academic performance caused him to leave the university without completing his degree. His father, concerned that Charles would become a ne'er-do-well (or, at best, a sometime-do-well), encouraged him to enroll at the University of Cambridge to become an Anglican cleric. For a dropout, upper-middle-class Englishman, the ministry was his last resort.

Darwin completed his theological studies and, immediately upon graduation and in spite of his father's protests, signed on to a two-year voyage on the *HMS Beagle* as a gentlemen's mate to Captain Robert Fitz-Roy. In the British navy during that time, aristocrats such as Captain Fitz-Roy were not allowed to socialize with the commoners who comprised the crew. To make his voyage tolerable, FitzRoy offered Darwin a position as traveling companion on a voyage to survey the wonders of Nature.

While at sea, the *Beagle*'s doctor, who was also the ship's official naturalist and in charge of wildlife survey, had a confrontation with young Charles. The doctor resolved the conflict by jumping ship in South America. Conveniently, Charles assumed the official post of naturalist as the *Beagle* sailed toward the Galapagos Islands for what would become a historic voyage of paradigmatic proportions. The two-year journey lasted five years, during which time Darwin immersed himself in his study of Nature.

Before the voyage, Darwin received a copy of *Principles of Geology*, which was published in 1830 and was, perhaps, the most important scientific publication since Newton's *Philosophiae Naturalis Principia*

Mathematica. Its author, Charles Lyell, was the most distinguished and influential scientist in the world at that time and for good reason. His *Principles of Geology*, published in three volumes in 1830 to 1833, established the science of geology and, in doing so, undermined the Church's Biblical interpretation of Creation.

Until that time, people held the sacrosanct belief that the Heavens, Earth, and life were the result of God's amazing six-day tour de force described in Genesis. The Church was so secure in its stand on this issue that it even offered, as a religious fact, the exact date that God gave birth to Earth. In case you were thinking of buying Gaia a birthday card, that was Sunday, October 23, 4004 B.C.E. James Ussher, an Anglican bishop, determined this date by calculating the lineage of Biblical begats back to the appearance of Adam.[3]

While most people of the day blindly accepted this date for Creation, geologists, led by Lyell, estimated that planet Earth had evolved through eons of gradual, yet dynamic, upheavals, which, in geological terms, resulted in a warping and repositioning of Earth's crust. Lyell concluded that the physical disposition of continents, oceans, and mountains was the result of slow, steady alterations by natural forces such as winds, rains, floods, earthquakes, and volcanoes.

Lyell's book contained four chapters dedicated to Lamarck's theories, which also suggested that life arose through a long, slow evolutionary progression over millions of years during which some organisms became extinct, a situation that explained fossils. To Lyell, evolution of the biosphere was a perfect complement to evolution of the physical planet. Lyell's writings did much to open the public's eyes to a whole new view regarding the origin, or Creation, of the world.

During his five-year voyage, Darwin immersed himself in Lyell's book and, in a sense, became a Lyell groupie, regularly corresponding with this prestigious scientific authority. The novel insights offered by Lyell and Lamarck helped shape Darwin's ultimate conclusion that the succession of life in Earth history should be ascribed, like geological phenomena, to natural causes.[4]

Darwin acknowledged the significance of Lyell's contribution to the formulation of his theory of evolution when he published the second edition of his *Journal of Researches* in 1845. Darwin dedicated this book to Lyell, with the following explanation: "The chief part of whatever scientific merit this journal and other works of the author may possess, have been derived from studying the well-known and admirable *Principles of Geology*."[5]

On October 2, 1836, Darwin arrived home in London. He met with and immediately became a lifelong friend of Lyell, who encouraged him to pursue his studies on the theory of evolution. As an upshot of their discussions, Darwin began to compile his first notebook on the *Transmutation of Species*, the title of which was also the original term for evolution coined by Lamarck in his *Philosophie Zoologique* in 1809.[6]

So, while Lamarck provided a scientific foundation for biological evolution and Lyell drew a correlation between that and evolution of the physical planet, Darwin focused on providing insight into the forces or mechanisms that drove or motivated the evolutionary process. He was specifically concerned with the reasons why new species should appear at all. Without an answer to that question, Darwin's theory languished for years until, ironically, he found the inspiration to advance his concept in the work of Malthus.[7]

Darwin wrote in his autobiography: "In October 1838, that is, fifteen months after I had begun my systematic inquiry, I happened to read for amusement Malthus on *Population*, and being well-prepared to appreciate the struggle for existence which everywhere goes on, from long continued observation of the habits of animals and plants, it at once struck me that under these circumstances favourable variations would tend to be preserved and unfavourable ones to be destroyed."[8]

In other words, Darwin was saying that, while Malthus focused on the selection process as a means through which the weak elements of a society are eliminated, he, Darwin, put his own spin on the selection process by emphasizing the survival of the stronger individuals. This was a politically savvy move because Darwin was a gentleman in Victorian England, a culture that had an upper class and a lower class. Rather than attributing the selection process to the influence of a menial lower class, Darwin emphasized that it was good breeding and heredity of the upper class—those having the "favourable variations" and presumably being the *fittest*—that drove evolution. Therefore, in his writing, Darwin rephrased what Malthus called "Nature's process of selection" in the elimination of society's unfavorable elements into what Darwin termed *natural selection*.

DARWIN'S INDELICATE ARRANGEMENT

By the early 1840s, Darwin began to develop his theory, but he did not share his conclusions with anyone, not even Charles Lyell. In 1844, Darwin wrote to the luminary botanist Sir Joseph Dalton Hooker, "at last gleams of light have come, and I am almost convinced (quite to the contrary of the opinion I started with) that species are not (it is like confessing to a murder) immutable."[9] The murder Darwin referred to was the murder of God. If the theory were valid that species individually descended through a process of evolutionary transformation, that would kill the legitimacy of the first book of the Bible, the part of the Scripture that defines the relationship between God and the human race. It is also interesting to note that Darwin wrote, "I am *almost* convinced" that species could mutate. Clearly, even he did not yet *believe* in evolution.

Later that year, Scottish journalist Robert Chambers anonymously published, *Vestiges of the Natural History of Creation*, a widely read book that championed evolution over creationism. Even though it was controversial and attacked by Victorian society, this book popularized the notion of evolution and broke the ice for Darwin to publish without professionally perishing.

Yet, Darwin kept stalling for more than a decade until prodded into action by a colleague's work. In June 1858, Charles Darwin received a package that would stir him to action. It was sent by Alfred Russel Wallace, an English naturalist working in Borneo. Wallace was a naturalist as good as or better than Darwin himself but was also, unfortunately, a self-educated, working-class commoner. To earn a living, Wallace caught specimens and sold them to museums, zoological parks, and wealthy collectors, and, in the process, became a great naturalist.

Wallace sent Darwin a copy of a manuscript titled *On the Tendency of Varieties to Depart Indefinitely from the Original Type* along with a letter requesting that Darwin review the material and, if he found it of merit, pass it on to Charles Lyell.[10] This manuscript was Wallace's theory of evolution. It was brief, elegant, academic, extremely well-written and would have qualified Wallace as the rightful "founder of the evolution theory," a title now attributed to Darwin alone.

Not wanting the prestige of formulating the theory of evolution to fall upon a commoner, Darwin beseeched Lyell for help to preserve his precious self-claimed priority in this profoundly important discovery. In a letter dated June 26, 1858, Darwin wrote: "It seems hard on me that I should be thus compelled to lose my priority of many years standing . . ."[11] Lyell came to the aid of Darwin, his distraught junior colleague, by engaging their mutual friend Sir Joseph Hooker in what was to become known as the "delicate arrangement" regarding "one of the greatest conspiracies in the annals of science."[12]

Lyell and Hooker crafted a letter in which they claimed that Darwin and Wallace were acquaintances. The letter stated that both "gentlemen having, independently and unknown to one another, conceived the same very ingenious theory . . . may both fairly claim the merit of being original thinkers in this important line of inquiry."[13] The simple truth is that Wallace had, in hand, a fully evolved written theory and Darwin had merely a long-incubated, but unhatched, idea! However, Lyell used his status to orchestrate fabrications, alter documents, and plagiarize so that Darwin, the aristocrat, would get first billing while Wallace, the commoner, would receive the dubious honor of being listed as second, or junior, contributor.

The theory of evolution—officially described as the Darwin–Wallace theory—was formally introduced at the Linnean Society of London on July 1, 1858, one month after Darwin received the package.

On the surface, this bit of skullduggery might seem to be trivial in regard to the history of humanity, but we can assure you this incident has had profound reverberations that continue to impact us today. The difference between whether Wallace or Darwin received credit for the theory is the evolutionary epitome of the glass being half full or half empty.

From the perspective of a commoner, Wallace recognized that evolution was driven by the elimination of the *weakest*, while Darwin interpreted the same data to mean that evolution resulted from the will to survive inherent in the *fittest*. The difference? In a Wallacean world, we would *improve* in order not to be the weakest, but in a Darwinian world, we *struggle* to acquire the status of being the best. In other words, had Wallace prevailed, there would be less focus on competition and more on cooperation.

A year after the delicate arrangement, Alfred Russel Wallace dissolved into the background as Darwin gained worldwide prominence with the publication of his masterpiece, *The Origin of Species by Means of Natural Selection*. The content of this best-selling book popularized the concepts of evolution and natural selection and implanted into the world the chilling notion that only the fittest survive.

What brought this book to the attention of the world more than anything else was its subtitle, which offered a more penetrating view of the Darwinism we would come to know. The full title is *The Origin of Species by Means of Natural Selection, or The Preservation of Favoured Races in the Struggle for Life*. It should be emphasized here, that Darwin was a product of his times. While he was radical enough to build on the geological implications of Lyell's work, he also accepted without question Malthus's conclusions, which we now know to be faulty. While biological success obviously comes from adapting to an environment, from the Malthusian standpoint, that adaptation primarily takes place in the fight over scarce resources.

The concept of *social Darwinism,* the term coined by philosopher Herbert Spencer—who, coincidentally, is also credited with inventing the term *survival of the fittest*—emphasizes the harsh implication of Darwinian theory. That theory encourages *improving humanity* by purifying the race, which, of course, means winnowing out *unfavorable genetic inferiors*. Taken to its fullest application, Darwinian theory became the state-sanctioned science and mission of Nazi Germany.

In his later years, Darwin moved away from academic Darwinism. Rather than emphasizing survival and struggle, Darwin readdressed his attention to focus on the evolution of love, altruism, and the genetic roots of human kindness. In addition, Darwin began to credit the Lamarckian concept of the environment as the driving force in evolution. Unfortunately, Darwin's disciples thought his new ideas were tantamount to sedition, undermining all that Darwinism had come to stand for. Darwinists simply held on to their version of the theory and dismissed Darwin's later ideas as the consequence of his creeping senility.

Within ten years of its publication, the majority of the world's scientists essentially accepted Darwin's theory as truth. But it had a much more powerful impact on the evolution of human civilization than most people realize, and that's because Darwin provided a missing piece that would change civilization's basal paradigm. Before *The Origin of Species*, monotheism shaped the cultural beliefs of Western civilization because it was the only source of truth that could provide satisfactory answers to each of the three perennial questions:

1. How did we get here?
2. Why are we here?
3. Now that we're here, how do we make the best of it?

While science was making miraculous advances and steadily eroding the Church's power base, it could not unseat monotheism as civilization's "official" truth provider until it offered "We evolved." as the answer to "How did we get here?"

HOW WE INHERITED SURVIVAL OF THE FITTEST

At the time *The Origin of Species* was published, the general public was very much engaged in breeding plants and animals and was quite familiar with hereditary alterations that influenced the structural and behavioral traits of offspring. It was not a far reach for laymen to accept Darwin's view that life on this planet evolved from a primitive ancestor who was followed by a long lineage of reproductive variations over millions of years. Consequently, the theory of evolution made sense and was readily accepted by both science and the populace. This acceptance put science in a position to provide a public-approved and satisfactory answer to that pesky perennial question regarding origins, an answer much more acceptable to the majority than the former view of Creation offered by monotheism.

Not surprisingly, the Church launched an aggressive campaign to counter the heresy of the godless evolutionists. The anticipated confrontation between religion and science came to a head only seven months after the publication of *The Origin of Species*. The showdown took place during a meeting held by the British Association for the Advancement of Science at Oxford University in June of 1860. The meeting was distinguished by the fact that two scholarly papers, based on the new theory of evolution, were to be presented for public consideration. A scheduled debate ensued between Bishop Samuel Wilberforce, representing the creationists, and Thomas Huxley, a friend of Darwin and a champion of his theory.

In a time before movies, radio, and television, debates commanded public attention for more than just the information they conveyed. Debates were entertainment. It was public theater wherein contestants would duel to the metaphorical death, verbally lashing each other with razor-sharp wit punctuated with high drama and biting satire. Bishop Wilberforce, a top-notch debater, was referred to as "Soapy Sam" because of the craftiness he displayed in gaining the advantage. In other words, Sam was slippery.

Wilberforce did not come to conquer evolution; he came to exorcise its evil spirit from the mind of the people. His expressed intent was to humiliate the evolutionists and reestablish in the public's mind the Church's belief in Creation. No record was kept of the actual debate, but Wilberforce apparently summed up his argument with a contrived question to make Huxley look like a fool no matter how he chose to answer it. A version of the question, which played upon Victorian reverence to family lineage and motherhood, went: "Let me ask Mr. Huxley one question. Is it through his grandfather or his grandmother that he claims descent from a monkey?"

Huxley, who was known as "Darwin's Bulldog," was hesitant to even attend the debate due to apprehension of being entrapped by Soapy Sam's rhetoric. However, he hit Wilberforce right between the eyes with his now famous reply: "I will answer your question, my Lord Bishop. An ape may seem to you to be a poor sort of creature, of low intelligence and stooping gait that grins and chatters as we pass. But I would rather have an ape for an ancestor than a man who is prepared to prostitute his undoubted gift of elegance and culture to the service of prejudice and falsehood."[14]

Huxley's magic bullet not only felled Wilberforce, it mortally wounded the Church. In a matter of moments, the debate—as well as the monotheistic paradigm—was over. After nearly two thousand years of overseeing the course of humanity, the Church was forced to relinquish the torch of knowledge and, with it, control of Western civilization's basal paradigm. The future was now in the hands of scientific materialism.

A DOG-EAT-DOG WORLD . . . NOT!

Prior to the 17th century, science viewed life as a harmonious process, one of the last vestigial beliefs of animism and its descendant, deism. But in the century before Darwin and in the years following his death, the cultural picture of Nature went from nurturing mother to violent jungle.

Largely, this change in image was based on erroneous conclusions derived from biased observations using distorted science. What we observe as violence in Nature is the result of both predator-prey relationships and rivalry over territory, food, and mates. However, the latter form of violence is rarely if ever fatal. Once dominance has been established and acknowledged in a territorial dispute, the defeated animal slinks away, still living. So it's most definitely *not* a dog-eat-dog world. Yes, it's a dog-eat-squirrel world and a dog-growl-at-dog world, but dogs just don't eat other dogs.

While we humans are, indeed, part of the web of life, we are, fortunately, perched atop the food chain. We no longer have natural predators and so, as more than one cynical philosopher has observed, we prey on one another. There is a distinct difference between the violence of hunting a deer, which is a natural process in the established web of life, and hunting a deer hunter, which is a behavior that falls far outside of Nature's inherent morality. Our fundamental preoccupation with violence as a way of life is truly a misinterpretation of Nature.

Whether by accident or design, the use of violence far predates Darwin as a lowest-common-dominator operating system, wherein might makes right. However, Darwinian theory offered humanity a scientific justification for inhumane actions, including individual violence and the collective use of force, especially if the latter helps eliminate the burgeoning, applecart-upsetting lower-class masses.

Darwinism also dealt the Church another low blow when it undermined the religious notion of morality in regard to justification of means and ends. In a survival-of-the-fittest mentality, Darwinian fitness is the ability of a population to maintain or increase its numbers in succeeding generations. Therefore, fitness through health or fit progeny represents an end. How we humans attain that end, be it through compassion or an Uzi, is entirely irrelevant.

In the end, Darwinian theory encouraged the "favoured races" to treat themselves to even more favorable treatment. Even worse, Darwinism gave tacit permission for each nation to advance its own "favoured race" at the expense of the whole. And so Darwinian theory delivered Western civilization from monotheism's laws of the scriptures to scientific materialism's law of the jungle. No rules or moral guidelines . . . just Darwinners and Darlosers.

While few people have actually read and understood Darwin's complete works, the phrase *survival of the fittest* is well known, but mostly misunderstood. The phrase isn't a scientific concept but a tautology, which is just a fancy way of defining what something is by stating what it is. For example, the dictionary defines the word *fit*, in biological terms, as being able to survive. When Darwinists invoke the mantra survival of the fittest, they are actually saying, "survival of those most able to survive." Well, yeah. But when fed into the human psyche, replete with images of lions chasing down gazelles, survival of the fittest takes on a more life-threatening, adrenaline-pumping significance.

However, if we take a look at the jungle, we find that the law of the jungle doesn't even apply there! When a lion takes off after a gazelle, the lion doesn't care about the fittest or capturing the one with the biggest antlers to later be a suitable trophy in his den. In fact, she goes after the *least* fit because she's hungry and wants to be sure she gets something to eat. More precisely, the law of the jungle is actually the non-survival of the non-fittest. By definition, to survive, you don't need to be the fittest, all you need to be is—well, fit. In another way of looking at it, consider the percentage of gazelles that *don't* get eaten by a lion every day.

An evolutionary lesson in not being the weakest is humorously portrayed in the story of two campers in the woods who wake up to find a bear in their camp. One starts putting on his shoes, and the other says, "Why are you putting on your shoes? You can't outrun a bear." The first one says, "Who needs to outrun the bear? I only have to outrun you."

THRIVAL OF THE FITTINGEST

As the path of humanity's evolution continues its swing toward a more balanced, holistic perception of life, we see that the new rules of quantum science apply to the theory of evolution as well.

Studies now emphasize that evolution occurs in the context of an environment—not separate from it. The progress of evolution can be seen as an environment constantly seeking to rebalance itself. For example, let's say organism #1 eats X in the environment and poops Y. As #1's population increases, its food source X necessarily diminishes, while its waste product Y simultaneously increases. While the loss of X and the buildup of Y throw the environment a little out of balance, the situation also provides an opportunity for the evolution of a new organism, #2, that thrives on eating Y and excreting Z. As #2's population increases, it causes the level Y to return to balance but at the cost of increasing the amount of Z in the environment, which, in turn, supports the future evolution of Z-eating organism #3. And so on, and so on. This is an oversimplified example and yet, as sophisticated systems theorists are showing us, it is, indeed, the case.

In his 1998 article in the prestigious journal *Nature*, British scientist Timothy Lenton provided important support for the Gaia hypothesis formulated by scientist, environmentalist, and futurist James Lovelock. Lovelock suggested that Earth, itself, is a living entity that uses evolution to regulate its own exceedingly complex metabolism. Lenton described how the sun has warmed by 25 percent since life on Earth began some 3.8

billion years ago, and, yet, the planet has somehow been able to regulate its climate and buffer that huge temperature differential. Lenton suggests that evolutionary traits that benefit the system as a whole tend to be reinforced, while those that alter or destabilize the environment in an unfavorable way are restrained.

Lenton concluded, "If an organism acquires a mutation that causes it to behave in an 'anti-Gaian' manner, its spread will be restricted in that it will be at an evolutionary disadvantage."[15] More to the point and applied to our current situation, Lenton is suggesting that if we humans don't find ways to evolve that are more harmonious with the planet, we may find ourselves homeless.

What we have failed to realize is that the real evolutionary principle is "thrival of the fittingest." Those organisms that best fit the environment by contributing and supporting global harmony get to thrive while the others—well . . .

THE ANSWERS LIE WITHIN

But, perhaps, the most cogent example of the real nature of life, the example that shows us the way out of the Malthusian dilemma of scarcity and points us in the direction of our next evolution, pertains to the origins and development of multicellular life forms on this planet.

Why is it, and how is it, that trillions of single-celled organisms were able to combine forces to become us?

To answer this question, we must remember that, for the first 3.8 billion years of life on this planet, the only life forms were single-celled organisms such as bacteria, algae, yeast, and protozoans.

Around 700 million years ago, cells started to assemble into primitive multicellular colonial organisms. By sharing information, new communal associations provided greater awareness of the surrounding environment and enhanced the life of their constituent cells. Simply, environmental awareness, which is a measure of evolution, affords an organism a greater opportunity to effectively and efficiently survive in a dynamic world. Two can live as cheaply as one, so joining forces is better than going it alone.

Initially, in the early stages of evolution, all the cells in colonial organisms carried out the same functions. However, there came a time when the number of cells that comprised an organism became so large that it was no longer advantageous for all cells to do the same thing.

Imagine, for example, that we're still a hunter-gatherer society and each morning eight million New Yorkers commute to Westchester County to forage for food. It is far more effective to split up life-sustaining responsibilities among the members of the tribe. In this case, hunters would go out into the world while others in the community would stay home and perform various chores such as cooking, raising the kids, maintaining tools, watching TV, and so on.

This is exactly what happened in the evolution of multicellular organisms. As their communal numbers increased to thousands, millions, and trillions, individual cells in the community took on specialized jobs to support the survival of the whole organism. Biologists refer to this division of the workload among constituent cells as the process of *differentiation.*

As the structures of the differentiating cell communities evolved further, they ultimately created a multitude of emergent species—an evolution unimaginable to the single-celled organisms that thrived in the first 3.8 billion years of life. The formation of multicellular communities was, in a sense, a quantum leap in the course of evolution on this planet. Therefore, we might be tempted to think the current sentient human organism represents the fully tweaked evolutionary endpoint. But, in reality, the human is actually at the beginning of the next and higher level of evolution, the emergent multi-human super-organism known as *Humanity.*

The notion of survival of the fittest has been applied in our individualistic culture to mean survival of the fittest individuals. The sad truth, however, is that Gaia couldn't care less about the fittest because she is more concerned about the impact the whole population has on its global metabolism, the environment. Regardless of how many Gandhis, Mother Teresas, and Leonardo da Vincis we produce, at the current time, our entire species is being measured, not for its fitness, but for its "fittingness." Perhaps we, like our single-cell forebears, must now leave our single-cell individuality behind and evolve into a coherent multicellular whole, wherein self-interest and planetary interest are one and the same.

FROM THE SELFISH GENE TO THE SELFLESS GENIUS

The current human society has taken to heart the notion of competition as a means to survival even though that word has been distorted and misinterpreted from its original Greek etymology where "to compete" meant "to strive together." To the Greeks, the notion of competition meant using the energy of each other's performance to enhance one's own; it did not imply that we should crush our opponents or try to win at any cost.

While exceeding one's personal best is certainly a worthy ambition, consider all the contests and games in which there are far, far more losers than winners. The movie, *Mad Hot Ballroom*, an excellent and inspiring documentary about teaching troubled inner-city students self-respect through ballroom dancing, unfortunately offered the downside caused by misinterpreting competition. Despite the learning, the enjoyment, and the growth that came from striving together in the dance competition, all but the final winners were reduced to tears because they failed to win. Now, how in Heaven's name does that make sense?

On the darker side, Enron, once heralded by *Forbes* magazine and *The Wall Street Journal* as the "company of the future" and, later, shown to be rotten to the core, made Darwinism their company credo. CEO Jeffrey Skilling touted his favorite book, *The Selfish Gene* by British science writer Richard Dawkins, as his Bible and, in true Darwinian fashion, took pride in culling the herd periodically at Enron in an effort to enhance corporate fitness. He would go into a division and tell the employees that he would fire the bottom 10 percent of producers during the next quarter. And he did exactly that. The pressure of the selection process created a ruthless, free-for-all atmosphere in which your best friend could become your worst enemy on judgment day.

The misunderstood notion of competition as a judge of evolutionary fitness was ferociously carried over into all of the company's dealings. If you have the opportunity to view the movie, *Enron: The Smartest Guys in the Room*, you'll hear and see traders gleefully talk about "screwing grandmothers out of their pensions," cheer for ravaging life-threatening fires that were increasing the value of their stocks, or celebrate the collapse of an entire state's economy as they reap windfalls from the victims.[16]

But that laughter was to die out abruptly because, in true reptilian fashion, Enron's corporate officers ate their young by sinking the company and running off with their employees' payrolls, pensions, and stock annuities. The fall of the house of Enron, and the resulting shock waves it sent into a blithely Darwinian business community, was an important wake-up call concerning the unworkability of short-term individual gain, including a paramount focus on next quarter profits. Yet, the very same faulty thinking behind the selfish gene still persists and keeps us from facing our true genius.

WE'RE ALL IN THIS TOGETHER

Perhaps the most important message offered by both quantum physics and field experiments is that everything is related. Our Universe is not hierarchical and linear; it's relational and fractal.

What do we mean by fractal? *Fractal geometry*, as we will see later, is the branch of mathematics that describes the patterns of Nature. When you look at a leaf, a stem, a branch, a tree, or a forest; or when you observe a seashore from varying distances; you notice a repeating, self-similar pattern at different levels of complexity.

Self-similar fractal patterns repeat themselves throughout every level of organization in the natural world. Hence, our cells, our selves, and our civilization all need oxygen, water, and food to survive. Why is this important? Because what is good for any one of these is good for all, and, conversely, what is damaging to one is damaging to all. This would seem to make great common sense, but, while under the spell of widely held myth-perceptions, common sense is sadly all too uncommon. The good news within the bad news is that the dire effects of having taken ourselves out of the web of life are beginning to wake us up.

Alarming issues like global climate change and species loss are telling us that no individual—no matter how physically or fiscally fit or how big the security wall behind which we live—can survive if the species doesn't. Polymath Arthur Koestler coined the word *holon* to describe the condition of "having parts" as well as "being part" of something else.[17] Humans are holons. We are made up of parts—cells, tissues, and organs. Yet, we are parts in something larger. We belong to communities, nations, and humanity. We even see ourselves as a cell of Mother Earth. The key to survival is thrival of the entire world system: healthy cells, healthy humans, healthy planet. Put another way, without Earth we're nowhere.

Therefore, what has been called the biological imperative seems to have two equally important concerns: survival of the individual organism and survival of the species. Generally, survival of the species is expressed as the drive to reproduce. However, when the species, itself, is threatened by environmental changes, reproduction not only is not an option, it makes no sense. We have now created an environment that, should we continue doing what we are currently doing, will no longer be able to sustain human life.

This means that the new biological imperative for humankind necessarily involves the understanding that we're all in this together and survival of the fittest must now give way to "thrival of the fittingest." That means we must adjust human activity to that which will cause the entire system to thrive. We now seem to have reached the level of complexity on the planet where seven billion human cells, operating unconsciously and using their energy at destructive cross-purposes, is no longer biologically functional.

Like the single-cell organisms that utilized environmental awareness in order to emerge into more complex and efficient organisms, human society must adopt a new paradigm of social and economic relationships. Paradoxically, this new level of cooperative awareness means maximum expression for the individual and maximum benefit for the whole. Only the seemingly impossible reconciliation of these misperceived opposites can create the emergent human that spiritual teachers tell us is our destiny.

CHAPTER 7

MYTH-PERCEPTION THREE: IT'S IN YOUR GENES

"The bad news is, there is no key to the Universe.
The good news is, it has been left unlocked."
— Swami Beyondananda

WE FOUND THE KEY TO LIFE—
BUT IT DOESN'T UNLOCK THE SECRET

The mission of modern science, as stated by Francis Bacon over 400 years ago, is to dominate and control Nature. Scholars were convinced that through an understanding of the material realm, humanity would acquire a mastery over the natural environment. Therefore, it's only natural that a materialist belief system would look for the key to human life in the material world itself—specifically in the gene.

In search of that key, the science of genetics assumed a myopic mission to identify the structure and behavior of the physical molecules that control the vehicular bodies we inhabit. Once endowed with an awareness of the mechanisms of biological heredity, science would be well on its way to dominion over Nature. Such an understanding would provide for the development of genetic engineering and offer science an opportunity to control life itself, including human life.

However, the same funny thing happened on the road to finding the key to life that happened on the way to establishing, with guaranteed certainty, the precept that all that matters is matter. The cosmic prankster leveled us with another cosmic joke of global proportions. Just when we thought we had the key to life in our hands, when we tried to unlock the secret, the key didn't work.

IS THE GENE THE KEY?

When Darwin put forth his heredity-based theory of evolution, the premise that traits were passed from parent to child made perfect practical sense to anyone who had ever bred animals: like begets like. Because the Newtonian view at the time emphasized the primacy of matter, it was seemingly assured that the secret of life would be encoded within the body's own molecules.

Based on the information available at the time, Darwin hypothesized that particulate gemmules, which programmed various physical and behavioral traits, were distributed throughout the body. During development, trait-attributing gemmules would somehow coalesce in the germ cells—eggs and sperm—which, then, enabled them to be passed on to the next generation.

Newtonian materialistic logic implied that the germ cells carry physical determinants within their molecules that control the traits of organisms derived from those cells. Combine this concept with the basic Darwinian notion of natural selection—that is, the traits that endure tend to be those that enhance survival of the species—and post-Darwinian geneticists had a challenge on their hands: to discover the physical elements that encode hereditary traits, to describe how they work at the cellular level, and then to use that information to design "designer humans."

It took nearly one hundred years of dedicated research efforts for genetic scientists to substantiate the speculations of Darwin in regard to heredity. German cytologist Walther Flemming made the initial advance by identifying the material elements of heredity in 1882. Flemming was a microscopist and the first to describe mitosis, which is the process of cell division. In his study, Flemming emphasized the reproductive importance of thread-like filaments found in the cell's nucleus. Six years later, in 1888, German anatomist Heinrich Waldeyer coined the term *chromosome* to describe these heredity-conferring filaments.

Shortly after the turn of the 19th century, American geneticist and embryologist Thomas Hunt Morgan became the first scientist to describe the rare event known as a genetic mutation when he found in his cultures of red-eyed Drosophilia flies a white-eyed fly that was able to produce similar offspring. From his observations on this and other mutant fruit flies, Morgan deduced that the genetic factors that control hereditary traits are arranged along the chromosomes in a precise linear order.

Further chemical analysis revealed that chromosomes are composed of proteins and deoxyribonucleic acid (DNA). However, the question as to whether the genetic key was the protein or the DNA remained until 1944 when Rockefeller Institute researchers Oswald Avery, Colin MacLeod, and Maclyn McCarty determined empirically that DNA was the molecule that encoded hereditary traits.[1]

Their experiment was both simple and elegant. They removed the chromosomes from bacteria species #1 and separated the DNA from the protein. Then they added either the isolated chromosomal protein or the chromosomal DNA into cultures of bacteria species #2. The results showed that when the DNA of species #1 was added into cultures of species #2, that species began to express traits that were specifically characteristic of species #1. In contrast, the addition of chromosomal proteins from species #1 did not have the ability to transform the traits of recipient species #2. While this study was the first to distinguish DNA as the heredity-controlling molecule, it did not offer any insight into how DNA accomplished this feat.

Interestingly, biologists were not at the forefront of the movement to uncover life's biggest little secret. Insight into the nature of DNA's mechanism was offered by the true mechanics of science—physicists. In his 1944 book, *What is Life*, Nobel Prize–winning physicist Erwin Schrodinger introduced the idea that genetic information could theoretically be encoded in the configuration of molecular bonds within crystalline molecules.[2]

Schrodinger offered a well-reasoned theoretical prediction of what biologists should look for in their search for the genesis elements. Inspired by Schrodinger's mechanistic vision, molecular biologist James D. Watson and physicist Francis Crick initiated a collaboration that would lead to one of the most important discoveries in the history of biology.

GENETIC DETERMINISM:
THE DOGMA THAT WOULDN'T HUNT

In 1953, Watson and Crick changed the course of human history when their article "Molecular Structure of Nucleic Acids" was published in the prestigious British scientific journal *Nature*. Working with x-ray crystallography, they found that the DNA molecule was a long linear strand assembled from four different types of molecular building blocks called nucleotide bases: adenine, thymine, guanine, and cytosine, which are abbreviated as A, T, G, and C. They also found that pairs of DNA strands assemble into double helices. Most importantly, they discovered that the sequence of A, T, G, and C bases along the length of the DNA molecule represented a code used to synthesize the body's protein molecules.

A gene, therefore, represents a length of DNA code that contains the nucleotide base sequences needed to make a specific protein. Protein molecules are the material building blocks of the cell and, as such, are responsible for an organism's physical and behavioral traits.

Based on the nature of the DNA coding mechanism, Francis Crick posited the concept known as the central dogma of molecular biology.[3] This central dogma, which is also referred to as the primacy of DNA, defined the flow of information in biological systems. The ATGC base sequences of DNA represent information—expressed as genes—that encodes a protein's structure. The cell makes the equivalent of a Xerox copy of a gene in the form of another type of nucleic acid called ribonucleic acid (RNA).

The RNA copy is the actual molecule physically employed to assemble the code into a protein molecule. Consequently, the information in the DNA is transcribed into RNA and then the information in the RNA is translated into protein molecules. Crick's central dogma mapped the flow of information in most biological systems as being one directional: from DNA to RNA to protein.

Because the original patterns for the trait-providing protein's structure are encoded in the DNA, this molecule was considered the primary determinant of our biological character. Hence, the central dogma, literally translates as DNA being the primary cause of our condition in life. Per Watson and Crick, the secret of life was finally reduced to molecular cascades that originate in the cell's nucleus by switching specific DNA genes on or off. This conclusion represented the epitome of biological reductionism—life emanates from material genes.

The central dogma became one of the most important tenets of modern science, one that significantly influenced the direction of genetic research for the next 50 years. The belief in a physical Newtonian world fully convinced biologists that life and its mechanisms were clearly the result of material interactions, akin to the old story of moving, interlocking gears within wind-up mechanical watches. Consequently, even before Watson and Crick were born, science had concluded that an assembly of physical molecules controls life. The only remaining question was, "Which molecules would it be?" When Watson and Crick reported their DNA results, the decision was a slam dunk: DNA molecules control life.

Scientists unquestionably accepted the central dogma's conclusions as true because they were already anticipating the result. Amazingly, biologists immediately adopted Crick's hypothesis even though its validity was never assessed. And it is both interesting and important to note that Crick referred to his DNA→RNA→Protein molecular information pathway hypothesis as dogma. By definition, the word *dogma* represents a "belief based upon religious persuasion and not scientific fact."

By adopting an unverified dogma and making it the very foundation of biomedicine, scientific materialism officially and ironically slipped into the realm of religion! The question as to whether or not modern science represents science or religion was now predicated on whether DNA actually controlled life. Before we go into every hotel room in the world and replace Gideon's Bible with a book on genetics, let's look into this question of the Primacy of DNA. Is it really true?

A key implication of Crick's central dogma is that hereditary information only flows in one direction, from the DNA to the proteins—DNA→RNA→Protein—and never goes in the opposite direction, which means, according to Crick, protein cannot influence the structure and activity of the DNA code. Here's the rub: the body that experiences life is made out of protein; because proteins cannot send information about life's experiences back to the DNA, then environmental information cannot change genetic destiny. This means that genetic information is disconnected from the environment.

The information flow predicated by the central dogma concretized the notion of genetic determinism, a concept that has influenced the lives of everyone on this planet.

Genetic determinism is the belief that genes control all of our traits—physical, behavioral, and emotional. It is the reason why we look for traits that run in families and why science keeps searching for genes that control this or that particular characteristic. Simply, it is the belief that our fates are locked in our genes and, because we cannot change our genes, we are truly, so they say, victims of our heredity.

However, as time went on, new discoveries undermined the surety of that belief.

In the late 1960s, University of Wisconsin geneticist Howard Temin was studying how tumor viruses hijack control of an infected cell's genetic code. The virus with which he was working contained only RNA as a genetic molecule. Consequently, when Temin published his research that suggested RNA information could flow backward and alter the host cell's DNA code, he was ostracized and declared a heretic. In this case, the religious connotation of the heresy label was an appropriate epithet in that he was guilty of challenging the dogma.[4]

At the time, no one was prepared for the profound implications of Temin's discovery, but we have since come to realize that the HIV viruses that presumably cause AIDS utilize the same heretical RNA genetic mechanism. Temin ultimately shared the Nobel Prize in Physiology in 1975 for discovering *reverse transcriptase*, the enzyme that copies RNA's information into the DNA code.

Temin's work broke the backbone of Crick's central dogma by proving that hereditary information flows in both directions: DNA sends information to RNA, and RNA can send information back into the DNA. The implication of Temin's work is that through reverse processing, hereditary changes can be made by design or environmental influence and not only by accidental mutation as had been presumed.

By 1990, another basic tenet of the central dogma and genetic determinism was deconstructed. As reported by Duke University biologist H. Frederik Nijhout, genes are not "self-emergent" and cannot "turn themselves on and off."[5] Nijhout's article emphasized that genes are simply blueprints, and the concept that a blueprint has an on-and-off quality is absurd. Imagine being in an architect's office, looking at a blueprint, and asking, "Is that blueprint on or off?" The appropriate question is: "Is that DNA blueprint being read or not?"

That's because genes don't read themselves, which means they are incapable of activating their own expression and are not self-emergent or self-actualizing. The next question then becomes, "What is responsible for reading a gene?" In Nijhout's words: "When a gene product is needed, a signal from its environment, not an emergent property of the gene itself, activates expression of that gene." Simply put, *environmental signals control gene activity*.

As we've already seen, biomedical sciences are being philosophically transformed by the new science of epigenetic control. The prefix *epi-* means "above," so the new science literally means control from above the genes. In other words, epigenetics describes how gene activity and cellular expression are ultimately regulated by information *from* the external field of influence rather than *by* the internal matter of DNA.

The inconvenient truth that genes do not control their own activity and that hereditary information does not flow in only one direction, as asserted by the central dogma, was established over 20 years ago. But, in spite of these flies in the ointment, basic science textbooks, the media, and, especially, the pharmaceutical industry continue to resist movement away from the notion of the central dogma. They, thus, perpetuate the layperson's view that genes control their lives. Apparently, if we continue to religiously feed it "dogma food," even a dead dogma can be kept alive.

Even though science has proven that the genetic-determinism dogma is invalid, mainstream media continues to focus on the concept that genes are controlling our lives. Every day, news articles claim that a gene has been found to control this trait or that trait. Anxious people queue up to glimpse their fate as offered by the latest, greatest gene-chip technology as revealed by a read-out of their individual genome. The concept of genetic determinism is so resonant with the prevailing dominant basal paradigm that even irrefutable scientific proof cannot dislodge it.

THE SELFISH GENE

The widespread appeal for Richard Dawkins' scientifically unsound book *The Selfish Gene* is a prime example of the remaining popularity of the dead dogma.[6] Dawkins' theory that genes created us to carry them around and provide for their own reproduction is not only an absurd parody on science fiction that takes logic to an illogical conclusion, but it also strains even the most severe reductionism by reducing organisms to mere biochemical vehicles designed to do the bidding of the genes.

After all, as he argues, genes persist through generations but we humans only last a lifetime. Genes are the driver, and we are merely the car that gets traded in for a new model after we hit 5 million miles or 120 years, whichever comes first. Dawkins' premise is similar to the old notion that a chicken is merely an egg's way of making more eggs.

But why the selfish gene? Because, maintains Dawkins, genes possess the same drive to survive as we do, and they promote their own survival without regard for the survival of the organism or even the species in which they reside. The evolutionary adaptations that occur over generations, Dawkins says, are not designed for the survivability of the organism but to enhance the generative power of the genes themselves. And even though those adaptations may or may not enhance the survival of the organism, to the selfish gene that doesn't matter.

And because the central dogma stipulates that everything emanates from the genes, it stands to reason—unreasonable as this reason may be—that, in Dawkins' words, "We are born selfish."[7] He also believes that natural selection favors those who cheat, lie, deceive, and exploit.

Therefore, genes that cause children to behave immorally or amorally have an advantage in the gene pool. Altruism, he maintains, is basically unworkable because it interferes with natural selection. The same goes for situations with child adoption, which he believes is "against the instincts and interests of our selfish genes."

Fortunately, few people have bought into (Dawkins') extreme and materialistic views. Nonetheless, as we have seen with the Enron example, his view provided what was, for him, scientific fuel and rational justification for the most ruthless excesses of social, commercial, industrial, and governmental Darwinism. Dawkins, a self-declared atheist, believes in neither a caring Creator nor a caring human. Unlike many humanists who don't believe in a personal God, he dismisses anything that is not purely deterministic, materialistic, and outright selfish.

If, according to Dawkins, survival equals success, then a metastasizing cancer is highly successful. Until, of course, it kills the host. But, by then, if we are to believe that our destiny is controlled by DNA, the selfish genes that caused the cancer have successfully established their survival by incorporating themselves into the genetic lineage of their host's offspring, in whom future copies of those genes are prepared to do the same thing again and again, thus creating more genetic determinism—to a cancerous degree.

From the standpoint of our planetary environment, it often appears that human enterprise has come to resemble that cancer, replicating and reproducing to the detriment of the environment as a whole. Now that we have developed space travel, we are preparing to survive by infecting other planetary systems while leaving our dear, dying Earth behind.

THE HUMAN GENOME

Meanwhile, the materialistic implications of genes as genesis led to one of the most ambitious scientific projects (and biggest disappointments) in the history of biology: the Human Genome Project.

The Human Genome Project (HGP) was launched in 1990 initially under the guidance of James Watson who headed the project on behalf of the U.S. National Institutes of Health (NIH), an agency of the U.S. Department of Health and Human Services. Ostensibly, at least in the public's mind, HGP was an altruistic project with three main objectives: to identify the genetic basis of all human traits, both positive and negative; to create a research database and tools for data analysis to be shared with the biotechnical industry and the private sector; and to foster the development of new medical applications around the world.[8]

The thinking went like this. With over 100,000 proteins in the human body and with a gene blueprint needed to make each protein, there had to be at least that many human genes, right? The masterminds behind the HGP believed that, by making a compendium of all human genes, they could use that data to engineer a human utopia.

But lest Richard Dawkins be dismayed by the project's apparent humanitarian goals, there was an ulterior motive to the project as well. Genetic scientists had convinced venture capitalists that a fortune could be made by identifying the 100,000 genes that comprise the human genome. By patenting the nucleotide base sequence for each gene and then selling that information to drug companies for use in drug discovery, the investment would reap phenomenal returns.

But once again Nature, with cunning clarity, played a trick on those who would mine its secrets for financial gain.

Based on the misassumption that genes control an organism's traits, HGP profiteers expected that the more complex organisms would possess a greater number of genes. Therefore, as a precursor to the project, scientists sequenced the genes of simple organisms that have been traditionally employed in genetic research.

They found that bacteria, Nature's most primitive organisms, usually contained between 3,000 and 5,000 genes. Next, they discovered that a tiny, barely visible roundworm, *Caenorhabditis elegans*, an organism with only 1,271 cells whose name is bigger than it is, had about 23,000 genes. So far, so good.

Moving up the complexity ladder, they then studied the more evolved fruit fly and surprisingly found it had only 18,000 genes. This conclusion did not make sense. How could the considerably more complex fruit fly have fewer genes than the simpler roundworm? Undaunted, they embarked on the Human Genome Project.

When the complete human genome was assayed, the results were so *under*whelming that what should have been a big fanfare came out as a weak bleating kazoo toot. We biologically complex humans, with our 50 trillion cells, have approximately 23,000 genes, almost the same number of genes found in the lowly roundworm.[9]

The project's results were released in 2003, and the event was, nonetheless, heralded as one of humanity's greatest accomplishments. In truth, the failure to find the anticipated 100,000-plus genes essentially led to a major downsizing of the bioengineering companies it spawned, Celera and Human Genome Sciences, and resignation of their CEOs.

Dr. Paul Silverman, a pioneer in genome and stem cell research and an early advocate and principal architect of the project, responded to the surprising results by concluding that science needed to rethink the notion of genetic determinism. Well, hello! Wrote Silverman: "The cell signaling process heavily depends on extracellular stimuli to trigger nuclear DNA transduction."[10] The short translation: It's the environment, stupid.[11]

Despite the failure of the Human Genome Project to find 100,000 genes and the discovery that genes are not self-emergent, the public continues to believe in genetic determinism. While the gene-as-blueprint metaphor is taken for granted, no one seems to be asking the more pertinent question, "Who's the contractor?" Or, just as importantly, "Where did the first selfish gene come from?" and "Who or what programmed it to be selfish?"

OF BABOONS AND BONOBOS

As with all the myth-perceptions, conventional wisdom has absorbed not only the notion that people are ruled by DNA but, also that selfishness, violence, and aggression have been programmed into the human hard drive. These conclusions have convinced humankind that the violence eroding our civilization is unavoidable because it is genetically encoded in the genome. After all, we humans are just naked apes right?

Actually, no. Two intriguing studies cast doubt on the conventionally established notion about the nature of human nature. In 1983, Robert Sapolsky, an American primatologist, was five years into a study of baboons in the Masai Mara Reserve in Kenya when disaster struck. An outbreak of tuberculosis killed half the troop's males. The source of the outbreak was a contaminated garbage dump, and the most aggressive and dominant males, those who were able to successfully compete for the food, were the ones who died.[12]

Sapolsky decided to abandon that troop for another with a balanced male-female ratio. Ten years later, he returned to the original research site and was surprised to find that all of the original males, not only the ones who died, were gone, and that the new culture was radically different. In contests of supremacy, bigger baboons no longer bullied smaller ones but picked only on others of the same size, and, unlike before, male baboons were less likely to attack the females.

During his initial study of the group ten years earlier, Sapolsky found high levels of hormones called glucocorticoids, which are the fight-or-flight hormones released in response to competition and aggression. However, Sapolsky's assessments of subordinate males in this new version of the troop revealed that the animals expressed far fewer signs of physiologic stress and had significantly lower levels of glucocorticoids.[13]

How did this new, more peaceful culture come about? Sapolsky hypothesizes that, with the old male leaders gone, the senior members of the troop were all female. These females then acculturated the younger males, apparently selecting those that exhibited less aggression and lower stress behaviors. Sapolsky has been watching the troop intently to see if invading or migrating baboon males will upset this delicate cultural balance, but so far the new culture has remained intact.

Regardless of whatever so-called selfish genes these primates may have inherited, a change in environment initiated a change in culture that has persisted, perhaps because it has contributed to a higher level of functionality.

An even more intriguing case involves bonobos, previously known as pygmy chimpanzees, which are thought to be one of our closest primate relatives. While other species of chimps generally live in societies in which dominator males bully smaller males and beat up females, bonobos enjoy a beautiful, living example of a make-love-not-war society. When faced with a potential conflict, bonobos engage in sexual activity that releases tension and reinforces safety and friendship. Although male-female sexuality is most common, polymorphous and polyamorous sexual activity also occurs. While chimpanzee males will literally kiss and make up after fighting, bonobos kiss before and, thus, prevent fighting from happening in the first place. And interestingly, even though bonobos have much more sex than their chimp cousins, their birth rate remains stable.

Male bonding among chimps and female bonding among bonobos provide another interesting contrast. In both species, adolescent females migrate to a new troop. Bonobo newcomer females immediately find one or two older females with which to rub genitalia, a behavior that creates a lasting bond between females in the troop and which encourages them to join together to prevent male bullying. In contrast, in conventional chimpanzee troops, bonding occurs primarily among males who then gang up on females, who are generally smaller than males. In bonobo troops, males and females are of comparable size, a factor that might also influence their gender equality.

However, those who study bonobos believe that environmental factors have kept this Garden of Eden chimp culture intact. As Dutch psychologist and primatologist Frans de Waal, author of *Bonobo: The Forgotten Ape*, suggests, the bonobos have never left the protection of the forest.[14] Like other chimps, bonobos are omnivores that hunt and kill small animals. But unlike the other chimps, they are blessed with what another researcher, Gottfried Hohmann, called "bonobo power bars." In their natural habitat, bonobos find an abundant herb, *haumania liebrechtsiana*, a high-protein plant that has defied Malthus by persisting through hundreds upon hundreds of generations of hungry bonobos.[15]

Most chimps have to work hard to secure their food because vegetation in most chimp forests is high in tannins and other toxins designed to protect the plants from being eaten to death. Amidst the abundance of their power bars, bonobos waste little time securing food or having to fight over resources.

So what can humans learn from bonobos? While the idea of making love in the face of conflict is intriguing—it would certainly change our courtrooms, not to mention hockey games!—the real message is this: when resources are abundant, fighting becomes less necessary. And when fighting decreases, resources become more abundant.

This is an especially important insight in a world that spends more than one trillion dollars a year on weaponry that could be beaten into plowshares. As we will see later, when resources are diverted from protection to growth, the result is a big boost in health and prosperity—both within society and within the body.

Other questions we need ask ourselves are: If the peaceful bonobos can live in abundance and balance, and a troop of otherwise violent baboons can find they enjoy peace more than war, what can we sentient humans, who have far more resources at our disposal, accomplish? Are we going to continually assume powerlessness and deny responsibility while blaming dire personal and world conditions on selfish genes? Or are we willing to use our intelligence intelligently?

It would be sad, indeed, for creationists and evolutionists alike, if our primate cousins actually evolve past us!

IT'S NOT THE KARMA, IT'S THE DRIVER

It seems that every week a medical article or study links one disease or another to a genetic defect. The cancer gene, the Alzheimer's gene, the Parkinson's gene are notions that feed the prevailing, stubborn belief that genetic determinism determines our fate. But when we delve deeper, we find that a relatively small percentage of illness actually can be attributed to genetic anomalies. Even as cancer researchers seek a magic bullet at the genetic level, the National Cancer Institute has determined that at least 60 percent of cancers originate from environmental causes.[16]

Probing deeper yet, we find that even when a close correlation exists between an environmental factor and a disease, relatively few of those exposed to the environmental factor actually contract the disease. A study some years ago revealed that when chronically exposed to asbestos, 1 in 1,000 people contracted mesothelioma, a deadly form of cancer. While this is an alarmingly high rate compared to the general population, the unasked questions are: What about the other 99.9 percent who are exposed but don't get the disease? What, if anything, are they doing or not doing that keeps them healthy? What other factors are involved in the expression of disease?

Modern medical science seems curiously incurious about the intangible and invisible characteristics of illness and healing. Thanks to 300 years of programming and the effects of the central dogma on modern medicine, we have come to see ourselves as biochemical robotic vehicles. When something is amiss, when we are experiencing symptoms, we cruise over to our local medical mechanic who tells us to stick out our tongue and say "aaah" and then takes a peek under our hood.

As Fritjof Capra points out in his book *The Turning Point*, mechanical medical practice generally consists of the physician's version of the 3 Rs—repair, replace, or remove.[17] Indeed, the history of modern biochemical medicine is founded on that mechanical metaphor. Ever since Descartes proclaimed that the body is a machine, even to the point where he insisted that animals don't suffer during vivisection experiments and likened their cries to "the creaking of a wheel," we have been under the sway of influence that says medicine has more to do with the parts than the whole.

While ancient Chinese medicine considers the heart to be the seat of the soul and Ayurvedic tradition sees that organ as the arbiter of Heaven and Earth, modern medicine remains satisfied with the antediluvian definition by the prominent Renaissance physician William Harvey that the heart is a mechanical pump. Twentieth-century scientific philosophers, such as British biochemist Joseph Needham, who said, "Man is a machine or nothing at all," and German-born physiologist and biologist Jacques Loeb, who added, "Living organisms are chemical machines," reinforced the perception of the body as a physical mechanism.[18]

The science of epigenetics recognizes that the environment, not the DNA in the nucleus, determines the actions of the cell. Information from the environment is translated into biological responses via the action of the cell membrane, which acts as the cell's skin as well as its brain.[19] Interestingly, the cell membrane is more accurately a "crystal semiconductor with gates and channels." Those words also define a computer chip, which reminds us that both computers and cells are programmable. And—drumroll, please—for each, the programmer is always outside the mechanism!

So, who or what is the biological programmer? Who or what is the genius behind the genes? Maybe the problem isn't with the karma but with the driver.

Let's say you have a standard shift car for sale. Someone unaccustomed to driving a stick shift buys it, and you watch the car jerk up and down the street as he drives away. A week later, the fellow calls you back and says, "Hey, that car you sold me has a bad clutch!" You tell him to take it to the "doctor," at an auto repair shop. "Yep," the mechanic tells him, "you have a bad clutch. We have to do surgery, a clutch replacement." The clutch transplant operation is successful. The vehicle's new owner drives off with the car bucking and lurching as before. Lo and behold, it isn't weeks before he's back in the repair shop claiming that new clutch doesn't work!

"Hmm," says the mechanic, "your car appears to have CCD; that's short for Chronic Clutch Dysfunction." He offers the owner a prescription for a new clutch to be refilled every two months. Thus the mechanic ignores the role of the driver and attributes the dysfunction to the vehicle's defective nature!

Now, consider that this is exactly how allopathic medicine perceives human disease—as an expression of an inherent physical defect in the body, most likely due to a genetic mutation. This diagnosis ignores the role of the body's driver, the mind.

Every motor vehicle bureau in every state has files and files of accident reports. In the space where the officer has to indicate either mechanical failure or driver error as the responsible agent, which one do you think is checked 95 percent of the time? Yep, you're right. It's driver error.

To extend the metaphor, do you think it might be worthwhile to offer driver training to each human "driving their own karma?" Perhaps a true "healthy caring system" would focus more on driver education than on having to clear away the debris from tragic, yet avoidable, accidents.

So what are the implications for a planetary spontaneous remission? Simply this. We humans have a lot more responsibility—*the ability to respond*—than we allow ourselves to believe. The programmer of the field, the genius behind the genes, is none other than our own mind—our own thoughts and beliefs.

To illustrate the extent of the invisible power of the mind, consider this extreme and amazing story. In 1952, Dr. Albert Mason, a young anesthesiologist in Great Britain, was working with a surgeon, a Dr. Moore, on a 15-year-old boy whose leathery skin was covered with so many warts it looked more like an elephant's hide than human skin. Moore was trying to graft clear patches of skin from the boy's chest to other parts of his body. Because Mason and other doctors had successfully used hypnosis to rid other patients of warts, Mason asked Moore, "Why don't you try hypnotherapy?" The surgeon replied sarcastically, "Why don't you?" So Mason did.[20]

Mason's first hypnosis session focused on one arm. When the boy was in a hypnotic trance, Mason told him that the skin on that arm would heal and turn into healthy, pink skin. When the boy came back a week later, Mason was gratified to see that the arm looked healthy. But when Mason brought the boy around to Moore, the surgeon's eyes became wide with astonishment when he saw the boy's arm.

It was then that Moore told Mason the boy was suffering, not from warts, but from an incurable and lethal genetic disease called congenital ichthyosis erythroderma. By reversing the symptoms using only the power of the mind, Mason and the boy had accomplished what had until that time been considered impossible. Mason continued the hypnosis sessions with further stunning results, and the boy, who had been mercilessly teased in school because of his grotesque skin, returned to his classes with healthy skin and went on to lead a normal life.

Mason published his case study in the *British Medical Journal,* one of the world's most widely read medical journals.[21] Word of his success spread, and Mason became a magnet for patients suffering from the rare, heretofore-incurable and lethal disease. But hypnosis was, in the end, not a cure-all. Mason treated many other ichthyotic patients, but he was never able to replicate the results he had had with the boy.

Mason attributed his failure to his *own* belief about the treatment. After the first patient, Mason was fully aware that he was treating what everyone in the medical establishment knew to be a congenital, incurable disease. Mason tried to pretend that he was upbeat, but he was not able to replicate his cocky attitude as a young physician who thought he was treating a bad case of warts. As he told the Discovery Health Channel in regard to his later patients, "I was acting."[22]

When we consider the astounding power of belief—and disbelief—to affect physical conditions, we must ask: "Might beliefs held in the mind be an area of untapped healing potential?" Put another way: "Could the power of belief produce results without costly drug trials, hugely expensive hospital facilities, or even medical insurance?"

As we will see, there are those who say that this potential for impacting the invisible field is inherent in human culture and might even be in—are you ready to believe it?—our genes!

The factor that has kept us from accessing this power is the same thing that has kept us from other transformational potentials: a false belief that healing power lies outside of ourselves. Those who benefit from our powerlessness reinforce this belief. And who might they be? Well, here's a hint: pharmaceuticals are a $600-billion-a-year industry.

Now that we understand there is, indeed, a playing field that most definitely impacts the material world and now that we realize that the spontaneous remission of our planet Earth involves a shift of our own mission from survival to thrival, we also see that we have the power and the responsibility to bring these changes about.

We have met the savior and He or She is us!

CHAPTER 8

MYTH-PERCEPTION FOUR: EVOLUTION IS RANDOM

"I believe we were created to evolve.
Otherwise Jesus would have said, 'Now,
don't do a thing until I get back!'"
— **Swami Beyondananda**

THE FALL AND RISE OF JEAN-BAPTISTE DE LAMARCK

Perhaps you remember the name Jean-Baptiste de Lamarck from high school biology, forever associated with the notion that giraffes developed long necks because of their desire to reach leaves and fruit in tall trees. The notion that primitive organisms have a consciousness through which they can influence their own evolution is ridiculous and makes Lamarck seem like a fool. But making Lamarck out to be a fool and discrediting his Bible-challenging heretical claims was precisely the intent of naturalist and zoologist Baron Georges Cuvier, the Church's and France's foremost scientist. In 1829, he fabricated this slanderous and cruel postmortem assessment of Lamarck's theory specifically to erase his work.

Jean-Baptiste de Lamarck was born in France in 1744. After being schooled at a Jesuit seminary, he served in the French army for seven years. He left the army as a result of an infection, attempted to study medicine, and, subsequently, found work as a bank clerk in Paris. There, Lamarck met the eminent philosopher Jean-Jacques Rousseau, who sparked in him a lifelong interest in botany and very likely infected him with the ideals of the Age of Enlightenment.

After laboring ten years in his spare time on a three-volume book on the flora of France, Lamarck won election to the preeminent L'Academie Francaise, the nation's academy of science. Although he was almost a commoner—an upper-class citizen with no money and, consequently, of low standing—Lamarck was subsequently appointed Royal Botanist during the reign of Louis XVI. In the wake of the French Revolution, which ended in 1799 when Napoleon Bonaparte took power, Lamarck was put in charge of transforming the deposed king's formal gardens, the Jardin du Roi (The Garden of the King) into a public botanical park, renamed the Jardin des Plantes (The Garden of the Plants).

The French Revolution offered Europe a brief window during which Nature became king and France became a republic. In an environment free of Church dogma, Lamarck's ideas about evolution and Nature's impulse toward perfection gained prominence. "Nature," he wrote, "in producing in succession every species of animal, and beginning with the least perfect or simplest to end her work with the most perfect, has gradually complicated their structure."[1]

Unfortunately for Lamarck, his ideas about evolutionary progress being part of the course of Nature had dangerous social implications. If Nature could progress, then it was natural for the lower classes of humanity to progress as well. So, when the French Revolution failed and King Louis XVIII restored the monarchy, Lamarck found himself out of favor with the Church and the ruling class, which didn't care for Lamarck's upstart notion at all. This ideological and theological disagreement was one reason why academic rival Baron Cuvier purposely distorted and misquoted Lamarck's work on evolution.

Other reasons were founded on clashes of personality and ego. At an earlier time, when Napoleon Bonaparte ousted the upper class, Cuvier, an aristocrat, had been demoted to a subservient position beneath the socially low-ranked Lamarck. Yet, Lamarck used his influence to assist Cuvier in getting established in Paris, a favor that Cuvier apparently found difficult to swallow.

After Napoleon's defeat, the disgruntled Cuvier was returned to power as head of the French Academy, where he became known as a reputation maker by virtue of his frequent work as a eulogist of departed Academy members. While his many other eulogies were fair and kind, *toasting* the contributions of his fellows, Cuvier seized the opportunity of Lamarck's death to not only *roast* his colleague but to slanderously destroy both the man and his new science of evolution. Cuvier's eulogy was so unflattering and filled with animosity toward the lower classes that the Academy refused to let him present or publish it. However, an edited version of it was later unveiled in 1832, three years after Lamarck's death and six months after Cuvier's.[2] But, even under those less-than-scientific circumstances, Cuvier's assessment of Lamarck and his ideas has ever since been cited as the document that justifies portraying Lamarck as a buffoon.

Had Lamarck been alive to defend himself, he would have emphasized that evolution was based on an instructive cooperative interaction among organisms in the biosphere that enables life forms to survive by adapting to changes in a dynamic environment. This becomes obvious when we observe the perfect relationship between organisms and their surroundings: furry polar bears do not live in the sweltering tropics, and delicate orchids don't grow in the frigid arctic. Indeed, Lamarck suggested that evolution was the result of organisms acquiring and passing on environment-induced adaptations needed to sustain their survival in an ever-changing world.

Interestingly, the misperception of Lamarck's work was predicated upon Cuvier's intentional misinterpretation of the French word *besoin*, which can mean either "need" or "desire." Lamarck maintained that evolutionary variations arise in Nature through the *besoin*—the biological need or imperative—of an organism to survive. But Cuvier wrote that Lamarck had used *besoin* to mean desire, as in "animals evolve because they wish to evolve."[3]

Cuvier claimed that Lamarck believed birds have wings and feathers because they wish to fly, that aquatic birds have webbed feet because they wish to swim, and that wading birds have long legs because they wish to keep their bodies dry. This misuse of *besoin* has led to the often-reproduced cartoon of a fish at the shore with a thought balloon above its head that reads: "I wish I had legs."

In light of Cuvier's denigration, Lamarck's ideas concerning evolution were ridiculed—no card-carrying scientist could accept the notion that fish have thoughts of evolving. Cuvier not only destroyed Lamarck's reputation as the distinguished founder of the sciences of biology and evolution; his slanderous eulogy is still used by contemporary biologists to attack Lamarckian evolution theory and its followers.

Ironically, more than 175 years after Lamarck's death, science is finding that evolutionary intention may be a lot closer to the truth than Lamarck ever imagined. But, between then and now, other scientists of their day also managed to push Lamarck and his ideas further into the background.

Three decades after Cuvier's nefarious eulogy, Charles Darwin published *The Origin of Species* and introduced his version of evolution in which he claimed hereditary alterations arise from random chance. Consequently, Darwin's theory generated another hotly contested attack. The issue was not raised by a creationist this time, but by a fellow evolutionist.

In staunch defense of Darwin's theory of random evolution, German biologist August Weismann helped propel Lamarck further into obscurity with his biased effort to disprove Lamarck's theory that organisms evolve by adaptation. Weismann mated male and female mice whose tails he had removed, arguing that if Lamarck's adaptive theory were correct, the offspring would also be tailless.[4]

The first generation of mice was born with tails, so Weismann used those progeny and repeated the experiment for 21 more generations. During five years of experiments, not a single tailless mouse was born. Now, anyone who has bred Doberman pinschers knows that clipped tails or ears do not show up in the offspring, no matter how many generations get clipped, which simply means that Nature never says, "Okay, you win. From now on, no tails."

Unfortunately for Lamarck and the rest of us, too, Weismann's conclusions were scientifically unjustified for several reasons. First, Lamarck suggested that evolutionary changes could take "immense periods of time," perhaps thousands of years. Weismann's five-year experiment was clearly not long enough to either prove or disprove Lamarck's theory. Second, Lamarck never claimed that every change would take hold. Instead, he said organisms hang on to traits, such as tails, that support survival.

Although Weismann didn't think the mice in his experiment needed tails, he didn't ask the mice if *they* thought tails were relevant for their survival! Nevertheless, Weismann's experiments bolstered Darwinian theory and ultimately served to debunk Lamarck, relegating him to the historical joke pile before slipping out of public awareness.

As a result of Weismann's studies, biologists began to dismiss the environment as an influential factor in both genetic mutations and the path of evolution. However, in light of recent advances in epigenetics and adaptive mutations, Lamarck's teleological, goal-oriented view of evolution is now proving to be more valid than once perceived. Yes, research still reveals that evolution utilizes a random process to rewrite genes, as Darwin and neo-Darwinists have maintained. However, as we will see, randomness occurs within a context. Every organism on the planet is part of a complex and, some say, intentional process to maintain balance in the environment.

RANDOM MUTATION? NO DICE!

At the time they lived, neither Lamarck nor Darwin was able to validate his theory on evolution and heredity because the necessary scientific technology wasn't available then. But, as later generations of scientists discovered and as we shall soon see, evolution actually embodies both Lamarckism and Darwinism.

The experimental science of genetics was officially launched in 1910, a century after Lamarck posited his theory. It was then that Thomas Hunt Morgan discovered that a mutated white-eyed fruit fly among a population of red-eyed flies was able to reproduce true copies of white-eyed offspring as described in the previous chapter.

Through his research on mutations, Morgan established that trait-controlling genes were discrete physical elements within the chromosome. While environmental influences, such as radiation or toxins, could induce genetic mutations, Morgan concluded that environmental insults apparently did not control or influence the outcome of such events. More sophisticated research protocols later led to the belief that genetic changes were unpredictable—just as Darwin had predicted.

In 1943, studies on bacterial genetics by researchers Salvador Luria and Max Delbruck appeared to prove, once and for all, that mutations were purely random events.[5] Starting with a genetically identical population of bacteria, they grew large numbers of colonies over many generations in a nutrient-rich broth. They then inoculated an equal number of these bacteria into a large number of culture dishes. Into these identical cultures, they added a solution of bacteriophages, which are viruses that infect and eventually kill bacteria. While this process leads to almost certain death for the bacteria, virus-resistant bacteria occasionally survived and developed into colonies.

To determine whether these life-sustaining mutations appeared in a purely random fashion or if they were the result of a directed cellular response to the threatening conditions, Luria and Delbruck assessed the distribution of surviving bacterial colonies among all the culture dishes. They reasoned that if these mutations were produced by a bacterial-adaptive response to the new environmental conditions, a similar and consistent number of surviving colonies would appear in each of the dishes. In contrast, if the mutations were the result of random processes then the number of surviving colonies would vary from one dish to another.

The results revealed that the number of surviving colonies differed significantly from one petri dish to the next, suggesting that mutations occurred in a random manner completely independent of environmental stimuli. Bacteria fortunate enough to survive acquired the right mutation solely by the luck of the draw. Over the next 45 years, many similar experiments confirming Luria and Delbruck's findings led science to adopt the assumption that *all* mutations were random events with regard to fitness.

Based upon these observations, science adopted the seemingly iron-clad tenet: when mutations occur, they are purely random and unpredictable events and have nothing to do with any need the organism might have in the present or in the future. Because evolution appeared to be driven solely by mutations, science concluded that randomly driven evolution has no purpose. The idea fit well with scientific materialism's belief in a purely materialistic Universe and helped shift the focus from intentional creation to merely a "throw of genetic dice." A human being is just another among the "accidental tourists" who materialized in the biosphere through random acts of heredity.

However, in 1988, internationally prominent geneticist John Cairns challenged science's established belief in random evolution. Cairns' novel research on bacteria, facetiously titled "The origin of mutants," was published in the prestigious British journal *Nature*.[6]

He chose bacteria with a crippled gene that made a defective version of the enzyme lactase needed to digest lactose, a sugar present in milk. He then inoculated these lactase-deficient bacteria into cultures in which the only nutrient was lactose. Unable to metabolize this nutrient, the bacteria could neither grow nor reproduce, so no colonies were expected to appear in any of the experiments. Yet, surprisingly, a large number of cultures expressed growth of bacterial colonies.

Sampling the bacteria that he started with, Cairns found that mutated forms did not exist in the original inoculum. Consequently, he concluded that lactase gene mutations followed, not preceded, their exposure to the new environment. Unlike the experiments of Luria and Delbruck, which relied on viruses killing the bacteria almost instantly, Cairns' experiment starved bacteria slowly. In other words, Cairns gave the stressed bacteria sufficient time to engage and activate innate mutation-producing mechanisms in order to survive.

In Cairns' study, life-sustaining mutations appeared to arise as a direct response to a traumatic environmental crisis. Interestingly, further assays revealed that only the genes associated with lactose metabolism were affected. In addition, out of five possible different mutation mechanisms, all of the surviving bacteria expressed the exact same type of mutation. Clearly, the results do not support the assumption of totally random mutations and purposeless evolution!

Cairns referred to this newly discovered mechanism as directed mutation. But the very idea that environmental stimuli could feed back into an organism and direct a rewriting of genetic information was an abomination to the central dogma, and the response from conventional science was swift and hostile. Both *Nature* and the American journal *Science* published editorials raging against Cairns' findings. The *Science* editorial title, which appeared in large bold font, proclaimed "A Heresy in Evolutionary Biology." This was a clear indication that the white-coated priests of scientific materialism were ready to burn Cairns at the stake. Nobody messes with the dogma![7]

Over the next decade, other researchers replicated Cairns' results, which should have increased the credibility of his work. However, the scientific community still considered his notion to be shocking and unacceptable. As a result, leading genetic researchers softened directed mutation to adaptive mutation then relegated it to beneficial mutation. Furthermore, science challenged Cairns to explain the mechanism through which mutations, whether labeled directive, adaptive, or beneficial, could occur in the first place.

Conventional science held that mutations only occurred as a result of copying accidents during the reproduction process. The billions of nucleic acid bases that comprise the genetic code have to be precisely copied so that each of the two resulting daughter cells will inherit a complete genome. However, the duplication process is fraught with numerous opportunities through which errors can be introduced.

In a sense, copying the DNA is akin to monks copying the Bible by hand before the advent of the printing press. Imagine how easily, among those millions of words, one could be misspelled. Imagine how a failure to include the word *not* would transpose a meaning.

Simple errors in transcription can completely change the meaning of the entire text. We've all heard the story of the monk who looks up from the scrolls visibly shaken and cries, "Oops! It says *celebrate*, not *celibate*."

Fortunately, Nature had already considered that possibility and ingeniously built into the genes a DNA-proofreading mechanism that repairs misread DNA sequences. If, by chance, a copying error should sneak past this repair mechanism, it would result in an altered blueprint, and rightfully be recognized as a random mutation. Darwinian theory emphasizes that evolution is ultimately derived from such accidental alterations in the DNA code.

But in Cairns' experiments, the original bacteria were unable to metabolize the lactose nutrient. They, therefore, lacked the necessary building blocks and metabolic energy needed to drive their normal reproduction processes. Consequently, these bacteria were not able to save their lives through the random mutation associated with conventional DNA copying errors. As a result, Cairns' starving bacterial cells apparently mutated their genes through a completely different mechanism than the one known to science. While we'd be hard-pressed to credit bacteria with consciousness, there seems to be some form of proactive, innate intelligence at work enabling them to rapidly adapt to a changing environment—per Lamarck.

We now know that stressed, non-dividing bacteria can purposely engage a unique error-prone DNA-copying enzyme to make mutated copies of genes associated with a particular dysfunction. Through this process of generating genetic variants, the organism attempts to create a more functional gene that will allow it to overcome the environmental stressors. Think of this mutation mechanism as a sloppy photocopy machine that intentionally makes mistakes.

Using this DNA-synthesizing enzyme to produce a large number of randomly mutated gene copies enables cells to accelerate their mutation rate in order to enhance their survival. Referred to as *somatic hypermutation*—rapid or excessive alterations of the genes in cells that form the physical body—this mechanism, which purposefully generates random mutations, represents the Darwinian part of the process.

The stressed bacteria end up with a large number of duplicated genes, each expressing a different variation of the genetic code. When one of these gene variants is able to produce a protein product that can effectively resolve the organism's stress, the bacterium cuts the original ineffective gene out of its chromosome and replaces it with the newly minted version. This is the Lamarckian part of the mechanism, the step in which an instructive interaction between the environment and the cell leads to the selection of the best version of the new gene.

Cairns' work and subsequent studies introduced the reality that organisms not only *adapt to an environment,* but that they intentionally *change their genetics* to enhance the adaptation of future generations. In other words, science is coming to realize that evolution is not simply an accident of blindly rolling Darwinian dice but a coordinated Lamarckian dance between an organism and its environment, a dynamic process in which organisms can continuously adapt to stressful circumstances.

Technologists have already taken advantage of this mutation mechanism by engineering bacteria to digest oil spills or to extract certain minerals from raw ore. Meanwhile, medical science has also been confounded and outmaneuvered by this same genetic mechanism that enables microbes to learn how to become resistant to our most powerful antibiotics.

So in regard to the question, "Does evolution occur by intention, or does evolution occur by chance?" the answer is a resounding "yes!" As with so much we are now learning, polar opposites, such as intention and chance, appear to operate simultaneously. Without getting too anthropomorphic—bacteria *hate it* when we do that—it would seem that bacteria have an intention to survive.

In fact, all life forms exhibit this inherent drive, which biologists identified as the will to survive. At the cellular level, this survival mechanism can unleash a cascade of random mutations until one hits the jackpot. No matter how many times these Cairnsian experiments have been repeated, researchers have found no consistent pattern within the DNA sequences of the successful mutations. So, in that regard, the process is random.

And, yet, it's not. Consider the interesting parallel between the process of hypermutation and the human endeavor of brainstorming. Imagine a group trying to come up with a name for a new product. By the rules of brainstorming, ideas are thrown out at random and put up on a board without editing or judgment. The brainstorming process allows for many supposedly wrong answers before someone suggests a name that resonates with everyone. Even though no one knows if five, ten, or one hundred ideas will be listed before the right one shows up, this *eureka!* is the expected—or intended—eventuality. And numerous different brainstorming groups, given the same task, will likely each take a different random path to ultimately reach the best possible resolution.

So, yes, evolution is a random process, but the randomness seems to have a purposeful destination. How do we know? Because in the case of the bacteria, when the appropriate adaptive mutation is found, the process stops. It's like the witticism: why do you always find a lost item in the last place you look? Because when you find it, you stop looking.

IN PRAISE OF TYPING MONKEYS

Applying pure randomness to the origin of life only makes sense in a purely material world where the notion of causative fields is ruled irrelevant. In this regard, recall the difference in appearance between iron filings haphazardly strewn on a sheet of paper and the patterned arrangement of those influenced by an invisible magnetic field. Is it possible that a similar influential field is involved with shaping single-celled organisms into elegant and coherent forms such as a tree, a dog, or one of us? Who or what told those cells what to do in order to do *that*?

As we've already learned, physics acknowledges that the nonmaterial field is, in fact, the sole governing agency of matter, which, of course, includes cells and people. So what, or possibly who, governs the field? Perhaps, as the greatest minds in quantum physics have historically remarked, we will soon discover that the Universe, like Descartes, thinks and, therefore, is. Perhaps we will come to realize that thoughts—more than inherited traits—do, indeed, manifest our reality.

However, for people who don't consider themselves creationists, questions regarding the origin of life and the biosphere must be predicated on the dynamics of a random Universe in which we humans somehow acquired our current form purely by chance. Unfortunately, dogmatic worship of the god of meaninglessness is just as disempowering as dogmatic belief in a God who is all-controlling. In either case, we surrender our power to something completely outside ourselves.

In a Universe derived from randomness and meaninglessness, the selfish gene would surely thrive. Why? First, because the moral authority inherent in a loving, harmonic presence in the Universe would be missing. Second, because, if there is no purpose to anything, it would certainly be permissible to create yourself as number one in order to justify treating everyone and everything else as number two.

Having bought into the ultimate realization that our Universe is an impersonal machine and that we were assembled accidentally, it is no wonder humans seem so docile when the machine commands that we compete, consume, be quiet, and obey. By telling ourselves, subliminally and audibly, that life is meaningless, we allow machine consciousness to transform our desire for personal improvement into some sort of naïve idealism. Over the past two postmodern generations, apathy and cynicism have become hip. These attitudes have squelched our quest for betterment, kept us from awakening to our positive role in the co-evolution of the planet, and blinded us from discerning the very patterns that will help us thrive.

WHEN RANDOMNESS MEETS DETERMINISM

We are now coming to realize that many of our fundamental cherished beliefs are not only false, but are blatantly destructive. This is especially true for the neo-Darwinist assumption that biology and evolution are based purely upon random mutation or chance, a belief that is disheartening and inaccurate. The fact that organisms, such as Cairns' bacteria, can engage adaptive mutation mechanisms in order to survive in stressful environments implies the notion of a purposeful evolution; that is, organisms will adapt in every way possible, including rewriting their genetic code. Consequently, as Lamarck envisioned, evolutionary processes are intimately connected with an organism's ability to actively respond and adapt to dynamic changes within its environment.

Therefore, we must ask, "Can we gain insight into the future of evolution?" At a time when civilization's future is blighted by the prospects of impending extinction, historical observation of our evolutionary path might forewarn us that we are already forearmed in our drive to survive.

But whether or not we choose to bear those arms depends on our belief in either an underlying order that shapes the Universe or in randomly appearing environmental dynamics, such as the collision of stars, Category 5 hurricanes, and the flight path of airborne pathogens.

We suggest that the answer is a balance of both.

By definition, a random Universe would evolve by chance or accident and its fate would consequently be totally unpredictable. The primacy of chance in shaping our existence is the essence of neo-Darwinian evolution theory. However, not everything that looks random *is* random—it may be chaotic. Random systems and chaotic systems outwardly resemble one another, so much so that we have come to use randomness and chaos as synonyms when, in fact, they are antonyms. Random systems operate by chance, while chaotic systems, although appearing random, are actually based on an underlying organization.

The difference between randomness and chaos is readily distinguished in the following scenario: imagine looking down on the main floor of New York's Grand Central Station at the busiest time of day. Throngs of people seem to be hurrying and scurrying in a random fashion, and yet, with very few exceptions, each individual has a specific destination. Had we access to the universal intelligence to read each person's mind, we would understand the purposefulness behind each of their stops, starts, and changes in direction. While appearing random, the traffic flow is actually chaotic because every individual's movement is based on an inherent plan.

However, imagine what would happen if, in the midst of that rush-hour traffic, someone were to yell, "FIRE!" At that moment, chaos would instantly transform into random pandemonium as people fled in all directions without really knowing where they're going.

The terms *randomness* and *chaos,* along with *order,* can be used to describe organizational complexity within a system. As illustrated below, randomness and order represent polar extremes with chaos as the midpoint of organizational structure.

System Organization

Randomness	Chaos	Order
	LIFE	
Uncertainty	*Predictability*	*Determinism*

In this continuum of life, randomness and order are on the extremes, with chaos as the midpoint. On a scale of predictability, uncertainty relates to randomness, and determinism relates to order.

Random systems are rife with uncertainty and, therefore, cannot support life because they lack the organization needed to provide a regulated and integrated physiology.

At the other extreme, life cannot arise out of a rigid crystalline system because it does not offer the dynamism necessary for living organisms. As with Goldilocks and the Three Bears, life requires a system that is just right—and finds it in the fertile predictability of dynamic, controllable chaos.

The ability to predict the fate of a system is based on the nature of its organization. When we are aware of underlying patterns that shape highly ordered systems, we can accurately predict the system's past and future conditions. In random systems, however, the inherently erratic behavior makes accurate prediction difficult, if not impossible. The organization of a system and, consequently, the ability to predict its fate are predicated on the mechanics—the physics—that govern its operation.

Systems that employ Newtonian physics feature determinism and order, while quantum-mechanics-based systems introduce uncertainty into the equation.

In contrast to both of these, chaotic systems are characterized by both order and disorder. Consequently, they are shaped by Newtonian physics and quantum mechanics. As emphasized in Chapter 5, *Only Matter Matters,* the adoption of quantum mechanics into the knowledge of science did not negate Newtonian physics but, rather, subsumed it. In regard to whether Newtonian or quantum mechanics influences chaotic systems, it is not a matter of either-or, it is a matter of both-and.

Perhaps you are beginning to recognize a recurring theme regarding the new awareness offered by science. Previously mentioned polar perspectives, such as intention and chance, Darwinian and Lamarckian theory, matter and spirit, and now Newtonian physics and quantum mechanics, are being united to provide a more holistic interpretation of our world. The fate of living systems is simultaneously influenced by the traits of both determinism and uncertainty.

PSST . . . THE GAME IS FIXED: PIERRE-SIMON LAPLACE

In the physical Universe influenced by the laws of Newtonian mechanics, material parts engage with the same dynamics of colliding billiard balls. In such a Universe, a mathematician or anyone with the acumen of legendary pool master Minnesota Fats can predict, or determine, the actions of all the balls after a collision.

In recognizing that the Universe's fundamental particles behaved as "nano billiard balls," French mathematician Pierre-Simon Laplace evolved the concept of *scientific determinism.*[8] To summarize Laplace: if, at one time, we knew the positions and speeds of all the particles—billiard balls—in the Universe, then we could calculate their behavior at any other time, past or future. With enough data about previous events and the use of appropriate mathematics, we could conceivably model dynamic systems and provide accurate predictions for future outcomes. The principle of scientific determinism implies that every state of affairs, including every human event, act, and decision, is the inevitable linear consequence of antecedent events.

However, there is a fruit fly in the ointment. According to Darwinism, evolution has been built on random mutations that occur independently of the environment. This would seem to contradict Laplace's model of a predictive Universe. Darwin's theory specifically emphasizes that the environment does not influence the outcome of a mutation. Chance-based evolution would represent the Universe's wildcard—like a moth that suddenly alights on the pool table and is run over by the cue ball, altering the course of what would otherwise be a fixed game.

Previously mentioned insights regarding Cairnsian adaptive mutations, through which organisms actively evolve to fit or mesh with the environment, challenge scientific materialism's belief in random evolution. Recent research on adaptive mutations revealed that genetically identical bacteria, when inoculated into cultures containing similarly stressful environments, followed parallel courses of evolution that unfold in the same way every time, governed by the available environmental niches.[9] These noteworthy findings support Laplace's notion of predicting the future; if it were possible to get enough data about the starting conditions in that stressful environment, we could, with high accuracy, predict the course of bacterial evolution in each of those cultures.

In a limited fashion, medical science has already been directing evolution for a hundred years. Every time physicians inoculate patients with a vaccine, they are controlling the evolution of specific genes in the immune system. By compounding selected viral or bacterial antigens in the vaccine, they can induce human immune systems to create precisely structured antibody proteins that specifically bind to and mark those antigens for destruction.

It's important to note that the genes that encode the structure of the induced antibody proteins did not exist in their specialized form prior to the vaccination. Rather, they were shaped through the same adaptive process of somatic hypermutation described above. Scientists specifically direct the mutation of an antibody gene and, in the process, control the immune system's evolution. Similarly, industrial microbiologists shape evolution when they introduce bacteria into specific environments in order to generate mutant forms that can digest oil spills and other contaminating toxins.

Working from the assumption of a deterministic Universe, MIT professor Edward Lorenz, an early pioneer in chaos theory, designed his own weather toy in 1960 using a set of relatively simple Newtonian physics equations. His goal was to mathematically model weather systems in order to make weather prediction more scientifically accurate. When Lorenz programmed the computer to solve his equations to an accuracy of seven decimal places, the printouts revealed a consistently predictable model.

However, Lorenz's most significant discovery came when he was pressed for time and he rounded off his data to four decimal places in order to speed processing time. On this particular run, the computer printed out a completely different result than what he had come to expect. In changing his data by less than a thousandth of a unit, Lorenz ended up with a vastly different conclusion. He observed that what appears to be an infinitesimal difference at start up could make all the difference in the world in regard to the result.

By using the rounded values, Lorenz accidentally stumbled on the concept of *sensitivity,* one of the most important insights concerning inherent behavioral patterns in complex dynamic systems. Sensitivity emphasizes that extremely small differences in initial conditions can lead to major consequences that are perceived as random changes. Consequently, much of what we have come to attribute to random events actually turns out to be quite predictable—if there is enough sensitivity in acquiring initial data.[10]

Lorenz's concept has become popularly known as the *Butterfly Effect,* which states, "A butterfly stirring the air today in Beijing can transform storm systems next month in New York." While such phenomena may be hard to imagine, Lorenz's discovery actually tells us that dynamic systems, which include weather patterns, ocean currents, and the evolution of the biosphere, while appearing to behave randomly are actually deterministic and, therefore, predictable.[11]

GOD THROWS DICE . . . AND THEY'RE NOT LOADED: WERNER HEISENBERG

Before you bet the farm on a vision of a deterministic Universe, it is necessary to temper that surety with a little insight from the eminent quantum physicist Werner Heisenberg. The classical view, put forward by Laplace, was that the future motion of particles was completely determined, if one knew their positions and velocities at one time.[12] This view had to be modified when Heisenberg's *uncertainty principle* revealed that it was not possible to accurately know both a particle's position *and* its speed because, in measuring one parameter, the observer distorts the other.

The uncertainty principle contradicts the surety implied in Newtonian determinism. Quantum mechanics does not negate Newtonian determinism; it does, however, temper it with the quality of probability. While one may never be able to accurately predict the future, with enough information the probability of a guess being correct can be extremely high.

For millennia, humans have observed that the sun rises in the east and sets in the west. One could predict that on a Monday one year from now, the sun will again rise in the east and set in the west. The odds for that are so good that no one is likely to bet against that feat of prognostication. However, although it's an improbable reality, a comet could hit Earth before then and cause the planet to spin in the reverse direction. The significance of our story is that the future is based on probability, not on surety. Einstein, very uncomfortable with the uncertainty principle in quantum mechanics, chose to believe that "God does not play dice with the Universe."

Darwinian theory emphasizes that evolution occurs through a series of infinitely gradual transformations over eons of time wherein one species evolves into another. In contrast, paleontologists Gould and Eldredge verified that evolution actually results from long periods of stability that are periodically interrupted by catastrophic upheavals. In the wake of each catastrophe, extinctions are followed by an explosive increase in the number of new species. The rapid origin and evolution of the new species occurs at a faster pace than can be accounted for by Darwinian mechanisms. In other words, evolution occurs by sudden leaps, not gradual transitions.

Sound familiar? Remember the quantum leaps that electrons experience as they jump from one energy shell of an atom to the next energy shell? This was the key discovery by Max Planck that created the science of quantum physics a century ago. Organismal evolution also reveals itself to be a quantum process in the sense that, at a certain level of complexity, entirely new emergent forms appear that could not have been predicted by the nature of their parts.

To imagine that a sperm and egg could become a human, if you really think about it, is a stretch of the imagination. But it is so universally accepted that there seems to be nothing unusual about it. Perhaps the next stretch of our imagination will be the appearance of an emergent human culture, scarcely predictable by the way people act and interact now, that will allow humans to survive and cooperatively thrive at a new level of complexity.

Insights into the nature of forces driving emergent processes have been provided by studies on the swarming behavior of insects, the flocking behavior of birds, and the schooling behavior of fish. What is it that enables these animals to act in accord with one another to instantly change patterns of behavior?

In an intriguing study of fish behavior, British researcher Iain Couzin and his team, using a mathematical model, found that schools of fish switch their alignment and relationship based on their proximity to other fish within the school.[13] When what is known as the alignment zone is negligible—meaning where fish aren't close enough to affect one another—they barely pay attention to each other as they swim around in random patterns. As soon as the quantity of fish reaches a critical number or they are forced closer together due to some environmental factor, the pattern changes. At a certain critical proximity, the fish begin following each other in a circular doughnut-like swarm. When their proximity reaches the next critical juncture, the pattern once again changes, this time with the fish swimming in parallel and forming schools. So, what causes these nonlinear changes in behavior patterns?

In search of an answer, Couzin and his team switched their study to ant swarms and began to find clues regarding group dynamics. Prior studies of herd behavior had indicated the presence of consensus decisions. For example, when 51 percent of a herd looked in a certain direction, the entire herd would advance in that direction.

Couzin, however, uncovered a more subtle distinction in what appeared to be leaders or trendsetters, which he called "experts," who seemed to have greater acuity regarding where to find food or where danger lurked. Larger groups relied on a smaller proportion of experts to influence the group's behavior. For example, 30 ants needed four or five experts, a ratio of 16 to 20 percent, while a group of 200 could also be led by just five experts representing a mere 2.5 percent of the population.[14]

Expert ants do not appear to have different physical traits from other ants. However, they seem to be better attuned to the field, and other ants seem to know that. Therefore, were Couzin a spiritual healer, he might have named them shaman ants, priest ants, or visionary ants simply because they appear to act in concert with the needs of the whole.

Correspondingly, it seems that evolution of the human swarm is also predicated on both its density and number of experts. As the mass of the human population reaches a certain density and we are forced to live and work in greater proximity to each other, the influence of a proportionally few creative cultural experts will guide us to abruptly change pattern and direction as we evolve to a more awakened, conscious, and life-affirming version of humanity. As Lamarck might have envisioned, these experts will help us save ourselves from ourselves.

SO WHAT *DO* WE KNOW, AND WHY IS IT IMPORTANT?

So, now that we've exposed and dismantled the Four Myth-Perceptions of the Apocalypse, what do we know? We know that even though scientific materialism would have us focus our attention on the material realm, it's the intangible field that governs the particle. When we expand our view to encompass the invisible field, we realize that both science and religion have been invoking the same invisible moving forces in regard to the factors that shape life. We know that any healthy worldview must acknowledge and encompass *both* visible matter and the invisible field, otherwise we leave out half of reality.

We also know that the Universe is relational. When we choose to gain at the expense of another person, we are clearly not operating at optimum efficiency. And, while survival of the fittest has enabled some in our species to do very well, survival of the individual at the expense of the whole now threatens the survival of the whole—which, incidentally, includes the individual.

We know that, by focusing on genetics as destiny, we have disempowered our impact on the greater portion of reality we can do something about. It has led to us giving our power over to a new priesthood of white-coated intercessors. The good news is, by acknowledging and learning to use our own inherent power, we can create a more effective, efficient, and survivable world.

We know that evolution, which mystified our ancestors for many generations, is not a random process, but one that follows predictable patterns inherent in chaotic dynamic systems. By recognizing these patterns, we can employ them, along with our own intelligence, to co-create with Nature. We might even say there is an *evolutionary imperative* that drives us forward, toward greater knowledge and experience—with an emphasis on continuation of life.

But, before becoming overly confident in our ability to make predictions, we would be wise to remember that the quantum character of the Universe, the cosmic prankster, emphasizes that predictions are more accurately probabilities and that quantum jumps may provide for the emergence of new forms or traits that could not have been otherwise predicted. Like the bacteria in John Cairns' experiment, which quickly learned to survive in a stressful environment, we humans must now engage in the adaptive mutation processes by brainstorming possible changes in beliefs and behaviors until we find viable solutions that will sustain our survival in face of the environmental challenges that lie before us.

We are fortunate, indeed, that the Internet, a rapid, almost instantaneous form of grassroots worldwide communication, now exists. This means that societal mutations that work in one place can be rapidly disseminated across the planet. The power inherent in the shared awareness is unparalleled in human history. In light of the fact that knowledge is power, humanity is now endowed with enough power to nurture and heal our planet and our selves in a predictable way.

An important aspect to fully expressing our shared awareness is to first become wholly aware of where humanity is now. After all, the first step in any recovery program is to acknowledge reality as it is. That's why trail maps have a "You Are Here" indicator. And where civilization is now—well, it ain't a pretty place. This is in a large part due to the institutionalized insanity that society created by supporting the obsolete and dysfunctional beliefs we have defined as the Four Myth-Perceptions of the Apocalypse:

Only Matter Matters
Survival of the Fittest
It's in Your Genes
Evolution Is Random

Although each belief seemed logical at one time, new science reveals that none is true. These failed paradigms unconsciously hold in place the current dysfunctions that threaten our survival. Once we release ourselves from these limiting misperceptions, we will be open to a whole new world of possibilities and opportunities. Radical thinking will open doors to an emergent future we cannot even fathom.

CHAPTER 9

DYSFUNCTION AT THE JUNCTION

"The truth shall upset you free."
— Swami Beyondananda

Even though we have bid farewell to the Four Myth-Perceptions of the Apocalypse, guess what? They're still here, and they are carrying us "fool speed ahead" down the wrong track. Even though these myths have been undermined by new science, they leave behind institutions and structures that were designed to support and propagate scientific materialism's paradigmatic wisdom. Over time, these institutions acquired a life of their own, and, as with any living organism, they are driven by the biological imperative to survive and re-create themselves. In this chapter, we identify these institutional agents of our cultural dysfunction in order to avoid an otherwise inevitable train wreck at the junction.

THE AMERICAN DEVOLUTION

The story of scientific materialism is reflected in the history of the United States, a nation originally conceived in the age of philosophical enlightenment, which was characterized by a balance between spiritual and material realms. As we have seen, the Founding Fathers of the United States were deeply spiritual, influenced both by perennial wisdom of the Western world and native peoples of North America. The institutional structures they designed for justice and self-governance were eminently practical—at least practical enough to last more than two centuries.

America's enlightened founding documents were pro-life in the most profound sense. At a time when almost all humans in what was considered to be the civilized world were living as subjects under the whim of monarchs and warlords, the colonialists of this upstart start-up nation offered a truly radical concept that all human beings have the right to life, liberty, and the pursuit of happiness. In the last two centuries, people suffering under the domination of might-makes-right governments have looked to the Declaration of Independence for light, guidance, and encouragement.

And yet, over the span of those 200-plus years, many would say the United States has regressed from a beacon of freedom to just another power-hungry empire that the rest of the world perceives as armed and dangerous. Are other countries jealous of our freedoms, as our government has asserted? Or have those cherished freedoms diminished to such an extent that the country's so-called free press is no longer willing or able to reflect America's shadow?

America, at its beginning, embodied the best the world had to offer: inalienable rights and freedoms—at least for white men. However, as pursuit of happiness morphed into pursuit of material, all of the promises became compromised. So what went wrong? How did this happen?

THE CHANGING OF THE GOD

As we have seen, each new basal paradigm brings with it a wave of functionality and resonant truth. Monotheism brought a sense of order and spiritual focus at a time of idolatry and superstition. Scientific materialism was a breath of fresh air in a world that had been stifled by religious hierarchy that promoted rigid belief. However, during each "changing of the God," some things were lost as other things were gained. As industrial societies replaced agrarian communities, the threads of communal connection that offered a common moral authority unraveled.

Remember, science, as pure knowledge, has no inherent morality or immorality but is values-neutral. Consequently, when scientific materialism cut us loose from the laws of the Bible, it created a moral vacuum. And, because human nature abhors a moral vacuum, something had to fill the void. Unfortunately, in the wake of Darwinian theory, the laws of the human jungle—laws with no moral code—replaced monotheism's moral authority.

Ever so gradually and ever so relentlessly, a new god, one with awesome temporal power, assumed dominion and introduced the unholy trinity of materialism, money, and machine. Not only do we worship the material, but we've accepted it as our savior. Despite urgent messages from reality that the opposite is true, conventional wisdom persists in reinforcing the beliefs that money will make us happy, weaponry will make us safe, drugs will make us healthy, and more and more information will make us wise.

The good news is these dysfunctional expressions of reality are not a result of hard-wired human nature but originate from the inhuman nature of thought, elevated to programmed beliefs.

The first step to deprogramming dogmatic dysfunction is to recognize the relationship between paradigms that are assumed to be true and the institutions and structures created to support those perceived truths. In deference to Einstein's dictum that "the field is the sole governing agent of the particle," consider that the field largely consists of invisible beliefs while the particles are the institutional structures that embody truths and convert thoughts and beliefs into things.

The second step is to realize the magnitude of the influence of these paradigmatic structures. These institutions shape the patterns of behavior that become accepted as fundamental parts of society's culture. They influence the world through industries, governments, schools, and organizations that foster and promote their beliefs. In other words, we're talking about a major part of society's mental and physical structure.

The third step is to identify and name the manifestations of these institutional structures within modern society. It's important to realize each of the myth-perceptions that we examined and debunked earlier in Part II has given birth to its own institutional entity.

- The belief that only matter matters has fostered *Moneychangers in the Temple.*

- The belief in survival of the fittest has empowered the *Lowest Common Dominator.*

- The belief that it's in your genes has created an *Unhealthy Care System.*

- And the belief that evolution is random has led to *Weapons of Mass-Distraction* designed to distract people from exercising their inherent Nature-given powers.

As we explore each of these institutions, we see that every one of them started out, more or less, in a functional balance between spirit and matter but became less functional as its truths moved further away from the balance point. Therefore, each had value in its time but then also lost value over time, giving way to the next valued thought system or belief.

By reviewing the development of each of these institutions, we can better discern the essential evolution that is also occurring in regard to the answers for those enduring perennial questions:

1. How did we get here?
2. Why are we here?
3. Now that we're here, how do we make the best of it?

MONEYCHANGERS IN THE TEMPLE

According to the New Testament and the chronicles of the historian Josephus, during the time of Jesus, the Pharisees, who were the ruling class in Jewish society, developed an elaborate pay-to-pray system. A half shekel admission price was required to partake in the Passover service, and moneychangers were stationed outside the temple to collect this fee and sell the cattle, sheep, and doves that would make the ultimate sacrifice so humans could get right with God.

In the only instance in the Gospels where Jesus showed anger, he reportedly took out a whip, overturned the moneychangers' tables, and scattered their coins. We can only imagine what Jesus would say today when the moneychangers are no longer stationed outside the temples but have, instead, set up tollbooths in front of just about every commodity that once contributed—for free—to life, liberty, and the pursuit of happiness. How big of a whip would Christ use, for example, within the boardroom of a company that declares its intention to wholly and completely own all of the world's food seeds? And how severely would Christ chastise Americans, 83 percent of whom profess to be Christian, for not even blinking an eye over such an outrage against the common rights of all humanity?

Monsanto Clause Is Coming to Town

In Yiddish lore, the classic definition of *chutzpah* is killing your parents then begging the court for mercy for being an orphan. But perhaps chutzpah has a new poster child.

Monsanto, a company once known for producing the deadly herbicide Agent Orange and, today, one of the largest transnational chemical agribusinesses in the world, produces a genetically modified seed, Round-Up Ready Canola.[1] When pollen from these genetically modified plants accidentally blows over to neighboring farms that use organic or other conventional canola seeds, it will fertilize those plants and introduce the engineered genes, making them essentially Round-Up Ready clones. When this happens, Monsanto sues the neighboring farmer for using their engineered genes without paying for them.[2]

Monsanto, which owns over 674 biotechnology patents—essentially proprietary life forms—has a unique business model. When farmers buy their genetically modified seeds, they must sign an agreement that stipulates they will not save the seeds or replant them. In other words, farmers must agree to buy seeds from Monsanto every year. To reinforce this agreement, Monsanto has unleashed an army of spies and investigators to make sure their seed doesn't get surreptitiously planted, accidentally or otherwise. According to investigative reporters Donald L. Bartlett and James B. Steele, Monsanto has launched thousands of investigations and hundreds of lawsuits. Most farmers, intimidated by the corporation's legal fire power, pay up without defending themselves, innocent or not.[3]

Farm-saved seed has been a staple of agriculture everywhere, representing today some 80 to 90 percent of seed used. However, Monsanto has other plans. According to Jeffrey M. Smith, author of *Seeds of Deception*, Monsanto envisions a world where 100 percent of all seeds are "genetically modified and patented."[4] Part of their plan includes intimidating farmers. Another strategy is to buy up conventional seed companies. Over a two-week period in 2005, Monsanto purchased Seminis, a company that controlled 40 percent of the U.S. market for lettuce, tomato, and other vegetable seeds, and Emergent Genetics, America's third largest cotton-seed company.[5]

While consumers and farmers worldwide are seeking to head Monsanto off at the pass, the company seems to have influential friends in high places. Supreme Court Justice Clarence Thomas was an attorney for Monsanto in the 1970s. In 2001, he wrote a key ruling on genetically modified seeds that benefited Monsanto and other companies that make genetically modified seeds.[6]

We could fill chapters, if not entire books, with horror stories of how privatizing privateers have brought their mining operations—"That's mine! That's mine! That's mine!"—to every corner of the globe. While the power of money is undeniable, that power is kept in place by our own largely unconscious agreement that it deserves to rule. For the last word on Monsanto and their ilk, we turn to Native American activist Winona LaDuke, who once explained genetic engineering to a group of Ojibwa elders. Their response was, "Who gave them the right to do that?"[7]

Who, indeed? Read on.

The Great Banking Robbery

To understand how completely our society has allowed not only the power of money but also the power of the speculative economy to rule, let's take a look at how money got swept into power along with scientific materialism.

Money has been with us ever since the advent of trade. Gold and other precious metals were pressed into coinage to represent goods that had real value in the world. Instead of having to say, "I'll give you a twentieth of this goat for that chicken," money became a convenient tool for commerce.

As merchants accumulated more coins than they could conveniently tote, they began to store the coins with goldsmiths, who issued paper money as IOUs or promissory notes. U.S. currency, for example, contains the acknowledgement: "This note is legal tender for all debts, public and private."

At some point, the goldsmiths made a happy discovery. At any given time, only a small fraction of merchants would come to collect their deposits. Thus began fractional reserve banking, which is the practice of loaning paper money in values up to ten times the actual amount of gold on hand. This practice is a fundamental characteristic of banking systems today.

Loaning money for profit was forbidden under the rule of the Church. However, in the 1500s, after the Protestant Reformation and after King Henry VIII relaxed the lending laws in England, the power of money accompanied civilization on its path into the material realm.

During the next century, the lending policy of loose money, followed by tight money, created an economic crisis in England. When loans were plentiful, people borrowed freely and loosely. But at some point, bankers said, "That's enough," tightened their lending practices, and called in their loans. People who had borrowed during good times of economic expansion found themselves unable to repay during times of contraction. Bankers then relieved those unfortunate indebted souls of their collateral, that is, their homes or other property, at pennies on the dollar and resold the repossessed collateral at a great profit.

War, which is another boon to bankers, led to the British Crown becoming the world's biggest debtor by the 1600s. But the bankers had a royal solution: create the Bank of England, which, in spite of its name, is not part of the British government but a privately held company owned by the bankers themselves.

The Bank of England had a perfect Ponzi scheme, a form of fraud in which belief in the success of a nonexistent enterprise is fostered by quick returns for the first investors from money invested by later investors. The bankers asked the British government to put up the initial one million pounds. They then loaned out ten times that much—ten million pounds—to their cronies who used this money, made out of thin air, to buy shares in this new bank. The bank agreed to loan the money back to England, securing interest debt with taxes paid by the people![8]

Meanwhile, off in the New World, the economy was thriving. Because precious metals were scarce, the colonialists had been forced to print their own currency, which they called "colonial scrip." This scrip was essentially fiat money, currency backed by nothing more than a commonly accepted agreement that the money had value. Because this currency was not debt-based but accurately represented the value of goods and services without interest, everyone benefited. However, a poorly timed boast by Benjamin Franklin squelched that currency and helped hasten the American Revolution.

While visiting England, Franklin was asked how he accounted for the prosperity of the colonies. He credited the issuance of colonial scrip, then added, "We control the purchasing power of money and have no interest to pay." That's all King George III and the Bank of England had to hear.[9]

By 1764, Parliament had passed the Currency Act, which prohibited the colonies from issuing their paper currency in any form. Without the currency to conduct daily business, the Colonial economy went into a severe depression. In 1766, Franklin went to London seeking the law's repeal, but to no avail. America's loss of sovereignty over issuing its own currency was a prime cause of the Revolutionary War and a reason why the Founding Fathers were adamant about not having a National Bank.[10]

In spite of those good intentions, a battle raged during the first 120 years of America's history over who would be in charge of issuing currency: the banks or the government. As the path of humanity led deeper into materialism, the power of the banks won out.

Consider that America went on the gold standard in 1873, only 13 years after evolutionist Thomas Huxley won his debate with creationist Bishop Samuel Wilberforce and, thus, elevated scientific materialism to the role of civilization's "official" truth provider. In both science and economics, the paradigm shift was official: the Golden Rule had been overruled by the Rule of Gold.

Meanwhile, civilization's trek into the material realm had a major effect in other arenas as well. In 1886, the U.S. Supreme Court issued a decision that, supposedly, gave corporations the same rights as persons. In actuality, a corporation is an anomaly: it is a nonliving entity with a birth certificate—its articles of incorporation—that allows it to exist forever. It functions in society, yet it is not subject to the moral constraints of humans.

What's even more anomalous is that, in reality, the Supreme Court never decided any such thing. The spurious ruling was actually the creative, if not malicious, deviation of J. C. Bancroft Davis. Davis was a lawyer, a diplomat, and former railroad president who was serving in the capacity of a court reporter during the case of *Santa Clara County v. Southern Pacific Railroad Company* in 1886.[11]

One function of a court reporter is to write headnotes for Supreme Court cases. Headnotes are summaries of the key legal points used by the court in rendering a case's decision. Headnote summaries represent a court reporter's interpretation of the case but are not official opinions rendered by the court. Lawyers use headnotes as a quick study guide in reviewing case content and court judgments

Prior to the *Santa Clara County v. Southern Pacific Railroad Company* case, the Bill of Rights and the Fourteenth Amendment to the Constitution stated that corporations as well as unions, churches, unincorporated business, partnerships, and governments had *privileges* while persons had *rights*. Davis introduced a falsified statement in his headnotes by writing: "The defendant Corporations are persons within the intent of the clause in Section 1 of the Fourteenth Amendment to the Constitution of the United States, which forbids a state to deny any person within its jurisdiction the equal protection of the laws." In other words, Davis's engineered summary elevated corporations from the privileges category and gave them the same rights as humans.[12]

Relevant to the story is that the issue of corporate rights was not even part of the trial. Chief Justice Morrison Waite reported that the Supreme Court "avoided meeting the Constitution question in the decision." However, no one took notice that Davis's fabrication about corporate personhood twisted the intent of the Fourteenth Amendment. Davis's fictionalized headnotes were subsequently cited in other court cases, and, in the process, they acquired the status of legal precedent.[13]

This headnote provided a giant step toward giving life to a money machine. In fact, President Grover Cleveland warned in 1888, "As we view the achievements of aggregated capital, . . . the citizen . . . is trampled to death beneath an iron heel. Corporations . . . are fast becoming the people's masters."[14]

A quarter century later, the bankers decisively won their battle to control America's currency. In 1913, during a Christmas recess when most members of Congress were on vacation, President Woodrow Wilson signed the Federal Reserve Act, the decree that set up a private company to issue public currency as debt. Just as the Bank of England is not really the bank of the English government, the Federal Reserve Bank is no more federal than Federal Express.

Perhaps Wilson was motivated by the status of the U.S. economy, which he described in his book *The New Freedom*, published in that same year. "We have come to be one of the worst ruled, one of the most completely controlled and dominated governments in the civilized world—no longer a government by free opinion, no longer a government by conviction and the vote of the majority, but a government by the opinion and duress of a small group of dominant men."[15] Although Wilson apparently believed he was stabilizing America's economy by signing the Federal Reserve Act, putting the bankers in charge of the nation's financial well being could not prevent the Great Depression 16 years later.

Currency has been issued as debt for nearly a century, and we have the red ink to prove it. America's national debt, as of early 2008 is $9.5 trillion—more than $31,000 for every man, woman, and child in America—and is increasing by a mind-boggling $1.85 billion per day. Meanwhile, America's total debt—for households, financial entities, businesses, and the government—is now over $53 trillion.[16]

Pursuit of Happiness? Looks Like It Got Away

The Happy Planet Index is a study that measures not only happiness but the cost of obtaining that happiness in terms of ecological impact and overall quality of life. The calculation is simple.

Life Satisfaction x Life Expectancy
÷ Ecological Footprint = Happiness Index

Put another way, the Happy Planet Index measures how efficiently a country converts the finite resources of our planet into the happiness and well-being of its citizens. The United States comes in at 150th out of 178 nations, trailing such countries as Ethiopia, Nigeria, and Pakistan to name just a few.[17]

Why does the United States have such a low rank? Well, call us bigfoot. Our ecological footprint is among the biggest in the world. In order to achieve the life satisfaction and life expectancy of a person in Costa Rica, which came in at number three in the index, the average American uses *four-and-a-half times* more resources! Now, that's inefficiency!

And yet, our financial system continues to spin its yarn, selling the unrealistic hope that doing more of the same—shop 'til you drop—will yield different results.

This fast track to economic suicide is reinforced by faith in another disproved myth, the survival of the fittest. In our collective affirmation that only material can save us, we have put our faith in the most insane, expensive, and harmful military machine in the history of humanity, and, in doing so, we have empowered a sinister force—the lowest common dominator.

LOWEST COMMON DOMINATOR

With the "changing of the gods," the law of the jungle replaced the law of the Bible as our moral guidepost. This didn't happen right away, nor is it accurate to say that people had ever actually lived by the laws of the Bible. Very early on, "thou shalt not kill" was modified to "thou shalt not kill unless done in extremely large groups."

Consequently, during the course of the 20th century, some 260 million human beings died as a result of warfare.[18]

That doesn't include the suffering of those who didn't die but were maimed, left homeless, or otherwise traumatized. Consider, too, the fears and traumas associated with these conflicts, both conscious and unconscious, which have been passed on to those alive on the planet now.

The staggering human cost of war in the 20th century, the first time we experienced two hot world wars and a very expensive cold one, is partly a result of officially institutionalizing the long-standing belief that might makes right, or what we refer to as the lowest common dominator.

The power of force has been in force so long that we assume it is natural. Looking at the whole of Western history, with a few exceptions we will explore later, we see that violence and domination have been internalized, externalized, and eternalized: violence has been declared a character of human nature for now and forever.

Human Nature or Inhuman Nature?

A major flaw in the mythos of an evil human nature becomes apparent when anthropologists assess prehistoric cultures and find quite the opposite is true. In her important contribution *The Chalice and the Blade* macro-historian Riane Eisler cites remarkable discoveries by archaeologist Marija Gimbutas of prehistoric societies in which no weapons were unearthed among thousands of discovered artifacts.[19]

Furthermore, as British archaeologist James Mellaart discovered in his excavations of the Neolithic site at Catal Huyuk, in what is now Turkey, early agrarian societies appear to have been egalitarian. Mellaart found that the sizes of their houses, the contents inside, and the funerary gifts buried in graves indicate few, if any, differences in class hierarchy and social status.[20]

As Eisler emphatically points out, these societies were not matriarchies, but egalitarian cultures. The title of her book, *The Chalice and the Blade*, comes from the distinction between the chalice, which is the vessel that represents life-generating and nurturing feminine powers, and the blade, which represents masculine rule.

Modern conventional wisdom would have us believe that, in a one-on-one, chalice-versus-sword contest, the smart money would be on the sword because, apparently at some point, sword-bearing warriors would overrun self-sustaining chalice-sharing cultures. However, as we are discovering, survival and thrival of our planet may yet depend on reawakening, revitalizing, and reinstating the nurturing chalice paradigm.

Unfortunately, in the wake of civilization's trek into materialism, that chalice has become dry. The rise of the sword and the loss of the chalice have been encouraged by society's two most recent basal paradigms, monotheism and scientific materialism, each of which has clearly valued the yang over the yin, the active over the passive, and the masculine over the feminine. The cost of this imbalance is so steep that it now threatens the very existence of our species.

Let's return for a moment to America's Founding Fathers. When Ben Franklin and his peers adopted the political structure of the Iroquois Nations, they left out one key element of Native American culture that would never have been accepted by their own tribe. As far as we know, no one ever proposed that Betsy, Martha, and Dolly serve on a Council of Grandmothers. As enlightened as our founders were and even though they embodied the feminine in the Declaration of Independence by declaring their respect and understanding for "the laws of Nature and Nature's God," the idea of actually handing women the moral authority to approve war or impeach chiefs was inconceivable—clearly the consequence of a European bias, not to mention nearly 5,000 years of discounting and disempowering the feminine.

From Lamb-o to Rambo

Yet, consider the consequences of a culture devoid of feminine power. Remember the bonobo chimps we talked about in Chapter 7, *It's in Your Genes?* Unlike other chimp societies in which males bond and bully smaller males and females, bonobo females bond with each other and, in the process, eliminate communal bullying altogether. It's not that the females dominate the males, but rather that they use their collective solidarity to counterbalance male power.

In *The Real Wealth of Nations*, Riane Eisler offers an enlightening quote from Elizabeth Cady Stanton, an American social activist and leading figure in the early women's rights movement: "The world has never yet seen a truly virtuous nation, because in the degradation of women, the very fountains of life are poisoned at the source."[21] That poison can be seen and felt in present-day American society where meanness is not only tolerated, but also cultivated so that the meek really don't stand a chance. Poor Jesus. If he returned now, he wouldn't recognize himself. Over the last two centuries, the religious right has managed to transmogrify his image from Lamb-o to Rambo. From Biblical accounts, we know that Jesus actually embodied a balance of masculine and feminine traits. Jesus was forceful enough to overturn the moneychangers' tables, steadfast enough to endure crucifixion, and yet he preached love and blessed the peacemakers. In contrast, those Christians who adopt the "God, Guns, and Guts" posture spend more energy on spiritually bullying the meek than in safeguarding their inheritance.

The Power of Money Meets the Power of Power

With the moral burden of love thy neighbor out of the way, the momentum of the materialist worldview created the unholiest of unholy alliances—the alliance between the power of money and the power of power.

During the years following the American Civil War and well into the 20th century, it was not uncommon for companies to hire their own armies to keep workers in line and prevent strikes. The Pinkerton guards began as a private army hired by the railroad corporations to protect their interests, the rail lines that crossed the nation.[22] They were later utilized as strike breakers by other companies.[23] Even famous automaker Henry Ford had his own militia, called Bennett's Boys in reference to Ford executive Harry Bennett a former boxer and reputed thug, to make sure the meek, such as the laborers who attempted to unionize, didn't get too emboldened.[24]

Although the Founding Fathers frowned on the idea of a standing army, a century after George Washington warned of "entangling alliances"—his code phrase for empire—America's armed forces were already in the employ of corporations looking to manifest their destiny overseas.

General Smedley Butler, an American hero and the most decorated Marine in U.S. history at the time of his death, spoke with regret of his role in war. In a speech delivered to the American Legion in 1931 and later published in a booklet titled *War Is a Racket*, Butler said, "A racket is something . . . conducted for the benefit of the very few, at the expense of the very many." Butler declared, "War is possibly the oldest, easily the most profitable, surely the most vicious [racket]. It is the only one which is international in scope . . . where the profits are reckoned in dollars and the losses in lives."[25]

The War to End All Wars . . . Does Nothing of the Kind

Not long after General Butler gave his speech, the world engaged in the second "war to end all wars." While historians instruct us to view this conflict as a battle against the evils of Nazism, the inconvenient truth indicates that it was as much about protecting America's empire in the Pacific Ocean as anything else.

The same American empire also contributed to the Nazis' rise to power in the first place. The German war machine was fueled by American industry and financed, in part, by American bankers including Averell Harriman and Prescott Bush, the father of U.S. President George H. W. Bush and grandfather of U.S. President George W. Bush.[26]

At the end of World War II, the United States emerged as the world's predominant super power. Unlike European states and nations of the Far East, the American mainland had suffered no bombing, no invasion, and no damage to its infrastructure. But perceived peace and tranquility was short lived because on July 14, 1949, the Soviet Union tested its first atomic bomb. America's response to that event launched the Cold War and set the U.S. on a karmic course that has led us to where America is today—armed to the teeth, ten trillion dollars in debt, and feeling less safe than ever.

That atomic test, plus the fact that the U.S. had actually used two atomic bombs to kill 220,000 Japanese civilians in Hiroshima and Nagasaki during World War II, created a tension unlike any that the world had ever borne. It was one thing for soldiers to battle soldiers with clubs, spears, or bayonets, and quite another for a mindless leader or reckless general to press a button and unleash a global nuclear holocaust. Or, as Albert Einstein succinctly stated, "I know not with what weapons World War III will be fought, but World War IV will be fought with sticks and stones."

So, let's look at the decision factors facing post–World War II President Harry S. Truman. Shortly after the war, aircraft manufacturers wrote letters to colleagues in the State Department, expressing their concern about their own economic fate in a postwar economy. State Department officials then convinced Truman that pumping money into military industry would avert another Great Depression.[27] Not that the convincing involved much debate. According to Noam Chomsky, "It wasn't really a debate because it was settled before it started, but the issue was at least raised—should the government pursue military spending or social spending?"[28]

Meanwhile, when it came to drafting policy, Truman was receiving conflicting advice from two of Secretary of State Dean Acheson's key advisers. One, George Kennan, had developed a reputation as an anti-communist diplomat assigned to the Soviet Union, but he did not see that nation as a military threat to the United States. Kennan concluded that the Soviet Union, under the rule of Joseph Stalin, was struggling to rebuild after the war and had no expansionist aims, and these facts were confirmed by CIA National Intelligence Estimates.[29]

The other adviser, Paul Nitze, had been a Wall Street investment banker and believed the key to America's economic and political security lay in creating a military-industrial state. On October 11, 1949, less than three months after the Soviets exploded their bomb, Kennan presented his view that the United States should forge an agreement with the Soviet Union that neither state would ever use the weapons. On that very same day, Nitze presented his own viewpoint. He said it would be "necessary to lower rather than raise civilian standards of living in order to produce arms."[30]

In early 1950, Truman directed Paul Nitze to fashion an elaborate blueprint for a Cold War economy. The document was titled "NSC-68: United States Objectives and Programs for National Security." And the rest is history—a sad history sustaining a precedent set by a document Nitze later called "appropriate for the mind of 1950."[31]

According to the aptly named illustrated exposé "Addicted to War," written by college professor Joel Andreas, since 1948, the U.S. has spent $15 trillion on the military-industrial complex, an amount of money greater than the value of all the factories, machinery, roads, bridges, water and sewage systems, airports, railroads, power plants, office buildings, shopping centers, schools, hospitals, hotels, and houses in the country added together.[32]

And for those of you who want to zero in on what $15 trillion looks like to an accountant, well, it's a number with a lot of 0s and commas—$15,000,000,000,000. That will buy a lot of bullets!

No wonder things seem a tad out of balance.

Gobble-ization

Undoubtedly, there are forces who seek to destroy American power, but those who profit from power have conveniently obscured and hidden the rationale for their destructive actions from view. Combine the power of the moneychangers and the power of corporations, back it up with the power of the most formidable military in the history of the world, and you have the relentlessly powerful, conscience-free machine gobbling up the world's resources in an unprecedented "mine-ing" operation.

While proponents of an international economy innocuously tout free trade as a benefit of globalization, they would be speaking more accurately if they called it "gobble-ization." That's because the same tactics that worked for the Bank of England and the Federal Reserve Bank—make money easy to borrow but hard to pay back—have paid great dividends to bankers worldwide.

And the two biggest worldwide bankers today are the World Bank and the International Monetary Fund (IMF), both of which came into existence in 1944 and 1945 in an attempt by 45 Allied nations to regulate international monetary and financial order at the conclusion of World War II.

Ostensibly, the World Bank provides financial and technical assistance to what are considered to be developing countries and nations recovering from conflict, natural disasters, and humanitarian emergencies. The IMF monitors global financial systems, exchange rates, and balances of payments.

While almost all nations on the planet participate with these powerful entities, critics maintain that their primary purpose is to support United States business interests around the globe and that their policies and actions actually contribute to global poverty by keeping developing nations in a state of permanent debt.

In his book *Confessions of an Economic Hit Man*, activist John Perkins describes his own role as an international banker in extending—or rather overextending—credit to Third World countries in a scam in which banks and their favored crony companies made billions at the expense of the poor. How? By purposely lending them more than the developing countries could possibly repay, then taking over key economic resources when they inevitably defaulted. Sound familiar? Yep, that's the same loose-money, tight-money ploy used by goldsmiths of the Middle Ages. When it comes to greed, bad pennies keep coming back.

But the alliance between money and power has an even darker side. Perkins explained, "Economic hit men are sent in first with plenty of money to grease the wheels." If the officials in question turn down the so-called opportunity, the situation is then "explained to them" by the other hit men, that is, CIA-sanctioned assassins whom Perkins called "the jackals."[33]

What might George Washington, Thomas Jefferson, and Benjamin Franklin think about U.S. participation in this turn of events? Would they wonder how a populace of free men and women could possibly turn their precious rights of life, liberty, and the pursuit of happiness over to the jackals?

Well, it happened at a very vulnerable moment in U.S. history. Emerging from the horror of World War II, goaded by the fear of communism, and kept in even greater fear by bomb shelter drills and threats of nuclear war, the American people were leveraged into agreeing to a mutual-denial pact. In a precursor to the U.S. military's policy of "don't ask, don't tell" in regard to sexual orientation of its soldiers, the public promised not to ask what was being done to keep them safe, and the government promised not to tell them.

In no way do we mean to suggest that totalitarian Marxist regimes were not a genuine threat. The most conservative estimates are that 20 million Russians died for political reasons during the Stalin regime and twice that many Chinese during the reign of Chairman Mao Tse-tung in China. But hiding behind those Marxist threats and taking unfair advantage of their manufactured fears were those same profiteers who have benefited from all wars.

So what is the good news? The good news is that no person or society has ever restored disease and disorder to ease and order without first acknowledging and diagnosing the malady's existence. As spiritual writer Eckhart Tolle wrote in *A New Earth: Awakening to Your Life's Purpose*, "The greatest achievement of humanity is not its works of art, science, or technology, but the recognition of its own dysfunction, its own madness."[34]

Congratulations! You have now taken the first small, but necessary, step toward healing—recognizing that something is wrong. Next, we will visit one very sick situation in which healing has already begun to occur.

THE UNHEALTHY CARE SYSTEM

Nowhere has the power of scientific materialism had more influence than in the medical system. Consequently, it should come as no surprise that health care, itself, is now gravely ill.

No doubt you or someone close to you has benefited from modern medicine. You probably know a number of individuals who wouldn't be on the planet today, living well and enjoying their lives, were it not for the intervention of surgery, drugs, or medical technology. As our cells have taught us, technology is a good thing. And yet, as we've seen with every one of the myth-perceptions, the same beliefs that are beneficial when they bring the system into balance can later become detrimental and throw the same system out of balance. The same scientific materialism that has given modern medicine its miraculous powers has also empowered its greatest flaw. Pharmaceutical corporations, whose primary interest is material gain, have diverted the path of medicine from healing to profiteering.

The past three decades have seen the rise of what medical journalist Jacky Law called "blockbuster medicine," that is, high-impact, high-priced drugs and treatments that have literally doubled the cost of health care in America over a 25-year period. In 2004, the United States spent $1.9 trillion on health care, which was 16 percent of its gross domestic product (GDP).[35] And what are we buying with that high-priced price tag? Please don't laugh, because it's not funny, but the number one—or maybe number three—killer in America is not cancer, not heart disease, but the practice of medicine itself.

Huh?

Using conservative estimates, a rare self-reflective article in the *Journal of the American Medical Association* acknowledged that, in 2000, the third leading cause of death in the United States was iatrogenic illness, which, ironically, is an "illness derived from medical treatment."[36]

However, the Nutrition Institute of America commissioned an independent review of medical practices and found that "the estimated total number of iatrogenic deaths—that is, deaths induced inadvertently by a physician or surgeon or by medical treatment or diagnostic procedures—in the U.S. annually is 783,936." These statistics are presented in a report appropriately titled *Death by Medicine*, co-authored by three medical doctors and two doctors of philosophy.[37] In comparison to these nearly 784,000 deaths per year attributed to iatrogenic consequences, the second leading cause of death, heart disease, was responsible for just under 700,000 deaths, while the third leading cause of mortality was cancer, accounting for 550,000 deaths. These figures emphasize that medicine, itself, might rightfully be designated as public health enemy number one.

But whether medicine is the number one killer or the number three killer is really irrelevant. Health care isn't supposed to be on the list of killers at all. And what might be even more alarming is that the health-care system, in a non-caring manner, refers to these patient deaths as the cost of doing medicine.

So how did our health-care system get so sick, and what is causing this seemingly unstoppable financial hemorrhage? The first place to look for the answer is in the persistent myth-perception that only matter matters and in what can best be called Newtonian Medicine.

Newtonian Medicine

Newtonian medicine began not with Newton but with Rene Descartes. With Decartes' clear distinction between body and mind, he essentially sawed a human in two—with one of the halves being invisible. At the time of Descartes in the early 17th century, the intangible mind, soul, and spirit were, per agreement, the domain of the Church, which left medicine in charge of the material realm of the physical, the mechanical, and the measurable. For the past four centuries, medicine has sustained an overriding Newtonian belief that matter controls its own destiny.

Given this worldview, it's no wonder that science would look for the causes of disease in matter itself. At roughly the same time Darwin was postulating his theory of evolution, French microbiologist Louis Pasteur made the connection between disease and microbes. Not only did germ theory fit well with the model of discrete physical causes for disorders, it also fit with the notion of dominate or be dominated. We are repeatedly informed that an army of deadly organisms, that is, germs and parasites, is standing poised to invade the temple of the body. It's either them or us!

As is the case with any basal paradigm in its ascendancy, scientific materialism brought great breakthroughs and benefits to a germ-troubled world. This was especially true of the rise of modern matter-based medicine that oversaw the eradication of many forms of infectious diseases and the development of miracle drugs, particularly penicillin and insulin. Over the last century, in the wake of such medical advances, the average life expectancy of Americans has increased by 30 years.

While these advances have been largely attributed to the miracles of medicine, this may not in fact be the case. Public health and social medicine researcher Thomas McKeown concluded that improved nutrition, sanitation, and other life conditions were the factors primarily responsible for the decline in mortality during the 19th and early 20th centuries.[38]

Not surprisingly, matter-based Newtonian medicine reached its greatest prominence in the late 1940s and early 1950s, right around the time that Watson and Crick claimed that the key to life was encoded in the DNA—the genes, as discussed in Chapter 7, *It's in Your Genes*. Traditional health practices, such as natural childbirth and breast-feeding, came to be considered hopelessly backward as the growing American middle class became "indoctor-nated" with the belief that the "doctor knows best."

In the Newtonian perspective of medicine, the causes and cures of disease came to be seen as the consequence of material things that only a medical specialist with an impressive number of letters after his or her name could understand. Even after allopathic medicine began to show diminishing returns, both in cost and effectiveness, its influence remains powerful. Why? As we will see shortly, the pharmaceutical industry is one of the most profitable endeavors in the world.

The High Cost of Profitability

Every day, millions of competent, well-intentioned people go to work as doctors, nurses, medical technicians, clerks, orderlies, and hospital staff. Thousands more work in laboratories as researchers, seeking cures or, at least, better treatments for maladies that range from minor aches and pains to lethal diseases. Very few of these people are derelict in their duty or intend to do harm, and, yet, as we have seen, the most expensive medical system in the world isn't anywhere close to being the most effective or efficient.

Despite the highest per capita expenditure for medical care in the world, America ranks close to the bottom for industrialized nations in actual quality of health care. The numbers are staggering—up from \$114 per person in 1960 to \$2,738 in 1980 to \$5,267 in 2002.[39] And, yes, all those figures are adjusted for cost of living. If you like your trends in percentages, the part of the nation's gross domestic product devoted to medical care has nearly tripled from 5 percent in 1960 to 14.6 percent in 2002.[40] As of 2008, 47 million Americans are uninsured, which means the playing field of health care is tilted—and not in their favor.[41]

How did this happen? The primary factor contributing to our unhealthy care system, the fatal flaw that negates so many good intentions, is that health care has become a for-profit business—and a very profitable for-profit business at that. In a system in which it is tacitly accepted that money matters most and profit rules, profit ends up making the rules.

As an example, a few years ago, when discrepancies between the prices of drugs sold in the U.S. and the price of the same drugs sold in other countries were revealed, Americans became understandably upset. When they found out the reasons for the discrepancies, they became even more upset. Drug companies sell drugs more cheaply elsewhere because they charge what the market will bear, and over there the market will bear less than it will bear over here. No problem. They just tame the bear market with a little bull about how privileged we are to pay more.

Consider the perceived victory for Medicare patients whose medications are now paid for by the federal government. The Medicare Modernization Act enacted in 2003 entitles persons 65 years of age and over to receive prescription medications free. Well, that's good, isn't it? Yep, until the taxpayer gets the bill, that is, and learns that he and she and all of us have to pay the piper to the tune of $400 billion over ten years.

Now, in case you thought the tab would only be a mere $400 billion, take a closer look at the fine print. One month after Congress passed the legislation and before President George W. Bush signed the bill into law, the Bush administration boosted the ten-year cost by an additional $134 billion over the amount approved by Congress.[42] While the lower amount was reportedly acceptable to fiscally conservative Republicans, the higher $534 billion price tag, had it been properly disclosed, would have likely led to the bill's demise. That's because the bill passed with only a five-vote margin, 220 yeas to 215 nays, as dawn was breaking over the Capitol dome and only after all-night wrangling by Republican House Majority Leader Tom DeLay and Speaker Dennis Hastert.[43]

But, hold on to your spectacles. The fine print gets even finer. Just a year or so after the law's enactment, the White House budget for the Medicare Modernization Act had doubled the cost of those supposedly free drugs to what is estimated to be a whopping $1.2 trillion.[44] Now, if that sounds like the economic hit man selling one of those dam—or is it damn?—projects to a Third World nation . . . well, it probably is. While American taxpayers are swallowing another bitter financial pill, Uncle Sam is cutting a big check to Big Pharma.

Not coincidentally, the drug industry is the most profitable industry in the world. In her book, *The Truth About Drug Companies*, Marcia Angell, M.D., the first woman to serve as editor-in-chief of the *New England Journal of Medicine*, reports that, in 2001, the top drug companies listed in Fortune 500 had an average profit after taxes of 18.5 percent whereas the other Fortune 500 companies averaged only 3.3 percent. Commercial banking, with profits of 13.5 percent, was the only industry that came close to Big Pharma.[45]

Even more amazing is that, in 2002, the $35.9 billion in profits earned by the top ten drug companies in the Fortune 500 were greater than the profits of the other 490 Fortune 500 companies combined![46]

Just Say YES to Drugs

The challenge for Big Pharma and its shareholders is that it's costly to develop, test, and market new drugs. Therefore, it's far more profitable to find new uses for old drugs, increase the marketability of existing ones, or make minor chemical modifications and sell the refurbished drugs as today's new model. Consequently, pharmaceutical companies have employed tremendous creativity in finding new ways to expand and extend the uses of their current drugs with minimal expansion and extension of their budget.

Consider the example of statins, a family of medications that are used to regulate the level of cholesterol in the blood. Over the last decade or two, increasing pressure has been put on the public to have their cholesterol levels measured and to do something about them if they are elevated above the FDA's guidelines. High cholesterol levels are a potent risk factor for cardiovascular disease, which can ultimately lead to unwanted and potentially fatal events, such as heart attack and stroke.

When first introduced, statins, which include brand medications such as Lipitor, Crestor, and Zocor, were prescribed primarily to people with heart disease. Over time, advertising to the public and heavy marketing to medical professionals have led us to believe that statins are appropriate for all people. As a result, statins have become a $20 billion a year worldwide market. While a huge stash of cash has been made on these drugs, is the touted life-saving reputation of statins really deserved?

An editorial in the premier medical journal *The Lancet* presented results of eight heart-disease-prevention trials that revealed statin therapy was not effective in reducing overall risk of death. The study found that risk of cardiovascular events was only minimally reduced by statin therapy. The data revealed that 67 individuals would need to be treated for five years for just one medical event to be prevented. One of the most startling findings of this review was that there was no apparent statin benefit seen in women of any age.[47]

In addition to their ineffectiveness, statins are quite dangerous. For example, the warning that comes with a prescription for the statin drug Zocor is 19 pages long, and, of course, it is all in fine print! The information is so lengthy that most users, as well as the doctors writing prescriptions, never read it.

Why is the fact that statin drugs are shown to be largely ineffective and potentially dangerous for the majority of people who take them ignored by medical authorities? Could it be politics and money? In 2004, the National Cholesterol Education Program (NCEP), an expert panel assembled by the National Institutes of Health, recommended that previously acceptable levels of cholesterol be lowered.

A scientific assessment of the NCEP's recommendations, subsequently published in the "Annals of Internal Medicine" in 2006, revealed: "we found no high-quality clinical evidence to support current treatment goals for [LDL] cholesterol." The report further acknowledged that the recommended practice of adjusting statin dosages to achieve recommended cholesterol levels was not scientifically proven to be beneficial or safe.[48]

Astonishingly, research has demonstrated that a balanced diet is as effective as statins to reduce bad cholesterol. Cardiovascular physician Dr. Dean Ornish has shown that changing lifestyle through diet, exercise, stress reduction, and social support can lower what is known as bad cholesterol (LDL) by nearly 40 percent.[49] Living a healthy lifestyle can even cause plaques in arteries to shrink, a feat that not even statins have been proven to do.

So, again, why were the new statin guidelines adopted? After its recommendations were made and accepted, it was revealed that eight out of nine members of the NCEP's panel had financial links to companies that manufacture statin drugs. Consider the reality that each time the cholesterol level guideline is dropped, the number of new statin prescriptions provides additional billions of dollars in profit for the insatiable pharmaceutical companies. The NCEP report's publisher described the omission of these clear conflicts of interest as "an oversight."

Yeah, right!

Ignoring the elephant in the room, the American Academy of Pediatricians recently established new cholesterol guidelines for children.[50] Children eight years of age and older who have high concentrations of LDL cholesterol in their blood are candidates for a lifelong regimen of statins in an effort to prevent the occurrence of cardiovascular disease in their adult life. With no real science to support the claim that statins prevent future expression of heart disease, addicting children to a questionable drug is morally reprehensible. Oh, we almost forgot the pharmaceutical industry operates, like many corporations, free of moral restraints.

Similarly, when the pharmaceutical industry needed to increase the profit margin by selling more blood pressure medication, it simply got the medical industry to change the definition of high blood pressure. For years, hypertension was considered to be blood pressure that measured above 140/90. In 2003, however, a new condition called pre-hypertension was introduced to describe patients whose blood pressure lies between 120/80 and 140/90. Voilà! The world now has a new condition that can be treated with the same old drugs, and the pharmaceutical industry has a brand-new market with many more new customers.[51]

And when the market became saturated with drugs used for old illnesses, Big Pharma also employed the ploy of creating new illnesses. A recent Big Pharma innovation was to collectively group several common components of normal everyday life, identify them as symptoms, and officially label them as a disorder.

The current list of new maladies identifies Intermittent Explosive Disorder as getting angry from time to time, Premenstrual Syndrome (PMS) as a dysfunction associated with any of 150 symptoms affecting a woman's physiology and behavior before the start of her period, Restless Leg Syndrome as an irresistible urge to move one's leg, and Social Anxiety Disorder as being uncomfortable in new situations. Well, sure, haven't we all been there and done that?

If you're feeling traumatized by these personalized disorders, the pharmaceutical industry would have you take heart because they have just the prescription for you. While medicine ads command you to "ask your doctor," we ask that you also realize your anxiety may well be the result of those TV ad campaigns to first sell the disorder, then the drug.

This is not a hard sell, considering that the American public has been programmed to believe that all ailments, whether a passing upset or chronic issue screaming for attention, can be whisked away by swallowing a magic pill.

The Self-Health Movement

In addition to adding costs to our already-overburdened health-care system, each newly defined disorder reinforces our acquired perception of being vulnerable and powerless in the struggle for survival. Fortunately, people are beginning to awaken to the myth of their implied frailty. Whether propelled by the high risk of iatrogenic illness or the skyrocketing cost of health care, more and more individuals are reclaiming control of their medical destiny.

In the early 1980s, the breakthrough book *The Aquarian Conspiracy* by Marilyn Ferguson explored the ramifications of introducing new science into society's institutions. Ferguson considered such questions as,

"What if we fully understood the implications of an Einsteinian Universe wherein invisible energy governs matter?" and "What would it mean to have this realization played out in education, economics, politics, business and health?"[52]

Ferguson predicted an impending radical change—an evolutionary awakening—by means of a more cooperative society and a new human agenda. Her message supported the long-standing spiritual maxim that what we believe, we manifest—believing is seeing.

When the book came out in 1980, Ferguson was optimistic that institutions would embrace this change. However, most have resisted and remained stuck in their material agenda. Yet, the one area where holistic ideas have taken hold is our own personal health.

Why? Because personal health is, well, personal, and dysfunctions within the medical system hit close to home, either within our own bodies or the bodies of our loved ones. The many people discarded and failed by the medical system—the uninsured and those diagnosed as terminal— have sought alternatives and, in the process, have become proactive managers of their own health.

The result is that currently more than half the population of the U.S. visits complementary practitioners. The reasons are quite simple: in many cases, alternative healing modalities have proven to be effective, less expensive, and significantly safer than the health care provided by allopathic medicine.

This realization comes not a moment too soon. We will need all the awareness we can muster to face the final frontier where the power of money and matter have already established an "in-post" in the invisible domain of our minds.

WEAPONS OF MASS-DISTRACTION

Inner Space: The Final Frontier

Before the downfall of the Soviet Union, a group of Russian writers touring America found something truly astonishing. No, it wasn't the magnificent skyscrapers or sleek cars or varieties of laundry soap at the supermarket. The thing they found so remarkable, after reading the newspapers and watching TV, was that almost all the opinions concerning vital issues were the same. One of the Russians remarked, "In our country, to get that result we have a dictatorship. We imprison people. We tear out their fingernails. Here you have none of that. How do you do it? What's the secret?"[53]

The secret is the use of weapons of mass-distraction and mass-deception to dominate without leaving the telltale marks of a dominator. The final frontier for planetary control is not outer space but inner mind.

As we've seen, power has evolved from brute force to economic power to the combination of the two. The power meisters of the new Information Age have figured out how to reach the innermost reaches of your consciousness in order to shape your life without you even knowing they've been there.

To begin to understand how that happened, let's look at the life and history of a master manipulator of the Information Age, Edward Bernays.

How the Brainwashing Machine Got Stuck in Spin

Certainly, you're familiar with public relations. Maybe you or your company has hired a PR firm. Maybe you work for, or even own or manage, one. However, do you recognize the name Edward Bernays? Probably not. Yet, Bernays is known as the "father of public relations" and is, no doubt, one of the most influential people of recent times.

Why? Drawing on the work of his uncle, Sigmund Freud, as well as Russian psychologist Ivan Pavlov—famous for his salivating dogs—Bernays was the first person to understand and apply subconscious programming to the art and science of mass communications. Not coincidentally, Bernays' work spanned much of the 20th century, from World War I to the Cold War, and starkly reflected the credo that, in an uncaring random Universe, only matter matters.

Bernays' first job as a young man during World War I was working for the Committee on Public Information (CPI), directed by George Creel. Bernays was impressed by the war propaganda created by that committee and with the newly emerging mass media's power to persuade and influence. In addition to the official advertising slogan, "Making the world safe for democracy," World War I propagandists gave us the classic poster that depicts a menacing German soldier and the caption, "Beat Back the Hun with Liberty Bonds."[54]

Propaganda poster that helped sell the American public on World War I

An important part of every war is to dehumanize the foe to such an extent that killing them is of no greater consequence than stepping on a roach.

The CPI invented atrocities and recycled lies from previous wars. They understood, as present-day purveyors of negative political ads know, that negative ads and stories are powerful because they mobilize an inner rage about anything and everything then focus that rage on a handy human target. That's why America engaged in a Cold War against the "Red Commies," and fought hot wars against the vile "Huns," "Japs," "Slopes," "Gooks," and "Rag Heads."

After the war, Bernays turned his attentions to the problems of peace. In his book *Propaganda,* he wrote, "It was, of course, the astounding success of propaganda during the war that opened the eyes of the intelligent few in all departments of life to the possibilities of regimenting the public mind."[55] Bernays would have called himself a progressive, but nonetheless considered the masses a "herd that needed to be led" and wrote frankly about his mission to "control the masses without their knowing about it."[56]

Have you seen a woman light up a cigarette lately? You can thank the genius of Edward Bernays for that, too. In the 1920s, a woman smoking was considered to be scandalous. Recognizing an untapped market in changing times, American Tobacco Company, the makers of Lucky Strike, hired Bernays to do something about it. Bernays, always a great self-promoter, called the result one of the greatest PR events of the century.

For the 1929 Easter Parade in New York and elsewhere, Bernays hired attractive young debutantes to parade as suffragettes while smoking, thus associating the modern and then-rebellious act of smoking with being fashionable and freedom-loving. Newspapers and newsreels ate this up, and it stood as a turning point in the acceptance of women as smokers. To Bernays' credit, however, once the toxic effects of smoking were known, he led the lobbying effort—unsuccessfully—to get the Public Relations Society of America to agree not to work on behalf of tobacco companies.[57]

One thing Bernays was not apologetic for, however, was his campaign a generation later on behalf of the United Fruit Company. He was hired by that company in 1951 to help them with a problem in Guatemala. The problem? Democracy. Newly elected president Jacobo Arbenz had vowed to initiate land reform, thus returning national wealth to the citizens of Guatemala. As the largest landowner in Guatemala, United Fruit took exception to even the most moderate reforms and hired Bernays to lobby the U.S. government on their behalf.[58]

Clearly believing his own propaganda, he framed the new Guatemalan government as a "Communist menace." In reality, President Arbenz was not a Communist; he was a reformer who vowed in his inauguration speech to turn Guatemala into a "modern capitalist country."[59] Nonetheless, Bernays arranged junkets for journalists to visit Guatemala, at United Fruit's expense, where they witnessed and reported on mocked-up communist riots that Bernays staged for the benefit of his corporate sponsors.[60] Of course, Bernays' job of convincing the journalists and the American public was made easier by McCarthyism, which was sweeping the U.S. at that time.

The result of this campaign? In 1954, a CIA covert action called Operation PBSUCCESS overthrew Arbenz and installed a military dictatorship, initiating a reign of terror that would last 28 years. Land reforms were overturned, and United Fruit and other corporations got their way.

During a series of brutal coups, rebellions, and repressions, which were precipitated by Bernays' PR efforts, thousands of Guatemalans died and a million became refugees.[61]

It's easy enough to admire Bernays for his brilliant and creative mind. He was neither immoral nor unscrupulous, but rather saw propaganda as a scientific way to influence for the good. The problem is, when all that matters is matter, science can be abused on behalf of material interests. We can only wonder what Edward Bernays would have said about the Pentagon paying a public relations firm, the Rendon Group, $397,000 for a four-month contract in 2001 to help sell the bombing of Afghanistan.[62]

As a result, the new law-of-the-jungle, extra-moral code has been all but emblazoned on stone tablets: Thou shalt lie, cheat, steal, and do anything you can get away with in pursuit of your own happiness.

So What Are We Being Distracted from, Anyway?

Those in the business of manipulating us understand that, in order to accept and live by their fear-based precepts, we must first be distracted from ourselves and our inherent goodness.

In spite of all those popular "Looking Out for Number One" and "Swim with the Sharks" books, most of us are not willing to treat everyone else like number two just so we can be number one. Maltreatment of others has to be learned, and the mind manipulators know this. Therefore, our society has been silently, and sometimes not-so-silently, programmed to believe that a conscience twinge is a sign of weakness.

A friend of ours was offered a well-paying job. When she found out the company produced and circulated false propaganda, she turned the job down. Her friends chided her and called her a fool, scolding, "Somebody has to get paid to do that. It might as well be you." This open chastisement of people who make conscious decisions on behalf of their own integrity for the common good indicates that, in the fog of massively meaningless information and the static of cynicism, many have learned to tune out the inner voice that longs for a more loving and sane world. That voice has been drowned out by manipulative dialogue that is little more than two dogmas barking at each other across an imaginary divide.

Could it be that this imaginary divide is something implanted into our consciousness to distract us from connecting with each other? To have liberals and conservatives, fundamentalists and atheists, hippies and rednecks sit across from one another and speak and listen to each other respectfully would be dangerous for the powers in power. People of apparently opposing positions might all get struck by en-lightening and discover their common—and uncommon—humanity!

In addition to our goodness and our desire to connect with others, there is something else we are being distracted from, perhaps the most important thing of all. That is our own power, beginning with our power to reprogram beliefs and mindsets that no longer work. While it may be temporarily convenient to blame those who have programmed us for their own benefit, once we realize we've been misled by myth-perceptions, who is responsible then? We are. The noise, the disinformation, the divisive puppet show are all designed to make sure we pay no attention to the person behind the curtain. But guess what? We are that person behind the curtain!

We unconsciously bought into cultural paradigms during our developmental years. But now we are awakening our consciousness to the power of subconscious programming, and we have the freedom to choose other, more life-enhancing programs.

When we individually and collectively divest ourselves from the acquired belief that money rules and matter comes first, we empower our *selves* to bring the curtain down on this tired old BS—er, Belief System, that is.

As a result, a new paradigm is emerging, and it's a paradigm that requires our full awareness, attention, and active participation—within our *selves*, of each other, and of our impending collective enlightenment.

Through this chapter, we have become aware of where we are, where we are going, and where we are likely to end up if we keep on treading the same track. Hopefully, the new insights we offer in *Spontaneous Evolution* will contribute to a cultural turning point because, in good conscience, we can no longer feed the dysfunctional paradigm of dispirited matter. Nor can we go back to the purely animistic paradigm of long-ago indigenous peoples. Nor to the lives and times of the Founding Fathers and the unadulterated Declaration and Constitution they created.

There is nowhere to go but forward. And going forward requires that we are ready to go sane.

CHAPTER 10

GOING SANE

*"If you can't take the craziness anymore,
there's only one thing to do. Commit
yourself to a sane asylum."*
— Swami Beyondananda

WELCOME TO THE SANE ASYLUM

As with any recovery program, the road back to sanity begins with acknowledging the problem. We have just taken a courageous journey through the shadow land of denied dysfunctionality. We have tracked false, obsolete, and unquestioned beliefs in the primacy of matter, survival of the fittest, genetic control, and random evolution to their illogical conclusions. We've seen what doesn't work.

By stepping outside the matrix of invisible beliefs that have silently governed and limited our lives, we recognize we have created a world in the distorted image of our worst fears and unconscious habits. Now that we have seen the awful truth, the rest of *Spontaneous Evolution* focuses on the other truth, which is the awesome opportunity we have as co-creators of our world.

Let's begin the second part of our journey by exploring the idea of sanity.

First, being sane and being normal aren't necessarily the same condition. Sanity is not a trait that can be tabulated by a show of hands. As psychologist and humanistic philosopher Erich Fromm reminds us, just because millions of people share the same vices doesn't make these vices virtues.[1] Sanity is derived from the Latin word *sanus*, which means "healthy." By sharing a common root, the meaning of sanity and healthy are bound by a strong relationship. That which makes us healthier, makes us more sane. And vice versa.

The healthy characteristic of sanity is represented by the soundness of an individual's judgment or reasoning—a soundness of mind. Individuals who continuously employ impaired judgment and reasoning would be operationally defined as being insane.

In a collective culture, judgments and reasoning are predicated on the perceived truths of the basal paradigm. Consequently, if the paradigmatic beliefs of a culture were untrue or flawed, then the population that knowingly operated under those faulty beliefs would collectively express unsound judgments and reasoning. In such a case, an entire population can be technically judged to be insane.

For example, let's say you hold an old belief that you are genetically destined to contract breast or prostate cancer. In light of today's new knowledge of epigenetics and psychoneuroimmunology, the reasoning you used to reach that conclusion would be deemed unsound—or totally insane. Fortunately, your condition would only be a temporary insanity because, with an awareness of how environment, personal perceptions, and lifestyle influence genetic activity and the immune system, you would be afforded the opportunity to actively influence and manage your health.

As illustrated in this example, cultural myth-perceptions can be personally disempowering and can lead to the collective insanity that currently threatens our survival. As we've suggested, however, civilization's insanity is only a temporary state, based on conditioning. As the population becomes aware of new-edge science's revisions of the Four Myth-Perceptions of the Apocalypse, they will be offered an opportunity to use judgment and reasoning that are more harmonious and supportive of our individual and collective survival.

Quantum physics reveals that despite our unconscious Newtonian belief in separation, which would have us believe one particle is a separate entity from another particle, everything in the Universe is actually connected in ways we can hardly imagine. The things we think of as solid and tangible, like matter and time, are nothing more than a set of relationships that only seem to become reality when experienced through our perceptions.

As we will see shortly, the patterns of Nature and, indeed, the patterns of the Universe repeat themselves at different levels of complexity. This means that our health doesn't end at our skin or, for you more metaphysical folks, at the outer edge of the aura. Just as there are 50 trillion cells in our bodies, each of us is a cell in the body of humanity. As above, so below. Healthy cells, healthy organs, healthy organisms, healthy organizations, healthy biosphere. Now, those are consequences of primal sanity.

Sanity cannot exist in an isolated pocket that conveniently denies the presence of the rest of the world. True sanity must face and embrace the insanity of today's world and, in the process, offer to the temporarily insane a new awareness and a pathway to achieve harmony.

As we encourage outbreaks of sanity everywhere, we add more power to a coherent morphogenetic field that has already begun to change the shape of the world. A new operating principle for a sane world might be this: life is a cooperative journey among powerful individuals who can program themselves to create joy-filled lives.

To take the connection theme a step further, sanity is about integrating opposites rather than taking refuge in one polarity or the other. Imagine living life with only half your wits about you! No wonder our institutions seem so half-witted. Sanity means full-wittedness, and that means bringing forth the holism hidden in the dueling dualities. For example, we may need to return to real old-time religion, a path that only makes sense when we evaluate the root meaning of the word *religion*.

As British political writer David Edwards points out in his book, *Burning All Illusions* the word *religion* derives from the Latin *religare*, which means "to bind together." The joining character of *ligare* is expressed in the word *ligament*, the structure that binds muscle to bone. While traditionally this binding has been linked to obligation—and some would say bondage—Edwards chooses a more sane interpretation. To him, religare means to rejoin the individual with society, the world, and the cosmos. This fundamental meaning of religion has nothing to do with a personal god, theology, or dogma. It is, above all, a term that implies coherent connection, a connection that doesn't necessarily require a priestly intercessor.[2]

Unfortunately, this deeper meaning of religion got buried under a pile of dogma-doo. Any spiritual or philosophical ligaments that remained to connect humanity to the world and cosmos were severed when scientific materialism superseded monotheism.

Instead of extracting the loving wisdom from both earthly and theistic paths, we threw the Baby Jesus out with the bath water. We invested our faith in the material world and allowed ourselves to believe that power could be a substitute for, and as good as or better than, love.

But now that humankind has recognized that worship of matter is an unmistakable mistake, we are becoming aware that the god of money can neither provide happiness nor end suffering.

Sanity, therefore, means that we graduate from a disempowering religion or, for that matter, a disempowering anything. Sanity means that we grow past the blind obedience of childhood and the blind rebelliousness of adolescence. Sanity means that we, as children of God, put aside childish things and finally become adults of God.

ADULTS OF GOD

The disillusionment in the post-Holocaust world caused people to seriously question traditional religious thought. Jews, as well as members of all Western religious traditions, found themselves thinking, "If God can allow this, who needs God?" Existentialists went a step further and simply proclaimed, "God is dead."

While old-time religion still thrived in the American south and rural areas, mainstream culture became more secular. As the 1950s gave way to the '60s, some interesting changes began to manifest. More housewives left home to join the workforce. Television became the all-purpose babysitter and, often, the focus of home life itself. The home-cooked meal eaten at the dining room table gave way to the TV dinner. For many, synagogues and churches became little more than social gathering clubs as congregants became more consumed with the values of materialism and getting ahead in the world than they were with spiritual enlightenment from the heavens above.

In the late 1960s and early '70s, the first waves of backlash began to hit the shore. Young people who had left home as hippie-radical wannabes came back a couple years later with beads, a mantra, and an unrecognizable Sanskrit name bestowed upon them by an Indian guru.

Others returned as born-again, Bible-thumping Jesus freaks, embarrassing their more traditionally religious parents with their passion and idealism for the doctrinal teachings of Christ, their Savior. Regardless of the direction taken, whether neo-Christian or neo-pagan, these young people had rejected the older generation's materialistic values and discovered a spiritual vacuum, which they sought to fill.

This trend played out differently in mainstream America. Through interviews with thousands of ordinary working people, Rabbi Michael Lerner concluded that, in a culture where money rules and the attitude of "dominate or be dominated" pervades the workplace, the populace experiences a spiritual disheartenment that is not addressed by either secular society or liberal politics. In his book *The Left Hand of God,* Lerner maintains that, in the 1970s, people began to feel the strain of unbridled materialism, loss of community, and loss of connection.[3]

Seeking refuge, these discouraged people flocked to spiritual communities in which savvy ministers offered an infusion of two things that had been lacking in the secular realm: genuine community and a tangible spiritual experience.

On the political front, liberals struggled to understand the phenomenon of Reagan Democrats, disheartened individuals who voted for values over their own economic interests. Meanwhile, conservative groups, such as the Moral Majority and the Christian Coalition of America, grew to fill the spiritual vacuum that they attributed to culture's secular humanism rather than to the real cause, materialism itself.

As Lerner points out, liberals simply didn't understand either the importance or the extent of the heartsickness that swept the heartland. As a result, liberal remedies focused on socioeconomic issues, while the deepest unmet needs of their constituents were primarily psycho-spiritual in nature.

At the same time, the rise of Christian conservatism further intensified the separation of religion from secular domains. While the conservative movement provided a welcome contrast to the values of the marketplace, it also fatalistically affirmed that was how the world is and how it is meant to be.

The bad news of the world was the good news for places of worship where people could get enough spiritual nourishment to fortify them for another week in the meat grinder. However, this spiritual "fix" had a downside. Just as conventional Newtonian medicine addresses the patient's symptoms without touching their problem, millions of worshippers found refuge from the bad, bad world—without having to do anything about it.

Meanwhile, the 1980s and '90s saw the birth of New Age and new thought spirituality, movements that focused on personal growth and largely avoided the worldly issues of social justice and economic balance. The personal-growth movement was just that—personal. In a society based on the primacy of the individual, the focus was on creating one's own personal reality. Politics? Why go there? However, more and more of those who sought to transcend the travails of life by prematurely ascending began to realize that *there* has come *here.* There doesn't seem to be a way to avoid the reality that we have collectively created!

Now, as we take on the prospect of going sane, we must accept our role as responsible co-creators of our world. Instead of using religious teachings to disempower ourselves, we must stop playing powerless and stupid. As philosopher and student of comparative religions Alan Watts said, "The common error of ordinary religious practice is to mistake the symbol for the reality, to look at the finger pointing the way and then to suck it for comfort rather than follow it."[4]

And that finger is pointing us toward the next level of human evolution. Can we teach those old dogmas new tricks? Here are four sane alternatives to consider:

Alternative 1. Move from Original Sin to Original Synergy: As we will discuss in more detail in Part III, *Changing the Guard and Re-Growing the Garden,* universal love is unconditional. Like the sun, it shines equally on everyone and everything. And yet, many in the Western world worship a conditional God who bestows or withdraws love and approval based on whether we follow certain man-made religious dictates. At the extreme, some religious sects practice self-flagellation by which people literally try to beat the hell out of themselves. We refer to these practices as "unsafe sects."

Persistent in the mainstream Christian thought field is the notion of original sin, which is the precept that all people are born sinners and that sinning is bad.

Interestingly, the word *sin* was originally an archery term that meant missing the mark and later evolved to mean falling short, or failure to live up to one's potential. In this sense, we humans are, indeed, sinners because we miss the mark and fall short of our potential much of the time, particularly while we are learning the lessons of life. You could probably say that those rapidly mutating bacteria struggling to digest the soup they're in are sinners, too. They kept missing the genetic mark until they finally found the mutational solution to their problem.

In the linear worldview, Heaven is a destination, far removed from life on this planet. In the quantum worldview, where time doesn't really exist and the only time we have is now, a heaven far removed in the future makes no sense. Likewise, all we can do in the now is be, which, in itself, *is* Heaven. In other words, Heaven is a practice, not a place. Perhaps the new spiritual bumper sticker should read, "Not Perfect, Just Practicing Being."

Therefore, in order to go sane, we must shift the focus of religion away from pleasing a conditional cosmic overlord to practicing Heaven on Earth.

Alternative 2. Move from a Punishment Model to a Learning Model: If sin means missing the mark, this suggests that, with practice, humans should be able to hit the mark more often. This concept calls into question the sanity of our society's focus on punishment.

Punishment is unnatural and is not found anywhere in Nature. Imagine the stomach recovering from an upsetting virus and the esophagus saying, "Virus, shmirus! You're lazy. And, for sending your regurgitation back up again, no more food for you!"

While punishment for mistakes doesn't occur naturally, consequences of mistakes do. For the 95 percent of us who aren't incorrigible psychopaths, it's more practical to focus on learning than punishment. We need to stop punishing ourselves or unconsciously asking for punishment.

The law of karma and the acceptance of consequences is an evolutionary step beyond punishment and self-punishment. Put another way, what if the bacteria, faced with the choice of mutate or die, stopped to flagellate themselves each time they tried a mutation that didn't work? Would that help them achieve their goal more quickly? No, we don't think so.

Reframing sin as learning creates compassion for ourselves and for others. It allows us to focus on the consequences of our lessons, take responsibility, and then take better aim.

Evolution of human culture, as well as individual humans, is a lot like the trial-and-error process employed by bacteria. Each step, whether we judge it as a brilliant breakthrough or a devastating error, is a mutation along the evolutionary pathway. Consider that Thomas Edison was only successful in inventing the light bulb through the process of trial and error. We move from victims to conscious participants when we learn from our errors and then apply our wisdom to act accordingly.

Alternative 3. Move from Victim to Free and Willing Participant: Princeton physicist John Wheeler, a colleague of Albert Einstein, when wrestling with the concept of humankind's role in the world came to this conclusion: "We had this old idea there was a universe out there, and here is man the observer safely protected from the universe by a six-inch slab of plate glass. Now we learn from the quantum world that even to observe so miniscule an object as an electron we have to shatter that plate glass . . . so the old word *observer* simply has to be crossed off the books, and we must put in the new word *participator*."[5]

Through these words, Wheeler is telling us that the implications of quantum physics emphasize that we create reality through our perceptions.

Extending Wheeler's notion to its logical conclusion reveals that *no particular future* is a certainty. There are some future scenarios that are probabilities and many more that are mere possibilities. The entangled field we all create with our collective thoughts influences all potential outcomes. What theologians identified as free will really represents our power as co-creating participants.

Ours is not a top-down Universe where reality is predetermined and dictated from on high, but a bottom-up Universe where collective thoughts assemble until they have the coherence to create one reality—or another. As a pertinent example, the dire condition known as Armageddon is neither an eventuality nor inevitability; it's a choice. If enough people on the planet believe Armageddon will happen, then, either directly or indirectly, they will likely find a way to make it happen. However, the same is true for the alternative reality of "Disarmageddon," if enough people choose that future.

So does God or some Divine Presence have any influence in this world? Theologian David Ray Griffin suggested that there is, indeed, a divine influence—and it emanates from our own hearts. Through our own free willingness to express love—through the simple practice of the Golden Rule—a loving God is made manifest on Earth. We don't even have to know what this loving God looks like or if He or She or It exists somewhere out there.

The hellish manifestation of the Holocaust, as well as the countless examples of collective compassion it inspired, are all expressions related to human choices. What we call the Messiah—"the promised and expected deliverer"—may be a do-it-yourself project, not a done deal from above. It comes down to what we collectively choose. As theologian Griffin said, "God is persuasive, not coercive."[6]

Alternative 4. Move from Separation to Connection: The Buddhists describe loving participation in the world as compassion, a word that is often misunderstood by the Western mind. We tend to think of compassion as a nice sentiment, like taking the time to feel bad about people who are starving somewhere. But in the Buddhist tradition, compassion is far more sophisticated in that it shows a deep understanding of both quantum physics and cellular biology.

In her book *A Call to Compassion*, Aura Glaser refers to compassion as the "practice of enlightenment." In other words, enlightenment is something we cultivate in daily life based on a sane understanding of the world and our relationship to it. The Bodhisattva, one dedicated to awakening heart and mind, Glaser said, cultivates the "two-pronged mind," the understanding that love of self and love of others are one and the same. "Compassion," she wrote, "is an expression of human freedom, flowing from a sound intuition of the unity of life and all living things."[7]

As we will see, this understanding of the relatedness of all things, as well as acting from that relatedness, offers the key to spontaneous evolution. Writer and lecturer Gregg Braden, author of *The Divine Matrix*, traveled to Tibet in search of a way to connect quantum physics and ancient wisdom. Through a translator, he asked the head of a Buddhist monastery, "What connects us with one another, our world, and our universe? What is the 'stuff' that travels beyond our bodies and holds the world together?"[8]

The *geshe*, or teacher, answered in only six words: "Compassion is what connects all things." The next day, another monk further clarified this statement. "Compassion," he said, "is both a force in the universe as well as a human experience."[9] In other words, compassion is both the field and the intention we put into that field.

To Buddhists, the freely willing choice of any individual to act in a particular way directly impacts humanity as a whole. The reverberation of our actions through time and space is called *karma*. The perception of selflessness sometimes associated with Buddhist compassion is actually a divine selfishness where two selves are served simultaneously. There is the small self of the individual and the greater Self of collective existence. This ancient belief fully conforms to our evolving awareness that each individual human is a sentient cell in the body of humanity and must simultaneously act in the self-interest of the individual and of the whole system. No wonder Glaser refers to Bodhisattvas as "citizens of the universe."[10]

Science has brought the world untold gifts. The fact that Gregg Braden and other citizens of Western civilization have been able to board an airplane and visit an ancient culture half a world away is only one example of the benefits of technology. While many shun technology, we see it is an inherent and fundamental element of evolution. Consider the fact that cells, in creating the human body, developed many technologies that are far more sophisticated than those yet derived from modern science.

The true wisdom dawning today is the realization that science devoid of spirit is limited. We must honor and acknowledge humanity's technological prowess. However, more importantly, we must also embrace our individual and collective power of compassion in order to use technology more wisely and with appropriate humility. This insight is illuminated in the classic scenario in which a scientist climbs the Mountain of Knowledge, finally reaches the top and sees Buddha quietly sitting at the peak.

"What are you doing here?" asks the scientist.

"What took you so long?" replies the Buddha, smiling.

EMBRACE OUR POWER WITH ALL DUE HUMILITY

The key to maintaining sanity in an insane world is to understand and maintain our relationship with reality. The reality we are talking about is not the diversionary reality of reality TV but the real reality that connects everyone with everything. As humans, we are not *all-powerful*, but we are *all powerful*. Understanding both the vastness and the limitations of that power and then acting accordingly, is the key to having our individual sanity contribute to the manifestation of a saner world.

We are neither subjects of a vengeful God nor victims of a random Universe. Just as every cell in our body holds all our genetic information, each of us holds a key to collective humanity. The program for a loving future is here; it only needs to be engaged through our awareness and our conscious actions. Those so-called sins we lamented about are nothing but mistakes—mutations if you will. Like bacteria facing the life-or-death issue of mutate or die, we humans can no longer sustain ourselves with the current form of insanity.

We have the power to choose new responses. While some of those responses could be viewed as mistakes or dead ends, eventually they will all collectively lead us in the direction of our emergent selves.

As adults of God, we now understand that healing the world comes from the inside out. Everything we do individually to become more coherent and compassionate will reverberate in the field like ripples on a pond. Like begets like. As you sow, so shall you reap.

Coherent and compassionate people have no need to dominate others, rather, they seek to empower cooperation rather than competition in everyone. Why? Because a coherent, harmonious world would be in everyone's best self-interest. Perhaps this is what Jesus meant by "the meek shall inherit the earth."

For those already involved with personal and spiritual growth, holistic health, and new thought, it is now time to apply that knowledge and wisdom to the world at large. It's time to move past the limitations of seeking our personal good fortune in isolation. It makes no sense to have a congruent life but not a congruent world. In fact, it's time for the self-empowerment movement to take an emergent leap front and center to test spiritual principles in collective reality.

Some 80 years ago, a 32-year-old would-be businessman stood ready to end his life. He had gone bankrupt, had failed at every venture, and had come to believe that his wife and family—and the world—would be better off without him. As he contemplated throwing himself into Lake Michigan, a wild thought crossed his mind. It seemed like a waste to throw away his life. Because he was about to discard it anyway, why not donate his life to science? Why not give his life to the world and live it as a scientific experiment?

That young man was Buckminster Fuller, and he lived another 55 years after that epiphany. He became a noted inventor and philosopher who gave the world the geodesic dome and the concept of Spaceship Earth. Perhaps in his life there is a cue for the rest of us. Maybe we are given our lives not just to live them, but to donate them to the world in a grand experiment to see if, together, we can achieve thrival. Like the bacteria's race against time, the human race is racing, too. The question is, "Will we achieve critical mass before we reach critical massacre?"

If the physicists are right, the only thing we can be certain of is uncertainty. Reality doesn't happen until we decide to make it happen through our collective beliefs. But we can be certain of our own loving intention. Our grand experiment involves applying that loving intention in our lives and our world. Put another way, the best way to accept the uncertainty in the world is with certainty in our hearts. We cannot be certain about the results, but we can be certain about our intentions, which, in turn, will affect the results. As Descartes *didn't* say, "I love, therefore I am."

As ancient spiritual traditions, from the Vedas to the cabala, reveal, the everyday world we think we see is an illusion. And as quantum physicists are coming to realize, there is, indeed, a field that projects what we call reality onto matter. The separation between us and them or between us and Nature that we so vividly experience in our reality is an illusion held in place by our beliefs.

Going sane means withdrawing our participation from this collectively created illusion. Going sane means that we stop enabling insanity with rationalizations, denials, wishful thinking, and misplaced hopes in someone or something outside ourselves.

Going sane is a choice. The good news is: there is a way to get there. All we need to provide is the will.

Based on the organization of a healthy, thriving human body, this model offers us a way to change the guard and re-grow the Garden. That is, we see that much of what we have been guarding ourselves from is based on programmed misperceptions and ancient memories.

Hopefully, that sane world will become so vivid by the end of *Spontaneous Evolution* that the bridge from here to there, or actually, from there to here, will become plainly manifest.

CHANGING THE GUARD AND RE-GROWING THE GARDEN

"Why don't we go for Heaven on Earth, just for the hell of it?"
— Swami Beyondananda

There's good news, and there's bad news. The bad news: civilization, as we know it, is about to end. Now, the good news: civilization, as we know it, is about to end.

True, the seemingly insurmountable crises that currently challenge our existence can be taken as an obvious portent of civilization's imminent demise. However, below the turmoil evident on the surface, there is an even deeper, more profound reason as to why our civilization is ending. The core beliefs upon which we have built our world are leading us to our own extinction—that's the bad news.

The good news is that new-edge science has drastically revised our current paradigm's core beliefs. By definition, revisions of paradigmatic beliefs inevitably provoke a profound transformation of civilization as its population assimilates the newer, more life-sustaining awareness.

More good news is that ours is not the first Western civilization to rise and then fall out of favor. Three earlier versions of civilization—animism, polytheism, and monotheism—preceded and contributed to today's culture of scientific materialism. So, there is precedent for the furthering of our evolution.

As with any living organism, the birth of a civilization is initially characterized by a developmental period during which novel cultural ideas are introduced to the mainstream public. As a society matures, effective life-enhancing beliefs become canonized and perceived as cultural law, and these concretized beliefs lead to rigidity in a society's behavioral patterns.

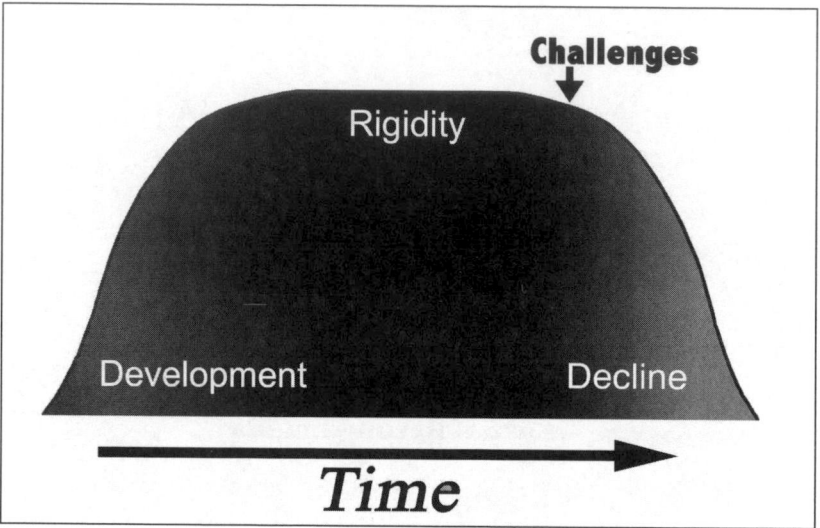

The lifespan of a civilization begins with new development, peaks with rigidity, and ends with decline.

Over time, a society's fixed beliefs inevitably precipitate irresolvable environmental challenges. At this stage of its life cycle, the cultural mainstream's inherent rigidity expresses itself as an active resistance to change, even when confronted with life-threatening crises. Inflexibility in a time of upheaval precipitates a rapid decline of the aging society.

Today's world situation reveals that we are deep in the throes of global life-threatening challenges that are directly linked to civilization's misperceived societal truths. We are entering a transition period between a civilization that is dying and one that is struggling to be born. From the ashes of the old civilization arises a new one—we are living the story of the Phoenix.

Every day, increasing numbers of people are awakening to the reality that civilization, as we know it, is going to end. This conclusion isn't exactly a surprise; a world in chaos with overwhelming crises can be taken as a reliable warning of imminent upheaval. Now that we have been fore-warned, are we *forearmed* to deal with the exigencies of such a massive social upheaval? Perhaps a more important question might be, "In the inevitable transformation of our world, will we be able to avert the trauma of revolution and, instead, opt for global healing through evolution?"

THE FORK IN THE ROAD

We are now speeding toward our third transit of the balance point between the spiritual realm and the material realm. What lies before us when we arrive will be defined by our choice between two alternative paths. We may choose to stay in the same familiar world of dueling dualities, wherein religious fundamentalists and reductionistic scientists continue to polarize the public. This path will obviously continue to take us toward the same destination we are heading to now—imminent extinction.

Or, as we return again to the balance point, we may choose to resolve our differences by seeking harmony over polarity. By combining formerly factious elements into a unified functional whole, we can open the door, transcend historic dualities, and experience an evolution that will provide for a higher-functioning, more sustainable version of humanity.

The potential behind such a seemingly miraculous resolution is not based on some pie-in-the-sky, Pollyanna thinking. The positive vision supporting this probable future is inherent in the wisdom offered by civilization's basal paradigm. However, we are not speaking of the wisdom of the current civilization's paradigm, a belief system with flawed myth-perceptions that directly contribute to today's global chaos. Rather, we are speaking of a new basal paradigm, one based on an integration of new science and ancient spiritual wisdom. While no official name has yet been designated to describe the next version of civilization, we will identify the new basal paradigm as *holism*.

As with civilization's previous paradigms—animism, polytheism, monotheism, and scientific materialism—holism must provide accept-able answers to the three perennial questions prior to becoming civiliza-tion's official basal paradigm:

1. How did we get here?
2. Why are we here?
3. Now that we're here, how do we make the best of it?

HOW DID WE GET HERE? THE HOLISTIC VIEW

Cosmologists agree that before the appearance of matter the Universe was comprised of an entangled matrix of invisible energy referred to as the field. After the Big Bang, estimated to have occurred 15 billion years ago, physical matter precipitated out of that energy field and has been entangled with it ever since.

The principles of quantum mechanics emphasize the primacy of energy fields in their influence over matter. Consequently, the Universe's matter is organized by information, represented as energy patterns contained within the field. The principles of quantum mechanics lend support to Socrates' notion that invisible forms, or souls, are responsible for shaping the physical realm.

Because the field's information existed prior to the material world, we can easily entertain the notion of *creationism* in which an organism's form existed in the field as a defined energy pattern before the physical organism appeared on the planet.

Over a period lasting billions of years, Earth's physical matter gradually assembled into complex physical forms that complement the field's invisible information patterns. In linear time, the first living organisms to appear on the planet were simple bacteria. Through the use of adaptive mutation mechanisms and epigenetic modifications, primitive cells were able to select and alter their genetic code in order to better accommodate their environmental niches. Heredity-modifying processes provided living organisms with a mechanism to continuously adapt to new and ever-changing environments.

The time-dependent process of assembling physical matter into cells followed by the assembly of cells into complex organisms, such as humans, represents the linear process of evolution. Therefore, it appears that the origins of the biosphere's organisms are derived from both creation and evolution processes.

In a paradigm of holism, former polar opposites are revealed to be entangled parts within one whole system. This especially applies to the dueling polarities of creation and evolution, processes that are inseparably entangled in the dance of life. Holism recognizes that both the creationist notion of a pre-existing pattern and the evolutionist theory of how this pattern is manifested over time are pieces of the cosmic puzzle that, when put together, approximate reality.

As we will learn in Chapter 11, *Fractal Evolution*, Nature has utilized a geometric formula to shape the dynamic assembly of communities of living systems. In contrast to Darwinian theory, which suggests evolution is random, the new science implies that evolution represents a purposeful process in which individual organisms survive by adaptation and thrive by becoming members of a larger community. Each participant is an interdependent member of the community, making a contribution to the whole and, in return, reaping the benefits.

WHY ARE WE HERE? THE HOLISTIC VIEW

As mentioned earlier, James Lovelock proposed the Gaia hypothesis in 1972. He theorized that the physical Earth and the living biosphere form a complex interacting system that can be considered as a single organism. The hypothesis states that the biosphere has a regulatory influence on Earth's environment, balancing and buffering the physical characteristics of the planet in order to sustain life.

Organisms introduced to an environment modify and disturb the original conditions of their ecological niche by engaging in life-sustaining biological activities such as eating, breathing, and eliminating waste. In an effort to restore environmental balance, Nature employs adaptive mutations and epigenetic mechanisms to shape the evolution of subsequent new species whose life activities contribute to the restoration of harmonious balance in the ecosystem.

The Gaia hypothesis emphasizes Nature's tendency to move toward balance and harmony. A fundamental example of Gaian harmony—one so obvious that we often fail to see it—is the entangled relationship between plants and animals. Plants require carbon dioxide for photosynthesis and excrete oxygen as a waste product, whereas animals breathe in oxygen for respiration and excrete carbon dioxide as a waste product. One couldn't survive without the other.

Humans, like every other organism in the biosphere, are here to support environmental balance, to buffer it, to sustain it, and to encourage harmony. Among Earth's organisms, human beings are unique in that we are consciously aware of our evolutionary process and potential. We are here to use our evolved awareness to support environmental harmony.

We can view the environment in terms of a delicately balanced seesaw. When a new organism is added at one end, the seesaw becomes unbalanced. To re-create balance, Nature will either eliminate the original organism or evolve a counterbalancing new organism at the other end of the seesaw.

The impact a species has on the environment's balance is directly related to how close it is to the seesaw's fulcrum. A species straddling the fulcrum can readily alter the balance by simply shifting its weight toward one side or the other. Humanity has evolved to the point of, essentially, standing on the fulcrum of evolution's seesaw, and we must recognize that we exert a truly powerful influence over the balance of Nature.

Ignorance of our responsibility to the planet's welfare has contributed to a number of life-threatening ecological crises. In light of new insights concerning humanity's role in planetary evolution, we must become consciously aware of our impact on the environment. We must redirect our awareness toward reduction of our environmental footprint so that we shift our influence toward greater sustainability.

As Lovelock suggests, the biosphere represents a giant living and quite aware organism comprised of all the world's cells, plants, and animals. Every cell is an aware sentient entity. Through the evolution of cellular communities, cells were able to greatly amplify the power of their awareness, and, in the end, create the advanced intelligence of the human mind. The history of evolution maps the developmental advancement of awareness through the expansion of community. Perhaps that evolutionary directive—accumulating awareness through expanding community—offers a clear direction for our currently evolving civilization.

NOW THAT WE'RE HERE, HOW DO WE MAKE THE BEST OF IT? THE HOLISTIC VIEW

We make the best of life by making the best life we can—for ourselves, for others, and for our planet. For insight on how to accomplish that, we need only look within our own bodies: a model community of 50 trillion individual cells that have learned to live and work in harmony. We humans can direct our conscious awareness to learn how to do what our cells already do—create a civilization endowed with health, harmony, and bliss.

Our destiny as human beings at the fulcrum of Earth's seesaw is to use our awareness to create sustainable technologies that enhance our survival and lessen our environmental impact. In Chapter 12, *Time to See a Good Shrink*, we will take a journey beneath our skin and observe exactly how societies of cells have created successful, life-enhancing communities. Human hubris would have us believe that we are Earth's most highly intelligent creatures and that all other organisms are less intelligent. In fact, many scientists might argue that primitive organisms, such as cells, display no intelligence at all.

This might be a good place to recognize this important fact: cellular technology created us! In designing the human body, cellular communities developed amazing technologies that were needed to manipulate, regulate, and precisely control their environment. Interestingly, most of the advanced technologies created by cells are still beyond the grasp of human science and awareness. Therefore, we argue, in contrast, that we have a lot to learn from cells.

Technology is an integral element in the evolutionary process. Considering that we are following an evolutionary path similar to the one taken by our cells, we are also destined to use technology to ensure our survival. This is counter to the arguments of Luddites who would have us forsake all of our technological know-how and return to the Garden as hairless pets.

Actually, our evolutionary destiny is to re-inhabit the Garden, only this time in full awareness of our journey. In the same manner that cellular technology provided for the success of cellular communities in a human body, we must recognize that human technology will provide for the success of human communities on our planet.

The chart below compares the beliefs of the current basal paradigm of scientific materialism with that of the evolving paradigm of holism. As is evident, the answers to the perennial questions are profoundly different, and the consequence is that civilization, as we know it, is about to divert from its present course of apparent self-extinction.

Perennial Question	Scientific Materialism	Holism
How did we get here?	Random acts of heredity	Via a combination of creation and adaptive evolution
Why are we here?	No other reason than to go forth and multiply	To tend the Garden and acquire awareness for humanity's evolution
Now that we're here, how do we make the best of it?	Live by the law of the Jungle	Live in balance with Nature recognizing that all is connected

The perennial questions, as answered by the scientific materialism paradigm and the holism paradigm

When civilization evolves into the paradigm of holism, we will have come full circle to reacquire the awareness once held by our animistic forebears. We will once again realize oneness with our earthly environment, and, at the same time, we will honor the influence of what we call field, or spirit, that shapes our material existence in every moment.

The human population is awakening with a rapidly growing awareness that the key to a healthy, happy life in a thriving Garden requires us to recognize that we are each and all cells in the body of humanity, that we are conscious and conscientious caretakers and cultivators.

The Universe appears to be in an ever-unfolding spiral of evolutionary development. Having reflected on the past and examined the present, we are now ready to consider the parameters of a healthier future. We stand ready to reject the programming of habitual fear that has enslaved us and inhibited our growth. We are learning that the path to healing and breakthrough necessitates that we unite polarities that have fractured civilization. Humans across the planet are on the threshold of accepting their "humanifest destiny" as conscious co-creators.

A STATE OF "EMERGENT SEEING"

As we've already seen, the old paradigm beliefs exert their influence invisibly through every institution in society as well as in beliefs firmly embedded in our own psyche. For transformation to take place, a critical mass of us must divest ourselves of these obsolete beliefs and then invest our awareness and activities so as to be in harmony with the new emergent paradigm.

But in order to re-grow the Garden, we must first change the guard. Those dated beliefs of scientific materialism that stand guard at our doors of perception must be retired and relieved of duty. We must welcome a new basal paradigm, one that is based on an integration of new science and ancient spiritual wisdom, one that weaves old dualities into a unified holistic worldview.

In Part III, we move from our current state of emergency and declare our desire for a state of "emergent seeing." We offer a story to help us emerge from our limiting identity as separate individual cells and come to recognize ourselves as unique and important interdependent cells in the body of humanity.

PART III

In addition to Chapter 11, *Fractal Evolution*, and Chapter 12, *Time to See a Good Shrink*, Part III contains four prescriptive and visionary chapters that apply fractal awareness and the wisdom of the cells to human economics, politics, individual consciousness, and collective spiritual understanding. Each chapter, built on the truths uncovered in new-edge biology and quantum physics, offers insights on choices that increase the likelihood of civilization realizing a life-sustaining spontaneous evolution.

The One Suggestion: Maybe Ten Commandments are too many. Maybe all we need is one suggestion: "We're all in this together." Chapter 13 is an exploration of the field, the mysterious and invisible shaping force that connects us all, which reveals that we truly are all entangled particles in the same field of dreams. This chapter affirms that humanity's survival in a holistic paradigm is predicated on adopting the Golden Rule as a universal operating system.

A Healthy Commonwealth: We are cells in the body of humanity as well as citizens of the biosphere. Consequently, we must declare that economy and ecology are one and the same. In fact, the English words *economy* and *ecology* both originate from the Greek *oikos*, which means "household, house, or family" and was, as it relates to both financial and environmental wellness, the basic unit of society in most ancient Greek city-states.

Chapter 14, *A Healthy Commonwealth*, provides new science and sustainable trends that offer a promise of a new economics that is harmonious with the planet and with true human needs. That's good *oikos*.

Healing the Body Politic: Chapter 15, *Healing the Body Politic*, prescribes a holistic treatment that contrasts the conventional Newtonian approach of temporarily masking symptoms through practices such as political repression. Instead, we consider a new system of justice—a balance—that stops us from wasting energy by suppressing symptoms and, instead, liberates that energy for actually solving problems. By accessing the healthy central voice of We the People, we bring to light vital, life-affirming elements that have been missing in our political conversations.

A Whole New Story: Chapter 16, *A Whole New Story*, focuses on the processes needed to release and complete the old story so that we can begin a new one. The new story integrates opposing polarities to maximize the benefit of each position while moving beyond static positions to solve problems at a higher level.

As we free ourselves from limiting and self-destructive programs on both the individual and cultural level, we become free to write a new story. What would our world look like if we declared an end to the old story of domination, greed, fear, and hatred? What if we dismissed all old grievances in a worldwide ceremony and declared ourselves healed? What if we finalized the old story by concluding, "and they lived happily ever after?"

Well . . . we could begin living happily ever after right now—immediately—by bringing our own happiness with us.

The possibilities we could unleash are beyond imagination!

CHAPTER 11

FRACTAL EVOLUTION

*"Once we understand the math of evolution,
we will understand the aftermath as well."*
— Swami Beyondananda

IS THERE A FUTURE IN FUTUROLOGY?

In Part I, *What If Everything You Know Is Wrong!*, and Part II, *Four Myth-Perceptions of the Apocalypse*, we provided a brief history of Western civilization as seen through the lens of an evolving basal paradigm. Our focus was on the nature of how personal beliefs influence our biology and how a culture's paradigmatic beliefs shape the fate of a civilization. In Part III, we leave the old stories behind as we weave the elements of a new story that will guide us through the uncharted territory of a truly new millennium.

When compiling the story of how we got here, we were afforded the armchair opportunity of assessing history through the lens of 20/20 hindsight. But Part III introduces a completely different kind of story—a vision into the future. Offering information as to what will be is clearly a different endeavor than providing a historical analysis. We are now entering into the domain of prediction, or, more formally, *Futurology:* a systematic forecasting of the future based on an assessment of societal trends.

A prediction may range from an outright guess to an astute inference. By its nature, a guess is based on insufficient information and, consequently, represents a chancy prediction. In contrast, an inference is based on evidence and reasoning and, therefore, represents a prediction that has a greater probability of being correct. Yet, the accuracy of an inference is dependent on perceived evidence and reason. Obviously, a presumably solid inference can totally miss the mark if the beliefs upon which it is founded are inaccurate or distorted.

The Ford Motor Company provided a powerful example of envisioning the future through a distorted lens. In 1958, Ford unveiled a $400 million venture designed to capture the public's attention and purchasing dollars. Using the best Madison Avenue marketing research, Ford designed a new line of automobiles touted as the car having "more YOU ideas." The Ford Edsel was engineered to complement public trends in styling, and its advertising was scientifically designed to elicit car buyers' motivations.

But the Edsel became the most famous marketing disaster in history. In fact, the name has since become synonymous with commercial fiascos, and other similarly ill-fated products are often comically dismissed as being Edsels. Marketing experts hold the Edsel up as a supreme example of corporate America's inability to understand the nature of the American consumer. One of the more interesting factors for the failure, as stated in *TIME* magazine's list of "50 Worst Cars," was that: "Cultural critics speculated that the car was a flop because the vertical grill looked like a vagina. Maybe. America in the '50s was certainly phobic about the female business."

Futurists who use conventional beliefs and reasoning to target a prediction sometimes widely miss the mark. Like an archer, they sin. The gravity of a prognosticator's sin can be measured in terms of the number of people who are misled. Consider the ramifications of a futurist's sin when that futurist is a politician, economist, or sociologist responsible for guiding the fate of civilization.

In a tragic example of misperception and misguidance, Secretary of Defense Donald Rumsfeld assured the world of a fast victory in Iraq with a war lasting no more than a few weeks. We now know that Rumsfeld's sin, based on distorted evidence and reasoning, has cost, and continues to cost, the United States dearly in what has been the Edsel of all wars!

A good futurist has the ability to assess data and identify inherent patterns. Therefore, pattern recognition is a primary component in the learning process and a necessity in projecting the future.

Below is an opportunity to test your skills at being a futurologist. Study the four sequences below and predict the number or letter that will fill the blank:

(1)   13 – 26 – 39 – 52 – 65 – ___

(2)   C – F – I – L – O – R – ___

(3)   7 – 3 – B – 16 – 2 – 9 – C – 0 – 4 – H – 1 – 1 – ___

(4)   3 – 1 – 4 – 1 – 5 – 9 – 2 – 6 – ___

Answers only become obvious after we observe a recognizable pattern. In sequence (1), the pattern reveals that each new number is derived by adding 13 to the previous number. In sequence (2) the pattern represents listing every third letter in the alphabet. If your answers for (1) and (2) were respectively, *78* and *U*, congratulations—you have seen into the future!

However, problems arise in predicting the future in sequence (3) because, apparently, there is neither rhyme nor reason to the pattern. Consequently, any answer you use to fill in the blank, by definition, represents an outright guess. Because this is a random equation, philosophically, any guess can be either right or wrong—and, as befitting a quantum Universe, the accuracy of that guess is dependent, of course, upon the observer.

For most readers, sequence (4) might seem to be yet another random sequence. Surprisingly, the answer is *5*. Perhaps you were sufficiently astute to have recognized this apparent non-pattern as the specific sequence of numbers that represent the mathematical formula for Pi (π). Equation (4), therefore, underscores a relevant concern for futurologists, that is, some components of Nature that appear to be random are actually *chaotic* in that they possess an underlying, but as yet, unrecognized pattern.

This simple exercise illustrates three fundamentally important points concerning futurology: first, if a pattern can be recognized, then the accuracy of predicting a future event is relatively high. Second, if events are found to be random, then all predictions are essentially guesses with an accuracy based on chance. Third, the apparent absence of a pattern does not imply the absence of a pattern. Some patterns are obvious, some patterns are not readily recognizable, and some things simply don't have a pattern!

Survival is dependent on pattern recognition. As a primal example, humankind's early knowledge of Nature's fundamental patterns included the day-night cycle, the lunar cycle, and the sidereal yearly cycle with four seasons. The ability to observe and forecast celestial patterns was fundamental to the development of agriculture and further evolution of civilization because this awareness provided humans with the means and motivation to plan future actions, such as planting crops in the spring then harvesting and storing food for the coming winter.

Likewise, early human cultures were able to connect the biological patterns of birth, growth, and death with the planet's cyclic seasonal patterns. These patterns were so important to survival that civilizations built great edifices and temples, such as Stonehenge, to observe and mark the transit of the sun, moon, and stars.

Today, the calendar serves as our monument to these daily, seasonal, and yearly patterns. With a calendar, a person anywhere in the world can know, for example, the propagation season for turtles laying their eggs on a Galapagos beach or the day swallows return to Capistrano.

When early humans connected astronomical patterns with patterns of human behavior, they recognized a link between Earth's cycles and human physiology. For example, the fact that the lunar cycle and a woman's menstrual cycle are each 28 days long is not a coincidence.

This link between the heavens and human biology and behavior led ancient societies to found the science and art of astrology. The practice in astrology of observing patterns and predicting human behavior proved to be so valuable that, from earliest recorded history to the present day, government rulers and leaders have consulted with astrologers to divine the future of their nations.

With the introduction of new cultural truths by the monotheists and, later, by the scientific materialists, civilization's awareness of Earth arts receded into history, relegated to the status of fanciful myths. Science today considers these ancient practices to be beliefs that are simply beyond the laws of Nature. And our current science-based society totally dismisses the ancient divining arts of seeing into the future as primitive metaphysical rituals.

But, perhaps, as new-edge science is revealing, these Earth practices are only beyond the limited vision of conventional scientists who still perceive the world through the flawed lenses of the four myth-perceptions. Fortunately, we have among us Aboriginal descendents who are still able to speak the language of the planet. But, the populations of these Earth stewards are rapidly diminishing, so we must act quickly to ensure that their wisdom will not be lost.

The character of today's civilization is primarily shaped by what scientific materialism presents as paradigmatic truths, which are really the beliefs originally adopted after Darwin introduced his version of evolution theory in the mid-19th century. In spite of their inherent faults, these perceived scientific truths nonetheless provided an important conceptual framework that enabled the development of technology and the growth of civilization. But, while these flawed beliefs once provided the miracles of our modern world, their shortcomings are a threat to human survival today.

The critical problems currently facing humanity are symptoms that reflect our inability to project into the future. Like a wayward rocket, civilization has been careening from one disaster to another, showing itself to be a forceful vector with no intentional direction.

Conventional wisdom is a contributing factor to history's erratic and often calamitous course. While this commonly accepted form of reasoning is used to envision patterns and project futures, it can also be distorted by faulty perceptions, especially when an accurate awareness of energy fields, genetic determinism, and the nature of evolution is required.

Therefore, in order to accurately see where we are going, we must first understand the patterns of how we got here. However, when consulting conventional science about inherent patterns in evolution, we must recognize that limiting Darwinian beliefs concerning random evolution will significantly distort their answers.

How does conventional science explain how we got here?

Oh—through billions of years of gradual evolution driven by random mutations and genetic accidents.

So, if that's how we got here, then can we predict where evolution will take us?

Perhaps on a joy ride . . . to Hell?

Seriously, if evolution is driven by random events, how can anyone predict where we are going? Any prediction, by definition, would be a sheer guess. For example, consider the fact that when the home computer rage first hit the public, futurists projected that, in the centuries ahead, humans would evolve smaller bodies and bigger heads from sitting at computer terminals all day. But, if we look at the current epidemic in obesity and dwindling intelligence, we see that that prediction was an Edsel of a guess!

WHEN IT COMES TO INVENTION, NECESSITY IS A MOTHER

In the face of global crises, new-edge science is introducing a new life-sustaining story, a different way of looking at the world. When we replace civilization's current faulty paradigmatic myths with the revised awareness offered by modern science, a whole new world of possibilities emerges. Seen through a corrected paradigm lens, unrecognized patterns come into sharp focus.

For example, consider the question of humanity's evolution in light of new scientific insights. In contrast to the Darwinian assertion that evolution is driven by random mutations, Cairns described beneficial mutations that certainly seem to be intentional. The hypersomatic mutation process provides a mechanism of evolution through which organisms are innately capable of adapting to dynamic changes in the environment by actively changing their genetic code.

Leading-edge evolution theorists have recently revived the 19th century concept of *ecological speciation,* which suggests the evolution of new species is driven by ecological pressures. These theorists point out that narrow, regional variations in an environment, such as in microclimate zones, influence an organism to rapidly adapt and change its biological shape and behaviors as well as its ability to survive and thrive in that altered environment. For example, we can split an identical population of either fish or snails into two groups and introduce each group into separate but identical environments. If we introduce predators that feed off fish or snails into one of the environments and follow the fate of both populations, we can observe how environmental alterations—the predators—profoundly influence the course of evolution within the fish or snail species. Similar results have been observed in natural ecosystems.[1]

Fish or snails in the altered environment will mature and reproduce earlier, and consequent changes in their structure and behavior will likely lead to different behavior patterns than those expressed by their unchallenged cohorts in the safe environment. The two subpopulations of species could even further disconnect from one another if some are forced by predation to live and feed in formerly unfrequented parts of their environment. Regardless of whether these changes are introduced by epigenetic mechanisms or by adaptive mutations, environmentally induced alterations may lead to such divergent developmental paths that organisms may no longer be able to recognize or breed with other members of the previously same species.[2]

The influence of environment in shaping evolution was recently demonstrated in long-term genetic studies on microbes. Trying to determine the role of chance in evolutionary development, researchers asked, "If the history of life could be replayed from the same starting point, would it unfold differently?" After introducing genetically identical bacteria into separate test tubes, each of which contained the same stressful environment, they followed the evolution of bacteria in each tube through 24,000 generations.

Researchers found that "these miniature adaptive radiations unfold in the same way every time, governed by the available environmental niches."[3] In some experiments, adaptations in different cultures were derived from different types of genetic processes. In other studies, the adaptations in different cultures were surprisingly reproducible, right down to the specific pattern of alterations in ATCG sequences in DNA.

Regardless of the path they took, microbes in each tube ultimately adapted to the same environment, generally using the same pathways. This indicates that identical populations faced with similar conditions follow parallel courses of evolution. Therefore, through this experiment and the others described above, new-edge science reveals that evolution is directly influenced by environmental determinants and, apparently, is not random.

If evolution is shaped by environmental conditions, as these experiments suggest, then, with enough awareness of environmental conditions, we should be able to envision the course of evolution. The question then becomes, "Can we predict environmental conditions in a dynamic world?"

While *dynamic systems* appear to behave randomly, Lorenz revealed that, with enough resolution of environmental data, even these systems are predictable. Dynamic systems express *deterministic chaos,* or, simply, *chaos.* In contrast to systems that display random behaviors, the fates of chaotic systems are predictable and, as Lorenz experienced, highly sensitive to initial influences.

DÉJÀ VU ALL OVER AGAIN

In addition to sensitivity, dynamical, or chaotic, systems are also characterized by another fundamental trait: *iteration.* Iteration simply means repetition of a pattern, be it a physical structure or a behavioral process. For example, if you take pictures of a coastline from a satellite, from an airplane, from a boat, and from standing on the shore, then if you trace the shape of the coast's outline in each image, all the tracings will exhibit a self-similar pattern. Likewise, at any level of its organization, a tree is made out of repeating self-similar patterns in a range of different sizes: the shape of the trunk is similar to the shape of a branch, which is similar to that of a twig.

In mathematics, iteration represents the repeated application of the same function or formula in which the output of each step is used as the input for the next repeated, or iterated, step. For example, consider this iterated equation:

$$\text{The length of a line} \div 2 = \underline{\quad}$$

For example:

$$12 \text{ inches} \div 2 = 6 \text{ inches}$$

Repeat the process:

$$6 \text{ inches} \div 2 = 3 \text{ inches}$$
$$3 \text{ inches} \div 2 = 1.5 \text{ inches}$$
$$1.5 \text{ inches} \div 2 = .75 \text{ of an inch}$$
$$.75 \text{ of an inch} \div 2 = .375 \text{ of an inch}$$

And so on with each resulting line being one-half the length of the previous line until such point as your pencil point is too large to draw the smaller and smaller lines. Yet, the iterating equation can still continue. You could use a microscope to see even smaller lines. And, if you were to use a computer you could iterate—repeat—this equation infinitely, creating infinitely smaller and smaller lines.

In this iterated equation, the use of a one-dimensional line merely produces a simple line of shorter length. However, if we apply an iterated equation to a two-dimensional object, such as a triangle, the results of iterating even a simple formula produce great complexity.

The creation of a more complex, two-dimensional Koch Snowflake is built by starting with a simple equilateral triangle and then applying this iterated equation:

On each surface, attach a new equilateral triangle; the perimeter of that triangle is equal to the length of the surface on which it sits.

By repeating this formula indefinitely, we can add smaller and smaller triangles to each newly created surface.

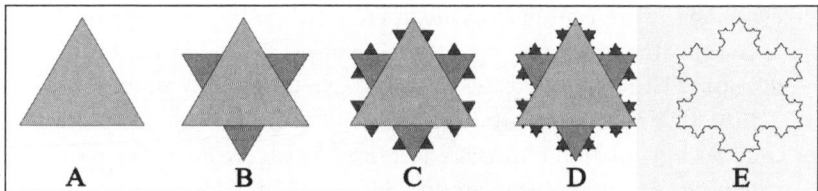

| A | B | C | D | E |

The Koch Snowflake illustrates that a simple geometric shape, such as an equilateral triangle, repeated multiple times, creates other figures of increasing complexity.

In the illustration above, the initial seed triangle A is light gray. The shading of the triangles becomes successively darker in each of the next three iterations (Figures B, C, and D). The complexity of the process is revealed in Figure E in which all the triangles are merged into a single image. As is evident by comparing the simple starting triangle with the result of each repeat of the equation, subsequent iterations vastly increase the complexity of the form.

The Koch Snowflake expresses an iterated pattern created by using a two-dimensional object. But dramatically more complex structures are produced when the iterated formula utilizes three-dimensional objects.

Consider the fact that all the variations of animals on this planet, from worms to sperm whales, represent multi-dimensional systems built from essentially iterated patterns of self-similar cells. These complex systems of living organisms, as well as the environment in which they are evolving, are chaotic. Yet, because of mathematical modeling, they are also arc you ready for this?—predictable!

This concept of predictable chaos is apparently what Galileo had in mind when he penned, "Mathematics is the language with which God has written the Universe."

FRACTALS—MATH AND AFTERMATH

Consequently, all we need to do is find out which mathematics was used to create the Universe and we will be able to understand how we got here and where we are bound. Because we are trying to discern environmental patterns, specifically as they relate to the biosphere, we need to discover the math Nature used to put physical structure into space.

Such a mission invokes the use of geometry because, by definition, this branch of mathematics is specifically concerned with the properties, measurement, and relationships of structure in space. Geometry is so fundamental to the organization of the Universe that long before Galileo's realization, Plato concluded, "Geometry existed before creation."

Until 1975, the general public was only familiar with the principles of Euclidean geometry, summarized in the 13-volume ancient Greek text, *The Elements of Euclid,* written around 300 B.C.E. This is the geometry most of us learned in school to plot structures such as cubes and spheres and cones onto graph paper. Euclidian geometry has enabled us to project the movement of heavenly bodies, construct great edifices and gardens, and even build spaceships and sophisticated weapons.

However, the mathematical formulae of Euclidian geometry are not readily applicable to Nature. For example, what kind of tree can you create using the standardized perfect forms of Euclidean geometry? Think back to the tree you drew in kindergarten, a circle sitting atop an elongated rectangle. Your kindergarten teacher, no doubt, recognized it as a representation of a tree, but in no way does it describe what a tree really is, no more than a stick figure describes a human.

With Euclidean geometry and a compass, you can draw a perfect circle. But you cannot use Euclidean geometry to draw a perfect or, at least, a realistic tree. Nor can Euclidian geometry describe the structure of a beetle, a mountain, a cloud, or any other familiar patterns found in Nature. Euclidean geometry falls short when it comes to describing the structure of life. So where do we find the type of mathematics referred to by Plato and Galileo, the math that describes the design principles inherent in Nature?

We were offered a clue about 90 years ago when a young French mathematician named Gaston Julia published a paper on his work with iterated functions. His was a relatively simple equation that used only multiplication and addition, repeated *ad infinitum.* To actually visualize the image encoded in his mathematical formula, Julia would have had to solve millions of iterations of the formula, a process that would have taken him decades. Therefore, even though he conceived of a fractal in mathematical terms, Julia never actually saw one.

The profound implications of Julia's formula were only revealed when his equation was solved with the aid of computers in 1975. Benoit Mandelbrot, a French-American mathematician who analyzed patterns in chaotic systems at an IBM computing lab, was the first person to observe what Julia could only imagine. Mandelbrot was awestruck by the strikingly beautiful organic and infinitely complex images generated by fractal formulae. He was the first to observe that fractal images possessed repeated self-similar patterns, regardless of the scale on which they were examined. The more he magnified the images, the more the structure appeared to be the same.

Inherent within the chaotic complexity of fractal images is the presence of ever-repeating patterns, nested within one another. The internationally popular toy, hand-painted Russian nesting dolls, provides a rough idea of the nature of a fractal's repetitive images. Each smaller version of the doll is similar to, but not necessarily an exact version of, the larger doll in which it is nested. Mandelbrot introduced the term *self-similar* to describe such objects that he observed in the new math, which he called *fractal geometry.*

Russian nesting dolls represent a fractal's repetitive image.

Within the complexity of his fractal images, Mandelbrot observed vivid patterns that resemble shapes common in Nature, such as insects, seashells, and trees. Historically, science had frequently documented the presence of self-similar organizational patterns at different scales of Nature's structure. However, until Mandelbrot introduced fractal geometry, these self-similar patterns were deemed to be merely curious coincidences.

Fractal geometry emphasizes the relationship between the patterns in a whole structure and the patterns seen in its parts. Recall the examples of the coastline and of the twigs, branches, and tree trunks cited earlier. Self-similar patterns are found throughout Nature and especially within the structure of the human body. For example, in the human lung, the pattern of branching along the large bronchus air passages is repeated in the branching structure of the smaller bronchi and even smaller bronchiole passages. Arterial and venous vessels of the circulatory system as well as the body's network of peripheral nerves also display repetitive, self-similar branching patterns.

Because fractal geometry is truly the design principle of Nature, the biosphere inherently reveals nested self-similar patterns at every level of its organization. Consequently, as we observe and become aware of patterns at higher or lower levels of an organization's structure, we can use fractals in the same way we use maps. Fractals can help us gain insight into the organization at any other level. In the biosphere, the fractal pattern of human evolution can inherently display a self-similar pattern of evolution experienced by structures at other levels of Nature's organization.

Ernst Haeckel, a famous embryologist and contemporary of Darwin, inadvertently reported the first inkling of a self-similar, fractal-like pattern in evolution in 1868. Haeckel published a now famous sequence of microscopic images that compares the stages of embryonic development of a number of species with that of the human. He noted that all vertebrate embryos, including the human embryo, pass through a series of similar structural stages. Haeckel argued that, in transitioning through their early development, organisms actually retrace every stage of their evolutionary ancestry.

Haeckel's theory, cryptically defined as *ontogeny recapitulates phylogeny,* literally means "development is a replay of ancestry." Unfortunately, when promoting his ideas, an overzealous Haeckel fudged his drawings to make the early stages of embryos appear more alike than they actually are.

Regardless of his flawed presentation, human embryos do morph through a variety of shapes before acquiring human form. In these transitions, the human embryo assumes a sequential series of self-similar structural patterns wherein it resembles embryos from earlier stages of vertebrate evolution.

The developing human embryo shape-shifts from one that resembles a fish embryo to one that resembles an amphibian embryo. It continues morphing until it takes on the appearance of a reptilian embryo and, later, that of a mammal before finally assuming a human shape. Evolving through the embryonic stages of its biospheric ancestors, human embryos offer a dynamic example of fractal-like self-similarity.

EVOLUTION DECODED

Is Nature really an expression of fractal geometry? Introducing simple mathematical equations into a fractal computer program and creating realistic landscapes and images of biological organisms provides evidence but does not prove that Nature is truly fractal in character. The appearance of self-similar patterns throughout the biosphere may, in fact, be merely a coincidence. The question then becomes, "Is there any functional reason as to why the evolution of the biosphere would be driven by fractal geometry?"

Nature is a dynamic system, founded on iterated processes and chaos mathematics, and subject to sensitivity. The fact that fractal geometry is the specific mathematics to model such a chaotic system supports, that Nature should be fractal, but it does not necessarily provide a reason as to why. However, there is another compelling reason, based strictly on mathematics, that suggests why the observed parallels between fractal geometry and the structure of Nature are more than coincidence.

Historically, Lamarck described evolution as *transformation*, a linear process that starts with primitive organisms and progresses upward toward what he described as "perfection." In his model, Lamarck envisioned evolution as an ascending ladder. Darwinists also acknowledged an upward progression in evolution, but they compared the process to a tree. They recognized that most random variations that generated new organisms are similar to a tree's lateral branches in that they do not necessarily contribute to vertical ascension of the species.

As a more current consideration, we would like to suggest that the path of evolution most closely resembles the shape of an exploding chrysanthemum. Species evolve in every direction with the innate drive to inhabit all available environmental niches. Organisms have evolved to live in glacier ice, at volcanic vents under the ocean, in bedrock many kilometers beneath the ground, and everywhere in between.

In the chrysanthemum model, it makes no sense to ask, "Where is evolution going?" It's going in every direction at once. To track the course of evolution, we must first define a parameter to be used as a yardstick to measure evolutionary advances. For example, the path of evolution of life in the sea has a different meaning than the path of evolution of life on the land or in the air. Humans do not rank very high in the evolution of water-breathing organisms or in the evolutionary hierarchy of egg-laying animals or flying animals. So what do humans excel at, evolutionarily speaking?

As both observers of and participants in evolution, we have selected a petal of the evolution-chrysanthemum to represent a trait we feel distinguishes us from lower organisms, and that trait is awareness. This is the same characteristic that Lamarck used when he emphasized the development of the nervous system as his evolutionary yardstick. Darwinists, likewise, illustrate their tree of evolution in a hierarchical ascendance of nervous-system development.

Unfortunately, as summarized in Chapter 1, *Believing Is Seeing,* and in more detail in *The Biology of Belief,* conventional science's understanding of evolution has been significantly distorted by its faulty misperception that the cell's nucleus and its enclosed genes represent the cell's nervous system.[4] Hence, science currently has a myopic preoccupation with measuring an organism's genome as representative of its evolutionary advancement.

As described earlier, the true brain of the cell is its membrane. Built into the membrane's structure are receptor proteins and effector proteins that serve as switches and which represent a measurable unit of perception. Consequently, an organism's awareness can be physically quantified by calculating the number of perception proteins it possesses.

In Chapter 12, *Time to See a Good Shrink,* we provide evidence that, because of physical restrictions, perception proteins can only form a monolayer in the membrane. This physical restriction means that an increase in the population of perception proteins is directly tied to an increase in the organism's membrane surface area. In other words, for an organism's awareness to multiply and to increase its brain power, it would have to increase its membrane power.

Simply, these insights reveal that mathematicians can calculate evolutionary advancement by mapping an organism's membrane surface area.[5] And how would that be done? According to William Allman, author of the "Mathematics of Human Life," an article in *U.S. News & World Report,* "Mathematical studies of fractals reveal that the repetitive branching-within-branching structure of a fractal represents the best way to get the most surface area within a three-dimensional space . . ."[6] Modeling evolution demands the use of fractal geometry because evolution wouldn't occur without it. Consequently the appearance of self-similar patterns in Nature is not a coincidence; it is a reflection of evolutionary mathematics.

The strikingly beautiful, computer-generated pictures of fractal patterns, such as those adorning the butterfly's wings on the cover of this book, should remind us that, despite our modern angst and the seeming chaos of our world, there is order in Nature. And because this order is inherently comprised of self-similar fractal patterns, there is nothing truly new under the sun.

The esoteric world of fractal geometry provides a mathematical model that suggests the arbitrariness, planlessness, randomness, and accidents that underlie Darwinian theory are outmoded. We believe that continued support of these outdated ideas represents a fundamental threat to the survival of humanity and should, as rapidly as possible, go the way of the pre-Copernican, Earth-centered Universe.

PURPOSEFUL PUNCTUATION

The fact that the biosphere is fractal in nature is no longer a question. The more important question before us now is, "Did biological organisms acquire their fractal character by accident or intention?" Conventional Darwinian theory suggests that evolution is driven by random mutations and Nature has taken on its current structure and organization simply by accident. However, the recent discovery of somatic hypermutation mechanisms reveals a process by which cells purposefully mutate their genes to actively engage in evolution.

Studies by Cairns and others on bacterial evolution, presented earlier, demonstrate that living systems have an inherent ability to induce evolutionary change to support their survival in a dynamically changing environment. This newly discovered gene-altering mechanism is variously referred to as *adaptive, directed,* or *beneficial mutations.* Regardless of the term, the meaning is the same: evolutionary changes appear to be purposeful, not random.

There is an inherent underlying plan to evolution in the form of Nature's fractal environment. Evolution is marked by periodic mass extinctions that were apparently caused by environmental upheavals, also known as punctuations, that disturbed periods of evolutionary stasis. Following these environmental alterations, life managed to survive, evolve, and, once again, flourish because of adaptive mutation mechanisms. The ability to intentionally mutate genes enabled surviving organisms to actively change their genetics so that they could survive by complementing and harmonizing with new environmental patterns.

The previous five mass extinctions were evolutionary punctuations that radically altered life on this planet. Just as suddenly as old life forms disappeared due to these catastrophic events, amazing varieties of new life forms came into existence.

This insight on the nature of punctuated equilibrium challenges another fundamental assumption of Darwinian theory: the belief that evolution from one species to another occurs through a series of infinitely gradual transformations over eons of time.

As mentioned earlier, paleontologists Stephen Jay Gould and Niles Eldredge have verified that evolution results from long periods of stability that are periodically interrupted by catastrophic upheavals. In their evolution theory, called *Punctuated Equilibrium,* Gould and Eldredge claim that each catastrophe is followed by an explosive increase in the number of new species at a rate faster than can be accounted for by plodding Darwinian mechanisms. In other words, evolution occurs by sudden leaps, not gradual transitions.[7]

The insights of Gould and Eldredge are absolutely pertinent to the current moment in our evolution, especially because scientists have now established that we are deep into the planet's sixth mass extinction.[8] Uh oh.

Will we make it? We are betting on the fact that when evolution theory is updated and the public becomes aware of the amazing insights offered by punctuated equilibrium, adaptive mutations, and epigenetics, civilization's evolutionary punctuation will turn out to be a highly positive and life-proclaiming exclamation point!

If bacteria can evolve purposefully, then why not us? Can we evolve with intention? *The answer is yes!* And that is what this book is all about.

FROM HUMAN TO HUMANITY

Before we look forward to see where fractal evolution might be taking us next, let's go back in time and take a deeper look at the history of evolution in terms of punctuated equilibrium. By assessing evolution as a series of repeating periods of stasis punctuated by upheavals and followed by evolutionary leaps, we can identify four fundamental punctuations that drastically changed the course of evolution. The recognition of these fractal punctuation patterns offer important insight into resolving the crises precipitated by our current punctuation.

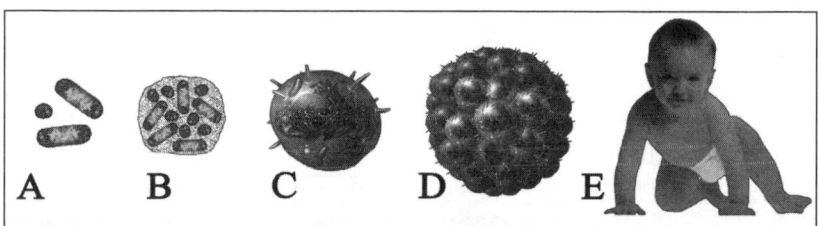

This figure traces the major evolutionary leaps that led to human beings. A: Individual, free-living prokaryotes. B: Community of prokaryotes within a biofilm. C: Single eukaryote evolved from a biofilm-like life source. D: Primitive colonial organisms, a simple community of eukaryotes. E: Differentiated multicellular community of eukaryotes.

Prokaryote Period: The first leap occurred within the first half billion years of Earth's fiery origin. This was when the first primitive cellular citizens evolved and began to colonize the planet's oceans. Called *prokaryotes,* these primal bacterial cells are generally the smallest and simplest cells, consisting of what could be called a bag of membrane filled with a soupy cytoplasm. Most prokaryotes are physically supported and protected by a somewhat rigid sugar-based capsule that envelops their fragile cytoplasmic bodies. External capsules physically constrain the size of prokaryotic cells and limit their ability to expand their membrane surface area.

Seemingly, the prokaryote's inability to acquire more membrane surface area and, consequently, more awareness-providing membrane perception proteins would signal the end of evolution. However, Nature had a bigger plan up its evolutionary sleeve. In response to increasing environmental pressures generated by exploding populations of cells, the biological imperative, the innate will to survive, served as a driving force to further prokaryote evolution.

At a moment in time, in what would amount to a spontaneous evolution, individual prokaryotes upgraded the mechanism of evolutionary advancement. Rather than trying to further increase the size and intelligence of the individual cell, prokaryotes assembled into communities to collectively share both an enlarged surface area and awareness. As communities, prokaryotes effectively became a group of species occupying the same environment.

While we generally perceive bacteria to be free-living cells, it is now recognized that unicellular prokaryotes live in functionally integrated but highly dispersed communities wherein free-living cells enhance their awareness by long-distance exchange of chemical information.

Over time, different species of bacteria acquired the ability to physically band together and create life-sustaining, controllable microenvironments by enveloping the entire community within a single protective membrane. This was Nature's equivalent of a gated community wherein the environment was maintained by the prokaryote population. The inhabitants of these membrane-encapsulated communities were a functionally complex and cooperative society of different bacterial species. Prokaryote citizens in the community enhanced their survival by collectively sharing their specialized functions and their DNA.

Within their encapsulated communities, called *biofilms,* bacteria were protected from antibiotics and other toxic elements in the external environment, the agents that would kill their free-living relatives who didn't have the good fortune to find residence in a biofilm.[9] The resistive and protective nature of the biofilms enabled these cellular communities to become the first life forms to leave the ocean and live on the land.

As a footnote, we want to point out that the bacteria that form tooth cavities are actually biofilm communities that resist our efforts to scour them from our teeth.

Eukaryote Period: The second punctuation that precipitated an evolutionary leap occurred when, over time, prokaryote biofilm communities evolved into a more advanced life form called *eukaryotes*. To do this, the former biofilm microbes transformed into cellular organelles, such as mitochondria and nuclei, that characteristically populate the cytoplasm in the large eukaryotic cells. Many biologists believe this organizational advance from a biofilm community to a eukaryotic community is one of the most significant events in evolutionary history; that's because Nature changed the strategy of evolution. Previously, evolution was mediated by influencing the amount of awareness in a single cell. The new strategy was based on collectively combining the awareness of a community into one new organism.

In her book *Symbiosis in Cell Evolution*, American biologist Lynn Margulis expanded on the notion that larger, more advanced eukaryotes initially derived from colonies of microbes.[10] Margulis contended that *symbiosis,* which is the assembly of individuals based on mutually beneficial relationships, is a major driving force behind evolution.

She suggests that Darwin's notion of evolution, driven by the survival of the fittest in a continual competition among individuals and species, misses the mark. In her opinion, cooperation, interaction, and mutual dependence among life forms allowed for the global expression of life. According to Margulis, "Life did not take over the globe by combat, but by networking."[11]

Stop for a moment and consider what a magnificent and paradigm-shattering advancement the evolution of eukaryotes was, and consider the awesome possibilities that a similar quantum shift, based on human cooperation and symbiosis, holds for our world today.

The evolution of eukaryotes diverged into two major paths: mobile animal protozoa, such as the amoeba and paramecium, and plant cells, represented by single-celled algae.

The animal versions evolved an internal flexible cytoskeleton for physical support and mobility. Unlike the more primitive prokaryotes whose size is limited by a constraining capsule, eukaryotes, equipped with an internal mechanical structure, were able to grow and expand their membrane in a manner similar to an inflated balloon. With internal cytoskeletal support, large eukaryotic cells have thousands of times more membrane surface area and a far greater awareness potential than individual prokaryotic cells.

However, even eukaryote size is ultimately limited because of an inherent fragility in the enveloping cell membrane. If a eukaryote grows too large, the pressure generated by the mass of its internal cytoplasmic content causes its fragile membrane to rupture, which leads to the cell's death. Ultimately, the eukaryote, like its primitive prokaryote ancestor, reached a size limitation and was unable to further expand its membrane-based awareness without jeopardizing its survival. The limits on expanding membrane surface area created a situation that represented another potential evolutionary endpoint.

Multicellular Period: For almost three and a half billion years, the only organisms on this planet were free-living prokaryotes and the more advanced eukaryotic cells. The third evolutionary leap occurred about 700 million years ago when individual eukaryotic cells, like their prokaryote precursors, began to share awareness by physically assembling into communities.

The first multicellular communities were simply colonial organisms, groups of identical cells hanging out together en masse to, we might say, "save on rent." But, because each cell represents a unit of awareness, the more cells in a community, the more potential awareness that community possessed.

However, as the population density of these eukaryotic communities increased, there came a time when it was no longer efficient for all the cells to do the same thing. The workload was subdivided, and eukaryotic cells in the community began to express specialized functions, such as muscle, bone, and brain.

Over time, the collective awareness within eukaryotic communities led to the evolution of highly structured and altruistic multicellular organisms capable of supporting the survival of communities consisting of trillions of cells.

Variations in the traits and functions expressed by these cellular communities led to the creation of cellular organizations with different structures, so that each multicellular organism had its own distinctive anatomy. Scientists use these anatomical characteristics to classify each version of multicellular community as a unique species. When we observe trees, jellyfish, dogs, cats, and humans, although we normally perceive them as individual entities, in truth, they are complex multicellular communities.

Societal Period: The current emergent version of evolution is characterized by a still higher order of communal assembly. This time, individual members of certain species—each of which is a multicellular community of eukaryotic cells, which, in turn, are each communities of prokaryotic cells—began to band together into social organizations to enhance their survivability. Fish assemble into schools; dogs into packs; bison into herds; geese into flocks; and humans into tribes, nations, and states. Social evolution provides for communities of species that take on a life of their own as super-organisms.

While, from our perspective, we tend to think of evolutionary leaps as producing new species, what we're really seeing is an evolution of increasing levels of communal complexity and interrelationships. This pattern suggests that the next phase of human evolution will not so much be about changes within individual human beings but about how human beings assemble into community.

Humans evolved millions of years ago. What lies before us now is the evolution of the next higher level, the community humans—humanity.

Apparently, the path of evolution is not a continuous ramp of gradual progress. Rather, its history is marked by long periods of nominal advancement, followed by quantum leaps wherein nested patterns of communal assembly provide for the emergence of properties or traits that could not have been anticipated before.

We see this in prokaryotes, the fundamental life forms that gave rise to individualized, membrane-bound communities called eukaryotes. Then, the communities of communal eukaryotes provided for multicellular species, such as plants and animals. Then, plants and animals subsequently assembled into higher order communities that we define as societal organizations.

If we were to illustrate this new perspective, we would see four tiers of gradual progression, with each tier distinguished from its evolutionary neighbor by a quantum jump:

A. Prokaryotes => Eukaryotes (evolution of single-cell communities)
B. Eukaryotes => Multicellular organisms (evolution of plants, animals, and humans)
C Multicellular organisms => Societal organizations (evolution of humanity)

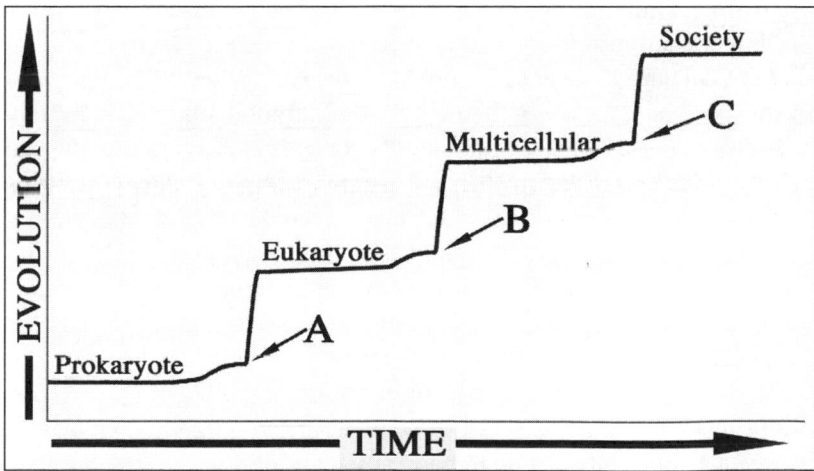

Evolution is not a steady slope but periods of stasis or gradual progression followed by quantum jumps.

We believe that human civilization, as a society, is struggling with its very existence. The pattern of evolution, as illustrated here, shows that we are on the threshold of experiencing the next evolution, the true expression of humanity.

NO NEW STORIES: OUR FUTURE
THROUGH A FRACTAL LOOKING GLASS

Based on Nature's fractal character, the pattern of structures within any one tier of organization is self-similar to the pattern expressed by structures at higher or lower tiers of organization.

Consequently, the structures, functions, and behaviors of a prokaryotic cell in Tier 1, a eukaryotic cell in Tier 2, a human in Tier 3, and society in Tier 4 express self-similar patterns in their evolution and organization.

The inherent nature of fractal self-similarity is the key reason why knowledge gained from studying the biology of cells can be applied to understanding human biology as well as communal society. More importantly, fractal evolution implies that an awareness of the organization and dynamics employed by cells in the community that comprises the human body can provide insight into the patterns required to create a similar harmony among the human cells who collectively contribute to human society.

Through millions of years of evolution, cellular citizens within multicellular organisms have worked out an effective peace plan that enables them to enhance their survival as well as the survival of other organisms in the biosphere. Consider the remarkable harmony among the trillions of individual cells living within the skin of a healthy human body. Our cells have apparently resolved any issues that would hinder cooperation so that our tissues and organs, which are the cellular community's equivalent of nation-states, tend to support rather than compete and fight with each other. For example, nowhere in medical literature is there documentation of the liver invading the pancreas in order to capture the Islets of Langerhans!

In coherence with fractal self-similarity, the assembly of humans into multicellular humanity expresses a similar pattern formerly used by cells to create a multicellular human body. The path of human evolution parallels the earlier path of animal evolution in which the animal kingdom progressed through two distinct phases: the primitive invertebrate phase followed by the more-advanced vertebrate phase.

As we shall see, the fundamental difference between invertebrates and vertebrates is the mechanism by which they support themselves. Likewise, the fundamental difference between early humans and advanced humans is also the latter's ability to support themselves and their societies.

Invertebrates: Multicellular invertebrate organisms, such as shellfish and insects, resemble prokaryotes in that they lack an internal skeleton and rely on external exoskeletal support, such as that provided by mineral shells or rigid chitin capsules.

In regard to the character of support, the earliest human civilizations were tantamount to invertebrates in that they relied on external support from Mother Nature. If She provided, they survived.

Vertebrates: In regard to support, vertebrate organisms, like their constituent eukaryotic cells, are physically supported from within by a rigid backbone.

The evolution of the vertebrate phase of human civilization correlates with the origin of technologies that enabled humans to support themselves through the prowess of their internal intelligence mechanisms. When civilization evolved to its internally supported vertebrate level, humans no longer relied on handouts from Nature—or so it seemed.

Similarly, vertebrate animals evolved through an increasingly more complex sequence that led from fish to amphibians, to reptiles, to birds, and to mammals prior to the origin of humans. Consequently, we can assume that, in a fractal Universe, the human community will likely evolve through a sequence of self-similar developmental stages that express the character of fish, amphibians, reptiles, birds, and mammals.

Fish: The fundamental character of fish is their dependence on a water environment.

Likewise, the earliest stages of self-sustaining human communities were fish-like in that they were physically restricted to the immediate vicinity of water. These *mariculture* societies flourished by harvesting food from oceans and water from lakes and nearby wetlands. Their highways were waterways, and they spread their civilizations by paddling or sailing from one coast to another.

Amphibians: While amphibians are birthed in the water, they are able to venture onto the land by acquiring mechanisms to take water with them.

Similarly, human civilization entered the amphibian phase and moved inland when people developed methods to convey water from lakes and waterways or extract it from subterranean aquifers. Through the rise of *agriculture,* these civilizations created and employed technology that enabled them to sustain and thrive in their new land-based environment.

Reptiles: From amphibians, which are relatively sluggish and vulnerable on land, came reptiles, which traded in the aquatic skills of their amphibian ancestors in favor of a superiorly designed, land-based physiology. Through adaptation, reptiles honed hardened bodies of great strength, speed, and dexterity suitable for their purely terrestrial environment. The digital character of a lizard's darting eyes and tongue and its mechanized gait attest to this machine-like nature.

The evolution of human civilization followed a self-similar path when the Industrial Revolution provoked humanity's transition from its earlier agrarian phase, which is comparable to the amphibian environment, to a more sophisticated, mechanized Industrial Age, which is reptilian in nature.

Dinosaurs: A unique branch of highly successful reptiles eventually evolved when Nature enlarged the blueprint of a 5-inch lizard to make a 50-foot dinosaur. While the lizard is a relatively small organism, a dinosaur was a giant killing machine. Interestingly, *dinosaur* is a Greek word that means "terrifying monstrous lizard."

But, while the dinosaur's body grew to massive size, its brain didn't. Consider that, if a 5-inch lizard requires ten muscle cells to move its leg in a certain way, the massive 50-foot dinosaur might necessitate 10,000 muscle cells to make the same movement. However, the brain of each creature requires only *one* nerve to activate that movement.

The point is this: as dinosaurs' bodies became enlarged, their brains remained quite small. The fact that lizards are still here today and dinosaurs are extinct suggests that the dinosaurs' undersized brain, although able to support amazing reflex behaviors, wasn't adequate to sustain survival of their massive bodies during times of environmental upheaval.

Bringing that situation forward in time, the successful nature of the Industrial Age enabled human industry to evolve from small mom-and-pop shops into giant international corporations. Analogous to dinosaurs, corporations have large bodies of administrative bureaucracies commanded by decision-making executives with small, reptilian brains.

Be forewarned: the patterns expressed in humanity's corporate dinosaurs are a reiteration of the same life-threatening flaws that led to the extinction of animal dinosaurs.

As was the case with dinosaurs, the so-called brains of conventional corporations are effective when controlling the reflexive behavior and growth of their organizations—as long as the environment stays stable. However, giant corporations lack the neurological ability to control and adapt their massive bodies to survive in environments that are in upheaval.

One example is the U.S. auto industry in which executive brains continue to push gas-guzzling sport utility vehicles on consumers who recognize the world is facing a global oil crisis. An indication of their threatened extinction is the current junk-bond status of General Motors' once-valuable stock.

We can only imagine that the final dinosaurs might have gone on a feeding frenzy when they witnessed others of their species running amuck and collapsing into tar pits of extinction. Similarly, we see colossal entities today engorging themselves at the expense of others, as was the case in October 2008 when the U.S. banking institution, a fiscal dinosaur, quickly and easily consumed $700 billion of U.S. taxpayers' money.

Another interesting similarity between the corporate dinosaurs of humanity today and real-life—er, real-extinct—dinosaurs of yore is the fact that modern civilization is fueled by oil, which is often referred to as the blood of the dinosaurs. As industrial organizations drink the last of the dinosaurs' blood, current dinosaurian corporations are facing their own imminent extinction and, if we're not careful, the extinction of civilization as we know it.

Fortunately, we can also find hope within the fractal parallels of biological evolution.

While dinosaurs were the first reptile descendents to rule the world, two other paths of evolution—birds and mammals—were arising in the shadows.

Birds: Birds evolved as a direct spin-off from the ground-bound dinosaurs.

A self-similar pattern of evolution expressed itself in human history when inventors and entrepreneurs, still at the growing-lizard size of industrialization, paved the path for humanity's bird phase. The first key event in this evolutionary path was the flight of Orville and Wilbur Wright over the sands at Kitty Hawk, North Carolina, in 1903.

Mammals: At the same time that birds evolved from the dinosaur lineage, a new species also branched from small reptiles. These novel furry species, called mammals, represented the origins of a new class of neurologically sophisticated organisms. In reference to the way they raise their young, mammals are characterized as nurturers who encourage growth, development, and thriving.

Until 65 million years ago, small reptiles and meek mammals were at the mercy of the ruthless monstrous lizards. At that time, a planetary upheaval led to the extinction of the dinosaurs and, for a short time, birds ruled the world. However, in the absence of those mammoth killing machines, the more sophisticated mammals seized the opportunity to evolve and become masters of the biosphere.

EARTH—FROM THE BIRD'S-EYE VIEW

Just as with the emergence of bird species, the advent of aviation radically altered the development of human civilization.

Prior to aviation, Earth's massive size, with its terrestrial and maritime barriers, seemed to be a formidable obstacle that made integration of the world's population unimaginable. However, within a decade of the Wright Brother's flight, and, by the end of World War I in 1918, aircraft were capable of flying high over mountains, deserts, and oceans. Technological advancements continued, and, with today's jets, physical distance between continents and nations is no longer a relevant factor whether engaging in business or personal travel, whether waging war or peace.

Humanity's bird phase reached its peak in the late 1960s when aviation technology provided civilization with a new, bird's-eye perspective of Mother Earth.

In October 1968, the crew of the Apollo 7 space mission beamed back the first pictures of our planet, one of which appeared on the cover of *TIME* magazine in January 1969. Another, titled "Earthrise—Apollo 8," taken in December 1969, is a dramatic image of Earth rising over the lunar surface.

But humanity's ingenuity toward flight reached an even higher summit in July 1969 when Neil Armstrong, Edwin "Buzz" Aldrin, and Michael Collins landed their Apollo 11 spacecraft on the moon. When Armstrong, clad in a bulky space suit, alit on the lunar surface and uttered, "One small step for man; one giant leap for mankind," he was making a statement both profound and prophetic in the course of human evolution.

These events marked the first time that every citizen in the world could actually experience the finite nature of our beautiful planet and its isolation in space.

When birds, aviators, and astronauts fly above the surface of Earth, they gain a greater perspective of the planet than their water-based and land-based predecessors. When astronauts transmit their view of Earth as a blue-green gem suspended in the black emptiness of space back to people on the planet, they share that new perspective with the rest of humanity as well.

And those images, from that perspective, have had such a powerful effect on civilization that they have caused a change in the course of human evolution. Those images fostered and concretized the hippie notion, professed by visionaries such as Buckminster Fuller, that we are all one people traveling through the galaxy on tiny, fragile Spaceship Earth.[12]

Those images of our Nest in the Stars induced a quality of self-consciousness in humanity that kindled and ignited an innate mammalian desire in responsive people to support survival by taking care of the environment; keeping our food and bodies healthy; and raising our children, families, and communities in an atmosphere of love and harmony.

Inspired by those initial photos from space, visionary John McConnell created the Earth Flag in 1969. In 1970, the United States celebrated the inaugural Earth Day and initiated the U.S. Environmental Protection Agency. And the 1970s saw the enactment of five major pieces of legislation to protect the nation's air, water, and land.

Simply stated, in response to the perspective provided by astronauts, an ever-increasing number of former reptilian-phase humans experienced an emergent leap in evolution wherein they became aware that survival is contingent on nurturing the planet and all species as well as our individual selves. These awakened persons become the seeds of our next evolutionary leap, the emergence of humanity's mammalian phase.

In that regard, the current state of civilization resembles the fractal iteration of a self-similar pattern that occurred millions of years ago in animal evolution, a time when dinosaurs, birds, and primitive furry mammals shared an uneasy coexistence. Such a vision evokes an image of movie director Steven Spielberg's *Jurassic Park* in which humans run for their lives as monstrous dinosaurs, the equivalent of all-consuming corporations, such as "Enron-osaurus Wrecks" run amuck and threaten the survival of the meek. At some point in Earth's prehistoric history, an undetermined event led to the extinction of the ruling dinosaurs and opened an opportunity for mammals, the meek, to inherit the earth.

Likewise, the current ecological, economic, and population crises that face humanity are portents of the demise of dinosaur-like corporations and the rise of green-friendly human nurturers.

As we project our fractal pattern into the future, we see it is likely that current global stresses will precipitate the planet's next evolutionary leap as marked by the emergence of civilization's nurturing mammals as the dominant life force on the planet.

FRACTALS UNDER OUR SKIN

While fractal self-similarity within the vertebrate evolutionary pattern may offer insight into our own evolutionary human destiny, this particular pattern does not provide adequate information regarding how we should navigate our course in order to secure survival.

For that pattern, we must examine the fractal image from a different perspective: rather than charting the dynamic unfolding of the image, we must focus on the structural patterns inherent within the fractal image itself.

Beneath our skin is a community of cells that is 700 times larger than the population of the entire Earth. If humans were to model the lifestyle displayed by a healthy community of human cells, perhaps our societies and our planet would not have to contend with the impending sixth mass extinction. Consequently, our next step is to explore the Universe beneath our skin through the lens of fractal geometry. This eye-opening journey will reveal striking parallels between human and cellular society, and it will offer informative insights for living a healthy, happy life in a coherent world.

CHAPTER 12

TIME TO SEE
A GOOD SHRINK

"You know, our cells just might be smarter than we are."
— Swami Beyondananda

Fractal geometry provides for infinitely complex structures assembled from simple repeating self-similar patterns. The deeper you look into a fractal image, the more detail you discover. A cell and a human body are self-similar fractal images that share self-similar functions and needs in their quest to survive. Therefore, the life of a cell in the body and the life of a human in civilization are parallel realities, fundamentally self-similar.

Because cells and humans find themselves in similar biological circumstances, it naturally raises the question, "How can 50 trillion cells live in harmony and peace while a mere 7 billion people are on the verge of annihilating each other?" The answer to that question can be found by studying the fractal structure of Nature.

From the fractal viewpoint, it stands to reason that the organizing principles responsible for the evolution of multicellular communities would be fundamentally self-similar to the principles that govern humanity's survival. Consequently, it behooves us to shrink ourselves down to the size of a cell and enter the body on a fact-finding mission to see how cellular communities have become so successful. What works for the cell, works for the human, and what works for the human, will work for humanity.

Reverse engineering is the process used to reproduce another manufacturer's product by carefully examining the details of its construction or composition. By reverse engineering the dynamics and principles used by 50 trillion cellular citizens to successfully create the human body, we can learn valuable insights that can be directly applied in our quest to sustain human civilization.

CELLS-Я-US

Throughout our journey, we have emphasized that the human body is not merely a single entity, but a conglomeration of trillions of cells. Cells are the individual units of life, and our body is the cell's expression of community. Because we are made of cells, our body's life requires that we also care for our cells' survival.

Therefore, simple logic says that our body and our cells have the same needs: oxygen, water, nutrients, a controlled environment to insulate life processes from the extremes of surrounding elements, and protection from other life forms, such as viruses, that would deplete energy and resources. Likewise, humans and cells have to work, that is, expend energy, in order to survive. People go to work to provide for their families, and cells work together for the health of the body.

Why? What is it that drives all life forms, from the first bacterium to human beings, to perpetuate this cycle of life? That mysterious force is the biological imperative, the inborn mechanism that unconsciously motivates organisms, regardless of their size, to survive.

A species's ability to fulfill its innate drive to survive is predicated on the following basic factors: energy, growth, protection, resources, efficiency, and awareness.

If we were to create a Survival Index formula to assess the survivability of an organism, the equation would look like this:

$$\text{Survival} = \left(\begin{smallmatrix}\text{Total}\\\text{Energy}\end{smallmatrix} - \left[\begin{smallmatrix}\text{Growth + Protection}\\\text{Expenses}\end{smallmatrix}\right]\right) \times \left(\begin{smallmatrix}\text{Resource}\\\text{Availability}\end{smallmatrix}\right) \times \left(\text{Efficiency}\right) \times \left(\text{Awareness}\right)$$

Total Energy: Total energy represents the total amount of energy available to drive the organism's life's processes. Energy generates the body's behaviors and movements. In fact, a body without energy is called a cadaver.

Growth Mechanisms: Growth expenses represent the energy expenditures used by physiologic systems to secure energy, maintain the body's health and well-being, and help it grow. These growth mechanisms collectively contribute to the organism's ability to find, ingest, and digest food;

absorb nutrients; and eliminate waste. Growth occurs when the organism uses energy to convert nutrients into complex molecules needed to rebuild or replace worn-out cells.

Protection Mechanisms: Protection mechanisms are indispensable to survival. In the human body, these mechanisms include the adrenal system's fight-or-flight reaction to external threats and the immune system's response to internal pathogens.

Environmental threats force an organism to withdraw a substantial quantity of energy from its energy reserves and reallocate that energy toward the protection of its very life. The more fear or stress an organism perceives, the more energy it diverts for protection. Because growth and protection behaviors are funded by the organism's energy reserves, the cost of protection curtails or inhibits growth.

That is why, in our Survival Index, growth and protection processes subtract energy from an organism's system. Simply put, an organism's survival is compromised by the amount of energy it must expend to protect itself, which is why an organism can be literally scared to death!

Resources: Organisms derive energy from environmental resources. In fact, survival is predicated on an organism's ability to secure external energy of equal or greater value than the amount of internal energy spent to acquire and process those resources.

The act of acquiring and processing resources from external sources is called work.

The primary resources for biological organisms are air, water, and nutrients, which come from both chemical energy and nonmaterial energy from environmental fields.

Until the evolution of human beings, organisms relied on renewable resources for survival. Under this arrangement, the environment's resources were continuously replenished and Earth's many species were sustained over eons of time. Even when an individual organism died, the recycling of its physical remains contributed to the energy available for other individuals.

Humans, however, altered the biosphere's balance and harmony by evolving into a technology-based civilization in which survival is dependent on extraction of the planet's nonrenewable resources. The current oil crisis is only one of many examples of how our acquired dependence on nonrenewable resources threatens our existence. This situation, in which society's survival is linked to ever-diminishing external environmental resources, has sapped our internal energy and compromised humanity's future. Logically—not a smart move.

Efficiency: Efficiency, which is the measure of work accomplished compared to the amount of energy put into that work, is essential to survival. The efficiency by which an organism utilizes its energy resources is a primary factor in determining its survivability.

Through evolutionary advances in structure and functionality, organisms honed their operational efficiency over time. And, by using energy more efficiently, they were able to invest their conserved energy into further evolutionary development.

Awareness: Awareness represents an organism's ability to perceive, interpret, and respond to environmental information. As the basis of intelligence, awareness ranges from simple reflex responses to conscious action, and then to the more advanced intelligence offered by self-consciousness.

The fundamental cellular units of awareness are the membrane's receptor proteins and effector proteins that serve as perception switches, as described earlier. Because perception proteins can only form a monolayer in the membrane, increasing the level of an organism's awareness is the direct result of increasing its membrane surface area.

Specifically, an organism's collective awareness correlates to the amount of membrane surface area that the organism dedicates to processing environmental perceptions.

$$\text{Survival} = \left({\text{Total} \atop \text{Energy}} - \left[{\text{Growth + Protection} \atop \text{Expenses}} \right] \right) \times \left({\text{Resource} \atop \text{Availability}} \right) \times \left(\text{Efficiency} \right) \times \left(\text{Awareness} \right)$$

In light of current global crises, it is apparent that human survival skills are questionable, at best. As mentioned earlier, energy is required to sustain life, and the loss of energy manifests in weakness, illness, and death. In contrast to human beings, all other organisms are proven models of energy conservation and efficiency. We know this because organisms that failed to properly manage their life energy reserves are extinct.

Humans, who are vastly more wasteful than any other organism in the environment, are facing the same eventuality. Unfortunately, humanity's destruction of the biosphere could also lead to the mass extinction of even those more intelligent and more efficient organisms that have lived in harmony with the environment for millions of years.

The Survival Index reminds us that we are asleep, inefficient, and expending too much energy on wanton, unwarranted growth and protection. Consider the exorbitant expense of security, whether of the in-home or homeland variety.

A consideration of the factors that contribute to the Survival Index emphasizes that, in order to survive, we must reduce our protection expenditures, switch to renewable resources, become considerably more efficient, and wake up.

Government and financial leaders, trying to mend the current global economic system by applying bandages here and loans there and a big dollop of bailout to boot, are behaving like stewards on the Titanic, arranging the deck chairs as the ship is going down.

Perhaps, as Einstein suggested, it is time to resolve our problems through new thinking. Perhaps, in pursuit of vital knowledge, we must learn from ancient sages who advised, "The answers we seek lie within." Einstein echoed that wisdom when he wrote, "Look deep, deep into nature, and then you will understand everything better."[1]

So, as we descend into the inner workings of biology, we will focus on the factors listed in the Survival Index. We expect to find that an awareness of social and economic patterns expressed by successful eukaryotic cells and multicellular organisms, such as our own human bodies, can help us create a template to promote a healthier, more successful version of humanity.

ENORMOUS INSIGHTS FROM THE LITTLE PEOPLE

Communal life increases survivability by encouraging greater operating efficiency and awareness. For example, if a single cell possesses an *awareness potential* of *x*, then a colony of 30 cells would have a collective awareness potential of at least 30*x*. That means that the collective information within a community offers each resident cell an awareness potential many times greater than that possessed by their independent, free-living, unicellular cousins.

It was the drive to increase awareness that provoked individual primitive prokaryotes to assemble into the first communities, the social organizations called biofilms. Biofilms later evolved into individual eukaryotic cells, such as an amoeba or algal cell, which represent evolved versions of prokaryotic communities encapsulated within a cell membrane.

Around 700 million years ago, Nature reiterated an old strategy to increase awareness: assemble single cells, eukaryotes, into multicellular communities to share awareness and efforts for the mutual benefit of all. In these close-knit eukaryotic cell colonies, individual cells essentially performed the same jobs and pooled their productivity.

As colonies exceeded certain population limits, it was no longer efficient for all cells to do the same work. Communal cells began to partition workload among themselves, delegating specific tasks to different cells, a process called differentiation.

These very same developmental patterns were played out in early human civilization when families lived and traveled together as a clan. In these small, undifferentiated colonial groups, all members participated in the same life-preserving chores, primarily procuring food.

As clans grew into larger tribes, it was no longer efficient for all members to perform the same job. Therefore, individuals took on specific, differentiated communal responsibilities: some hunted, some gathered, and some protected the young and elderly. And as the size of tribes grew, the workload was further subdivided among the population, which resulted in a hierarchy of specialized workers.

Differentiated cells in a cellular community are akin to craftsmen. In the same way that human craftsmen organized into guilds, differentiated cells form tissues and organs whose products and services are required for the community's survival. For example, a differentiated cardiac muscle cell is a master of contraction, and organized guilds of cardiac cells comprise the heart. In exchange for their specialized cardiovascular services, cardiac cells receive complementary services from other guilds of highly skilled cells: nutrients from the digestive system, oxygen from the respiratory system, protection from the immune system, waste management through the excretory system, and world news through the nervous system.

The first heart, the first liver, and the first kidney represented the first businesses on Earth. The heart is the energy industry and its constituent cardiac cells are employees. Likewise, the immune system is the equivalent of the Environmental Protection Agency, and the white blood cells are its agents. The kidney is a waste-management organization with an amazing recycling program.

And here's the important lesson we can learn from these early enterprises: The success of these systems, as businesses, is not based on *competitiveness* with other organs and tissues. Rather, success is measured by how well each organ fulfills its job of *cooperating* with other systems.

The number of undifferentiated eukaryotic cells in primitive colonial organisms ranged from fewer than 30 to several hundred. From these humble roots, community planning and management enabled eukaryotes to create phenomenally successful multicellular organisms with cell populations numbering in the trillions.

Each individual cell in a giant multicellular civilization has the same physiologic functions, drives, and needs as individual humans in society. Cells are the equivalent of miniature people, each having personal lives while sharing the experience of community—and that's not just a metaphor.

The remarkable harmony displayed at the cellular level is the one truly noteworthy character that distinguishes successful eukaryotic cell communities from the current state of human society. Cellular societies that comprise our bodies truly exemplify the United States motto, *e pluribus unum*, "out of many, one." Each cell is an individual, yet they all behave and support one another.

Unity does not mean uniformity. A liver cell does not physically or functionally resemble a muscle cell, which, in turn, does not look like a nerve cell. The cells, while functionally forming a whole, are subdivided by borders into communities that we distinguish as uniquely different tissues and organs. Each community contributes a task, talent, or mission that supports the body's survival.

Each nation and culture on the globe is the equivalent of a tissue or organ in the larger super-organism referred to as humanity. In the manner that each organ system contributes to the economy of the body, each nation contributes to the economy of whole of humanity.

The cells that populate an organ may look different and live by different rules than neighboring cells just across the organ's border. The valuable work they do has more to do with their differences than similarities!

Across the globe today, countries see each other as rivals, and many countries are preoccupied with making other countries simply disappear altogether. If that behavior occurred within the body, it would be tantamount to your internal systems taking sides with the intention of banishing a particular organ or tissue. Which of your vital organs would you choose to banish out of existence? How might that impact your ability to thrive, let alone survive?

If it seems like a stretch to compare organs with nations, consider this fractal image: Built into the cell membrane, which is the skin that surrounds each eukaryotic cell, are protein perimeters that delineate territories. Within each of these membrane boundaries are selected populations of proteins that engage in specific functions. Partitioned membrane territories are the functional equivalent of specialized nano-organs. If these protein territories were stained using different colored dyes, their groupings in the membrane of the spherical cell would curiously resemble the outlines of national territories on a global map.

ARE OUR CELLS SMARTER THAN WE ARE?

We can learn far greater insights regarding the nature of successful communities when we focus our vision even deeper and observe the lives of cells on a more intimate level.

Consider the awesome job our cells do to bring us into the world every day. Then compare that with the mediocre job humans do in the category of "works and plays well with others." With that self-assessment, we might actually have to adjust our self-aggrandized intelligence downward a few notches and recognize that our cells are smarter than we are.

Observing the day-to-day operations of our cellular citizens may come as a blow to our collective ego because just about everything we humans do, including the development of technology, our cells did first and, to this very day, still do better.

For example, cells have:

- A *monetary system* that pays cells according to the importance of the work they do and stores excess profits in community banks.

- A *research and development system* that creates technology and manufactures biochemical equivalents of steel cables, plywood, ferroconcrete, electronic circuitry, and high-speed computer networks.

- An *environmental system* that provides air and water purification treatment that is more technologically advanced than humans have ever imagined. Ditto for the *heating and cooling system.*

- An exceedingly complex and extremely fast *communications system,* like the Internet, that sends zip-coded messages directly to individual cells.

- A *criminal justice system* that detains, imprisons, rehabilitates, and, yes, in a Kevorkian way, even assists with the suicide of destructive cells.

- *Full health-care coverage* that makes sure each cell gets all it needs to stay healthy.

- An *immune system* that protects the cells and the body like a dedicated National Guard.

TECHNOLOGY: CELLS HIT THE INDUSTRIAL AGE AGES AGO

As human technological innovations were introduced to the world, biologists frequently equated each new emerging technology with the mechanisms displayed by the body's systems. The steam engine led pioneering physiologists to compare pressure-creating pneumatics with the body's mechanical operation. When physicists first understood and harnessed electricity, biologists of that day equated the electrical power grid with the nervous system. More recently, neuroscientists have compared supercomputers with the brain. And computer scientists are so enamored with cell's information processing technology that they are currently incubating nerve cells on computer chips to meld their technologies.

It is important to recognize that there is a lot more to the marvels of the body's technology than just the cells. In the same manner that humans utilize engineered materials to construct buildings to house themselves and their enterprises, cells do the exact same thing. Here are a few examples.

Approximately one half of the body's mass is comprised of extracellular matrices, known as collagen. Collagen is a thread-like protein secreted by the cells into their surrounding environment. In much the same manner that a spider spins a web from its body to outside its body, the cells construct this extracellular structure around themselves. The shape of every organ, blood vessel, nerve, muscle, and bone is maintained by this supporting matrix of woven collagen protein fibers. In fact, if all the cells were removed from a human body, the extracellular collagen would maintain the body's structure intact as though it were a flexible, fibrous sculpture.

Collagen proteins are an engineering tour de force: these organic filaments can be woven into a fabric with the softness of silk, a trait characterized by a baby's bottom. But changing the weave pattern creates collagen textiles with the bullet-resistance of Kevlar. To gain an appreciation of the body's technological skill, collagen filaments spun into rope-like fiber, such as those that comprise tendons and ligaments, have vastly more strength, flexibility, and far less weight than equal-sized filaments of steel.

The collagen secreted by specialized bone-forming, body-architect cells, called osteoblasts, is like magnificent steel girders that shape massive skyscrapers. In the assembly process, osteoblasts decorate their collagen girders with proteins that cause the spontaneous formation of crystallized calcium, the body's equivalent of marble. These result in lightweight, extraordinarily strong calcified collagen grids that form bones.

To gain an appreciation for the body's ability in this endeavor, consider that a cell looking at a six-foot human body sees an object as proportionally as tall and magnificent as does a person gazing up at a 10,000-story marble building—including the mezzanine, the thirteenth floor, and the penthouse.

Chondrocytes are cells that manufacture cartilage, the body's equivalent of concrete. Pouring cartilage into preformed shapes molded by collagen matrices, chondrocytes create freestanding sculptures such as the nose and earlobe. Cartilage, like concrete, is fragile. Given a good bust in the nose, it quite literally fractures into pieces.

Fragility is an issue for the cartilage disk that the body uses as a cushion between individual vertebral bones in the spine. Ordinary cartilage in that position would be crushed to the consistency of gravel under the pressure of the backbone's weight-bearing movement. Therefore, eukaryote freemasons learned to reinforce their cartilage with steel-like collagen filaments, thus creating fibrocartilage, the organic equivalent of rebar reinforced ferroconcrete. The importance of this weight-bearing composite material in forming the intervertebral disk is generally only appreciated after one of them happens to slip.

Within the skin-enclosed body environment, inhabitant cells are the equivalent of marine organisms that live and breathe in a watery environment. Ingenious plumbing and filtration mechanisms, which include the lymphatic and circulatory vessel systems, continuously purify and recycle the body's life-providing water. Cellular technologies in the liver, kidneys, lungs, lymph nodes, and spleen provide the most advanced and efficient filtration systems on the planet. These organs eliminate and detoxify waste products, replenish vital life-sustaining components, and defend against invasive organisms with effectiveness far beyond that offered by human designers.

Sophisticated engineering feats, pioneered by the body and later created by humans for surgical implant and replacement operations, include hydraulic and mechanically operated valves, osmotic pressure pumps, countercurrent-exchange systems, mechanical leverage systems that utilize universal joints and linkages, and self-regulating feedback and feedforward information loops.

A more familiar technical innovation first created by the body's cells is color television. Human eyes are endowed with the same fundamental red-green-blue color system that creates full-color images on human-manufactured TV sets.

In the short history of computer science, electrical engineers have introduced transistors, capacitors, and batteries to high-speed, parallel-processing information networks, stereoscopic 3-D vision, and computer-generated imagery. And while these are amazing technological advancements, we must recognize that eukaryotic cells first put those systems into motion millions of years ago.

Perhaps the most amazing feat of the body's collective cellular citizens is the human brain, the most powerful computer system designed and created . . . ever! In an ongoing zealous endeavor to adapt human physiology to the human environment, building an information processing system that can rival the power of the human brain is the ultimate mission of every driven computer engineer.

In fact, scientists in the emerging field of *biomimicry* are reverse engineering biology's age-old technological advances in an effort to create new technologies that will sustain life on the planet.

THE CELLULAR ECONOMY: NO CELL LEFT BEHIND

The movements of protein molecules that provide bodily functions require energy to empower their actions. We become personally aware of the body's energy expenditures through the heat it both generates and conserves to keep the system at the proper operating temperature.

Cells in the body manage their energy needs by exchanging molecules of adenosine triphosphate (ATP), an adenosine molecule with three phosphate chemical groups attached to it. ATP is the molecular equivalent of a rechargeable battery, similar to the battery used in a mobile phone. Cells tap the energy from ATP molecules to empower cellular functions.

ATP molecules release a unit of energy when one of their three phosphates is clipped off. Discharging the energy in an ATP molecule causes it to become adenosine diphosphate (ADP), an adenosine molecule with only two phosphates. Through the efforts of their work, cells can recharge the ADP molecule by reattaching another phosphate and turning it back into an energized ATP molecule. Cells work to make ATP and expend ATP to do work.

ATP molecules are exchanged, like a currency, among the body's cells. Interestingly, biology textbooks often refer to ATP as the "coin of the realm," a reference to the fact that energy in human society is equated to money. The more dollars one has, the more energy one has to create and support life.

Insights into managing a sound economy are available if, as economists might say, we "follow the ATP." In exchange for ATP salaries, cells work for the system and pool their productivity. Cells can bank extra energy savings by storing ATP coins in their cytoplasm. ATP salaries are commensurate with the cell's contribution to the body. Cells whose efforts are more vital to the community get paid more ATP and may even be provided with cellular entourages that support their specialized functions. While cells are on different pay scales, every cell is provided with the basics of life: food, shelter, health care, and protection.

Excess energy, the equivalent of cellular profits, is stored in what might be called regional and national banks, physically represented by reserves of adipose, or fat cells. By their nature, energy reserves are true deposits. However, savings are not stored in individual accounts. Rather, all energy reserves are available for use by the entire community. At the behest of the body's government—which we will describe later in this chapter—energy reserves can be sent anywhere in the system where they are needed to build, upgrade, or repair the body's infrastructure. With this system of equity, cells freely contribute their efforts to the community and never have to worry about where their next ATP paycheck will come from.

In regard to ATP/ADP exchange, the body is a closed system, which means there's no external lending mechanism or procedure from which the body can borrow energy. Because there is no Federal Reserve Bank with power to coin ATP, when the system needs emergency funds, that energy must come from resources that already exist within the community. This means that cells cannot charge debt on an Ascended MasterCard to be repaid in a future lifetime—with or without interest. Therefore, true fiscal conservatives will be happy to know that the body's energy budget is always balanced.

A HEALTHY CENTRAL VOICE:
THE CELLULAR INTELLIGENCE AGENCY

Every cell that comprises the human body is an independent, intelligent, sentient being that, when given a proper environment, is self-sufficient and can survive on its own. However, a multicellular organism is not simply a bunch of self-serving eukaryotic cells crowded together under one skin; functionally, they form a community.

Community, by its nature, represents an organization of individuals who share common interests, attitudes, or goals. The key word is share. As a member of a community, a cell defers its own personal interests and agrees to support the whole. In return, the cell's survivability is enhanced by increased awareness and energy efficiency that comes from the cooperative community.

Survival is predicated on one's ability to accurately assess and respond to environmental information. Dispersed primitive prokaryotes in the first level of the biosphere's evolution communicated information across distances by releasing signals into the environment, and other prokaryotes received and responded to these signals.

Information exchange was enhanced in the next level of evolution when closely packed eukaryotes acquired membrane junctions that enabled them to physically connect, or plug in, to one another. Cell junctions are functionally analogous to computer cables used to create a network among a number of individual computers.

Increasing the population density in multicellular organisms led to many cells existing in the organism's internal regions without direct access to external environmental cues. This created a need for cells on the interior to receive messages from cells on the exterior.

Therefore, through differentiation, a new breed of eukaryotic cells, the nerve cells, formed in the skin where they could perceive environmental conditions and relay that information inward. This subsequently led to development of the nervous system, which is an information network that interconnects the cells in the community, regardless of their location, and enables two-way communication from internal organs to the skin and from the skin to the organs.

This flow of information between the external environment and internal cells makes the nervous system's regulatory function tantamount to the body's government.

The governing nervous system does not tell the other body cells how to do their jobs. The heart cells beat and cells of the digestive system process food because of their own built-in intelligence. Distributed within each organ system are clusters of nerve cells called ganglia. Ganglia resemble state governments that process local organ-related information, as distinct from the brain, which functions as the central government and manages what might be called the affairs of the "Federation of Organs."

As an example, if we were to remove the entire digestive system, mouth to anus, from the body and place food into the esophagus, the local nerve ganglia would move that food through the entire digestive process to the elimination of waste without any input from the central nervous system.

In addition to coordinating the functions within an organ system, ganglia exchange information with the brain, which integrates and coordinates data derived from the body's other systems. As the central information processing system, the brain trusts that the organs and organ systems will regulate their own functions, and it continues to operate under that protocol until it receives an indication that a job isn't being performed properly.

The allocation of management responsibility is analogous to the original intent of the U.S. Constitution, which states that anything not specifically designated as a power of the federal government is left to the regional authority of the states.

The nervous system not only perceives and organizes the body's response to environmental stimuli; it also learns and remembers information from past experiences. The efficiency gained by working in community enabled the body to invest significant energy to support an amazingly large population of nerve cells specifically dedicated to processing and memorizing learned perceptions. The enhanced information-handling capacity provided by the networking of a trillion cells in the brain enabled humans to learn how to rub two sticks together to create fire and, subsequently, to use fire to propel a rocket to the moon.

It is profoundly important to emphasize that the nervous system is not a top-down means of authoritarian control but, rather, an interactive communication system. In the same manner that a nation's government can generate rules and legislation for the populace, the brain can regulate certain bodily functions. In much the same manner as news networks, the brain broadcasts the perceptions of the day to every one of the body's 50 trillion cellular citizens.

But, again, good governments and healthy bodies operate with a two-way information exchange. Citizens can express their opinions by making telephone calls or sending letters to their legislators, by voting, or by protesting in the streets. Likewise, cellular citizens respond to information stimuli within the body by voicing their opinions to the central nervous system via communications that we perceive as emotions and symptoms—some of them gentle and some of them violent.

If the brain engenders wise and supportive governance, it will respond to the cellular community's feedback with leadership that offers each cellular citizen a life of healthful bliss. But, as is frequently demonstrated in our own world, if the brain is uninformed, out-of-touch, and unresponsive, it can stress a cellular community to the point of breakdown, disease, and death, which are the body's equivalent to anarchy, destruction, and warfare in civil society.

GROWTH, PROTECTION, AND THE BALANCE OF LIFE

For the last 150 years, Western civilization has chosen material science as its source of truth and wisdom about the mysteries of life. Allegorically, we may picture the wisdom of the Universe as resembling a large mountain. We scale the mountain in order to acquire knowledge, and our drive to reach the top of that mountain is fueled by the notion that, with enough proper knowledge, we could become masters of the Universe. And that image of an all-knowing master may simulate the iconic vision of a guru seated in a lotus position atop the mountain of wisdom.

Scientists are professional seekers, forging the path up the mountain of knowledge. Their search takes them into the Universe's uncharted unknowns. With each scientific discovery, humanity gains a better foothold to help scale the mountain. Ascension is paved one scientific discovery at a time. Along the path, science occasionally encounters a fork in the road. Do they take the left or the right? When confronted with this dilemma, the direction science chooses is determined by the consensus of scientists who are interpreting the acquired facts—as they were understood at the time.

Occasionally, scientists embark in a direction that ultimately leads to an apparent dead end. When that happens, they are faced with two choices: continue to plod forward with the hope that science will eventually discover a way around the impediment, or return to the fork in the road and reconsider the alternative path. Unfortunately, the more that science, and especially humanity, invests in one particular path, the more difficult it is to release the beliefs associated with that path, even if the chosen path leads to oblivion.

In *A Study of History*, a 12-volume analysis of the rise and fall of civilizations, British historian Arnold Toynbee introduced the notion that the cultural mainstream clings to fixed ideas and rigid patterns even in the face of imposing environmental challenges. He maintained that threatening challenges would inevitably be resolved by what he described then as *creative minorities*. Known today as cultural creatives, these active agents of change transform old, outdated philosophical truths into new, life-sustaining cultural beliefs.[2]

A Google search reveals that, currently, hundreds of thousands of cultural creatives are working around the globe, each actively participating in a communal effort to transform humanity. These cultural creatives will very likely be the bearers of information that will bring about spontaneous evolution.

The fundamental factors that cultural creatives must consider when assessing the survivability of humanity or any other living organism are elaborated in the Survival Index presented earlier. Using this formula's fundamental determinants to score the current viability of human civilization reveals that we are failing on many fronts.

$$\text{Survival} = \left(\begin{smallmatrix}\text{Total}\\\text{Energy}\end{smallmatrix} - \left[\begin{smallmatrix}\text{Growth + Protection}\\\text{Expenses}\end{smallmatrix}\right]\right) \times \left(\begin{smallmatrix}\text{Resource}\\\text{Availability}\end{smallmatrix}\right) \times \left(\text{Efficiency}\right) \times \left(\text{Awareness}\right)$$

In regard to the factor of global Resources, civilization is currently facing a grim future as shortages of nonrenewable materials threaten our way of life. Awareness of the threats posed by trashing the planet has led to a recent spate of survival-oriented books, videos, Websites, and activist movements, each offering green, life-sustainable alternatives. Every day, awakening cultural creatives contribute to the development of renewable energy resources, recyclable products, and the return to organic farming.

Considering the Efficiency factor, human civilization unequivocally receives the lowest score of all the living organisms on Earth. The United States and, to a lesser degree, other Westernized cultures are trampling the biosphere with an enormously large footprint in regard to the planetary costs of maintaining their existence. The inefficiency of a fossil-fuel-driven civilization and its cost in terms of planetary desecration are legendary. The act of indiscriminately fouling Earth's oceans, lakes, and rivers, and then paying exorbitant prices for a bottle of supposedly clean drinking water, is humanity's inefficiency Edsel. The good news is that cultural creatives are currently out in force, providing new ideas and thought to support humanity's pass-or-fail crash course in Efficiency 101.

The Protection factor directly influences the equation's resources and efficiency categories. The fact that we have spent $15 trillion worth of energy and environmental resources on the military-industrial complex to fight one another is the most egregious example of inefficiency ever displayed in the biosphere. Humanity will not survive if it continues to waste more people, money, and resources on what amounts to self-destruction. The self-healing process of turning our weapons into plowshares begins with this awareness.

The Awareness factor is not only important to survival, it is the driving force behind evolution. Throughout human history, civilization has trod a tortuous path where every twist and turn has been guided by an evolving and self-correcting collective awareness. The radically revised awareness of the Universe and its operating principles offered by new-edge science indicates that humanity is primed for an imminent and major course correction.

The Internet, one of civilization's most important technical advances, is set to play a profoundly important role in humanity's evolution. This information network offers every human cell with access to the technology an opportunity to instantly receive and disseminate new life-enhancing awareness throughout the community. In this sense, the Internet serves as humanity's peripheral nervous system that interconnects humans from all over the globe and integrates their collective awareness.

Energy is the last, but certainly not least, of the factors affecting our survival. As the Survival Index emphasizes, energy is life. Consequently, the judicious use of energy is a fundamental consideration when determining an organism's fate. The energy factor relates to the differential between the energy spent by an organism and the energy its life processes generate. Second-grade arithmetic clearly demonstrates the consequences of spending more than what is earned.

LET THEM EAT GUNS

Growth and protection represent energy-expending work that is necessary for organismal survival. Over the course of human history, there has been a gradual, yet steadily increasing imbalance in the energy expenditures allotted for growth versus that spent on protection. Physiologists recognize that similar imbalances in the body's energy distribution represent a primary cause of disease and death. The fractal reverberation of that unbalanced pattern is also having a negative effect on the vitality of civilization.

An organism's life-sustaining functions can be conveniently divided into those that support growth, which include reproduction, and those that provide protection. From a study of individual cells in a culture dish, we can observe a physiologic conflict between growth and protection behaviors.

When nutrients are placed in front of a cell, the cell will move toward the nutrients, open and ready to assimilate them. When toxins are placed in front of a cell, however, the cell will close down and move away from the threatening stimulus. Growth behaviors, expressed as openness and forward movement, are completely opposite of closed, retreating protection responses. Therefore, being open *and* closed or moving forward *and* backward at the same time are mutually exclusive, impossible behaviors. Simply, a cell cannot be in a state of growth and protection at the same time.[3]

The first organisms to appear on Earth were free to abound in the absence of threatening predators. Consequently, the primary physiologic processes to evolve were those designed to support growth. Later, the advent of species that lived off of other organisms necessitated the development of effective protection behaviors, which were primarily designed for emergency situations.

Ideally, energy is expended for growth and reproduction with as little as possible spent on defense. This simple differential in energy allocations is due to the fact that energy used for growth nets more energy for the system while energy used for protection offers no return on investment.

That is why Nature designed protection systems with the hope that they would never be used or, at worst, used sporadically to help organisms escape the occasional clutches of life-threatening predators. Certainly, the body's defense mechanisms were never intended nor designed to be used 24/7, as is too often the case with great numbers of humanity today.

Therefore, if an organism's need for protection is out of balance and plagued by chronic ongoing fears and threats, the excessive energy resources required for protection directly compromise energy reserves needed to sustain health.

Based on functional responsibilities, cells that comprise the body can be divided into two populations: those that contribute to the viscera and those that comprise the somatic system. The viscera are the fundamental organs related to bodily growth and maintenance, such as the digestive, respiratory, nervous, and reproductive systems. The somatic system, represented by the arms, legs, and outer wall of the body, provide protection, support, and mobility.

When the body is in growth, the system primarily sends its energy to the visceral organs while the somatic system plays a secondary role. In contrast, when faced with external threats, the body sends more blood to the somatic system to energize fight-or-flight responses while the visceral organs take a backseat to the action.

When the body's central intelligence identifies threatening signals from the external environment, it activates a specialized system called the Hypothalamus-Pituitary-Adrenal (HPA) axis. Regulatory signals released by the HPA axis primarily include stress hormones, such as adrenaline and cortisol. These chemical signals constrict the blood vessels in the viscera, which preferentially redirects blood flow to the somatic system. There, the extra blood provides the energy, in the form of nourishment, to the muscles and bones used to protect the body from those external threats. When the HPA axis is activated, the suppression of visceral blood effectively reduces energy supplies that would normally be used for growth.[4]

In severe situations, an organism will fight or flee until all of its accessible energy reserves are depleted and it falls victim to the predator. In the best-case scenario, the intended prey escapes and is later able to shut down its protective HPA functions. The consequent cessation of stress-hormone secretion then allows an ample amount of blood to, once again, flow through the visceral veins, nourish the body's growth mechanisms, and replenish expended energy.

These same physiologic processes also apply to the cells of humanity when a nation's central voice signals a threat of attack. When danger is imminent, activation of the HPA axis has the same effect on a nation as it has on individual citizens. Under such circumstances, a country diverts its energy reserves from growth to defense.

This was strikingly apparent in the United States in the days following September 11, 2001, when fear of further attacks inhibited the country's growth processes to such an extent that the economy stalled. Unaware of growth-protection dynamics, President George W. Bush challenged the nation's innate biological intelligence by going on national television and trying to coax growth by announcing, "America is open for business."

Similarly, the U.S. Department of Defense is the nation's functional equivalent of the body's protective adrenal system, which provides adrenaline and cortisol to fuel and mobilize fight or flight. When feeling threatened, the country preferentially directs its energy reserves to the military.

Of course, this means the country must redirect funds from growth-oriented agencies, such as the Department of Health and Human Services as well as the Environmental Protection Agency, which is the equivalent of the body's immune system. Budget cuts in these departments inevitably compromise the growth and maintenance of the country's infrastructure. And, as with any living organism, a country that drains its resources by maintaining a prolonged defense posture is susceptible to disruption and collapse.

A vivid illustration of how regulated growth and protection responses affect a nation was evident in the United States in the 1950s and '60s when the government scared the population into believing that Russia represented an imminent threat to survival. In those years, people across the country were subjected to frequent air-raid drills during which blaring sirens signaled the public to flee to underground bomb shelters. Up to the moment of the warning signal, communities were generally engaged in pleasurable and productive growth processes. However, after the air-raid alarm was sounded, people ceased their growth-related endeavors and sought the protection of the shelters.

After the all-clear signal sounded, people returned to their jobs and the community resumed its growth activities. However, consider the consequences if those were actual alerts and there was no all-clear signal. In that scenario, the population would be forced to stay in the protection posture. How long could they survive that way? For as long as their reserve of food, water, and other energy-sustaining supplies held out. After that, they would die.

It's easy to see that time spent in the bomb shelter is time away from commerce and other constructive human activities. However, shutting down growth processes insidiously worsens the situation because workers in a state of protection are unable to re-provision their necessary, life-sustaining resources.

With this human example, we see, again, as we did by watching cells presented with nutrients and toxins earlier, that protection and growth are mutually exclusive behaviors. As an example, the current protracted War on Terror that is being waged by the United States has bankrupted its reserves and profoundly compromised its survival. Based on government-created fears, the U.S. has chosen guns over butter and, as a consequence, no longer has resources for either.

We have linked the nation's adrenal system to the role of the Department of Defense. But let's also consider that the name of this department and its functions of war do not accurately reflect the parallel role played by the body's adrenal system. While the adrenal system is used for protection responses, it is also the primary system engaged when carrying out external rescue responses, such as running into a burning building to save a child or pulling people to safety from raging floodwaters. Occasionally, the Department of Defense engages in such life-sustaining efforts when it serves in disaster relief operations or delivers food and medical supplies in humanitarian exercises, but, in contrast to the adrenal system, the military is more often engaged in a war campaign.

Perhaps we should rename the military establishment as the Department of Mobility, a title that more accurately reflects the role of the adrenal system. Motivated by that name, we could maintain the function of a military-capable organization without expressing our society's collective belief in the perpetually adrenalizing necessity of war.

MEN ARE FROM PROTEIN, WOMEN ARE FROM LIPIDS

Delving deeper into the fractal pattern of life and culture reveals it is no coincidence that a civilization dominated by patriarchal authoritarian governments is preoccupied with protection while matriarchal civilizations focus on growth and fertility.

Over the last several thousand years, human nature has tended to perceive the world in terms of opposing polarities: good-bad, right-wrong, black-white, male-female, and spiritual-mechanical are just a few examples of these dueling dualities. But there is one profound and enduring duality that actually reflects a basic property of chemistry.

Two fundamental classes of molecules created from elements in the periodic table exhibit profoundly different physicochemical properties. Referred to as polar and non-polar molecules, their differences are best understood in terms of water and oil.

Water molecules are polar, which means they have localized regions of positive and negative charges. In that regard, they are analogous to magnets, which are also distinguished by their opposing north and south polarities. Because opposite charges attract and form tight bonds, polar molecules can physically assemble into large, rigid structural complexes.

Even though the chemical bonds that hold the atoms of an oil molecule together are highly energized, lipid molecules are non-polar because their polarizing charges are evenly distributed throughout the molecule and, consequently, do not possess localized sites of positive and negative charge.

Chemical bonds that hold atoms together in a non-polar lipid molecule possess six to ten times more energy than chemical bonds in an equal weight of polarized protein and carbohydrate molecules. This means that Nature uses non-polar lipid molecules to store biological energy, a fact that is reflected in the body's accumulation of fat. The relative absence of localized sites of attractive and repulsive forces in non-polar molecules allows them to form fluid communities. However, the same non-polar character prevents lipids from assembling into rigid structures.

Filling a beaker with non-polar molecules is like filling it with atom-sized ping-pong balls. Because they do not bind to one another, each ball is free to move and form fluid-like associations. In contrast, a beaker of polar molecules more closely resembles a beaker filled with nano-sized magnets that automatically assemble into a solid, tightly packed mass in which molecules align and couple their polar charges.

Upon throwing a mixture of ping-pong balls and bar magnets into the same beaker, the tightly coupled polarized magnets would clump together and separate from the loosely organized ping-pong balls. This molecular imagery reveals why water's polar molecules physically separate from oil's non-polar molecules and why water droplets bead up while oil droplets flatten to a thin film.

Interestingly, the first differential between masculine and feminine traits is manifest in the difference between polar and non-polar molecules. Non-polar molecules express a characteristic similar to females: when assembled together, they create a harmonious fluid community. In contrast, males resemble polar molecules: when mixed together in a group, they engage in a power struggle as the molecules self-assemble into a polarized, strongest-to-weakest hierarchy.

The interaction of polar and non-polar molecules over time provided for the four fundamental types of macromolecules, which are complexes comprised of very large numbers of atoms. The fundamental building blocks of cells are macromolecules that include proteins, fats, sugars, and nucleic acids.

Proteins are polar molecules; fats are non-polar lipids; and, interestingly, the reproduction-related nucleic acids, DNA and RNA, represent the union of polar amine groups and sugars derived from non-polar lipids.

The origin of life was totally dependent on the cooperative interactions of polar and non-polar chemistry because, together, they created the primal biological organelle, the cell membrane. The basic building block of the cell membrane is the phospholipid, a molecule assembled from a polar phosphate chemical group and a non-polar lipid. Phospholipids simultaneously express both polar and non-polar traits and, in that capacity, are able to physically interface with both realms.

By providing a water-impermeable lipid boundary, the cell membrane's feminine lipids created a controllable internal environment, the primal womb, which, by definition, represents a place of origination and development. However, life only arises within this womb through the cooperative action of polarized masculine proteins that physically support the cell membrane and, more importantly, generate movement, that is, the work that creates physiology and life.

The cytoplasmic organelles created in the original cellular womb can be divided into two functional categories based on whether they support the cell's visceral functions or somatic functions. Visceral cytoplasmic elements are the membranous organelles associated with growth and maintenance. The cell's somatic elements are primarily represented by a matrix of fibrous polar proteins that provide support and motility. The membranous visceral organelles reflect the expression of the feminine traits: growth and reproduction. The fibrous matrix of the somatic system expresses masculine traits: physical support, protection, and movement.

V=Visceral realm: membranous organelles responsible for growth and reproduction
S=Somatic realm: protein filaments responsible for support, protection, and movement

Visceral and somatic functions are complementary. In a state of growth, the membranous feminine visceral organelles are the primary contributors while the masculine matrix functions as support. However, when a cell is in danger, these roles are reversed. In a state of protection, the masculine proteins protect while receiving supportive energy from the viscera.

The structure and functions of the human body reflect a self-similar fractal pattern to that of the cell. Our organs of growth and reproduction are contained in our viscera, the gut, and our arms, legs, and body wall comprise our somatic system.

The human male body is physically defined by its polarized proteins, the primary macromolecules that characterize muscle. The musculature is a physical feature that reflects the male's primary role in providing support and protection. In contrast, the human female body shape is defined by non-polar lipids, which are energy-laden fat deposits that distinguish a woman's figure from a man's.

The evolution of the super-organism that is humanity also reveals a masculine-feminine duality. Western civilization's focus on the physical material realm and technology reflects masculine traits that emphasize structure, protection, and polarity. Eastern cultures were built on feminine characteristics associated with spirituality, energy, growth, and harmony. The potential derived from male-female cooperation is implied in the old adage, "When East meets West."

In *The Chalice and the Blade*, Riane Eisler's impressive research emphasized that the earliest European civilizations were feminine in character; they were egalitarian, worshipped a Mother Goddess, and focused on agrarian endeavors. According to Eisler's thesis, these cultures were systematically destroyed some 5,000 years ago by invading Kurgans, who were wandering cattle herders from the steppes of central Russia. These mobile tribes were technologically advanced and violent warriors who overran and destroyed Europe's peaceful egalitarian agrarian civilizations. In the wake of the Kurgan invasion, civilization adopted its current masculine character of worshipping warring male gods in a society controlled by a hierarchy of male powermongers obsessed with control, protection, and technology.[5]

The survival of civilization has been threatened by nearly five millennia of testosterone-driven patriarchal authoritarian dominance. This one-sided distortion in leadership has led to a gravely out-of-balance world that emphasizes the masculine trait of protection at the expense of the feminine's life-giving contributions for growth.

In order to restore life and vitality to our world, it is now necessary to reintegrate the complementary values of the sacred feminine. Whether seen as a reunion of East and West or a reunion of hemispheres—as with the South American mythology of the condor and the eagle—a balanced masculine-feminine field is the first step we must take to restore planetary health, love, and harmony.

As we will learn in our unfolding conversation about how the body politic can model the success of the human body, an important key to our evolutionary emergence resides in the reconciliation of what we currently perceive as opposites. Only by integrating formerly dueling dualities can we attain the unity that will shape our hopeful future.

In the next chapter, we will play in the playing field where this integration will take place.

CHAPTER 13

THE ONE SUGGESTION

*"We are all one with the same One,
the inescapable Oneness. The Universe
has us surrounded. Might as well surrender!"*
— Swami Beyondananda

Having submerged ourselves deep into the world of the micro—assessing the fascinatingly functional civilization of our cells—it's now time to get macro and focus our attention on the environment that stretches way beyond our skin. Epigenetic science reveals that the story of life doesn't end at the edge of our body; it only begins there. That's because the fate of a living organism is directly influenced by information gleaned from its surrounding field.

Biological behavior and genetic activity are directly formulated to complement an organism's perception of its environment. In human biology, cell-controlling environmental stimuli are perceived and processed by the brain and interpreted by the machinations of the mind. The mind's consciousness is then converted by epigenetic mechanisms into the physiology that controls the health and fate of cells that comprise the human body.

As Einstein emphasized, "The field is the sole governing agency of the particle." In human biology, the field is represented by the mind and the particle is the body. While the brain is a physical mechanism, the mind represents a brain process and is, itself, a non-physical field of information. While properties of physical matter, such as the brain, conform to the principles of Newtonian or classical physics, the operation of the mind's energy fields employ the fundamental mechanics of quantum physics. As described below, the mind is a primary factor in shaping the character of our lives. And, as spiritualists have long believed and physicists have discovered, much of what we call reality might more accurately be seen as a figment of our imagination.

HOW REAL IS REALITY?

The fact that the mind of the observer influences the outcome of experiments is one of the most profound insights introduced by quantum mechanics. This new physics acknowledges that we are not merely passive observers of our world but, rather, we are active participants in its unfolding. While almost everyone thinks that the physical world we observe is real, quantum physicists have verified as fact that the world we observe is not real. Astrophysicists Sir Arthur Eddington and Sir James Jeans recognized this immediately when physicists adopted the principles of quantum mechanics in 1925.

Commenting on this mind-boggling insight, Jeans wrote: "the stream of knowledge is heading toward a non-mechanical reality; the Universe begins to look more like a great thought than like a great machine. Mind no longer appears to be an accidental intruder into the realm of matter . . . we ought rather hail it as the creator and governor of the realm of matter."[1]

Interestingly, Einstein came to the same conclusion; however, he personally couldn't accept it as truth. Consequently, he spent the rest of his life—without success—trying to repudiate this disconcerting implication inherent in quantum mechanics.

Quantum physics has absolutely verified that information processed by our minds influences the shape of the world in which we live. With all that that implies for the meaning of human existence, why has this profound awareness not become part of our everyday world? As Eddington explained, "It is difficult for the matter-of-fact physicist to accept the view that the substratum of everything is of mental character."[2] Physicists have shied away from this truth simply because it is so alien to their everyday perception of life.

Conventional physics courses suggest that the principles of quantum mechanics that govern wave-particle interactions only apply at the level of atoms. By restricting quantum physics to the subatomic world, it has become a general assumption that quantum mechanisms do not apply to our personal lives and world affairs. Therefore, today's physicists have completely failed to inform the public of the purely mental nature of the Universe.

Fortunately, leaders in the field, such as Johns Hopkins University physicist Richard Conn Henry, are addressing the misperceptions about the perceived primacy of the material world. Henry offered an elegantly simple definition on the true nature of the Universe, "The Universe is nonmaterial—it is mental and spiritual. Live, and enjoy."[3]

Our minds actively co-create the world we experience. Consequently, by changing our beliefs, we have an opportunity to affect world change. While this profound insight represents a soundly grounded scientific principle, the questions remain: "Does it work in practice? Are there studies or observations that actually demonstrate that quantum mechanical principles apply to people and society? Does the energy field of the human mind truly influence the physical character of our world?"

Theoretical physicist Amit Goswami sought an answer to these questions by designing an experiment to see if human behavior is influenced by quantum mechanical activities. Goswami chose to work with the quantum principle of *nonlocality,* a fundamental property displayed by subatomic particles such as photons and electrons. As defined by this principle, the physical traits of particles become intimately connected, or entangled, once they interact with one another. If a characteristic of one of a pair of entangled particles is altered, for example, the change of its rotational spin from clockwise to counterclockwise, the other particle instantly responds with a complementary change of its spin—even though vast distances may separate the particles. Einstein referred to nonlocality as "spooky action at a distance."

Goswami's experiment was designed to see if the operation of the human mind expressed the quantum property of nonlocality. Specifically, he asked whether human brains could behave as entangled particles so that a change in activity of one subject's mind would induce a complementary change in the mind of an entangled partner. Goswami had pairs of subjects engage in a meditative interaction in which they were instructed to maintain direct communication, that is, to feel each other's presence at a distance.

The subjects were separated by a distance of 50 feet and placed in electromagnetically shielded Faraday chambers where their EEG activity was monitored. Goswami flashed a strobe light into one of the subject's eyes, inducing an *evoked potential,* which is a distinctive electrical pattern that reveals the brain's response to a sensory stimulus.

When individuals were mentally linked by meditation, eliciting an evoked potential in one partner instantly induced an identical evoked potential in the entangled partner's brain even though the second individual did not physically experience the stimulus. This experiment demonstrates that activity in one person's brain can influence the activity in the brain of a separated entangled partner. The non-local transfer of potentials from brain to brain reveals that the brain has a quantum nature that operates at the macro level.[4]

Large numbers of studies have observed that the minds of presumably frail and powerless humans consciously and measurably influence the field, which, in turn, shapes our world. In this chapter, we will explore further evidence that, in the real world of human actions and events, an invisible moving field does, indeed, exist—and that our thoughts, emotions, and actions are important in how that field is shaped. We will provide information regarding how our thoughts, empowered by feelings in our hearts, can be harnessed to bring about peace and harmony in our world.

We end the chapter with a suggested path of action—a human operating system, if you will—that will support the success of our species. The one suggestion that we suggest is based on information that has been handed down by spiritual teachers throughout the ages, information that is now resoundingly confirmed by new-edge science.

THE FIELD EXPERIMENTS

History acknowledges that the Wright Brothers flew a heavier-than-air aircraft in 1903. But it wasn't until seven years later, when people actually saw a photograph of President Theodore Roosevelt in an airplane that the average American finally realized that flight was possible. If you had the opportunity to ask the typical person on the street up to the moment that picture appeared, "When will humans fly?" the answer would likely have been, "When pigs fly!" In a similar way, the average person today is unfamiliar with the new sciences that incontrovertibly demonstrate the existence of an invisible energy field that influences life.

Since the founding of modern science, researchers have been on a mission to understand the domain of the observable and measurable Universe. That which could not be seen—and could not be measured—was, by definition, outside the realm of science. While mystical and religious thought has always expressed belief in what physicists named the field, it is only in the past century that science has developed the instrumentation to definitively measure the field's existence and its influence.

Biomedical scientists bold enough to explore outside the bounds of conventional Newtonian explanations are now discovering a vast and uncharted *playing field* that seems to defy the conventional laws of the physical Universe. That this playing field is also a *praying field* indicates that experience and knowledge are leading us into a domain where science and spirit merge to become cooperative evolutionary forces.

Just as surely as we are aware of the presence of an invisible field when we observe iron filings arranging themselves around a magnet, we can now actually see the presence of life-influencing invisible energy fields through use of advanced medical scanning technologies such as CAT scans, MRI scans, PET scans, and sonograms.

While scanned images may reveal cancers and symptoms of other diseases, it is important to realize that scans are not actual photographs of physical tissues and internal organs; if they were, the images would show only external skin. Rather, scan images are visualizations of invisible radiant energy fields, and the characteristics of the invisible field are an energy complement of the body's physical reality.

Most scan technologies are employed to read the character of energy fields within the body. However, there are a number of new technologies that actually read energy fields that radiate from our bodies into the environment. Instruments have been designed that detect a beating heart's powerful electric and magnetic fields meters away from its source. Field-influencing electromagnetic messages broadcasted from our hearts have been shown to entangle with the hearts of others in the field.

Similarly, a new scanning system, magneto-encephalography (MEG), actually reads the brain's neural energy patterns through a probe that is some distance from the body. MEG technology provides physical proof that brain activity is broadcast into the environment in the same way that a tuning fork radiates a sound through the field.

TIME ISN'T WHAT IT USED TO BE

Just as surely as we humans thought we knew a century ago that we couldn't fly, most of us today have been programmed to believe that time is an absolute that moves in only one direction. Well, maybe. Maybe not.

As startling as it may seem, researcher Dean Radin, author of *Entangled Minds,* and journalist Lynne McTaggart, author of *The Field* and *The Intention Experiment,* offer proof that sometimes we respond to future events ahead of time. Consider the experiment where subjects are wired to biometric equipment that registers emotional reactions. They are shown a succession of slide images, the vast majority of which are peaceful and pleasing. But about 3 percent of the pictures—randomly interspersed—are shocking images portraying sex or violence. Subjects registered an emotional response to the disturbing images seconds *before* those pictures actually appeared on the screen. How can this be, given our current concept of linear and progressive time?[5]

Or, consider Dr. Radin's surprising studies with random number generators, which are computers programmed to continuously generate sequences of numbers in an erratic fashion. When graphically mapped out, the computer's number sets display a random pattern—except on rare occasions. Exceptions are distinguished by the fact that, at those times, the number sets are no longer random but unexpectedly express pattern and coherence.

The amazing part of the story is that the loss of randomness usually occurred when there was a global event that simultaneously captured the attention of a vast number of people. Apparently, it doesn't seem to matter what or how people think or feel about the event, only that their attention is coherently focused on the same event. This commonly occurs each year at the time of the Super Bowl, but it has also been noted during three events that had the world's focused attention: the O. J. Simpson trial, the funeral of Princess Diana, and the attack on the World Trade Center.[6]

Now here is where Einstein's "spooky action at a distance" becomes even spookier. When the pattern of spikes in global coherence is mapped on to a graph, it creates a typical bell-shaped curve. Nothing unusual about that, except that, in this case, the devices that plot the bell-shaped graph over time reveal that numbers begin to get more coherent at a particular time *before* the event. Thus, it was that two hours prior to when the first plane hit the World Trade Center on September 11, the number generators were already *responding* to *pre*-verberations of the shocking moment![7]

Helmut Schmidt, a German-born physicist and psi researcher of purported psychic abilities, had long been interested in the relationship between the observer and the observed phenomenon. Having observed that the observer could influence random events through intention, Schmidt posed a deliciously intriguing question: could an observer influence the outcome of that event—even if it had already happened?[8]

Schmidt connected his random number generator to an audio device that would record a click in either the left or right ear of a set of headphones. He then made a number of recordings of the number generator's left-right output; making sure that no one, including himself, could observe the results. A day later, a volunteer was given a recorded tape and told to mentally influence the outcome so that more clicks would occur on one side than the other.

Schmidt compared the distribution of left-right clicks on influenced tapes with those on uninfluenced control recordings. While control tapes showed purely random results, to his surprise, Schmidt found that his subjects influenced the distribution of clicks on tapes recorded two days earlier!

Interestingly, this time travel experiment only worked if the recorded clicks went unobserved until after the volunteer had a chance to influence them. If anyone observed the original results before the time the experiment was conducted, their observations could not be subsequently influenced.

The implications of this experiment are mind-boggling and paradigm busting. Sometimes psychic healers report healing a condition by going back to a time before the condition existed. While this sounds like a bunch of woo-woo hoodoo, the laws of quantum mechanics suggest it may, in fact, be possible. If nothing else, Radin's and Schmidt's experiments provoke us to seriously reconsider the commonly accepted idea of linear time because that concept now appears to be a bit shaky. And what is it that exists beyond time? The field.

THE PLAYING FIELD AS A PRAYING FIELD

Not only do these studies challenge our concept of time, this research also calls into question our notions of distance and space. Interestingly, some of the most far-out, woo-woo experiments have been in the service of the most practical matters—like national defense. In his book *Miracles of Mind*, physicist Russell Targ describes his participation in CIA-sponsored *remote viewing* experiments at the Stanford Research Institute.

Remote viewing is a specialized practice of clairvoyance that was developed by the military to explore enemy installations halfway around the globe. Persons adept at remote viewing are told a latitude-longitude coordinate. "Adepts," as they are called, then enter into what amounts to be a deep meditation. While in that altered state, the adept can actually describe landscapes and structures at the provided location even though they have never been there.

According to Targ, one of the more gifted remote viewers was Pat Price, who had been the Police Commissioner of Burbank, California. In an experiment sponsored by the CIA, Price was given only the latitude and longitude of what turned out to be a Soviet nuclear weapons laboratory in Siberia. With nothing but those coordinates to go on, he was able to sketch the plant with incredible precision. Satellite photos later confirmed the remarkable accuracy of his sketches.[9]

These and similar remote viewing experiments demonstrate that the field transcends distance as well as time. The implications are profound, not only for long-distance spying but also for long-distance healing.

Genetic determinism aside, Russell Targ's willingness to apply science to the mysteries of life was passed down to his daughter, Elisabeth Targ. Elisabeth was a rigorously trained medical doctor, scientist, and psychiatrist who was curious about the emerging science of psychoneuroimmunology, the study of how an individual's psychology controls the activity of their immune system.

The Institute of Noetic Sciences recruited Elisabeth in 1995 to conduct experiments on the effectiveness of remote prayer on healing. Having grown up in a household where science was considered to be religion, she had a natural skepticism about the value of prayer in any form. Nonetheless, she had observed from her father's work that there were, indeed, mysterious ways through which the mind could influence the field.

Elisabeth's directive was to design an impeccable experiment that would determine if positive or negative thoughts actually influence events. To answer that question, Targ and her co-researcher Fred Sicher chose to study if prayer could influence the progression of AIDS. As subjects for their experiment, Targ and Sicher selected a homogenous population of AIDS patients who were expressing the same degree of illness.

They employed 40 religious and spiritual healers, from evangelical Christians to Native American shamans and just about everything in between, in a double-blind study wherein no one but the healers knew which patients were receiving healing prayers. All healers had one thing in common—they all had a history of successfully treating what the medical community referred to as hopeless cases.

Twenty patients were divided into two groups. Each group received the exact same standard medical treatment, but only one group was the focus of remote healing prayers. The healers never met their patients and were only provided with a name, a photo, and a T-cell count. Each of the 40 healers was asked to "hold an intention for the health and well-being" of a patient one hour a day, six days a week, for ten weeks. With 40 healers praying for ten patients, each patient was the recipient of healing prayers from four different healers over the ten-week period.

The results of the study were so astounding that Targ almost didn't believe them. After six months, four of the ten patients in the control group that did not receive prayers group had died. In contrast, all ten patients in the healed group were not only still alive, they all reported feeling better, and this subjective assessment was substantiated by objective medical analysis. Targ and Sicher repeated the experiment with 50 separate control factors that could possibly influence the outcome. Once again, those who received healing prayers scored significantly healthier in all parameters measured.[10]

Targ and Sicher's experiments confirm and extend similar results from a number of other investigations on the effectiveness of healing prayer. In all studies, it didn't appear to make any difference in regard to the remote healer's religion or method of prayer, the healer had only to convey a healing intention. The most successful healers expressed humility by stating that some higher force was working through them.

THE SCIENCE OF PRAYER

One thing should be clear by now. While we may not know exactly how the field operates, we do know it exists. And, although we cannot quite take the field apart like a Swiss watch to see what makes it tick, we can still use it to influence our reality. After all, it's been hundreds of years since Newton described gravity, and, even though we still cannot explain it, we use gravity every day to keep things from flying off our table.

In addition to those published by Elisabeth Targ, a large number of scientific reports have also assessed the power of prayer. Medical doctor Larry Dossey, author of *Healing Words* and *Prayer Is Good Medicine*, reviewed more than 60 scientific studies that provide evidence of prayer having a measurable impact on healing. These studies collectively reveal that, regardless of which religion or form the prayer takes, without love and compassion, the prayer has little or no effect. Dossey concluded that the best healing attitude is expressed by the Buddhist injunction, "Have good heart!" According to Dossey, this means "caring deeply with no hidden agendas."[11]

Dossey states that prayer is not something we do—it is what we *are*. Gregg Braden derived a similar conclusion. While in the Himalayas, Braden asked a Buddhist abbot to explain the intention of monks chanting for 14 to 16 hours a day. Specifically, he asked, "When we see your prayers, what are you doing?" The monk replied, "You've never seen our prayers, because a prayer cannot be seen. What you've seen is what we do to create the feeling in our bodies. *Feeling is the prayer!*"[12]

Similarly, Braden once asked a Native American rainmaker what he did when he prayed for rain. "I don't pray *for* rain," the shaman corrected him. "I *pray rain*." In other words, the shaman embodied the experience of rain. He felt what it felt like to have rain fall onto his body, his bare feet in the wet mud. He smelled the rain and imagined himself walking through rain-nourished fields of corn. From his extensive research on the nature of prayer, Braden concluded that we communicate with the field through the language of emotion, by experiencing the intent of the prayer as if it has already occurred.[13]

Mentally and emotionally experiencing the desired outcome of a prayer before the reality exists makes sense in the world of quantum mechanics. Physicists acknowledge that the mind is a primary influence when creating reality. Consequently, consider the state of an individual's mind when he or she is praying for something. That person is manifesting a mental field characterized by lack or need. Because the field influences the shape of the material realm, a field that emphasizes lack will contribute to the creation of a complementary reality that embodies lack. In contrast, if the person's mind were to manifest a mental and emotional experience of already having realized his or her desire, that mental field would transform the prayer into a matching physical reality.

Dossey and Braden agree on one thing in particular and that is the importance of non-attachment in prayer. The apparent paradox that seems to hold the key to breakthrough is to care deeply and yet not be attached to the outcome. In *Secrets of the Lost Mode of Prayer*, Braden reports a discrepancy between the classic Biblical injunction on the nature of prayer: "Ask and ye shall receive" and the original Aramaic translation: "Ask without hidden motive and be surrounded by your answer—be enveloped by what you desire that your gladness be full."[14]

The original Biblical instruction on how to pray offers, as a first step, "Ask without hidden motive." This is the same directive that Dossey attributes to the Buddhist prayer intention of having ". . . no hidden agendas." This simply means not having attachment to the outcome or how that outcome must manifest. Interestingly, the secret to successful prayer-making leaves us with a crazy-making paradox: "In order to have something, you must at once desire it, yet not be attached to getting it."[15]

Braden offers a thoughtful reason behind the necessity of detachment when he suggests that most prayers are ego-based wishes for individual selves who are rarely aware of the consequences that realizing those personal desires may have on the lives of other individuals or on the greater good. The intelligence of the field, expressed Biblically as "Thy will be done," often has a much bigger plan up its very, very big sleeve.

The second caveat of the Bible's injunction on creative praying reads, "be surrounded by your answer."[16] This simply means to physiologically and emotionally experience the desired intention as if it already has occurred. This is precisely the activity of Buddhist monks and Native American shamans who pray by internally creating the experience of what they desire, as if it already existed. Modern physicists offer the same insight on prayer and manifestation, even though they prefer to consider it in terms of fields influencing matter.

Engaging an emotional experience plays an important physiologic role in the manifestation of prayer. Emotions link consciousness with the experiential physical realm because they represent the bridge between thought and the chemistry of feelings. Now we truly come to the heart of the matter—for the heart is the mind's powerhouse that amplifies and broadcasts our emotional information into the Universe.

THE SACRED HEART AND COHERENCE

In the world of scientific materialism, the heart is merely a muscle—a very important muscle, but a muscle and nothing more. However, in Chinese medicine, the heart is considered the center of wisdom, and, in the ancient Vedic tradition, the heart is the mediator between Heaven and Earth.

Ancient Ayurvedic philosophy contends that the body possesses seven chakras, which are force centers considered to be focal points for the reception and transmission of the body's vital energies. The powerful heart chakra lies in the center between three higher and three lower chakras. The higher crown, third eye, and throat chakras are energy centers of consciousness and communication. The lower solar plexus, sacral, and root chakras represent the physical domain and bodily emotions. If ever there were a gateway between the *above* and the *below*, the heart chakra would certainly be it.

Once again, modern science is confirming ancient wisdom, this time in relation to the influential role of the heart. In 1992, stress researcher Doc Childre founded the Institute of HeartMath as a scientific research center dedicated to investigating the notion that the heart possesses powerful wisdom and might hold the key to the spontaneous evolution of our species.

Childre and a cadre of HeartMath researchers amassed data from a variety of new scan technologies that reveals the ancients were right in regard to the heart's influence on life. In their book, *The HeartMath Solution,* Childre and co-author Howard Martin concluded, "Heart intelligence is the intelligent flow of awareness that we experience once the mind and bodily emotions are brought into balance and coherence."[17]

To paraphrase an old Connie Francis song, our heart does, indeed, have a mind of its own. In the 1970s, physiologists John and Beatrice Lacey of the Fels Research Institute discovered that the heart possesses its own independent nervous system, which they referred to as "the brain of the heart." At least 40,000 neurons in the heart are used to communicate with consciousness-related brain centers including the amygdala, the thalamus, and the cerebral cortex. When first discovered, scientists assumed these cardiac neurons were used to simply process signals sent from the brain above.[18]

The Laceys' research revealed an entirely different scenario. Their studies showed that the heart does not automatically obey the brain's messages but that it actually interprets neural signals and bases a response on the individual's current emotional status. The Laceys concluded that the heart employs its own distinctive logic and that heartbeats are not merely the mechanical rhythms of life but, rather, represent an intelligent language.[19] Analyses of EKG patterns demonstrate that the heart has far more to do with perceptions and behavioral reactions than Western science has ever imagined.

HeartMath researchers confirmed what religion, poetry, and our own intuition have been telling us since the beginning of human awareness. The heart is the interface between consciousness and the physiologic responses that generate emotions. What's more, they found that the impact of love, itself, is real and biochemically measurable.

Childre and Martin's research led to specific techniques for accessing what they refer to as *coherent heart intelligence.* When subjects focus their attention on the heart and activate a core heart feeling, such as love, appreciation, or caring, these emotions immediately shift their heartbeat rhythms into a more coherent pattern. Increasing heartbeat coherence activates a cascade of neural and biochemical events that affect virtually every organ in the body.

Studies demonstrate that heart coherence leads to more intelligence by reducing the activity of the sympathetic nervous system—our fight-or-flight mechanism—while simultaneously increasing the growth-promoting activity of the parasympathetic nervous system. The relaxation response produced by heart coherence reduces production of the stress hormone cortisol and redirects its chemical precursors to produce the anti-aging hormone dehydroepiandrosterone (DHEA). Cultivated feelings of love, compassion, caring, and appreciation influence our physiology so as to provide us with healthier, happier, and longer lives.[20]

Science has actually tracked the pathway by which love heals! By focusing attention on our heart, we increase synchronization between the heart and brain, which, in turn, calms our nervous system and deactivates the stress response. When operating in a state of heart coherence, the body conserves vital energy for growth and maintenance.

The heart's influence on the field is empowered by its own electromagnetic activity that is 5,000 times more powerful than the brain's electromagnetic field. Current technology can read the heart's energy field up to ten feet away from the body. Feelings such as love generate measurable, quantifiable heart field coherence, while negative emotions create incoherence and disharmony in the heart's field.

The heart broadcasts our emotions into the world around us and is, likewise, influenced by emotions broadcast by others. When an individual connects with another person through either physical touch or simply by caring, the electrical activity of the two communicating hearts and brains become entangled and begin to entrain with one another. This research offers even more profound implications for activating a coherent worldwide healing field because it reveals that the healing coherence of love is contagious and can rapidly spread throughout a population.

These observations suggest that the emotional coherence or incoherence of large groups of people can profoundly influence the greater field. The Institute of HeartMath has recently launched a worldwide experiment to test this hypothesis by enlisting the efforts of large numbers of participants across the planet. Their Global Coherence Initiative is a science-based initiative designed to assess the coordinated influence of millions of people who consciously practice what they define as "heart-focused care and intention to shift global consciousness from instability and discord, to balance, cooperation and enduring peace."[21]

Can our intentions purposefully change Earth's field? Please stay attuned.

ENTRAINING WHEELS FOR THE NEXT CYCLE

HeartMath's Global Coherence Initiative is not the first study to measure the impact of focused coherent concentration by large numbers of people on the physical world. Practitioners of Transcendental Meditation (TM), a technique brought to America by Maharishi Mahesh Yogi, launched an experiment in two dozen American cities in the early 1970s. The Maharishi claimed that when the square root of one percent of a given population practiced this form of meditation, there would be a reduction in crime in the surrounding area.[22]

While this might seem like an outrageous claim by someone who supposedly was the subject of the Beatles' song "Fool on the Hill," it turns out that the Maharishi Effect is, indeed, real. Interestingly, not only is crime significantly reduced while these studies are going on, but other markers of coherence, including a decline in emergency-room visits, are experienced as well.

In a well-documented 1993 study, TM practitioners converged on Washington, D.C., during the hot summer months of June and July. Despite a near-record summer heat wave—something that statistically correlates with a higher crime rate—crime began to decrease and continued to decrease throughout the duration of the experiment. When the experiment was over and the meditators went home, curiously enough, the crime rate immediately began to rise again! The observed decrease in crime in that area, as substantiated by FBI Uniform Crime Statistics, could not be accounted for through analyses of any other known variables. Statistically, the likelihood that these results could be attributed to coincidence is less than two chances in a billion.[23]

Are these results something that can only be achieved through Transcendental Meditation, or are there other ways and techniques for impacting field coherence?

Two different coherence-creating projects, Lynne McTaggart's Intention Experiment[24] and Common Passion,[25] are seeking answers to that question.

Joe Giove, executive director of Common Passion, wrote: "Imagine a massive global collaborative of peace-creating groups whose purpose is social harmony, comprised of members from every religion, meditation practice, and indigenous group. They would come together locally and globally, learn how to apply the findings of prior social studies, and develop an open-source technology that validated the social harmonizing effects of their combined efforts."[26]

Giove proposes an ambitious, yet worthy, undertaking that offers individuals the opportunity to gather and focus human love under one big intent. As is often the case when a new context emerges, evidence of the phenomenon begins to appear everywhere.

In his recent book, *Awakening into Oneness,* Arjuna Ardagh reports on what he named the Oneness Blessing, a practice referred to as *deeksha* in India. According to Ardagh, the blessing is a form of coherence that can be transferred from one individual to another. Ardagh reports that the Oneness Blessing, based on the work of Sri Bhagavan and his wife Sri Amma, founders of Oneness University in India, produced a profound local transformation in the vicinity of the university that is strikingly similar to the Maharishi Effect.

When Sri Bhagavan originally moved his center to near the small village of Varadaiahpalem, it was typical of the poor towns in that part of India. In addition to poverty—most families lived in one-room mud huts with no running water, sewage, or electricity—there were rampant social problems, including alcoholism, physical violence, and spousal abuse. Bhagavan proposed adopting villages and offering residents instructions on the Oneness Blessing so they, too, could increase their happiness.

At first, only 30 or 40 people from surrounding villages took the invitation to learn this technique. However, coherence is contagious. Soon, more and more people began attending, and, within 5 years, as many as 6,000 residents were attending Oneness Blessing classes. According to Ardagh, who visited the villages and interviewed the inhabitants, alcohol consumption was reduced more than 80 percent of what it had been five years earlier and drunken brawls in the streets had become a rarity. Numerous community work projects were created and employment was available for anyone who wanted to work.[27]

As with so many reports regarding the healing power of love, prayer, and coherence, Ardagh's account is officially anecdotal, based more on personal observation than scientific rigor. For those who've experienced such phenomena firsthand, the need for rigor might seem redundant or unnecessary. Yet, there is something profoundly transformational when science, itself, explores the blurred boundary between the visible and the invisible, particularly when it comes to measuring something as immeasurable as love.

WHAT'S LOVE GOT TO DO WITH IT?

Two other notable experiments offer evidence regarding how something as supposedly unscientific as emotions can have a measurable physical impact on matter—at a distance!

Let's begin with the intriguing research of Bernard Grad, a Canadian biologist who carried out experiments in the field of paranormal healing. Rather than studying human patients, Grad focused on plants. He found that when a psychic healer transmitted energy to a beaker of water, seeds soaked in that water grew noticeably taller and more rapidly than plants from control seeds grown in psychically untreated water. In another of his studies, Grad had psychiatric patients, including one severely depressed man, hold beakers of water that would later be used to sprout seeds. The water held by the patients, and in particular by the depressed man, clearly inhibited the plants' growth.[28] Further studies showed that healers actually produced a physical change in the structure of water that was assessed by studying its spectroscopic absorption of infrared light.[29] These changes demonstrated greater structural coherence of the water molecules after it was exposed to the hands of the healer and a lesser coherence when the depressed man influenced the water. Grad extended these studies and found that healers could also provoke a slowing of the growth of tumors in laboratory rats.

Further evidence that thoughts and emotions can alter cellular reality is provided in the work of physician and healer Leonard Laskow. Like so many of those who find themselves at the forefront of this new paradigm, Laskow began his career in traditional medicine. It was a twist of fate that changed his direction and led him to a healing experience so profound that his life work took off in a totally unpredictable direction. In 1971, Laskow was a successful OB/GYN and surgeon with a thriving practice in Northern California. A pain in his shoulder led to x-rays that revealed a lesion, which is often an indication of bone cancer.

As a doctor, Laskow already knew the treatment protocol was amputation. And, while there had been a one-armed outfielder who played major league baseball when everyone else was in the military service during World War II, it's exceedingly difficult to perform surgery single-handedly. While awaiting his test results, Laskow accepted that, even with one arm, he could still be of service as a health counselor.

A few weeks later, the test results showed the lesion to be a simple benign cyst. However, over the interim, Laskow pondered his fate and decided that a change was in order. He left his stressful medical practice and focused his attention on studying the mental and emotional facets of healing.

A short while later, Laskow received the following message while in a meditation: "Your work is to heal with love." The message left him awestruck and humbled. He realized that his decision to go into medicine in the first place was predicated on the desire to be a healer, and traditional medicine was the accepted mode. Laskow's meditation awakened him to a new healing vision, "I believe that we all have to learn, in some point in our evolution, to heal with love."[30]

A few years later, Laskow found himself at a retreat where his roommate was a young man suffering from metastasized cancer. When the young man woke up in the middle of the night in pain and with troubled breathing, Laskow wanted to help but was unsure what to do. "Acting purely on intuition," Laskow reported, "I placed my hands on the sides of his chest and visualized a radiant ball of light coming down through the center of my head to the level of my heart, then down my arms and out through my hands."[31]

The young man calmed down, told Laskow his pain was gone, and slept through the night. Fast-forward 11 years and Leonard Laskow found himself at another conference where this same young man was singing on stage. He told Laskow about a miraculous spontaneous remission he had about six weeks after his encounter at the previous retreat. Did Laskow's work precipitate the healing? Or was it a *pre*-verberation of what would happen six weeks later? Clearly, there was a relationship, and it caused Laskow to engage in some intriguing experiments in healing with love.

While Laskow has reported amazing anecdotal results of his healing work with patients, his most scientific experiment involved working with cancer cells in a petri dish. This protocol was chosen because cultured cells could be biochemically monitored in a laboratory. Laskow held three culture dishes that contained tumor cells in his hand while maintaining a state of focused healing consciousness. As an experimental control, a non-healer in another room held in his hands three other Petri dishes, inoculated with the same tumor cells. The non-healer was assigned a reading task while holding the cultures so that he would be distracted from influencing the cultured cells with his own intentions.

Laskow experimented with several different emotional intentions while holding the cells, all of which sought to activate the natural force of coherence in the Universe. The most effective intention, the one that caused the cancer cells to diminish their growth by 39 percent, was: "Return to the natural order and harmony of the normal cell line." When Laskow added visual imagery to the intention, the healing effect doubled.[32]

So, what's love got to do with it? As Laskow reports in his book *Healing With Love,* his intention was not to destroy the cancer cells but to allow them to exist as part of universal creation. Love, he explained, is the "impulse toward unity, non-separation, wholeness. While love can take many forms, its essence is relatedness."[33] Laskow believes that the opposite of love is not hate but separation. While there are many different modes for accessing and using healing energy, Laskow's protocol involves connecting with the condition instead of separating from it.

When we experience an illness or a life condition that we would prefer not to have, our first impulse is to cast it out. We tend to think of illness as a foreign invader that attacks us rather than something we co-create. However, when we truly own our participation in the condition, even if we don't understand the reason, we become responsible participants in directing our fate.

With the awareness that our mind shapes our biology, we can recognize that we have the opportunity to change our minds and, thus, create a healthier biology. Given what we now know about the intelligence and functionality of our cells, maybe we can begin by humbly apologizing to our inner citizens and thank them for putting up with us! When we take the step of consciously loving our cells, we affirm that we are co-creating participants, not victims of life.

An illness or disharmonious condition occurs when something is mis*form*ed or de*form*ed. Healing, therefore, involves trans*form*ation to change the dysfunctional form. Here is Laskow's simple four-step transformational healing process:[34]

- **Step One:** *Inform* yourself about what has already materialized in form. Telling the truth is the first step toward responsibility.

- **Step Two:** *Conform* to the condition by loving it rather than creating separation. Resonating with the form allows us more influence over its organization.

- **Step Three:** *Unform* the condition by releasing it. "It is the observer's intent," said Laskow, "that converts particulate matter to its wave form and its wave form back into matter."

- **Step Four:** *Reform* the released energy to conform to our purpose and desire. This is the letting go part where we send our intention into the Universe without attachment.

Even when releasing the diseased condition, there is connection and not separation. Laskow wrote: "When you accept and love the parts of yourself you want to reject or change, you create an opportunity to discover the positive life force behind them."[35] That old Biblical word *atonement* can be reinterpreted as *at-one*-ment through which we make ourselves *at one* with whatever condition we would have otherwise rejected.

In the quantum Universe where everything is connected, love is the glue that holds things together. Said Laskow, "Love is a universal pattern of resonant energy."[36] In this sense, two or more tuning forks vibrating together are in love with each other, just as two or more humans can resonate in a palpable field of connectedness, joy, and even ecstasy. Love, he said, "is the universal harmonic."

Leonard Laskow's work brings up an intriguing and transformational question. If we can "love a cancer cell to death," or at least to the point of relative harmlessness, can we also love terrorists and other human sociopathogens and render them harmless, too? Can embracing these individuals, groups, and even nations as a manifestation of our own need to heal be the key to a new quantum politics?

THE ONE SUGGESTION

Science suggests that the next stage of human evolution will be marked by awareness that we are all interdependent cells within the super-organism called humanity. And just as surely as the seeker who climbs Mount Awareness and finds Buddha patiently waiting at the top with his words of wisdom, there is an equally valuable one suggestion waiting for us when we boil most religious thought down to its golden essence. The nearly universal suggestion offered by most of the world's spiritual systems is to practice some version of the Golden Rule.

Cited below are a few examples of how the Golden Rule has been incorporated into the world's major religions:[37]

- **Buddhism:** Hurt not others in ways that you yourself would find hurtful. (Udana-Varga 5,1)

- **Christianity:** All things whatsoever ye would that men should do to you, do ye so to them; for this is the law of the prophets. (Matthew 7:1)

- **Confucianism:** Do not do to others what you would not like yourself. Then there will be no resentment against you, either in the family or in the state. (Analects 12:2)

- **Hinduism:** This is the sum of duty; do naught onto others what you would not have them do unto you. (Mahabharata 5:1517)

- **Islam:** No one of you is a believer until he desires for his brother that which he desires for himself. (Sunnah)

- **Judaism:** What is hateful to you, do not do to your fellow-man. This is the entire Law; all the rest is commentary. (Talmud, Shabbat 3id)

- **Taoism:** Regard your neighbor's gain as your gain, and your neighbor's loss as your own loss. (Tai Shang Kan Yin P'ien)

- **Zoroastrianism:** That Nature alone is good which refrains from doing another whatsoever is not good for itself. (Dadisten-I-dinik, 94:5)

Could these spiritual practices be trying to tell us something? Perhaps the most profound difference between children of God and adults of God is that children of God worship the lawgiver while adults of God strive to live the law.

Again, while the Golden Rule is only a suggestion, it is based on experience. Robert Thurman, Professor of Buddhist Studies at Columbia University, emphasized, "Buddhism isn't a religion, it's a practice."[38] What makes the practice practical, said Thurman, is that it works.

Thurman stated that Buddhism is based on rationalism because Buddhists believe human fate is not determined by God, but by a causal system called karma. Thurman said, "In the karmic system, one kind of action is systematically more successful than another in enhancing a being's existence."[39]

As we come to understand the relatedness of all things, we see that actions are related to consequence. The Buddhist understanding of karma resonates with both Jesus' message to love thy neighbor and the Jewish concept of *tikkun olam,* "the healing of the world."

Although the one-suggestion operating system has been passed down throughout the ages by great religious teachers, up until now, in the face of fear, manipulation, and disempowering programming, humans have done everything possible to avoid putting it into operation. Now, with species' survival at stake, we must recognize, once and for all, that the tired argument of religion versus science can no longer be used to avoid accepting our own power and responsibility as conscious co-creators of our reality.

Those citizens among us who have been infected with the dominator virus have convinced the rest of us that their inhuman nature is the only form of human nature. However, now that we have insight into the nature of our programming and have seen the very wide range of behaviors that humans are capable of expressing, we must recognize that we can choose the nature of our human nature.

There is the famous story of a Native American grandfather talking to his grandchild. "There are two wolves fighting inside of me," said the grandfather. "One is the wolf of love and peace, the other is the wolf of anger and war." "Which one will win?" asked the grandchild. "Whichever one I feed," was the grandfather's reply.

In a certain sense, all the complexity of philosophy and human history that we have been relating in *Spontaneous Evolution* boils down to this one simple choice. We can divert and delude ourselves into waiting for an external messiah with a magic wand, or we can withdraw in resignation to the chaotic evil of this world.

Or, better yet, we can take a hint from the Buddhists who emulate the bodhisattvas; these are persons able to reach nirvana but delay doing so out of compassion and in order to save suffering beings. Referred to as "working messiahs" by Robert Thurman, these spiritual practitioners work for "the complete welfare, liberty, and happiness of every living being." Bodhisattvas have chosen to embrace Heaven as a practice, not a destination.

Buddhists have a meditation practice they call *tonglen,* which is Tibetan for "taking and giving," that offers a way to internally digest the toxins of the world and use them to feed the wolf of love and peace that resides within all of us. The practice involves visualization in which one person takes in the suffering of others and releases into the world one's own peace, love, and happiness.

Again, this suggestion has nothing to do with promoting Buddhism as a religion—even the Dalai Lama insists it's a practice, not a religion. Spiritual practice should be the most private and intimate of all matters rather than self-proclaiming righteousness that always seems to come out as self-righteousness.

Instead, consider the practice of loving thy neighbor as just one of the tools in our do-it-yourself Messiah kit that apparently is as much a part of our inheritance as is a perceived propensity toward evil. All that is required is that we take the challenge to step away from the comfortable discomfort of being a victim and graduate to the more productive discomfort of being a co-creator.

In the remaining chapters of *Spontaneous Evolution*, we will look at the practical matter of living in this ever-entangled physical world as we adopt the one suggestion as our new operating system. We will explore how economics can approximate the cellular wisdom of the body and emulate the efficiency of Nature itself. We will see how political and social relationships reflect the ultimate truth of the quantum Universe, which is that we're all in this together. And we will offer insight into how the universal field of compassionate wisdom can be accessed in order to process and eliminate the toxic beliefs of domination, exploitation, fear, manipulation, injustice, and programmed ignorance that have been passed down to us through millennia.

Finally, we will get a glimpse of a future, a time when we move beyond the old story and write new stories for ourselves, our children, and the world, a time when we see a worldwide spiritual authority that reflects the healthiest and most coherent central voice of humanity, empowered as our own Iroquois forebears foresaw by freedom at the grassroots.

Are you ready to engage the one suggestion—that we are all *one* with the same *One?* If so, be prepared because all Heaven is about to break loose.

CHAPTER 14

A HEALTHY COMMONWEALTH

*"In Nature's economy,
the Golden Rule overrules the Rule of Gold."*
— Swami Beyondananda

The original draft of this chapter warned of a pending financial meltdown and the potential for global economic collapse. In the fall of 2008, before the manuscript was completed, this negative potential exploded into reality as our house-of-credit-cards economy, based on unlimited borrowing and a diluted dollar, began its precipitous collapse.

While the financial crisis can understandably feel life-threatening, we will come to see that it is a necessary adjustment, a convulsive labor pain that will propel us to birth a higher evolutionary version of humanity— one that operates on the one suggestion that we're all in this together.

This chapter explores the exciting domain offered by a truly natural economy in contrast to the current economic structure that is based on outdated, irrelevant paradigms of only matter matters and survival of the fittest.

But, to begin transforming our crisis into opportunity, some long-standing and unquestioned myth-perceptions about economics must first be set aright.

Just hearing the word economics might cause brain fog for those who recall a mystifying subject never fully grasped in high school or college. For others, the complexities of economics might be boiled down to the simple description offered by comic faux priest, Father Guido Sarducci, "You buy something for less—you sell it for more."

Aristotle first defined economics as the science of household management, the study of the dynamics necessary to sustain individual or family survival. As households joined together in community to enhance their collective survival and prosperity, family economic principles were extended and applied to the well-being of the entire village. Villages with successful economies subsequently grew into cities and, later, evolved into more encompassing nation-states that employed essentially the same economic principles. As nation-states further evolve into the new organism called global humanity, in which all must share the finite resources of one planet, it is again necessary for us to revise and expand our understanding of economics.

Historically the field of economics has been associated with the dynamics of property exchange among members of human communities. But in a fractal Universe, the same economic principles apply to all living systems, be they households, nations, businesses, or the communities of cells that comprise a human body.

THE NATURAL ECONOMY: WHAT WOULD OUR CELLS DO?

Over the last three millennia, human civilizations have periodically risen and fallen as their economic systems played out a repetitive pattern of growth, death, and renewal. Current global economic crises punctuate the ending of another cycle, another death, and it is painfully clear that civilization has not yet acquired an awareness of what constitutes a sustainable, stable economy suitable to serve as a basis for the next renewal.

Fortunately, ancient wisdom and modern science conspire to point us toward the solution of our economic woes. From the past, we receive enlightening insight from the old adage "The answers we seek lie within." Paradoxically, the same guidance comes from the new science of fractal geometry, which tells us that the fundamental elements of the eminently successful 50-trillion-celled community that is the human body can lead us to a successful human economy as well.

The effectiveness of the cellular economy has stood the test of time in that it has supported the survival of the human body for millions of years. Additionally, the body's economy has proven to be durable and flexible enough to support human adaptation to the widest range of environmental challenges. Consequently, understanding economic exchanges among the body's cellular community will, logically, help us design a more successful model of human economic management.

At its most basic level, cellular economics is simply the study of how living systems apportion and use energy in order to work and produce. While the units of exchange may range from dollars to donuts, all economies are based on an exchange of work, which, of course, equates to energy.

To maintain itself and empower its functions, a body expends energy as it works to procure and process food, as we learned in Chapter 12, *Time to See a Good Shrink*. Cells, then, extract energy from that food and store it in the form of stable ATP molecules, which is the cellular equivalent of money. ATP coins are exchanged among the community's cells as salaries to cover the cost of expended energy for operations such as digestion, respiration, neural processing, movement, reproduction, and waste elimination.

Energy produced in excess of the body's needs, by definition, represents wealth. The body transforms surplus energy into energy-rich oil molecules that are banked as fat deposits, which are the body's equivalent of a financial savings account. The body deposits and withdraws fat molecules to keep ATP money circulating and to fund the cellular community's functions, growth, and maintenance.

A healthy economy can only exist when a community of individuals generates wealth by creating more energy than it consumes. For example, before a farmer can contribute to the village economy, he must first grow enough food to sustain his own household. When he produces extra food, the farmer generates surplus, which, by definition, represents wealth. Circulation of the farmer's wealth facilitates production, consumption, and transfer of energy by and among others with various other skills within the village.

Considering our culture's preoccupation with the material realm, it is not surprising that we measure wealth in terms of physical possessions, particularly money. Aristotle recognized an inevitable problem of equating money with wealth over 2,500 years ago when he wrote, "He who is rich in coin may often be in want of necessary food." In other words, Aristotle understood that people who become avaricious and pursue money for the sake of merely having money confuse the instrument of wealth—money—with wealth itself.

So what is wealth, really? The term *wealth* is derived from the Old English word *weal*, which means "well-being." In its original context, wealth literally represents comfort, health, happiness, or satisfaction. The Founding Fathers were clearly aware of the meaning of wealth when they penned in the Declaration of Independence that individuals "are endowed by their Creator with certain unalienable Rights, that among these are Life, Liberty, and the pursuit of Happiness."

By contrasting the successful cellular economy with the failing global fiscal economy, we can identify four fundamental principles of economics in which human policies profoundly differ from cellular practices. These deviations are in regard to our human perception of wealth and how it relates to well-being, ecology, efficiency, and currency stability.

PRINCIPLE ONE: WEALTH IS WELL-BEING

In his treatise on human economics, Aristotle wrote that a city *originates* for the sake of basic survival, but it *exists* for the sake of living well. The same consideration holds true for the human body. The cellular community that is our skin, bones, blood, and so on originated for the sake of the basic survival of individual cells, but it exists for the sake of the body's entire well-being.

A fundamental difference between successful cellular economics and the failing human economy concerns a polar opposite perception of the meaning of well-being. When cells assembled into communal life forms, the economic emphasis was not on the wealth of the individuals but on the well-being of the collective, that is, the common, or shared, wealth of all.

Even though America's Founding Fathers valued individual freedom, they understood that a healthy commonwealth—the governmental form in which power is held by the people—would be essential if individual citizens were to thrive. Unfortunately, after a century and a half of scientific materialism and Darwinism, the concept of commonwealth has fallen by the wayside, replaced by competing individuals seeking "uncommon wealth."

The wealth of a healthy economy is measured in terms of abundance, which is a community's ability to produce in excess of its needs for survival. In a natural economy, cellular communities possess wealth only after the basic needs of each cellular citizen are met. Therefore, cells in one part of the body do not hoard energy while cells in another part of the community are in need.

Human economics completely misses the mark—it sins—in regard to this fundamental principle of cellular economics. Our unnatural human economic policies are tainted by the Darwinian misperception that life is an eternal struggle for existence. This aggressive notion emphasizes competition among individuals as the primary driving force in evolution. When programmed into our beliefs, this misperception encourages and condones selfishness at the expense of community. An economy driven by the survival-of-the-fittest mentality honors individuals like Indian industrialist Lakshmi Mittal and Mexican telecommunications magnate Carlos Slim Helu, each of whom has amassed personal wealth of \$50 billion while 80 percent of the world's population struggles to survive on less than \$10 a day.[1]

The current situation in human economics completely conflicts with the successful cellular principle that the community's first level of investment is to assure the health and social welfare of its citizens. Cellular logic is quite simple: a healthy, happy population inevitably produces more wealth and prosperity for all because individuals consume less to survive. The consequence of failing to make the community's well-being a first priority seriously threatens human survival.

Warfare, the health-care crisis, and the disproportionately large number of imprisoned citizens are expressions of civilization's lack of well-being. The loss of productivity due to a disabled workforce combined with massive expenditures to fund the war machine, tend the ill, and control the incarcerated has drastically drained America's wealth.

Our economic collapse is further exacerbated by a cultural program that equates well-being with economic prosperity and self-worth with net worth. Such behavioral conditioning unconsciously drives us to acquire more stuff as a means of ensuring happiness and life satisfaction.

The validity of this programming has been profoundly challenged by the surprising results of a 2003 World Value Survey of people in 65 nations, published in the British magazine *New Scientist*. The data revealed that Puerto Rico and Mexico, although economically deprived, were the world's happiest countries, populated by the world's most satisfied citizens. The proudly prosperous Americans scored an embarrassing 16th on the list! Clearly, economic prosperity does not directly translate into well-being.[2]

One factor shared by all the happiest nations in the survey is a strong sense of community, a true representation of what is meant by commonwealth. Furthermore, research suggests that when an individual's basic needs for security, safety, and health are met, their happiness and satisfaction with life is most significantly impacted by the quality of their personal relationships—with themselves, their partner, family, friends, and community.

The survey data was bad news for consumption-oriented Westerners because it revealed that consumerism, instead of facilitating the pursuit of happiness, might actually be chasing happiness away. Prosperity-driven cultures are working longer hours than ever before to earn enough to buy the stuff they think they need to make themselves happy. In the process, they become so busy chasing money they don't have the time to invest in the personal relationships that actually generate well-being.

PRINCIPLE TWO: ECOLOGY AND ECONOMY ARE THE SAME

For the past 1,200 years, Western civilization has been conditioned to believe that humans are separate and distinct from the environment in which they live. That's because, according to the perceived truths offered by the previous monotheistic paradigm, humans arrived on this planet in a separate act of Divine intervention after the creation of all animals and plants.

When scientific materialism commandeered civilization's basal paradigm, Darwinism offered a completely different story of origins but with essentially the same conclusion: we arrived on the planet for no other reason than sheer accident, the result of an improbable lineage of random mutations.

The distorted perceptions of origins promulgated by both monotheistic creation and scientific evolution imply that human beings exist separate from the environment in which they are immersed. While monotheism teaches that mankind was given dominion over the biosphere, scientific materialism contributes to our separation from the environment by suggesting that the mission of science is to govern and control Nature.

Our misperceived detachment from the environment introduced life-threatening flaws into the way we manage our economy. Specifically, we have failed to acknowledge the reality that the environment is the primary source of wealth. Our monetary wealth originates from the sun's energy, which fuels the growth of all life in our biosphere. Our further monetary wealth comes from the finite resources of Earth and through processes that lie outside the human economic marketplace and are not funded by, or considered part of, the human economy.

In the words of scientist-turned-economist Frederick Soddy, "Chlorophyll was the original capitalist."[3] Chlorophyll molecules are responsible for *photosynthesis,* the process through which the sun's energy transforms water and carbon dioxide into nutritional sugar molecules. Plant cells harvest their solar-powered sugar molecules and use them for both metabolic building blocks and life-sustaining energy.

The growth of a cornstalk, from a sprout to the height of an elephant's eye, is made possible by the accumulated nutritional wealth manufactured by the plant's chlorophyll. Almost all life on this planet, including our own, is dependent upon photosynthesis-created sugar molecules.

Economists Carl H. Wilken and Charles Walters demonstrated how all wealth enters an economy as raw materials provided by Nature. Wilken declared, "All new wealth comes from the soil."[4] Whether fruit on trees, berries on bushes, crops in fields, animals raised or in the wild, or minerals from the earth, everything of tangible value can be found on, in, or coming from the ground. Even in today's cyber economy, without the production of goods from the soil, life would perish.

Charles Walters offers a powerful example of how Nature produces wealth in his book *Unforgiven*. Imagine one spring you place a kernel of corn in the ground. With proper sun and rainfall, in a few months the resulting corn plant will yield several ears of corn, each bearing hundreds of kernels with the same potential to produce. Where else can one multiply wealth a thousand times in such a short period? The environment is truly a cornucopia of ever-producing wealth.[5]

Walters, whose magazine, *Acres,* serves the dwindling population of small farmers, has seen in his lifetime, the virtual disappearance of family farms. In their place, more and more factory farms operate monoculturally outside the rhythms of Nature, producing de-natured food and toxic waste. Meanwhile, science and technology have given civilization the opportunity to wantonly mine Gaia's wealth in order to support the excesses of the human monetary economy.

However, our ignorance of the planet's fragile web of life has blinded us to the profound damage and havoc we wreak by pillaging the environment's resources and then, adding insult to injury, contaminating that environment with discarded waste.

The wealth of the ecosphere, like that of any living organism, is a direct reflection of its health. Decimated rain forests, festering open-pit mines, species harvested to extinction, toxic smog, pharmaceutically poisoned waterways, discarded radioactive waste, and many other man-made catastrophes have compromised the environment's well-being and devalued its ability to produce health and wealth. Our misperceived efforts to dominate and control Nature have unwittingly disturbed the ecosphere's natural balance and exacerbated environmental crises that now threaten our survival.

In the holistic paradigm we are now moving into, we can no longer separate the money game that we call economics from that game's planetary consequences, especially when those consequences disrupt and threaten the natural environment.

Nature provides human society with a diversity of life-sustaining benefits that economists would classify as *goods and services*. The basic goods are food for sustenance and building materials for shelter. The services are water purification, storage, and delivery; waste assimilation; balance of atmospheric oxygen and carbon dioxide; and regulation of climatic forces, to name a few. Environmentally provided goods and services are collectively referred to as *ecosystem services*. And, whether you want to believe it or not, humanity's well-being is totally dependent on the continued flow of Nature's ecosystem services.

The cost of producing environmentally derived goods and services are borne by Mother Earth. If we actually had to pay for ecosystem services, the costs for commodities would be immensely higher. But, because the costs of environmentally produced goods and services are not factored into the global pricing system, renewable ecosystem services are often given little consideration when making economic policy decisions.

Whether we like it or not, global crises are now forcing us to give Nature's contributions adequate weight in our economic decision-making processes. Humanity is beginning to realize that neglecting the role of ecosystem services may ultimately compromise the sustainability of human life itself.

In 1997, the journal *Nature* published an extensive study that incorporated the work of biologists, climatologists, economists, and ecologists from universities across the United States. This study attempted to do what no one had done before—put an actual price tag on the natural world's contribution to our economy. From a survey of 17 fundamental ecosystem services, the group estimated that the current monetary value of the environment's contribution to our welfare conservatively comes to $33 trillion dollars per year. This startling massive figure is about twice the gross national product (GNP) of the entire world economy. To determine this astronomical figure, the study attempted to calculate the financial contribution made by ten sub-ecosystems, from oceans to forests to wetlands to deserts, and, yes, even urban environments. The value of these systems was based on the natural services that we take for granted as part of life—what the ecosystem does to clean our air, supply and distribute our water, produce our food, and provide us with natural recreation.[6]

Because all economies on Earth would crash without the services provided by ecological life-support systems, the environment's actual value to the economy is infinite. Or, to paraphrase a popular credit card advertisement: Biosphere life-support systems, $33 trillion; Nature's contributions to existence, priceless.

The establishment of a monetary value for ecological services provides an eye-opening factor when calculating the value of ecosystem services lost versus potential project gains.

To provide for a sustainable economy, civilization is being called upon to walk in the footsteps of our animistic ancestors and honor Mother Earth by tending her Garden. Our survival necessitates that we employ economic strategies that factor in the environment's substantial contributions and, consequently, fund remediation and preservation measures that enhance the wealth and well-being of both Nature and human civilization.

PRINCIPLE THREE: EFFICIENCY IS THE KEY TO THRIVAL

Living systems, from cells to the humans and living entities they create, must successfully manage their energy economy in order to sustain survival and ultimately prosper. To paraphrase Father Sarducci, an organism's wealth is based on its ability to generate more energy than it uses.

As emphasized in our Survival Index in Chapter 12, *Time to See a Good Shrink*, the success of any organism—and this includes humanity—is predicated on how efficiently it utilizes energy resources. For persons conditioned to believe that environmental resources are limitless, the notion of efficiency, for all practical purposes, is irrelevant—there's always more, or so they say. In the rule-of-gold economy, which is empowered by the current materialistic paradigm, populations have found it totally acceptable to extract and spend irreplaceable natural wealth and define that practice as economic success. This self-serving shortsightedness has unhinged our economic system from the natural world that sustains it.

Because we are part of Gaia, the living Earth, we are accountable for everything we extract from the planet and release into the biosphere. For millennia, this responsibility was not well-understood because our little ol' species couldn't extract or excrete enough to make a difference in this big ol' world.

All that has changed. According to a 2006 report by the World Wildlife Fund and the Global Footprint Network, humans are devouring Nature at an "unprecedented rate." If the present trend continues, by the year 2050 we will need the natural resources of two Earths to sustain our survival.

WWF Director General James Leape added, "If everyone around the world lived as those in America, we would need *five* planets to support us."[7]

The natural limit to this unnatural growth comes when an organism finds that it has devoured all its available food. The scientific term for this situation is *extinction.*

Human beings are the most wasteful organisms on the planet. In contrast to sanely pursuing a more harmonious relationship with the environment, profit-driven corporations actually encourage greater inefficiency as a boon to their own short-term profits. Consider, for example, the pirates of the petroleum industry who plunder Nature's oil reserves while simultaneously coercing automakers to manufacture bigger gas-guzzling SUVs—good for profits, bad for life.

On the other hand, we can diminish or even balance our debt through the development of technologies that enhance efficiency. We have only to think back to our lives before the days of computers, the Internet, cell phones, and answering machines to see how technology has improved efficiency in the workplace while making a less-demanding demand on the environment.

A fundamental drive behind the creation of community is to promote well-being, or what the Founding Fathers identified as "the pursuit of Happiness." In contrast to that beneficent concept and to support their own well-being at the expense of the rest of the world, corporate interests have programmed the public to believe that life satisfaction depends on possession and accumulation of material wealth. All we really need to be happy is a Ferrari; a Rolex; and a diamond-studded, 18-karat-gold beer-can opener. None of these, in themselves, represents, let alone ensures, being well. And if you spend your money to buy them, you're not likely to be wealthy, either.

As the ads exhorted, "What better way to show you love her than to buy a diamond ring?" In the end, we will find that writing love letters or poems may be more heartfelt and life-sustaining than a diamond ring that, on a simple, functional level, is primarily useful only for cutting glass or playing old phonograph records.

Maybe what we are after isn't so much the goods, but the goodness we think these things will provide. Once we acquire this awareness, the most efficient economy will be one that provides the greatest happiness and well-being bang for the energy buck.

PRINCIPLE FOUR: CURRENCY MUST REPRESENT REAL WEALTH

Ever since life evolved on this planet, organisms have had to sustain their existence by working and investing their energy to empower behaviors that produce more life-sustaining energy. Once communities became large enough for a division of labor, it became necessary to develop a system of exchange so that an individual could acquire goods and services that were created through the energy investments of other individuals in the community.

Necessity is the mother of invention, and, in this case, the invention was money. Money, or currency, is any instrument that is used as payment for goods and services and the repayment of debts. Money is defined by three functions: it is a medium of exchange, it represents units of account, and it is a store of value.

Let's compare that definition with ATP molecules, which is, as you know, the energy-storing currency exchanged among cells within a living organism. In doing so, we will see that ATP molecules are the planet's first currency, and they provide all three functions that characterize money.

Function 1, Medium of Exchange: ATP is a medium of exchange that can be transported across both space and time. Both cash and ATP units are exchangeable and help us avoid the inefficiencies inherent in a barter system, whether internally or within society. Consider the difficulties when only goods are exchanged: Today's Special: "Oil Change and Tune-up—Only Three Chickens and Half a Trout!" Or, "I'll trade you three fat molecules in exchange for eight digestive enzymes."

Function 2, Units of Account: Each ATP molecule represents a defined amount of consumable energy. Consequently, ATP is a unit of account because it is a standard numerical unit of measurement that can be applied to the market value of goods, services, and other transactions. Units of account simplify the exchange process: Oil Change: "15 ATP. Tune-up: 35 ATP. Today's Special: Save 10% on Both—Only 45 ATP."

This is easier than figuring the standard numerical value for half a trout.

Function 3, Store of Value: ATP is also a store of value, which means it's a commodity or form of currency that can be reliably saved, stored, and retrieved, and, upon retrieval, it is predictably useful. The energy value of an ATP molecule stored for a million years is exactly the same today as it was when first created. In contrast, the dollar, franc, euro, and yen change value almost every minute.

ATP represents *commodity money,* which is a currency based on the value of the commodity out of which it is made. In contrast, the principal currency in human civilization is *representative money,* which is currency that stands in direct and fixed relation to the commodity that backs it, while not itself being composed of that commodity. An example of representative money is the U.S. dollars that, at one time, were known as silver certificates because they represented a dollar's worth of silver, even though the notes were made out of paper.

Today, the U.S. dollar, like most currencies, is *fiat money,* which is a form of paper or coin currency whose value is determined by a government order, a *fiat.* The usefulness of fiat money comes not from any natural value or guarantee that it can be converted into silver, gold, or other precious metal, but is derived from a legal decree that it must be accepted as a means of payment.

In most countries, fiat currency is no longer backed by silver or gold and has become a medium of exchange with no intrinsic value. If you doubt this, try eating your money. While it might be high in fiber, it is very low in nutritional content. And, even more amazing—a hundred dollar bill has no more nutritional value than a one dollar bill!

Thomas Jefferson expressed concern regarding the value of representative money when he wrote: "Paper is poverty, . . . it is only the ghost of money, and not money itself."[8] Jefferson recognized that the nation would face an ill fate if it used representative money because they who issue that money, and they alone, would control its availability and determine its value.

It is important to remember here that the colonial scrip we referred to in Chapter 9, *Dysfunction at the Junction,* was, indeed, paper money, and that this fiat currency—intrinsically worthless—was nonetheless an important key to the colonies' prosperity. Why is that? While it didn't have the backing of silver or gold, it had something ultimately more valuable than precious metals; it had the genuine value of the natural goods and productive services the American colonies were ready, willing, and able to produce. To understand the difference between this natural prosperity and the economic situation we are in today, we have to follow the money.

FOLLOW THE MONEY

So, where does money—be it in dollars, pounds, francs, or euros—come from? Why, from the Federal Reserve Bank, the Bank of England, the Swiss National Bank, and the European Central Bank, respectively. The titles of these money-issuing entities sound very impressive and give the notion they are government institutions whose mission is the well-being of the commonwealth. Not so. Each of these banks is a privately held corporation imbued with the primary corporate mission to make a profit for its fortunate shareholders!

To understand how a bank brings money into existence, consider what happens when you go to a bank for a loan. Perhaps you think the money you borrow is another person's savings, invested in the bank to earn interest. That is not the case at all. Money-issuing banks operate on a *fractional reserve system,* which means they can print a quantity of bank notes equal to nine times the value of their customers' deposits. They literally create 90 percent of the money out of thin air!

How do privately owned banks fulfill their corporate mission to make a profit? They loan money for which they charge interest—10 percent interest equals 10 percent profit.

So, let's say you borrow $1,000, the privilege for which you must repay the bank $1,100. Where do you get the extra $100? Well, from selling your goods or services to other people. True—but where do they get the money to pay you? Oh, yes—they borrow from the same bank, which, of course, charges them interest, too.

Let's say a country has a population of one million people and each citizen borrows $1,000 from the bank to create an economy based on currency exchange. Collectively, the bank loans the country $1 billion in bank notes. In return, the country owes the bank $1 billion dollars for the loan's principal, *plus* another $100 million for the interest. So where does the country get the extra $100 million in currency to pay the bank? It doesn't. It can't.

That's because the country can only borrow and repay money—not create it—and because only banks can create money.

This issuing of a national currency solely by private banks results in a debt-based economy in which there is never enough money in circulation to pay both the principal and the interest. It's only through *continual economic growth*—and the demand for new loans—that enough money can be created to repay the original loan. In other words, borrowing can only beget more borrowing.

Inevitably, the compounding of the debt leads to a situation in which creditor insolvency motivates banks to foreclose on loans. The debtor's property, used as collateral for the loan, is confiscated and distributed to the bank's shareholders. Because the money loaned by the bank was never equal to the value of the collateral, the shareholders happily accept foreclosures.

This persistent pattern in the money game can be traced back to ancient Babylon. Centuries before Jesus cast the moneychangers from the temple, the priests of Baal had their own money racket. Each spring, they would extend credit to farmers to plant their crops. At harvest time, the priests expected payment. However, because the priests also regulated the money supply, they made sure there was never enough money in circulation for all the farmers to repay their loans.[9] This led to more credit being extended, which meant that, at the next harvest, the debt was even greater. Repeating the same game plan over a number of years inevitably led to the farmers becoming indentured servants to the priests, who produced nothing. The Babylonian civilization eventually collapsed when the productive elements of their society were reduced to little more than slaves.

Visionary economist Richard Kotlarz recognized that the same pattern of exploitation, that is, "borrowing money into circulation, then withholding more money to make debt service impossible," reverberated throughout ancient societies of Persia, Greece, and Rome with the same effect.[10] The practice later found resurgence in the era of colonialism and empire. It can be seen today in the monetary policies of the World Bank, the International Monetary Fund, and other international financial institutions. Their economic hit men of the globalization era hit on underdeveloped nations, promising freedom through credit for development but delivering slavery through debt. The consequence of such exploitive economies is that they always end up killing the proverbial golden goose from which the tangible value originated.

We see the same sad scenario being played out today as executives with golden parachutes bail out of once-productive, but now indebted companies, closing factories and leaving workers unemployed. Even though real wealth—the productive potential of available resources and willing workers—is in place, the means of exchange, the currency, has been extracted from the system. There isn't enough money available to purchase goods or pay workers for their services.

No wonder visionaries like Thomas Jefferson and James Madison fought against the establishment of a national bank in the United States. They understood that political freedom was not possible under a system of economic exploitation. Without the ability to coin debt-free currency based on the value of natural wealth, an entire society would eventually fall into the perpetual in-debt status of those farmers in ancient Babylon.

Jefferson was quite prophetic when he wrote: "If the American people ever allow the banks to control the issuance of their currency, first by inflation, and then by deflation, the banks and corporations that will grow up around them will deprive the people of all property, until their children wake up homeless on the continent their fathers conquered. The issuing power of money should be taken from banks and restored to Congress and the people to whom it belongs. I sincerely believe the banking institutions having the issuing power of money, are more dangerous to liberty than standing armies."[11]

As the current economic crisis reveals, the amount of money in circulation doesn't necessarily represent the wealth of a society. For example, consider that America's farm production during the Depression in 1933 was roughly the same as it was in 1929 before the stock-market crash. And, yet, the monetary value of total farm income in 1933 was half of what it had been four years earlier! As economist Carl H. Wilken points out, the harvest of 1933 had the same number of calories as the harvest four years earlier. If our currency was truly a store of value, the value of farm production would not have been reduced by half.[12]

The variable nature of our money's value has profoundly undermined our natural economy and given rise to a totally unnatural one. David Korten, author of *Agenda for a New Economy*, bluntly described our current financial system as a "money game in which the players use money to make money for people who have money, without producing anything of value."[13]

Citing Kevin Phillips' book, *Bad Money*, Korten compares the economy of America at its peak of global power in 1950 with the economy today. In 1950, manufacturing accounted for 29.3 percent of the United States gross domestic product (GDP). By 2005, manufacturing was down to a mere 12 percent, while so-called financial services, meaning money invested into money markets, accounted for more than 20 percent of the GDP.[14]

Hedge funds, an example of a financial service that was barely a shrub on the economic landscape 20 years ago, have now grown to over $1.8 trillion in assets. These risky ventures, which essentially use borrowed money to borrow more money, totaled some $14 trillion in 2006.[15]

The new word for borrowing is leverage, and the now defunct and discredited Lehman Brothers was leveraged 35 to 1, meaning that it had borrowed $35 on every dollar of its equity! Lehman's bankruptcy has left its unsecured creditors with over $200 billion in losses.[16]

In the world of money marketing, Wall Street's short-term gain ends up as Main Street's long-term loss. Korten reported that, over a period of roughly three decades, "the benefits of productivity gains in the Main Street economy were captured by Wall Street players as interest, dividends, and financial service fees."[17]

In an attempt to make ends meet in an economy where the real value of the dollar was plummeting, the American consumer began to borrow money to pay for their consumable goods. Why, you can even use your credit card to purchase fast food, adding debt while you add calories. Financial institutions were all too willing to extend credit, and, by 2007, personal household mortgage and credit card debt stood at $13.8 trillion, which is roughly the equivalent of that year's GDP! Time for another round of foreclosures!

BEYOND THE OLD NEEDY-GREEDY: REAL MONEY BASED ON REAL WEALTH

In the sobering light of where we are today, it's natural to ask who is responsible for this sorry state of affairs. Do we blame the bankers, the capitalists, the corporations, or politicians? Certainly, the money machine called the corporation bears some responsibility because corporations have conveniently disconnected profits from the environmental cost of those profits. But, if we just identify one or two or three villains, we've missed the real lesson: essentially, we humans are collectively responsible for these conditions because, time after time, we have agreed to them.

This is particularly true in modern society where the poor dream of winning the lottery, the middle class uses credit to pay for instant gratification, and the rich accumulate far more wealth than they will ever need.

Thanks to survival-of-the-fittest programming, the fear of not having enough—which we call "scare-city"—is so pervasive that it's difficult to imagine any other state of life. Programs of scarcity have compounded, like interest on debt, as materialistic science and Darwinists gathered abundant historical evidence that neediness and greediness are, so they say, part of human nature.

Human civilization has been following the money for 3,000 years. What would it be like to have money follow human life for a change?

While we are at it, what would we like to have instead of the old needy-greedy? Fortunately, a large number of *imaginal cell* economists have come forward to help us see outside the money matrix and design something new.

As one example, Stephen Zarlenga of the American Monetary Institute has proposed a monetary reform platform that would likewise resonate with populist conservatives, libertarians, and America's founders:[18]

1. End the private creation of money by the Federal Reserve Bank and replace it with debt-free money that reflects the value of the general wealth of the nation.

2. End the fractional reserve banking system and allow banks to make money by lending only money they have on hand.

3. Add new money to the system, not as debt, but as national grants to rebuild the infrastructure and thus create jobs that create real value.

Zarlenga's plan may sound radical, and it is. However, the situation we face is grave, and, as with any emergency, everything is on the table. While we're awakening to and dismantling our other no-longer-useful paradigms and programming, we might as well do the same with our obsolete beliefs about what money is and what money does.

As long as the discussion of making big changes is in the air, Richard Kotlarz suggests we also reinstitute the Jubilee. In the Old Testament, every 50 years marked a *Jubilee Year* when debts were forgiven and slaves freed. This was done to make sure the fabric of society didn't unravel due to vast discrepancies in wealth.

A Jubilee today might create some much-needed jubilation. Without the burden of debt, imagine the worldwide potential for self-sufficiency, creativity, and genuine, life-promoting enterprise. It is conceivable that we might actually be able to free up the resources to actually re-grow the Garden.

In addition to long-term monetary reform, we can adopt three short-term strategies that will bring about a healthier commonwealth: create and use alternative currencies, increase local self-sufficiency, and empower an economy based on growing happiness.

Alternative Currencies: Valueless, debt-based representative money is a major contributor to the current global economic crisis. To paraphrase Einstein: We cannot solve the economic problems with the same money that created them. A more functional currency must evolve before a sustainable economy can be established. Toward that end, creative economists are coming forward with revolutionary ideas regarding new units of exchange to transform the world's current currency dilemma.

In his book *Access to Human Wealth: Money beyond Greed and Scarcity*, Bernard Lietaer, a Belgian economist who helped design the euro, offers a short-term solution for our economic problems in the form of *yin currency.* Yin currency is designed as a complement to the dominant money, *yang currency,* represented by the dollar, the yen, the franc, the euro and so on.[19]

Lietaer emphasizes that the nature of what constitutes workable, beneficial money is defined by agreement within a community. Therefore, people are free to create their own currencies to complement the yang monetary system. Without even realizing it, we make use of complementary currencies all the time. Lietaer cites frequent-flyer miles as an example of an agreed upon complementary currency—and you don't even need to fly to earn them.

Yin currency represents a form of money that allows time-rich but money-poor communities to contract needed services from those willing to provide them. Currently, nearly 4,000 communities around the world use yin currencies, most often as a means of funding nurturant care in communities where there isn't enough yang money to pay for social services.

A specific example of yin currency is Japanese *fureai kippu*, which means "caring relationship ticket." Instead of relying on expensive nursing homes, Japan has created the *fureai kippu* currency to pay for elderly care not covered by national health insurance.[20]

Here's how it works. Let's say an elderly man who lives on your street cannot go shopping by himself. You do his shopping, help him prepare food, and assist him with his ritual bath, which is an important part of Japanese culture. In exchange, you earn credits that can be put in what might be termed a *fureai kippu* savings account. You can draw on your credits when you're old, or you can transfer them to your elderly mother who lives in another city so she can pay someone else to look after her.

Surveys indicate that Japanese seniors overwhelmingly prefer services provided through *fureai kippu* to those paid for in yen because they more closely express the heartfelt essence of community.

Interestingly, the word community is derived from the Latin *cum munere*. *Munere* is "to give," and *cum* means "among each other." Community and *fureai kippu* share the same meaning—"to give among each other."[21]

Another highly successful version of organic money is the Local Exchange Trading System, or LETS, developed by Australian James Taris. Much like other yin currencies, LETS offers a clearinghouse for individuals within a community who want to enhance the quality of their lives by exchanging caring services, skills, and talents. For example, it allows an auto mechanic or professional babysitter to enjoy a massage or a home-cooked gourmet dinner, things they couldn't afford in the dollar economy. As of this writing, there are currently more than 1,500 LETS and community currency groups in over 39 countries, a number that will have surely increased by the time you read this![22]

Local Self-Sufficiency: The buy-local movement represents another promising natural economic trend. No, this is not an anti-foreigner phenomenon. Rather, it represents the recognition of two cost-effective principles. First, locally produced products are economically and energetically more efficient simply because they eliminate transportation charges. Second, and equally important, locally owned endeavors add to the quality of life and uniqueness of an area while literally multiplying that area's wealth.

Two recent studies bear this out. The first study concerned four types of businesses in San Francisco: books, sporting goods, toys and gifts, and limited-service dining. The study's results conclude that a mere 10 percent shift in retail spending from large chains to local stores resulted in nearly $192 million in increased economic output, $72 million in new income for workers, and more than $15 million in new retail activity.[23] A second study in Austin, Texas, concluded that if each household shifted $100 of holiday spending from chain stores to local merchants, it would have a $10 million positive impact on the local economy.[24]

How are these financial benefits possible? Big-box and chain stores take their earnings out of the community. In contrast, locally owned businesses recirculate money close to home: they hire local labor, buy goods and services from regional merchants, support community charities, and spend their profits with neighboring stores.

According to a study by the Go Local organization of Sonoma County, California, when purchases are made from locally owned businesses as opposed to national chains, the proceeds circulate three times longer in the community.[25]

To counter the daunting task of raising enough food for all 6.5 billion of us, the Go Local movement also has evolved a grow local branch that offers a simple and natural solution. The goal is for every community to become sustainable through food and energy self-sufficiency. And, because the sun and soil are the sources of all wealth, then a healthy, wealthy commonwealth begins with every community having access to this abundance.

Even in the most urbanized and ghettoized areas of our country, food can be grown locally and provide a thriving business opportunity. When inner-city residents have access to vacant lots, rooftops, or a corner of a schoolyard or park, they also acquire the possibility to grow, process, sell, and deliver food up the economic food chain.

Growing Happiness: To take the garden notion one step further, in a sense, each neighborhood, community, city, state, and nation is a garden with the potential to grow not only food but also other forms of renewable wealth, including intangibles like happiness. Perhaps we need to follow the lead of the Buddhist kingdom of Bhutan, where, back in the 1970s, King Jigme Singye Wangchuck decided the true measure of wealth is Gross National Happiness (GNH).

And what exactly is happiness? To the Bhutanese, it's a change in perspective. "The underlying message," according to an article in *Developments Magazine,* "is that the country should not sacrifice elements important for people's happiness to gain material development." In short, GNH takes into account not only the flow of money but also access to health care, free time with family, conservation of natural resources and other non-economic factors.[26]

In keeping with the Buddhist idea that the ultimate purpose of life is inner happiness, the Bhutanese society has decided to curtail the excessive use of consumer goods, essentially eliminating the corporate middle man, and cultivate the greatest good of all—happiness. Bhutan's lead begs the curious question: what if each nation, each region, and each community had a mission for maximizing happiness in the world, in its own unique way? Yes, what if?

We cannot underestimate the economic impact of well-being intangibles like love, happiness, imagination, and awareness. In an evolving economy, these are the multipliers that help us achieve what Buckminster Fuller would have termed a *dymaxion economy,* which means an economy based on "deriving maximum output from a minimum input of material and energy."

As we learned in the previous chapter, indices of well-being—love, happiness, peace, and equanimity—are contagious. For example, one person can walk into a room with love, and hundreds or maybe thousands absorb that love and carry it out of the room with them. The love of the original bearer is not only undiminished but has, very likely, increased. If ever there was a formula for applying the miracle of loaves and fishes, this is it!

As with every other aspect of the newly emerging holistic paradigm, the resolution of our economic predicament will inevitably involve a global decision made by the collective. How are collective decisions made? And how reliable are they? Are they made through some kind of Orwellian new world order in which we humans become little more than pre-programmed voting machines? Or are they made through something far more intelligent in the collective conscious that simultaneously generates maximum freedom and maximum connection?

The surprising answers to these questions, offered by modern science and from America's founders, are discussed in the next chapter.

CHAPTER 15

HEALING THE BODY POLITIC

"Imagine . . . going to the polling places
and being able to vote for the greater of two goods."
— **Swami Beyondananda**

Just as surely as our guardian beliefs about money and economics are up for re-examination and revision, our unconscious and unexamined beliefs about politics will also have to be transformed if we are to become the emergent organism called humanity.

To understand how fundamental the change in politics must be only requires a trip to the dictionary. Politics is commonly defined as "winning and holding control over a government" and "competition between special interest groups for power and leadership . . . characterized by artful and often dishonest practices." In a world that believes in dueling dualities, competing interests, and every cell for itself, it's understandable that the meaning of politics would come to represent competition, control, and unsavory means toward selfish ends.

The consequences of such self-serving politics are destructive. In an article titled "The Industrial System Isn't Intended to Bring Out the Best in People," environmental scientist Donella Meadows wrote: "Every day decent people clear cut forests, fish the oceans bare, spray toxins, bribe politicians, overcharge the government, take risks with the health of their workers or neighbors or customers, cheapen their products, pay people less than a living wage for a day's work, and fire their friends. 'If I don't do it, my competitor will,' they say regretfully, and they're right."[1]

That attitude exemplifies politics as a self-serving endeavor that, as we now know, has been shaped by Newtonian and Darwinian philosophy.

But, delving deeper into the dictionary, we find a less common usage of the term that aligns with our emerging holistic paradigm: "politics is the total complex of relations between people living in society." With that definition, we can see that our 50 trillion cells are a model community. And the wisdom of our cells to create harmonious politics within can be applied as new rules in the creation of a healthy body politic in which we organize, relate, and act together.

As we learned in Chapter 11 *Fractal Evolution,* and Chapter 12 *Time to See a Good Shrink,* cellular politics is characterized by:

- Unity combined with diversity through which each of the body's 200 different cell types perform diverse functions for the benefit of the collective whole

- A central intelligence system that coordinates all of the body's physiologic systems with the needs of individual cells

- A healthy balance between beneficial growth systems and occasionally necessary protection systems, both of which consume energy resources

These principles of unity and diversity, central intelligence, and balance between growth and protection, as expressed within the body, can be applied to the body politic to provide a new, more holistic definition: politics is how we organize, relate, and act together to promote the health of the whole of humanity and *every* individual in it.

And, by contrasting the social well-being of cellular politics with the crises generated by dysfunctional forms of human political organizations, it is obvious that a political evolution is in order.

So, how do we evolve politically? To explore this question, we first consider the obsolete and harmful consequences of Newtonian-Darwinian politics practiced today. Then we, once again, revisit the wisdom of America's Founding Fathers who set an example for a better way.

NEWTONIAN–DARWINIAN POLITICS

Modern medicine as based on Newtonian-Darwinian philosophy, perceives the body as little more than a physical machine in which equal and opposite forces push and pull against one another and every action provokes a reaction. When we encounter a symptom in our bodies that we don't like, doctors simply mobilize an opposing pharmaceutical force to overwhelm it. Frequently, the counterforce unintentionally unleashes other forces that produce negative consequences known as side effects.

The mechanics of Newtonian-Darwinian politics operate in a similar way. If a disturbing symptom, such as an inconvenient uprising of economically deprived peasants or spiritually disenfranchised terrorists, occurs, the response is to apply a counterforce. And, if the force doesn't work, then more force is added.

Often, in combat, the counterforce unleashes negative consequences, or side effects, that are deceivingly listed as *collateral damage,* which means civilian casualties, and the oxymoron *friendly fire,* which is the term for bullets and mortar that kill one's own troops.

The process of employing ever-escalating counterforces, followed to its illogical end, assures mutual destruction. Perhaps the most hilarious—but not really funny—representation of this behavioral absurdity and its inherent ineffectiveness can be seen in a scene from a Stan Laurel and Oliver Hardy film in which the two hapless heroes get into a fender bender with another car. In classic Oliver Hardy fashion, he twiddles his tie and says to Stan, "Let me handle this." Ollie then steps out of his vehicle to confront the other driver. Starting with finger-pointing, one thing leads to another, and, eventually, the other driver yanks the mirror off Ollie's car. In response, Ollie rips off the other car's headlight. This is followed by the other driver pulling the fender off Ollie's car. Every action provokes an escalated reaction until both drivers systematically and thoroughly dismantle each other's vehicles.

This scenario is now unfolding in the long-running non-comedy, The Iraqi Horror Picture Show, which has played an extended engagement in the Middle East. It is the story of every war in history, only more so. As horrible as wars have been, the increasing power to destroy combatants has had the side effect of causing more and more civilian casualties.

According to Norman Solomon, author of *War Made Easy,* civilians accounted for 15 percent of the casualties in World War I, 65 percent in World War II, and, now, more than 90 percent of the casualties in Iraq.[2] If this trend continues, the only way to assure personal safety will be to enlist in the military.

Conventional political policy conforms to the machinelike nature of a Newtonian-Darwinian Universe—and a Laurel and Hardy comedy—and encourages cyclic action-reaction responses to community disturbances. From a reductionist perspective, we tend to perceive each occurrence of civil unrest as a separate and unrelated event, merely the natural consequence of an eternal struggle to survive. But, in a holistic world in which we are all part of an interrelated Oneness, this is simply not true.

Consider how the destructive policies of the U.S. government's so-called *war on terror* would play out within the human body: Terrorist cells reported in the liver? Well, bomb the liver! They are too deeply entrenched? "Well, then, nuke the liver and radiate those terrorists! That'll teach the liver to harbor terrorist cells. Oh—the gall bladder and the pancreas are the liver's allies, part of an axis of evil. Nuke them, too!" And so on, until every last radical terrorist cell is dead. The unfortunate side effect of this strategy is that it would kill 90 percent of the innocent civilian cells in the process and, essentially, destroy the body. How's that for collateral damage?

The Newtonian-Darwinian Universe emphasizes a mechanism of distinct independent physical elements. In contrast, the quantum mechanical Universe demonstrates that everything is connected and that separation is an illusion.

In a Newtonian-Darwinian Universe, a cancer is perceived as an enclave of deviant cells living irresponsibly among normal body cells. To fight a cancer, medical doctors employ nuclear radiation, a military-like shock-and-awe response that releases chemotherapeutic poisons into the general cellular population. And, in the character of the military, the conventional medical paradigm dismisses the fact that many innocent, healthy cells will become collateral damage as an unavoidable side effect of these hostilities—this nuking of radical, irresponsible cells.

Because Western medicine equates the body with a machine, it is, therefore, concerned with dominating and controlling that machine. But Eastern medicine takes a completely different approach. Ayurvedic and traditional Chinese medicine see the body as a quantum holistic system. Rather than attacking a cancer with the intention of killing it, Eastern medicine first attempts to restore natural balance and harmony to the body. When an individual's internal environment is in a state of well-being, the biological terrain simply does not encourage nor support disease-producing disturbances.

Had the United States responded to the attack on the World Trade Center by using the cellular approach of simultaneously isolating the sociopathogens while encouraging greater health and harmony within the world environment, humanity might have taken an evolutionary step forward.

Following the lead of holistic practitioners, holistic politicians would have first tended to the several causes of the imbalance that inevitably precipitated the symptom—the attack. They would have regenerated harmony by dealing with grievances before they could manifest as grievous, retaliatory anger.

It is important to note that a *symptom*, whether in civil society or a cellular civilization, is not the *cause*, but a *consequence*. Failure to appreciate that distinction is the inherent folly in modern politics and modern medicine, both of which focus on eliminating, covering up, or masking the consequence while ignoring the cause. Reacting to the consequence without understanding the cause is the first step toward an inevitable escalation of continuous Newtonian-Darwinian, action-reaction responses.

Terrorist violence is a symptom of a much deeper social problem. In the case of The Iraqi Horror Picture Show, Western civilization's manipulation of and interference with Middle Eastern culture has created a tremendous social imbalance. The West's imperialistic attitude that *those people* are living on that sand above *our oil* has generated a deep sense of humiliation among Arabs and great disrespect for their invaders. The foolish attempt to eradicate terrorists has actually caused more terrorists and more terror, which is a situation that political leaders must address if there is to be a resolution.

Regarding the two current hot spots, Iraq and Iran, the U.S. seems to be suffering from a self-serving case of political Alzheimer's, conveniently forgetting that the Central Intelligence Agency (CIA) was responsible for manipulating politics and leadership in both countries. The CIA masterminded the regime change in Iraq in 1963 that brought Saddam Hussein's Ba'ath Party into power while making him head of Iraq's secret service.[3] The CIA literally put the fox in the hen house—until he was no longer an asset—then abetted President George W. Bush and his top aides who contrived an illegal invasion to fetch him out.

Similarly, the CIA overthrew Iran's popular and democratically elected ruler, Prime Minister Mohammed Mossadegh, in 1953 and installed its own candidate, General Mohammad Fazlollah Zahedi, and reinstated the monarchy of Mohammad Reza Pahlavi as the Shah of Iran.[4]

The Shah, who was pro-West, remained in power until 1979 when he was overthrown by a fed-up populace. The nerve of those Iranians to take back control of their own country! But, in a Newtonian-Darwinian political world built on opposing forces and counterforces, it is not surprising that the new leader, Sayyid Ruhollah Musavi Khomeini, the Ayatollah, proved to be an equally onerous political despot.

In addition to destabilizing Iran, Iraq, and other Middle East nations, Western political self-interests have equally disrupted the social systems of Central America, South America, Southeast Asia, and Africa. A century of Newtonian-Darwinian, push-pull political polarities have created such global tensions that civilization is now on the verge of a spontaneous combustion.

Fortunately, in the light of emerging new awareness, we have an opportunity to dissipate these political tensions and, instead, redirect their forces toward a spontaneous evolution. A major key to help us manifest a healthy order and a balanced body politic is embedded in America's founding documents.

THE AMERICAN EVOLUTIONARIES AND A *NEWER* WORLD ORDER

America's founders, as evolutionaries, intuitively understood the animistic worldview—the beneficial relationship of the individual, the collective, and the field—that new-edge science is beginning to realize and confirm. If we, as members of modern society, set aside the harmful practices of Newtonian–Darwinian politics in favor of a newer form of those original Native American beliefs, we can continue the evolution engendered by the men and women who transformed 13 individual colonies into a Constitutional nation designed to generate and safeguard the common good of all.

Influenced by the enlightenment philosophy of John Locke and Jean-Jacques Rousseau, the perennial wisdom of hermetic spiritual traditions, and interactions with Native Americans, the deistic founders sought to live in harmony with Nature.

Likewise, they perceived tyranny as an unnatural imbalance and, therefore, sought a positive political structure that ensured individual freedom along with that of a healthy, thriving society. In America's founding documents, they specifically emphasized four traits they believed were necessary to accomplish their goal: liberty, justice, truth, and equality.

- **Liberty:** As deists, the Founding Fathers understood liberty to be the free will of life that encourages growth and evolution. However, they also realized that, in order to sustain survival, liberty must be balanced with justice.

- **Justice:** Justice balances liberty because it tempers domination and recognizes each individual as free, equal, and worthy of fair treatment, a situation that justly secures the freedom of the whole. In short, justice is the Golden Rule codified by law.

- **Truth:** Truth preserves and nourishes justice both within the body and the body politic. Just as immune cells must correctly read internal signals and properly distinguish false threats from real danger, We the People, need clear, unspun information to accurately assess global situations and make decisions that are life-sustaining and not life-threatening.

- **Equality:** Equality is the balance between each and all combined with the lasting change that emerges from a critical mass of enlightened individuals.

Our forefathers recognized the value of *the commons,* an area within communities set aside for discussion in which the voice of each individual counts as much or as little as another's and where wealth and status are not used to judge one's worth. Through observation and participation in such discussions, they knew that creating a nation in which citizens respect each other as equals increases the chances that healthy individuals will voluntarily work together to benefit the entire commonwealth.

America's motto, *e pluribus unum,* "out of many, one," serves as a reminder that the one is not created through top-down imposition or kingly whimsy in a hierarchy of power but, rather, from the coherent effort of healthy, cooperative, sovereign individuals. It is an organization that is voluntary, not coercive.

THE CENTRAL VOICE OF DEMOCRACY: UNCOMMON COMMON WISDOM

Just as America's founders understood the animistic worldview, as described in the previous pages, they also believed in the power of free individuals to call forth a more coherent order. Today, more and more people are also recognizing the combined benefits of greater individual freedom and common wisdom.

Here are examples of how professionals, from journalists to software designers, from business executives and management consultants to therapists and faithkeepers, are applying or documenting that philosophy and changing the world's perspective.

American journalist James Surowiecki opens his book, *The Wisdom of Crowds,* with the tale about British anthropologist Francis Galton, the founder of *eugenics,* the science of genetic defects and presumed undesirable inheritable traits. As a scientist who had spent his life measuring human capabilities, Galton had concluded that humans simply didn't measure up. He found "the stupidity and wrongheadedness of many men and women being so great as to be scarcely credible."[5]

In 1906, the 84-year-old Galton was at an agricultural fair near his native Plymouth, England, when he observed a weight-judging competition in which individuals placed wagers and guessed what would be the total weight of an ox after it was slaughtered and dressed. While the bettors included butchers and farmers, most were average citizens with no familiarity of the meat packing business. Cynically, Galton described these people as a typical cross-section of the public who cast ballots in elections.

He decided to conduct an investigation that he ostensibly believed would prove the incompetence of the average individual who seemed so incapable of self-governance. After the contest was over, Galton assembled the 787 legible entries, added the contestants' estimates, and calculated the mean estimate, which was the average weight guessed by the crowd as a whole. Galton was completely surprised by the result. The average guessed weight was 1,197 pounds, only one pound less than the actual dressed weight of 1,198 pounds!

While not even the individual whose ticket won the wager came that close to guessing the actual weight, there was something about the collective guesses of average people that provided an awareness that not even an expert could match. Interpreting this phenomenon, Surowiecki suggests that each individual has limited knowledge, but when "aggregated in the right way, our [collective] intelligence is often excellent."[6]

Just as certain statistics, when charted, tend to plot as a bell-shaped curve, we might reasonably imagine that, when the judgment and perspective of a large enough sample of individuals are combined, their mean estimate would approximate the real answer or the best possible solution to any given problem.

Another example of mass common wisdom occurred during the aftermath of the tragic explosion of the space shuttle Challenger in 1986.

Because the launch was televised, people saw it as it happened and news of the disaster spread instantly. When reports of the accident hit the Dow Jones newswire, investors immediately began unloading stocks in the four companies responsible for building the Challenger and its engines: Lockheed, Martin Marietta, Rockwell, and Morton Thiokol. But by the end of the day, all the companies' stocks had begun to rebound except Morton Thiokol's, which remained 12 percent down.[7]

This market reaction indicates that traders sensed Morton Thiokol was responsible for the accident, even though no one really knew which company's part had failed. Six months later, investigators of the crash determined that faulty O-ring seals on the booster rocket caused the Challenger disaster. Morton Thiokol made those seals. How on Earth—or, how in space—did the investment public intuit that result months before the experts released their findings?

Surowiecki's research led him to conclude that three factors influence the accuracy of a crowd's common wisdom: diversity, independence, and decentralization.

Diversity: In Newtonian-Darwinian thinking, the political atrocity of ethnic cleansing is considered to be good because it rids a nation of persons—*others*—who might look different or disagree with *our way of thinking.* The same misperception applies to blackballing an individual from a group. In contrast, the evolving holistic view realizes the benefit of diversity.

In decision-making or problem-solving situations, the perspectives of a diverse group offer more accuracy than a homogeneous group of specialists. That's because people who are more intelligent or knowledgeable about a particular issue tend to think alike, whereas a group with a variety of perspectives will exhibit a broader range of wisdom.

Surowiecki concluded, "Adding in a few people who know less, but have different skills, actually improves a group's performance."[8] In other words, a large group that includes individuals with different life experiences will generate more precise forecasts and make more intelligent decisions than even those considered to be skilled decision makers.

Independence: The second factor that influences crowd accuracy is independence. When groups talk among themselves, they tend to prematurely come to consensus and conform to a norm. Generally, however, agreement on what are perceived to be normalized responses does not imply that the conclusion is right, proper, or beneficial. In situations where an individual or individuals have a higher standing within a group, members of that group tend to follow the leader. And the more people in a group who conform to an opinion, the harder it becomes for those with minority views to have their opinions considered.

In contrast, consider the independent thinking of the people who guessed the weight of the ox. Individually, each offered an answer, secretly scribbled on a piece of paper, without conversation and without expert testimony from those who—apologizing in advance for a very bad pun—had some kind of ox to grind. The result was a common wisdom, generated by independent thought, collectively stated through what was, in effect, a ballot process.

Decentralization: Conventional thinking holds that ownership and control of solutions is good. This applies to businesses seeking greater profit or to individuals desirous of higher status or praise on the job or recognition within their families or social groups. To that end, corporations, for example, often sequester a group of in-house specialists to work on a specific problem, to the exclusion of external points of view. And individuals may retain secrets they believe will give them an edge.

In contrast, decentralization demonstrates that collective problem solving is actually a better process for health and wealth of both the individual and the community.

All three of these factors—diversity, independence, and decentralization—are found in the concept of *shared awareness,* which has inspired the profoundly efficient and effective wiki Internet software that allows collaborative editing of Webpage content and structure by all members of a population. This facilitates awareness and rapidly accelerates the learning curve for all. The best-known wiki Website is Wikipedia, the constantly expanding living encyclopedia.

In *Wikinomics: How Mass Collaboration Changes Everything,* Canadian business executive Don Tapscott and consultant Anthony D. Williams described wikis as, "self-organizing, egalitarian communities of individuals who come together voluntarily to produce a shared outcome."[9] Thanks to the power of computers and the reach of the World Wide Web, problems can now be exposed to the expertise and wisdom of a whole world of independent minds.

Tapscott and Williams tell the remarkable story of Goldcorp, a small Toronto-based gold mining company that defied precedent by making its proprietary information public and offering $575,000 in prizes to those who could best help them locate "the next 6 million ounces of gold." This *open source strategy* provided so much awareness that Goldcorp transformed from a $100 million company to a business worth over $9 billion.[10]

Surowiecki cites another wiki success in the story of Linux, the highly productive open source software system designed by Finnish software designer Linus Torvalds in 1991. Rather than holding on to the proprietary rights of his system, Torvalds revealed his code to the world and sought feedback for improvements from all interested computer scientists. Almost immediately, he received suggestions from programmers around the world. Thanks to the common wisdom offered by individuals working in their areas of interest, Linux has become an ever-learning, growing, and increasingly robust system.[11]

Open source wisdom offered by wikis may, in fact, provide the key to solving society's most challenging problems that have, until now, been exacerbated by the secrecy of a for-profit-first—rather than a for-the-good-of-all—mentality. What better way to think globally and act locally than to have ideas from one place tried elsewhere with both successes and failures reported for everyone to see? After all, life itself is open source.

How can open source systems influence our collective political wisdom? Tom Atlee, founder of the Co-Intelligence Institute and author of *The Tao of Democracy,* confirmed and expanded on Surowiecki's findings that the crowd tends to be wiser than its wisest members. Atlee suggested that specific skills can be cultivated that help extract wisdom from groups. Not surprisingly, these skills invite openness and suppress domination by an individual or an idea.

Atlee cited an experiment reported by management consultant Marilyn Loden in her book, *Feminine Leadership.* Small groups of executives were given a simulated wilderness problem to solve. Teams comprised only of females arrived at better solutions than all-male teams, not because the women were smarter individually but because their natural collaborative style made them collectively smarter. In contrast, male groups were hampered by individuals who asserted their own solutions and inhibited access to group wisdom.[12]

And what exactly is wisdom in regard to political situations and collective decision-making? Atlee defined it as "seeing beyond immediate appearances and acting with greater understanding to affirm the life and development of all."[13] Perspective offers wisdom. Therefore, communities have greater potential for wisdom than do individuals. "Communities are wise," Atlee explained, "to the extent they use diversity well in a cooperative, creative interplay of viewpoints that allows the wisest, most comprehensive and powerful truths to emerge."[14]

Atlee said the tool to access wisdom is *co-intelligence,* which he defined as, "integrating the diverse gifts of all for the benefit of all."[15] Clearly, our body, our organs, and our cells are co-intelligent, a trait that enables them to co-evolve with their environment. Likewise, when applied, co-intelligence enables ordinary people to access extraordinary wisdom through which we can, hopefully, practice evolution and reach transcendent solutions.

TRANSCENDENT SOLUTIONS: PRACTICING EVOLUTION

A primary function of politics is to develop policies that preempt conflict. Conflict is a natural part of human life and social interactions and should not be confused with violence, which is the most dysfunctional way to handle conflict. Conflict derives from incompatibilities between two or more opinions, principles, or interests. Because conflict usually involves contradictory goals, resolution can occur when something—the goals or expectations regarding those goals—is changed.

In the classic book on negotiation, *Getting to Yes,* authors Roger Fisher and William Ury suggested that breakthroughs in conflicts come when positions are deconstructed and transformed into expressions of legitimate interests. Once disagreeing parties clarify their interests, they can reframe the conflict as a shared problem and, thus, see each other as colleagues working together to resolve that problem.[16]

Careful and respectful listening by all participants is required for this process to occur, continue, and be successful. When a party to the discussion makes an emotional statement or raises an objection, it is an opportunity to ask, "What is your concern?" The response may be rational or irrational, but either way, it must be heard and recognized as an insight that could lead to a key breakthrough.

The result of this process, whether resolving conflict or developing a policy to preempt conflict, is often an emergent solution that could not have been predicted at the start of the process. When a solution is sought at a higher level of consciousness than that which created the problem, it facilitates access to this higher wisdom.

Tom Atlee tells the story of an Indiana farmer who found his neighbor's dogs killing his sheep. Too often the way of solving such problems involved confrontation, threats, lawsuits, barbed wire fences, and, potentially, shotguns. This particular farmer had a better idea. He gave his neighbor's children lambs as pets. This out-of-the-box solution established a win-win proposition: for the sake of the children's adorable pets, the neighbors voluntarily tied up their dogs, and the families became friends.[17]

Johan Galtung, a Norwegian pioneer in peace and conflict resolution, made a career of finding what he called *the fifth way*, or *fivers*. Galtung recognized that every conflict has five potential resolutions:

1. I win. You lose.

2. You win. I lose.

3. Negative Transcendence in which the problem is solved by avoiding it entirely.

4. Compromise in which each wins by agreeing to lose a little.

5. Transcendence, which produces a resolution above and beyond the problem.

Conventional politics seeks to resolve issues through compromise, which, at best, leaves everyone equally dissatisfied. In contrast, the transcendent fiver solution generates a positive feeling among all parties. The first step in bringing forth a fiver is the intention between two opposing polarities not to meet in the middle but to join forces and move forward together toward an optimal solution.

The power of Galtung's fiver approach is exemplified in negotiations he mediated over a 55-year-old border dispute between Peru and Ecuador. What was the emergent solution to a polarized border dispute? No border at all! Today, the contested area is a thriving bi-national zone run by and for both countries, and it even includes a jointly administered nature park.[18]

This is holistic politics at its best because it involves the practice of evolution, seeking emergent both-and solutions that are beyond the dualistic either-or conflict.

Atlee supports the power of pooled and cooperative experience. He acknowledges that, as a society, we "have reached the limits of an atomistic approach to citizenship—in which individual perspectives simply add up when we agree, or cancel each other out when we do not."[19]

A MISSING PERSONS REPORT ON WE THE PEOPLE

The current opposing-party system of politics is designed to manipulate public opinion rather than cultivate public wisdom. As a result, the public usually has to choose between two less-than-satisfying alternatives. If ever the world needed a fiver worldview, now is the time.

So what is stopping us? Given the inherent wisdom of crowds, why does our collective political judgment, particularly recently, seem so flawed and so easily manipulated?

One answer is corporate media, which is the right-hand helper of the current Newtonian-Darwinian political structure and is not the central voice of democracy.

In the current atmosphere of privatized falsehood masquerading as truth and intentional distortion to exploit and dominate the public, it's easy to forget that the Founding Fathers didn't design freedom of speech and freedom of press so that we could utter George Carlin's "seven words" on TV or get porn in our inbox. The real reason for these freedoms is to ensure that sovereign citizens have all the information, perspective, and viewpoints needed to effectively respond to the issues of the day—so we can better come up with our collective fivers.

Another answer is the belief of some in *cynical realism,* which holds there is no truth. Adherents of this philosophy emphasize that "Life is a battle of all against all," a belief that stems directly from Darwin's survival of the fittest and is an example of Galtung's Negative Transcendence, which, entirely and pessimistically, avoids the problem of truth or not truth.

Meanwhile, even those addicted to mainstream news have a gnawing sense they are being lied to. Consequently, an undercurrent of cynicism—you can't believe *anything*—creates another level of self-disempowerment. Because nothing seems to be true, why bother to exercise discernment or integrity? Philosopher Aldous Huxley offered an important insight on the negative consequence of this ideology when he wrote: "Cynical realism—it's the intelligent man's best excuse for doing nothing in an intolerable situation."[20]

Thus, we see that the current political dysfunction is kept in place by our own disempowering developmental programming and the politicians, corporations, and media moguls who benefit from that programming.

While We the People could rightly be faulted for apathy, the truth is that the average adult is far busier nowadays than his or her counterpart half a century ago. How ironic that back in the '50s, people imagined that by now we'd be living a paradise, working a three-day week. In the United States today, the average family needs two breadwinners working full-time . . . to barely make it. Civic life? Who has time for it? Consequently, in the transition from town hall to global village, the resonant central voice of We the People has been drowned out by the massive media voice of we, the very, very select people.

THE SYSTEM IS THE PROBLEM

To evolve the revolutionary vision of America's Founding Fathers one evolutionary step further, we must now wake up our minds and see the light of our new awareness, the need for an intelligent central voice, and the inherent wisdom of the crowd.

A key to that wake-up call comes from business consultant Jim Rough, author of *Society's Breakthrough! Releasing Essential Wisdom and Virtue in All the People.* Rough uses a technique he named Dynamic Facilitation to replace mutual stuckness with common wisdom. To demonstrate how to transcend the current political structure, which is designed for battling, he asked an audience to select a contentious issue and assured them he would facilitate a resolution within 30 minutes. The group chose the highly charged topic of abortion.

At first, participants expressed the usual binary pro-life and pro-choice positions that demand a divisive this-or-that resolution. Once all the either-or positions had been stated and written on a board for all to see, Rough asked for other possible suggestions. A period of silence ensued as the group pondered unfamiliar territory outside the box.

Thus, Rough motivated them to look beyond the symptom, that is, abortion, and seek the cause of the dispute. At the end of 30 minutes, despite having voiced sharply different views, the group came to a breakthrough question that defined the real problem: "How can we achieve a society where all children are conceived and born into families who want and love them?" Rough stated, "This kind of consensus, a pulling together of what everyone thinks, *can always be reached.*"[21]

However, in order to truly understand the power of Rough's process and how it can transform politics in America and elsewhere, let's begin with the universal conclusion arrived at in every one of his group sessions: the system is the problem.

This is not intended to slough off personal responsibility but, rather, to acknowledge that, in the absence of a coherent voice of We the People, a heartless, soulless, self-perpetuating system persists.

In order to understand how America arrived at this position, let's go back to the radical notions of America's Founding Fathers. While they believed that government must serve the people, the new government they created stopped short of actually giving power to the people. Instead of a democracy, they actually created a republic.

The subtle, yet profound, distinction between these two terms can be traced to their etymologic roots. The word democracy comes from the Greek *demos*, which means "the people," and *kratia*, which means "power." And the word republic comes from the Latin *res*, which means "thing," and *publica*, which means "of the people." The distinction is that a democracy is ruled by the power of the people while, in a republic, people empower a thing to rule them.

Participatory democracy is a government in which people govern directly, and decisions, such as starting or ending a war or raising or lowering taxes, require a vote of the people. In subtle contrast, a republic is an *indirect democracy* in which decisions are made by the people's elected representatives. In this manner, America's founders carefully crafted a balance of power that not only protects the many—We the People—from the few who would control but protects the few from the many who might transform into a rebellious mob.

That is all well and good, but the problem today is that the system, as it has evolved toward Newtonian-Darwinian thinking, no longer holds elected representatives accountable. Consequently, they are no longer obligated to govern and vote on behalf of the people they were elected to represent, and they can just as easily vote to further the interests of special interest groups, big corporations, or even themselves.

This is why the Constitution, as it has been amended and interpreted over the decades, no longer defines the country as being either a democracy or a republic. Rather than ensuring that We the People govern through our representatives, it now allows our representatives to govern us and make decisions detrimental to the common good.

Fortunately, thanks to instant global communication through the Internet, more functional ideas and individuals are coming to the fore and gathering support.

THE SHAPE OF POLITICS TO COME?

At the beginning of this chapter, we posed the question: "So, how do we evolve politically?" To answer that, we compared Newtonian-Darwinian politics with the beneficent formula of politics established by America's Founding Fathers. We also showed a comparison between the intentions of the founders and the extent to which their intentions have devolved.

Here's another comparison that will help us answer that question and understand the shape of politics to come.

Jim Rough suggests that, throughout history, civilizations have employed some form of governance that can be depicted by geometric shapes: triangle, box, and circle.[22]

Triangle: The first form of governance is top-down: rule by chiefs, kings, or emperors. Rough depicts this form of governance as a triangle, which represents dependence.

As a form of leadership, the triangle is elementary, if not infantile. Just as children depend on parents for sustenance, order, and discipline, an uninformed populace depends on an appointed leader to do the same for them.

This is the form of governance imposed by historical English kings and queens on their subjects and colonies around the world.

Box: The second form of governance involves a set of rules and agreements created by the populace rather than the arbitrary rule of a top-down hierarchy. Rough depicts this form of governance as a box, which represents the metaphorical container into which the rules, such as the U.S. Constitution, are placed and held sacred. This form of governance relies on the will of free people and therefore represents independence.

Just as adolescents break loose from parental authority to explore their own power and resources, our Founding Fathers offered their fellow colonialists the wherewithal to be independent individuals, an offer that broke loose as the American Revolution.

While America's founders offered a vast improvement over King George's monarchy, their republic was still a thing. Yes, it was created by independent, sovereign citizens and codified by the Constitution and the rule of justice, but it was still a machine that had no inherent moral authority. Like any machine, it could be used for purposes dictated by those who sit in the driver's seat. Over the last two centuries, We the People have gotten so far away from the actual driver's seat that we are now hostages in the backseat, if not locked in the trunk. The thing that the people created is being driven by the self-interests of those who perceive themselves as the politically fittest in the struggle for survival.

More distressing is the fact that the machine called government is now being ruled by itself to perpetuate itself. This situation is eerily similar to that in Stanley Kubrick's movie *2001: A Space Odyssey* in which the spaceship's onboard computer, HAL, takes over control of the ship and locks out the crew to pursue its own machine-like interests. Our own box-like creation, a self-serving and self-perpetuating unaccountable government has likewise locked out and disenfranchised the American public. Things feel so out of control because the intrinsic moral values of 95 percent of Americans have been overridden by the sociopathic values of a mere 5 percent of the population. Two hundred years ago when the founders were designing this government, their fear was mob rule. Thanks to the absence of the central voice, the new threat is mobster rule.

Circle: Fortunately, there is a third shape of governance—a circle—that can enable our species to achieve "humanifest destiny." Every point on a circle is equidistant from the center and is equally important to maintain the shape of the circle. Therefore, the circle represents interdependence. Not to be confused with co-dependence, interdependence means a community of capable, diverse, and co-equal individuals who recognize that self-interest and mutual interest are one and the same.

And, while both James Surowiecki and Jim Rough view independence as something good to be appreciated, we must also recognize it as merely a necessary stepping-stone on our path of evolution that has led us from the triangle's political childhood to the box's political adolescence and is now leading us to the circle of political adulthood.

The power of the circle as an access point to a field of higher wisdom was first recognized by Earth's indigenous people. Oren Lyons, faithkeeper of the Turtle Clan of the Onondaga Iroquois, described tribal council sessions during which everyone sits in a circle this way, "We meet and just keep talking until there's nothing left but the obvious truth."[23]

A Native American elder, storyteller, and author named Manitonquat, whose name means Medicine Story, uses the same circle to turn around the lives of hardened criminals. Manitonquat runs a highly successful program in New England prisons. He wrote: "Our people noticed long ago that the circle is the basic form of Creation. In the circle, all are equal; there is no top or bottom, first or last, better or worse."[24]

Manitonquat stated that the golden key in this process is respect. He said, "Most of these prisoners have never in their lives been listened to with respect. Very few have persons in their experience who have shown them respect in any manner at all."

To ensure respect, Manitonquat employs a talking stick, held by the person speaking, to empower and liberate that person to speak freely and to remind others in the circle to listen intently. He tells prisoners, "No one was ever like you in all of the universe, and there will never be another one like you again. Therefore, only you have your special gift, and you are the only one who can give it away . . . the rest of us need to receive your gift and hear your story."[25]

Only 5 to 10 percent of convicts who complete Manitonquat's program ever return to prison as compared to a recidivism rate of 65 to 85 percent for the general prison population. This wildly effective rehabilitation program is amazingly inexpensive. As a volunteer, Manitonquat serves 120 to 150 inmates in seven state prisons for only $100 a month in travel expenses.

Many convicts who complete the program return to their home neighborhoods with the desire to, as Manitonquat described, "replace the pyramid of domination with the circle of equality and respect."[26]

Box in Circle: The next evolutionary form of governance may be represented by a box within a circle. Under this visionary plan, inside-the-box governmental paradigms would still hold elections and make and enforce laws. However, the box, which contains our Constitutional independence, would exist inside the interdependent circle of We the People.

To encircle the box of government with collective wisdom and co intelligence, Tom Atlee, Jim Rough and others propose citizen deliberative councils or citizen wisdom councils. These or similarly named groups of randomly selected persons focus on issues and policies that are mired in conflict then glean common wisdom and make it available to the entire community or nation.

These councils are holistic in two ways: First, they seek input from the broadest range of information and points of view, even ideas that seem outside the box. Second, they seek solutions that address the well-being of the whole versus that of special interest groups. In contrast to the static positions that typify binary politics where one party is pitted against another, citizen deliberative councils offer dynamic, emergent solutions.

One example occurred in 1997 when 15 citizens who represented Boston's diverse population convened to consider that city's telecommunications policies. The group's membership included a high-tech business manager, a homeless person, and people of various other social and financial strata. The group spent two weekends becoming familiar with the issues and, then, two days listening to expert testimony.

After deliberating, they came up with an impressive consensus statement, which they presented to the public. Even though none of these individuals were experts—or, perhaps, because of that fact—they were able to process the testimony into workable policy. Dick Sclove, the lead organizer, reported that, by the end of the process, these average citizens knew more about telecommunications issues than their elected representatives who vote on them.[27]

Jim Rough says that wisdom councils that employ the principles of Dynamic Facilitation can provide "a nonjudgmental, heartfelt, energy-driven creative thinking process in which people seek to invent new options that work for everyone. Instead of negotiating agreement on particular points or discussing ideas back and forth, people seek breakthroughs everyone can support."[28]

While such councils have the inferred power of moral authority and could recommend new solutions to the public, they do not possess coercive powers associated with the authority to pass legislation. Yet, Tom Atlee reports that citizen deliberative councils have been used by the Canadian government and by the Danish Parliament to generate recommendations for legislation and new policy.[29]

Regardless of the level of government or community in which they are used, such councils and their evolutionary principles offer society a vision of what a healed body politic might look like. And with that vision, we will hopefully see that new form of governance, the box that is the rule of law inside the circular, coherent, central voice of We the People.

Then, the next questions become: How do we get there from here? How do we bring mistrustful and long-separated parties together? How do we lift ourselves from the habits of separation, mistrust, hatred, and retribution? And what is the new organizing principle for the body politic?

HEARTLAND SECURITY

In the final chapters of the book, and particularly this chapter, we have used our cellular community to reflect on the body politic. However, there is one body part that we have not yet addressed in Part III, and it is now time for the discussion to get to the heart of the matter—or, more accurately, the matter of the heart.

We have seen how a body politic that has lost connection with its heart and soul can lose its way. To emerge a new political order in which each individual is viewed as an equally valuable cell in the body of humanity involves shifting our focus from a fear-based homeland security to a love-based heartland security.

In her aptly titled book *Waking the Global Heart: Humanity's Rite of Passage from the Love of Power to the Power of Love*, author and therapist Anodea Judith wrote that "the rite of passage into the future" is through an awakening of the global heart. If future generations are alive to tell the human story, "it will only be because the best of humanity prevailed and pulled together with a love so profound that the seemingly impossible was achieved."[30]

The best of humanity to whom Judith refers isn't some righteous elite but, rather, the potential that each of us holds within. Perhaps love—the invisible force that can induce a cancer cell to slow its growth—is humanity's secret peaceful force that will enable us to transcend survival and live in thrival. If so, it's the most underutilized tool in our political toolbox and the one ripest for development. As discovered by HeartMath researchers, coherent hearts entrain with one another. Consequently, it is feasible that we can entrain our hearts to collectively focus love energy into a coherent healing force.

Indigenous cultures and medieval villages often had a communal hearth at the center of the village. Initially, the fire was used to keep predators away. Over time, it came to represent the presence of spirit looking over the community. In Western culture, where tending the spiritual fires has been left to religious authorities, people have become disconnected from their common spiritual bonds. The only time the masses experience a collective connection is when an extraordinary event occurs, such as a man walking on the moon, or when tragedy strikes, as in New York on September 11, 2001.

What would it be like to have a preemptive secular, yet spiritual, connection in every neighborhood, city, and nation to affirm the values that the vast majority of people have in common?

Such a network has been quietly evolving in Reno, Nevada. Launched in 2003, an organization called the Conscious Community Network (CCN) brings together diverse elements of the city and surrounding region to improve the communal, economic, and spiritual quality of life in the area. Without fanfare—but with lots of fans—CCN has based its work on what it called "the universal spiritual virtues of Love, Integrity, Courage, Service, and Respect."[31]

The CCN organization and its leadership mobilized local and state governments to establish Independents Day, an awareness campaign to encourage the public to buy local goods and services. They created a Local Food System Network of local producers and consumers that birthed an alliance of persons with diverse religious beliefs who share a common desire for organic produce.

By weaving together common sense traditional values with the global understanding that we're all in this together, the Conscious Community Network created what is termed a *third force,* a political entity that more closely resembles the circle than the conventional American political box. CCN's work supports transpartisanship, which acknowledges the validity of truths across a range of political perspectives and seeks to synthesize them into an inclusive, practical unity outside of conventional political dualities.

CCN relies on grassroots volunteers who work directly with people, thus sidestepping the government or other established institutions. This completely organic and non-coercive, self-generating project offers an evolutionary model for non-governmental governance that expands awareness by creating community.

Business owner Richard Flyer, the organization's visionary founder, described this new awareness network as "an intentional community without walls, with a desire to open hearts and build bridges between people of diverse beliefs and backgrounds."[32] Flyer sees himself and his organization as a weaver of health-enhancing, life-affirming, joy-producing elements in the community.

Flyer's communal matrix offers a largely invisible infrastructure of relationships that support individual, community, and planetary health. Flyer suggested, "By connecting the dots between 'like-hearted people' who want to uplift humanity—people found within every local community and in all social groupings—we release the 'creative intelligence' to grow a new society within the old."[33]

People in Reno and in countless other communities where wisdom councils, world cafés, and other active listening groups form are discovering two profound truths. First, the connection in the heart is far more powerful than divisive beliefs in the head. Second, the circle of inclusion is much more beneficial than the box of separation.

The heart of humanity is calling for a safe, generative environment of respectful communication, which is the foundation for a healthy and sane political structure. As with so many other aspects of this new, transformational story, We the People are being called upon to release our either-or polar positions and embrace both-and opportunities.

LIFE IS PROGRESSIVE . . . AND CONSERVATIVE

Here's another reason why true security originates in the land of the heart. As modern life becomes more stressful and overwhelming, people tend to over-identify with their beliefs. When these beliefs are polarizing, inaccurate, or downright false, they are even more problematic because they become life-threatening.

Consider the commonality as well as the distinction between progressive and conservative. Both are natural impulses and elemental components of life. However, when they become beliefs—and rigid ones at that—they can harden into opposing polarities that keep the system from growing.

Since the cultural upheaval that followed the war in Vietnam, Americans have divided themselves into two combative factions: blue-tribe progressive Democrats and red-tribe conservative Republicans. Locked in a dysfunctional conflict, these two groups spend much of their vitality and energy arguing about whether it's more wrong to kill the born or to kill the unborn. Meanwhile, survival of both the born and the not-yet-born is in danger because planetary web-of-life-threatening issues aren't being addressed.

If we rise above and beyond these dueling dualities, we see that both progressive beliefs and conservative beliefs align with the natural forces of growth and protection. Fundamentally, life is progressive because it is ever-growing and ever-evolving. Life is also conservative, as evidenced by a husk that protects its vulnerable seed. A seed in its husk, like an egg in its shell, represents the harmonious and collaborative integration of progressive and conservative functions. Both are necessary for life to successfully move forward.

However, in our society, progressive and conservative factors are profoundly out of balance. The old story of domination has been so pervasive in our culture that the structures of protection that we've built now endanger the progression of life. The social imbalance we are afflicted with might appropriately be diagnosed as MIC, Military-Industrial Complex. MIC is a self-destructive auto-immune disorder that is threatening the well-being of civilization.

As emphasized earlier, Nature intends for us to use protection behaviors as little as possible. That's because, while protection provides life-saving responses, it also consumes massive wealth and compromises the system's life-sustaining growth processes.

That is why when we learn to rise above opposing polarities and create a state of "emergent seeing," we'll recognize that, by enhancing community awareness, we reduce the need for protection. This is the exact motivation that led 6 Native American tribes to form the Iroquois Confederacy and 13 American colonies to form the United States. And please note the words they chose to describe those entities: confederacy means "an alliance for a common purpose," and united means "a single entity in harmony."

While life and evolution seek to progress toward greater common purpose—harmony and community—there is a conservative impulse born of the American Revolution that wants to ensure that freedom of the individual doesn't become overwhelmed by the needs of the collective. Moreover, in the past century, conservatives have become overly sensitive to the utopian dreams of Soviet and Chinese communism that devolved into dystopian totalitarian nightmares. In the face of worldwide financial and military power, conservatives are rightly concerned about the notion of an even more horrific new world order based on the same top-down control by the powerful elite.

However, the new holistic world order would be circular and profoundly different because it would arise from the bottom up as a functional matrix for mutual benefit, connection, and community. It would be an evolved perspective that would actually enhance individual freedom. The less we need to protect ourselves from one another, the more freedom and wealth we will have to pursue happiness. And the wonderful side effect is that more happiness on the planet will mean less need for protection from each other.

To build on the work of imaginal political philosophers and activists such as Tom Atlee, Jim Rough, Richard Flyer, and other healers of the body politic, we will find ourselves cohering around the new moral authority of *we're all in this together*. From this perspective, progressive and conservative will shift from being two opposite polarities, seeking to dominate, and, instead, become fully empowered dance partners, working in concert. Imagine what it would be like were we to collectively ask and answer the questions: "How do we wish to progress?" and "What do we choose to conserve?"

Thanks to the Internet's ability to connect the global village, these conversations are already underway. Politics is, indeed, on the cusp of achieving its highest purpose: to promote and sustain a healthy humanity on a wealthy planet where every cellular soul thrives. All that is needed now is the willingness of a critical mass of humanity to participate in changing our story.

CHAPTER 16

A Whole New Story

*"It's time we put our energy into fruitfully re-growing
the Garden instead of fruitlessly scrapping over the scraps."*
— Swami Beyondananda

We have now come full circle. Our journey began with a story about the power of stories, particularly invisible ones that permeate our consciousness and filter our experiences without our even being aware of their existence. Myth-perceptions distort our stories and have led us down the road to societal dysfunction and destruction of our sacred habitat.

Now that we have explored suggestions for a new story based on new-edge science and perennial wisdom, we are presented with a challenge: How do we change the old story and write a new one? How do we shift from a way of life based on obsolete understandings to one based on truer truths? How do we participate in the conscious evolution of the new super-organism humanity?

As the name implies, humanity is a life form defined by the trait of being *humane*. Throughout history, there have been exemplary humans who lived by the humane values of compassion, philanthropy, kindness, tolerance, benevolence, charity, and generosity. However, as a consequence of developmental programming, profoundly influenced by myth-perceptions, too many humans live lives characterized by indifference, intolerance, cruelty, spitefulness, and even barbaric behavioral traits that are far from humane. Today's civilization, by strict definition, more accurately represents inhumanity than humanity.

From an evolutionary standpoint, we can no longer point to the best among us as evidence of our fitness. As we find our civilization precariously perched on the Endangered Species List, our biological imperative is unconsciously driving us to adopt humane traits so that humans may fully evolve into the life-sustaining organism defined as humanity.

Great idea, but how?

It is evident that the current basal paradigmatic beliefs offered by scientific materialism, yet disproved by new science, are not able to meet our challenges. Given this understanding, the first step is to collectively detach from the limiting beliefs that prevent us from realizing our true human potential.

What if we changed our beliefs? After all, as we have seen, we are living in a world of make believe, that is, we make what we believe. To make something different, we must believe something different. Consider the alternative realities that might arise by releasing the collectively agreed upon conventional beliefs that only matter matters, that the law of the jungle rules, that we are frail and powerless slaves to our genes, and that we are here because of a random throw of the evolutionary dice.

Not only must we dismantle the obsolete story and replace it with a more viable one, we must also heal the wounds the old story has inflicted over the ages. Reprogramming and healing must occur on both an individual level and a collective level. In a fractal—as above, so below—reality, there cannot be an evolved organism without first having evolved cells.

The intention of this final chapter, titled *A Whole New Story,* is not to provide a detailed version of civilization's new story. We offer, instead, an outline based on new insights from new-edge science with the hope that it will serve as the foundation for an evolving wiki on humanity's evolution. This wiki will inevitably be written and rewritten a great many times over the next decade as we evolve into the new millennium. This whole new story will not be only about ourselves or our tribe or our nation, not even only about humanity, but about the whole of existence. Before we get too far ahead of ourselves, though, let's review what we now know as well as the implications of that knowledge, in other words, "What's so!" and "So what?"

WHAT'S SO!—SO WHAT?

Once, a friend stopped by while on a pilgrimage from Los Angeles to San Francisco. Our friend and six other seekers were en route to a New Age mega-conference that featured wisdom luminaries such as Deepak Chopra, Wayne Dyer, and Louise Hay, among others. As is our habit, we greeted and hugged our friend and each in his entourage as they exited their van. One of the women in the group, with furrows between her eyes as deep as the Grand Canyon, was so stiff that, when hugged, she elicited a response from us that she should relax. That sparked an immediate and irritated response, "I am relaxed!" and anger at the very suggestion that she was not.

After we gently reminded her of the negative physiologic consequences of tension, she rattled off a laundry list of comments about stress, tension, and health. Had this been an oral exam for a New Age wisdom course, this woman would have received an A+ grade. However, because of the anger she generated in her defense, she would have failed the experiential laboratory portion of such a course.

Similarly, we have been to environmental and sustainability conferences where the trash cans were filled to the brim with empty plastic water bottles.

The point is that, while our conscious minds may easily learn new life-enhancing information, that information may never make it below the neck and into the domain of action. This is understandable when we remember that subconscious programs control 95 percent of our behavior.

If this book were part of an academic course in school, we might say, "Okay, close your text and take out a pencil and paper for a quiz." Clearly, many of you would score an A by rehashing the scientific data we have provided. But, while this book offers interesting new insights to ponder, the relevance of this information is predicated on the reader's consideration of this fundamental question: "How would my life be different if I incorporated this awareness into my behavioral programming?"

Civilization is now confronted with major scientific upheavals that profoundly impact our story and our lives. The new insights are not matters of supposition; they are matters of fact. Consequently, the story offered by new-edge science does not suggest that we change our collective behavior; it demands that we change it!

The scientific principles that necessitate behavioral change are derived from many disciplines. The new science of holism emphasizes that, in order for us to transcend the parts and see the whole, we must acquire an understanding of Nature and the human experience.

The conventional idea that biology, physics, and mathematics represent entirely different fields of knowledge has become an evolution-limiting misperception. All systematic studies on the structure and behavior of the natural world are intimately entangled and fall under the one roof of science. The knowledge accumulated under that roof can be assembled into a structure that resembles a multi-tiered building, with each floor built upon the scientific foundation provided by the supporting lower levels.

The floors of the building, as illustrated below, represent the basic scientific disciplines. The ground level is mathematics, upon which is assembled physics. Built upon physics is chemistry. Chemistry serves as the platform for biology, which is the basis for psychology, the building's fifth and, currently, top level.

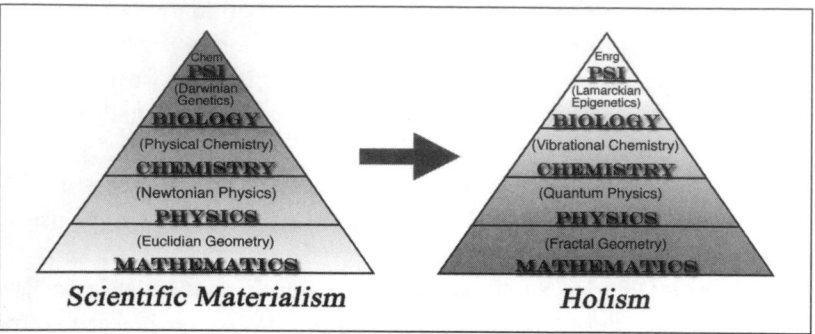

Each level of science is based upon previously established levels of science.

This hierarchical structure illustrates that a science on a lower level is more fundamental than a science on a higher level. As an example, Newton created the science of physics only after he evolved the branch of mathematics known as differential calculus.

This structural organization reveals an important insight: if the belief system within a lower level of science changes, it is imperative that the belief system on the higher levels change accordingly. However, when the belief system of a higher science changes, those changes may not apply to lower levels.

Civilization's current awareness and, consequently, its behavior are shaped by truths postulated under the roof of scientific materialism. The insufficiencies of these truths are contributing to and, in many cases, are solely responsible for the crises that currently threaten human survival. In the waning days of our civilization, the emergence of revisionary science is leading us to a more evolved science, holism—a structure built on a much firmer foundation.

In children's education, students are provided with a curriculum that requires them to tell, "What's so," by reciting memorized facts. As students mature, however, they learn to ask the more valuable question, "So what?" They begin to consider, "If such-and-such is so, what are the implications and applications of this knowledge in regard to my life?"

Likewise, the question before civilization now is, "What do new scientific revisions mean to humanity on Earth?" Listed below, are several relevant new science facts about "What's so" along with the more relevant question, "So what?"

Mathematics: *What's So:* The principles of fractal geometry describe the structure of Nature. *So What?:* Fractal geometry, the scientific foundation for fractals—as above, so below—emphasizes that self-similar patterns of organization are found at every level of the Universe's structure. In light of the success of Nature, the survival and thrival of human civilization is assured if we consciously follow her lead.

Physics: *What's So:* Matter and energy, that is, spirit, are inseparable. *So What?:* Everything in the quantum Universe—be it physical or non-physical, for example, energy waves or thoughts—is entangled and embedded within an invisible energy matrix called the field. The field's forces influence the shape of the physical Universe similar to the way a magnet rearranges iron filings. No structure, from a drop of water to a human being, can ever be separated from the field, which is the Source, All That Is, or, to some, God. *What's So:* Quantum mechanics acknowledges that the observer creates the reality. *So What?:* We co-create reality with our beliefs, perceptions, thoughts, and feelings.

Biology: *What's So:* Epigenetics controls genetics. *So What?:* Epigenetic molecular mechanisms represent a physical pathway along which consciousness makes us masters of our own health and well-being. Our field of beliefs and perceptions, individually and collectively, determine our biology and our reality. *What's So:* Evolution is derived from adaptations that provide Earth with an integrated, balanced, and harmonious ecological community. *So What?:* Human evolution is not an accident. We are here to tend the Garden through our cooperation with each other and the environment.

Psychology: *What's So:* The subconscious mind controls 95 percent of our behavior and gene regulating cognitive activity through programs obtained primarily from the field of beliefs. *So What?:* When we take command of our own subconscious beliefs and emotions, individually and collectively, we take back creative control over our lives.

To summarize the really big "So what?" question about "What's so," we find that the story we tell ourselves and each other about reality and our place in it profoundly impacts not only human civilization but the planet itself. Even though we perceive ourselves as small and insignificant, our collective conscious and unconscious beliefs are actually arranging the particles of matter that we call reality.

We referred to the field's influence on matter through the example of invisible magnetic fields that organize the distribution of sprinkled iron filings. However, the field's influence over the particle is not the whole story because the iron particles actually alter the shape of the magnet's field as well. Even though the influence of each miniature iron particle is negligible, the individual filings, if compressed into one, solid iron bar, will measurably distort the field.

Similarly, throughout evolution, Earth's energy fields have shaped the organization of primitive biological organisms and also influenced the fate of humans. In turn, individual persons, like iron filings, have had a small, perhaps seemingly negligible, impact on the field through their unique spheres of influence.

However, the origin of human self-consciousness represents a profound change in the story of evolution. Self-consciousness is the neurological mechanism that endows individuals with the choice to respond or not respond to environmental fields. Freedom of choice translates as human free will. So, while iron filings have no capacity to self-assemble into an iron bar, human beings can consciously pursue coherence and create a field-impacting unity called humanity.

Also, an iron bar's influence on a magnetic field is static. In contrast, humans have the ability to dynamically and creatively change Earth's field through conscious intention. Through collective consciousness, civilization can transform crises into a new sustainable reality. We can truly re-grow the Garden and create Heaven on Earth.

How do we create that coherence that will enable us to realize our "humanifest destiny"? How do we become participants in evolution, rather than mere bystanders?

The first step is to rewrite the fundamental story that civilization currently uses to create reality. That starts, not with a story imposed from the top down, but with an outline from which the new story can emerge from the bottom up. It happens by looking at promising directions through which we can realize our evolutionary destiny.

HEALING THE OLD STORY

Self-similar fractal patterns of organization reverberate throughout the Universe. As part of Nature, human culture is also built on repetitive patterns. One such pattern that has repeated itself throughout human history is that of violent domination, exploitation, and warfare. Almost every ethnic group has been both victim and perpetrator in this long-playing tragedy.

While we can find numerous examples of courage and selflessness in these war stories, the patterns of suffering expressed in both our conscious story and our subconscious memory are the ones that seem to have most influenced our culture. In reflecting this reality, human development researcher Joseph Chilton Pearce defined culture as "a set of beliefs and practices centered on physical survival," which he bluntly called, "a mutually shared anxiety state."[1]

Thanks to thousands of years of dominator programming—and lots of historical evidence with visual reminders—we viscerally believe it's us versus them. And, when push comes to shove, we inevitably resort to pushing and shoving. While paying lip service to the love-based Golden Rule with our conscious mind, the Rule of Gold rules in the profoundly more dominant subconscious, particularly when it is fueled by fear and backed by coercion. How do we address this seemingly overwhelming programming?

By making the unconscious conscious. When we recognize we can be programmed by fear, we are less susceptible to manipulations by those who benefit from mass conflict. Nazi leader Hermann Goering acknowledged this quite plainly at the Nuremberg trials when he testified, "Naturally the common people don't want war . . . But, after all, it is the leaders of the country who determine the policy, and it is always a simple matter to drag the people along, whether it is a democracy, or a fascist dictatorship, or a parliament, or a communist dictatorship . . . All you have to do is tell them they are being attacked, and denounce the peacemakers for lack of patriotism and exposing the country to danger. It works the same in any country."[2]

Those words should hold a particular relevance in the United States after the preemptive war in Iraq failed to accomplish its touted goal of finding weapons of mass destruction and brought the country to the brink of financial and moral bankruptcy. We can rightfully refer to the eight-year Bush-Cheney Administration as an intense fear-based educational experience for which both the U.S.A. and the world paid a very high tuition.

Evolution is synonymous with learning, and learning is based on pattern recognition, which is why we derive awareness by recognizing patterns and understanding their meaning. Situations perceived as problems or puzzles only exist until their underlying patterns are identified and understood.

But once we acquire information from a learning experience, we can memorize it and take it into our consciousness so that former or similar problems or puzzles need not be re-experienced. And with that learning, we are free to release the old story.

One reason that history repeats itself is that humans have consistently insisted on not learning the lessons. Instead, we opt for blame and vengeance, which is why it is not enough to merely debunk or dismantle old limiting or destructive stories with new learning. We must also come to an understanding—even an appreciation—that the victims and villains who have played roles in this drama have acted out of their own programming. The culprit isn't necessarily the individual, but the repeating pattern of behavior.

The suggestion that we release the actors from their drama is, for many, untenable and may even provoke anger. That's because these stories, while intellectually perceived in the mind, are simultaneously encoded with bodily emotions. Joseph Chilton Pearce emphasized that emotions that hold stories in place must be addressed before the stories can be released, and that resolution requires us to acknowledge and heal the spiritual, psychological, and emotional wounds.

History also reveals that forgiveness doesn't come easily. It seems as if an 18th century couplet by poet Alexander Pope, "To err is human; to forgive, divine," is deeply implanted in our collective consciousness. Lacking a perception of our own divinity, most people conveniently leave forgiveness in the hands of God and neighborhood divinities, such as Jill, who is acclaimed as a saint for forgiving Jack!

However, new-edge science reveals we are intimately entangled and one with All That Is. Being fruit of the Divine, forgiveness is truly within our domain. The Biblical injunction, "Forgive them; they know not what they do," is reaffirmed by the new science that tells us that 95 percent of our behavior is unconscious. With that in mind, ponder this thought: if either party in a personal dispute were conscious, the whole affair would have never occurred. When we truly become aware that most of our behavior is invisible to ourselves and that our perceptions can be distorted by our beliefs, we can logically forgive others who, like us, honestly know not what they do. While forgiveness can be based on truth and logic, healing is driven by love.

Earlier, we documented some extraordinary feats of ordinary human beings, such as lifting cars and helicopters to save a loved one's life. Then, in Chapter 13, *The One Suggestion*, we examined Leonard Laskow's experiments in which love shrunk cancer tumors. In our need to metabolize the political toxins that have accumulated from our histories of mutual perpetrations, might we be able to once again call on love to do the heavy lifting?

One of the most visionary experiments of the past two decades was the use of love, truth, and forgiveness to heal centuries of colonialism in South Africa. In 1989, Nelson Mandela, leader of the African National Congress, which was the revolutionary movement to end apartheid in South Africa, was freed after 27 years in prison. While spending more than a third of one's life behind bars might breed bitterness and rage in most people, Mandela managed to transmute his experience into spiritual wisdom and compassion. Upon his release, Mandela vowed to create a peaceful and respectful transition from apartheid to multiracial rule.

As president of South Africa in 1994, Mandela created the Truth and Reconciliation Commission (TRC) because, in his words, "Only the truth can put the past to rest." The purpose of this commission was to acknowledge political crimes committed by both the government and revolutionary forces and to allow perpetrators to confess these crimes and seek amnesty in exchange for their truthful testimony. Anglican Archbishop Desmond Tutu, Africa's foremost spiritual leader and proponent of the traditional tribal philosophy of *ubuntu,* was chairman of the TRC.

Ubuntu in the Bantu language represents the connection between the individual, humanity, and the world, which is reminiscent of the interpretation of *religare,* as described in Chapter 10. African historian and journalist Stanlake J. W. T. Samkange lists three maxims that characterize *ubuntu*:[3]

a. We affirm our own humanity by recognizing the humanity of others.

b. When faced with the choice of human life or wealth, we choose life.

c. The king owes his status to the will of the people under him.

Hmm. That sounds a lot like the Golden Rule, Jesus overturning the moneychangers' tables, and government empowered by sovereign citizens. Traditional *ubuntu* philosophy clearly contributed to the creation of the African reconciliation movement with its intention to repair the fabric of the community.

While citing the South African state as the primary culprit for apartheid, the TRC's final report acknowledged and condemned atrocities on both sides. The commission's evolutionary mission, driven by the healing intentions of both Mandela and Tutu, paved the way for a peaceful transfer of power in South Africa. The love and forgiveness that the commission advocated was not nicey-nicey sentimentality; rather, it required real courage and spiritual fortitude.

The intent for reconciliation was tested even before Mandela was elected president when his African National Congress associate Chris Hani was assassinated in 1993. With the country on the brink of retributive violence, Mandela addressed the nation with these words: "Tonight I am reaching out to every single South African, black and white, from the very depths of my being. A white man, full of prejudice and hate, came to our country and committed a deed so foul that our whole nation now teeters on the brink of disaster. A white woman, of Afrikaner origin, risked her life so that we may know, and bring to justice, this assassin . . . Now is the time for all South Africans to stand together against those who, from any quarter, wish to destroy what Chris Hani gave his life for—the freedom of all of us."[4]

Imagine how different the world would be today if an American President had given this kind of address in the wake of the September 11, 2001, attack on the World Trade Center. Might it have precipitated reverberations of love and functionality at a time when America had the world's sincere compassion? We think so.

Mandela's spiritual leadership prevented a new nation from dying in childbirth. In spite of its limitations, the truth and reconciliation process enabled an entire nation to participate in forgiveness. The TRC also inspired other projects and ventures to bring love into the political sphere.

In 2000, Dr. Fred Luskin, director of the Stanford Forgiveness Project and author of *Forgive for Good,* brought a small group of Protestants and Catholics, all of whom had lost loved ones in the war in Northern Ireland, to California as part of a project he called HOPE—an acronym for Healing Our Past Experience.

For some, their loss had occurred more than 20 years earlier, but their grief had never gone away. The first breakthrough came as both Catholics and Protestants recognized that the grief they shared in common transcended the oppositional sides on which they found themselves. When the weeklong project ended, participants filled out questionnaires to assess emotional and physiological change. The participants reported that they felt lower levels of hurt, anger, and depression. In addition, they experienced a 35 percent reduction in physiological symptoms of emotional stress such as irregular sleep patterns, unusual appetite, low energy levels, and physical aches and pains.[5]

While these results are heartening, the question still remains, "Can love really heal toxic emotions, particularly the malignancy of hatred?" Leonard Laskow's loving cancer cells in a petri dish is one thing, but what happens in the real world when hatred is actually at your doorstep?

In *Not by the Sword*, Kathryn Watterson tells the story of Michael Weisser, a Jewish cantor, and his wife, Julie.[6] They had recently moved to their new home in Lincoln, Nebraska, in June 1991 when their peaceful unpacking was interrupted by a threatening phone call.

Shortly afterward, they received a package of racist flyers with a card that announced: "The KKK is watching you, scum." The police told the Weissers it looked like the work of Larry Trapp, a self-described Nazi and local Ku Klux Klan grand dragon. Trapp had been linked to fire bombings of African American homes in the area and a center for Vietnamese refugees. The 44-year-old Trapp, leader of the area's white supremacist movement, was wheelchair bound and had diabetes. At the time, he was making plans to bomb B'nai Jeshurun, the synagogue where Weisser was cantor.

Julie Weisser, while frightened and infuriated by the hate mail, also felt a spark of compassion for Trapp, who lived alone in a one-room apartment. She decided to send Trapp a letter every day with passages from Proverbs. When Michael saw that Trapp had launched a hate-spewing TV series on the local cable network, he called the Klan hotline and kept leaving messages: "Larry, why do you hate me? You don't even know me."

At one point, Trapp actually answered the phone and Michael, after identifying himself, asked him if he needed a hand with his grocery shopping. Trapp refused, but a process of rethinking began to stir in him. For a while, he was two people: one still spewing invective on TV; the other talking with Michael Weisser on the phone, saying, "I can't help it, I've been talking like that all my life."

One night, Michael asked his congregation to pray for someone who is "sick from the illness of bigotry and hatred." That night, Trapp did something he'd never done before. The swastika rings he wore on both hands began to itch, so he took them off. The next day, he called the Weissers and said, "I want to get out, but I don't know how." Michael suggested that he and Julie drive to Trapp's apartment so they could "break bread together." Trapp hesitated, then agreed.

At the apartment, Trapp broke into tears and handed the Weissers his swastika rings. In November 1991, he resigned from the Klan and later wrote apologies to the groups he had wronged. On New Year's Eve, Larry Trapp found out he had less than a year to live, and, that same night, the Weissers invited him to move in with them. Their living room became Trapp's bedroom, and he told them, "You are doing for me what my parents should have done for me."

Bedridden, Trapp began to read about Mahatma Gandhi and Dr. Martin Luther King, Jr., and to learn about Judaism. On June 5, 1992, he converted to Judaism—at the very synagogue he had once planned to blow up. Julie quit her job to care for Larry Trapp in his last days, and when he died on September 6th of that year, Michael and Julie were holding his hands.

The lifting of cars, the lifting of karma. With love, both are possible. Both are extraordinary examples that point the way to spontaneous evolution. We—and the power of love we possess—are bigger than our stories. Yet, it takes more than good intentions to activate the power of love. While a worldwide healing ceremony to metabolize the accumulated toxins of human history would be a breakthrough, each of us—like a little piece of iron—must individually confront our own programming in order to transform evolutionary possibility into reality.

CHANGING THE INNERSPHERE

Civilization's quest for freedom has permeated the history of the world and, specifically, America for the last two centuries. Over that time, citizens in Western society have acquired unprecedented freedom to travel, to experience, to explore, and to learn.

Now, a different type of freedom is evolving. This one is more internal than external, more at the heart of humanity's evolution. It is freedom from limiting and unwanted subconscious programming.

New science is echoing the ancient truth that the human mind is the ultimate prison. Programmed in the mind's information field are behaviors that bind and restrain us like manacles and chains. Like the baby elephant that inaccurately learns it cannot break its tethering rope, we, too, are often tied up in "nots," a matrix of negative beliefs that we are incapable of achieving our dreams or fulfilling our destiny.

Many people seek personal freedom by consciously and diligently devouring self-help book after self-help book, only to end up feeling more discouraged and helpless. Somehow, great ideas on paper too often fail to materialize in life. The problem relates to the fact that, while the contents of the books are read and understood by the conscious mind, the information rarely integrates into or modifies preexisting behavior-controlling programs in the subconscious. What can we do about that?

The first hugely liberating step is to truly realize that each of us, regardless of how spiritually evolved we may imagine ourselves to be, engage in largely invisible shadow behaviors. Consider the number of gurus, politicians, and self-proclaimed moral guardians who have been literally caught with their pants down. Our clearest path to learning is not to make such people either villains or victims but to use the opportunity to cultivate humility and forgiveness. Once we understand how much of our behavior is unconsciously controlled by the beliefs of others, each of us can legitimately be released from the shackles of blame and shame.

Another step is to own responsibility for the stories in our lives. Denying responsibility for our participation acknowledges victimization, which, by definition, makes our situation one of helplessness. Only when we own responsibility do we have an opportunity to cultivate processes and practices that empower us to respond differently the next time we are revisited by previous stressful situations. Life success is predicated on navigating our actions with conscious decisions rather than engaging in reflexive, preprogrammed subconscious behaviors.

Those seeking conscious control over their lives are finding support for their efforts from both ancient and modern resources. While an in-depth exploration of processes for consciously managing our lives is beyond the subject of this book, we suggest that the pathway for change involves at least three fundamental elements: intention, choice, and practice.

Intention: Intention serves as a great declaration of purpose and direction. As the old saying goes, "If you don't know where you are going, you are likely to end up there." In the case of our personal evolution, a suitable intention would be to weave our talents, loves, and mission to support the newly emerging butterfly organism. Ancient and modern spiritual teachers collectively recognize that setting an intention draws new experiences to us like a magnet. If necessity is the mother of invention, intention is most likely the father.

Choice: Setting intentions may set things in motion on the subconscious plane, but, for true change, intentions must also be reflected in our daily conscious choices. By accepting the implication within *Spontaneous Evolution* that we are all cellular souls in an evolving super-organism called humanity, we need to ask, "What daily choices can I personally make to reinforce this emergent worldview?" For some, the answer might mean changing careers. For others, it might mean growing a garden or performing a kind act each day. Each individual's choice will be unique and represent the highest form of self-expression in these transformational times.

Practice: As suggested earlier, Heaven isn't a destination, it's a practice. To facilitate our maturation from children of God to adults of God, we can engage in practices and exercises that create congruency between our inner selves and our outer expression. We can support our evolution by selecting a practice or process that harmonizes the outer world with our inner well-being.

Fortunately, there are many very old and very new resources and processes to support conscious transformation. The variety of approaches simply reflects the fact that no one size fits all. Selecting a practice to maximize our potential is truly a matter of personal choice.

One of the most ancient practices to regain conscious control over one's life is Buddhist mindfulness. Fundamentally, mindfulness is a training exercise to rein in the conscious mind's wandering into the past and future in order to focus on the present moment and make aware choices in the now. Essentially, mindfulness disengages automatic subconscious programs so that the conscious mind, the seat of our personal wishes and aspirations, can generate behavior that is coherent with our intentions.

While mindfulness generates harmony by focusing on mental exercises, some harmonizing practices specifically focus on bodily sensations and movement. Meditation, yoga, breath work, relaxation, tai chi, and qigong cultivate inner harmony and coherence.

A classic, but generally insufficient, approach of modifying sabotaging subconscious behaviors invokes various forms of Cognitive Behavioral Therapy, which is talk therapy that provides a mirror for observing, understanding, and altering limiting subconscious programs. Recently, a very effective new practice called Body Centered Therapy has evolved from the integration of talk therapy with the meditative physical practices.

Other modalities that facilitate rewriting of subconscious programs include affirmations, conventional clinical hypnotherapy, and a number of new *energy psychology* modalities. Energy psychology is an exciting innovation that helps manage limiting beliefs. Interventions are based on recognition and manipulation of the human vibrational fields derived from the interactions of the neural and cardiac biofields, the chakra energy centers, and the energy pathways that include acupuncture meridians.

Most amazingly, energy psychology practices—of which there are many, including Holographic Repatterning, the BodyTalk System, as well as the one with which we are most familiar PSYCH-K—have been shown to make lasting behavioral changes, frequently in a matter of minutes. A partial list of belief-changing modalities is included in the Appendix.

Meanwhile, organizations like the Institute of HeartMath are developing new practices to entrain brain and heart functions that reduce stress while profoundly enhancing neurological processing powers. Similarly, the Oneness Blessing described by Arjuna Ardagh represents a prototype for group practices that create healthier, more coherent human fields worldwide.

The power of group coherence was illustrated on May 20, 2007, a date designated as Global Peace Meditation and Prayer Day.[7] More than one million people in 65 countries meditated and prayed for peace at a synchronized moment in time. The results were similar to those random number generators (RNGs) that shifted into coherence during events like Princess Diana's funeral or the attack on the World Trade Center. In fact, Global Coherence Initiative researcher Roger Nelson reported that monitors around the world recorded measurable increases in the coherence of RNGs while the meditation was in process. Yes, coherent consciousness impacts Earth's fields!

The implications of these initial findings are profound. Could meditations and group intentions such as these provide a template for creating a human awareness strong enough to influence the planetary field in the same way that iron filings compressed into an iron bar can influence the force field of a magnet? Could the vision of a coherent civilization whose collective consciousness is focused on love, health, harmony, and happiness truly create a field strong enough to manifest Heaven on Earth?

Yes, we think so. In fact, they are.

But it's important to keep in mind that these changes aren't happening on the level of cosmic consciousness alone. Rather, this connection and coherence manifests daily as millions of random and not-so-random acts of kindness and functionality. Like the multiplying of loaves and fishes, each of these acts, in turn, ripples outward and creates more of the same.

But what if you have no interest in meditation or spiritual practice, believe that therapy is good only for strained muscles, and have no compulsion to go poking around your own subconscious for beliefs to reframe? Research reveals that you can still manifest positive results by simply changing your story.

That story we tell ourselves can have direct bearing on the quality of our lives and our health. Dr. Gail Ironson, professor of psychology and psychiatry at the University of Miami, found that HIV patients who believed in a loving universal power remained healthier longer than those who believed in one that was punishing.[8] Sounds like a prescription for creating our own placebo to counteract the prevailing nocebo generated by our culture's negative stories.

Problems arise in this intellectually based freedom story when seemingly bad things are happening to you. At such times, it is difficult to experience the world as a friendly place. How can one generate positive feelings when there is no reason to be happy?

Author Marci Shimoff offered a provocative suggestion in the title of her book *Happy For No Reason*. Shimoff wrote: "When you're happy for no reason, you *bring* happiness to your outer experiences rather than trying to extract happiness *from* them."[9]

If this seems like simplistic let-a-smile-be-your-umbrella happy talk, consider this scientific reality: Your facial expression actually triggers bodily production of emotional chemistry that is related to both happiness and unhappiness. Emotions specifically shape physiological and physical responses that accompany our behaviors. Conventionally, we tend to perceive that emotions are the driving force behind our behavioral experiences. However, new science has revealed an amazing discovery that our physical expressions can drive emotional responses.

French physiologist Dr. Israel Waynbaum discovered that frowning triggers the secretion of the stress hormones cortisol, adrenaline, and noradrenaline, which are neurochemicals that inhibit the immune system, raise blood pressure, and increase susceptibility to anxiety and depression. Smiling, on the other hand, reduces secretion of stress hormones and raises the production of endorphins, which are the body's natural feel-good hormones, while simultaneously enhancing the function of the immune system by increasing T-cell production.[10]

When downloading learning experiences into memory, the brain links emotions with behavioral responses. The biological reactions involved with this process can generally flow both forwards and backward, which means that an emotion can drive an experience and an experience can elicit an emotion. This is an important characteristic relative to memory-capture.

Scientists have recently identified a particular class of visuomotor nerve cells called mirror neurons. Research involving monkeys shows that these nerve cells fire both when a monkey does a particular action and when it observes another individual, be it a monkey or a human, doing a similar action. Identical mirror neurons are also found in human brains. Have you ever squirmed while watching a movie in which a giant spider is crawling on an actor? Have you ever cried in response to someone else's tears or laughed when they did? If so, you were responding to the function of mirror neurons, which replay learned personal responses derived from our own experiences when we observe others having similar experiences.[11]

When we act, we intend to reach a goal. Conversely, when we observe someone else act, mirror neurons translate their behaviors so we can often infer their intentions. Neuroscientists listening in on brain cells suggest that mirror neurons are at the root of empathy, which is the ability to discern others' thoughts and intentions.

Mirror neurons play a major role in the creation of coherence in an evolving human population. Consider the consequences of seeding individuals in a population who express love, joy, happiness, or gratitude. Mirror neurons in the brains of the observing public would stimulate them to experience the same sensations. These neurons would initiate a neurological chain reaction through which an entire population would catch the healthy vibe of positive feelings. This is why charismatic leaders, such as Nelson Mandela, John F. Kennedy, and Martin Luther King, Jr., have such a profound effect on the public's emotions and attitudes.

The "So what?" component of these insights is that our attitude and our interpretation of circumstances profoundly influence the outcome of our experiences. According to Dr. Martin Seligman at the University of Pennsylvania's Positive Psychology Center, optimistic responses can be learned. A self-described born pessimist, Seligman maintains that modern society reinforces victimhood and learned helplessness. He suggests that helplessness can be reprogrammed by choosing a healthier perspective in the face of challenges. For example, Seligman recommends reframing bad events as temporary setbacks, isolated to particular circumstances that can be overcome by one's efforts and abilities.[12]

Marci Shimoff offers her own reframe prescription. She advises that, when plagued by a persistent negative thought, lean into an equally true positive thought about the same situation. To seek equanimity, she suggests repeating the advice of Zen masters who pray: "Thank you for everything. I have no complaints whatsoever."[13]

We chose not to fill this chapter with information on techniques for addressing the *innersphere* because the accelerated evolution in this field would necessitate frequent revisions. Like rapidly mutating bacteria seeking to adjust to environmental challenges, human cells in the newly forming organism called humanity are actively experimenting with practices to secure freedom from limiting beliefs. Such practices are topics ideally suited for a dynamic worldwide wiki. The Web's platform offers the public access to the best, latest, and most helpful transformative practices that are being tried, tested, and continuously revised.

FROM DUELING DUALITIES TO DYNAMIC DUO

Beyond the need for individual and societal reprogramming, spontaneous evolution necessitates at least one more significant cognitive leap. We have been programmed with the myth-perception of the world as a battleground for eternally dueling dualities: progressive versus conservative, competition versus cooperation, science versus religion, creation versus evolution, growth versus protection, spirit versus matter, wave versus particle, and eagle versus condor, among many, many more versuses.

For millennia, the polarization of life's traits has fractured civilization by forcing individuals and groups to take sides. And, while this list of polarized pairs could go on for many pages, the few examples here emphasize that the world is derived from the integration of opposing tendencies.

Evolutionary unity now necessitates that we own the awareness that opposing characters are actually cooperative partners in evolution's dynamic dance. At no time is this "up-wising" needed more than when resolving the perceptual dysfunction that masculine and feminine represent oppositional forces. After 5,000 years of dominator programming, the battle of the sexes is taken as a given, with, of course, the man on top.

Conventional biology still perceives of Nature in terms of the Darwinian nightmare of a world eternally engulfed in life-threatening competition. Geneticists apply this perception when they refer to battles of dominance waged between male genes and female genes. But the dominator story makes no biological sense at all. When a sperm and egg unite to create a new life, does one defeat the other? In Glynda-Lee Hoffmann's groundbreaking book, *The Secret Dowry of Eve: Woman's Role in the Development of Consciousness,* she wrote: "There is no hierarchy between a germ and a husk. They work together or they don't work at all."[14]

Scientific insights from physics and biology on the nature of polarized traits reveal that, while these traits appear to be separate and opposing entities, they are actually rooted together in a unity. Interestingly,

Eastern philosophers grasped the truth of this unity almost 4,000 years ago when they defined the relationship between yin and yang.

The yin-yang symbol contains two separate, but entangled, entities: one white and one black. However, a black spot resides in the white entity, and a white spot resides in the black entity, an indication that both entities are made out of the same elements. Externally, we see males and females, regardless of species, as being physically different, but, internally, both males and females have masculine and feminine hormones.

The yin-yang symbol consists of two separate entities, black and white, yet each entity contains the seed of the other.

In recognition of this inherent equality portrayed by yin and yang, the notion of masculine primacy makes absolutely no sense. Hence, the entire concept of a battle of the sexes makes as much sense as a battle between the particle and the wave. The integrated worldview in which both the masculine and feminine principles are in full balanced power is the key to the birth of a new humanity.

CAN HUMANS ACHIEVE HUMANITY?

There are those who insist that human consciousness is not up to this evolutionary task. Spiritual determinists, for example, insist we are hopelessly flawed sinners who can only be saved through Divine intervention. Intellectual elitists point to massive ignorance on the part of the masses and to our all-too-obvious failings as a humane species.

Yet, indications suggest we may have underestimated the extent of the current state of awakening. In Our Own Words 2000, a comprehensive research project published by the Fund for Global Awakening in 2007, reported that 85 percent of Americans believe, "underneath it all, we're all connected as one." A whopping 93 percent agree that "it's important to teach our children to feel connected to the earth, people, and all life."[15]

The election of Barack Obama as President was an important evolutionary milestone that transcends anything that Obama can or will do in office. Buckminster Fuller once said that an audience applauds not so much in recognition of the individual onstage, but in recognition of one another. In this case, the support given Obama the man was in reality support for his well-articulated vision of hope, change, and global communal cooperation. The election of Obama, as the voice of imaginal cells everywhere, is a sign that we have withdrawn our investment of time, energy, attention, and intention from the caterpillar and are now casting our fate with the butterfly. As a world leader, Obama's words echoed the conclusion in Chapter 13, *The One Suggestion:* "We're all in this together."

There is one more factor in Obama's election that has evolutionary significance, and that is his background as a community organizer. The very trait disparaged by those who cling to an obsolete paradigm represents the pathway to humanity's spontaneous evolution. Remember, all evolution moves forward by increasing community and expanding awareness.

If this evolutionary step toward planetary coherence seems huge, perhaps we need an even bigger perspective: The evolution of humanity is not an ending; it is a beginning. This stage of humanity's development completes the evolution of our planet. Through the evolution of humanity, we will come to see Earth not as a physical planet but as a living cell. What happens when a cell fulfills its evolution? It assembles into colonies with other evolved cells to share awareness.

Upon completing its evolution, Earth will connect with other aware Earth-like planets to continue the process of expanding awareness about who we are, what we are, and the nature of the Universe in which we live.

Meanwhile, back in the here and now, we are the leaders we've been waiting for. Although we may be inspired by the election of Obama and basking in the warm breeze of political climate change, at this evolutionary crossroads, the emphasis is not on individuals who lead from the top. The emphasis is on the awakening of all cellular souls who create a coherent loving field so empowered leaders can be attuned to the healthy central voice of the super-organism that is humanity.

Consequently, the real challenge for the individual is to practice evolution, to learn the lessons of the old stories so we no longer need to repeat them, and to remind ourselves that the critical mass of humanity involved with this evolution will change the world from the inside out. We are living in a positive future, practicing Heaven, and designing a bridge across which the whole of humanity will walk.

This is our love story—a universal love story for the entire Universe: you, me, everyone, and every living organism, too. And, now, on to Act V!

ACKNOWLEDGMENTS

Collective Acknowledgments:

We want to express our love and appreciation to Mountain of Love Productions, Inc., whose generous support and encouragement transformed our vision into this book. Margaret Horton, president, and Sally Thomas, office manager, were wonderful midwives. Their mental, emotional and spiritual support facilitated the birth of this work.

The spirit of this book would not have been fully realized without the superior editorial skills of Robert Weir. We have come to see word craft as a performance art and honor Robert for the maestro he is. We are also thankful that he maintained the patience of Job and a sense of humor for all those times we tested him. http://www.robertmweir.com/

Robert Mueller the brilliant artist who created the beautiful cover art for *The Biology of Belief* has provided us with another masterpiece. Robert fully absorbed the content of this book and magnificently translated its essence into a collage of art and science. Robert's commentary on the story behind the art is appended at the end of the book. www.lightspeed design.com

We wish to express our deepest appreciation to our agent, Ned Leavitt, and to Reid Tracy, president-CEO; Patricia Gift, director of acquisitions; and Laura Koch, acquisitions editor from Hay House. It is a true pleasure working with Hay House for they are an exemplar of the cooperative conscious corporations needed to revitalize civilization.

To our beta readers, colleagues, and friends who contributed their valuable time to review the manuscript, we extend our heartfelt appreciation. Their questions, comments, and critiques were major contributions in refining this book so that its message is loud and clear: Nicki Scully, Diana Sutter, Robert Mueller, Thea and Vaughan Wiles, Omri Sitton, Terry and Christine Bugno, Patricia Gift, Theodore Hall, Rob Williams, Mary Kovacs, Ben Young, Shelly G. Keller, Brian Kelly, Russel Walder, Sherill Burton, Georgia Kelly, E. Carroll Straus, Margaret Carswell, and Aura Glaser.

Bruce's Acknowledgments:

Spontaneous Evolution is a grand synthesis derived from the people I have known and places I have been, so the book is as much other people's stories as it is mine. Everyone in my life has contributed to the creation of *Spontaneous Evolution,* and I would love to cite them all, but practicality necessitates a more abbreviated listing.

I want to thank some good friends whose wisdom and insights contributed to this book: Curt Rexroth, Ted Hall, Rob Williams, Ben and Millie Young, Shelly G. Keller, and Terry and Christine Bugno.

A special place in my heart and mind is reserved for my dear friend and spiritual brother, Gregg Braden. I have had the joy of sharing the stage with Gregg in public and the honor of being privy to his wisdom in private. Margaret and I are blessed to be recipients of his Light and Love.

I want to thank the visionary Board of Trustees of the New Zealand College of Chiropractic and, especially, President Brian Kelly for including me in their bold new vision of academia. Their program is a powerful testament to the power of community.

A special thank you to my friends and landlords Stuart and Carol Roscoe, for hosting my extended visits to beautiful New Zealand. Their home, nestled between the wild Tasman Sea and a "dinosaur" rainforest, offered the ideal backdrop for writing a book about Mother Earth.

To Steve and Trudy Bhaerman . . . we laughed, we cried, and then we laughed some more. It has been a fabulous adventure as we have evolved from friends to family.

Speaking of family, as I evolved along this journey, I was delighted to find that when I turned around, my own family had evolved right along with me. If we can do it—there is hope for the whole world! With love for my mother, Gladys; my brother David; his wife, Cindy, and son, Alex; my sister, Marsha; and my brother Arthur—survivors one and all!

This book was especially written for my lovely daughters, Tanya and Jennifer, and their families. They will inherit this world, and I hope this contribution will leave it a better place for them.

Most importantly, I want to acknowledge my beloved Margaret Horton, my best friend, my life partner, my love. You inspire and fulfill me, darling. I love you.

Steve's Acknowledgments:

First of all, I want to thank the Universe for giving us this assignment, and the grace to complete it.

Next, I wish to acknowledge all of the people who supported this endeavor in any and all ways, offered us encouragement, and kept us nourished with their enthusiasm. I'd also like to thank those who gave their time and expertise, in particular Brian Bogart for his historical perspective and Richard Kotlarz for his economic wisdom. Thanks to Ruth Harris who took on research assignments, my office manager Annette Toivonen, and my friends who have been wondering when I'll be able to come out and play.

My deepest appreciation goes to my colleague Bruce Lipton and his partner, Margaret, for their friendship, perseverance, and good humor in taking on this joint venture—that really took us on. Finally, I am especially grateful for my wife, Trudy, and her steadfast support for this book since the beginning, for her love and faith, and for always bringing out the best in me.

BELIEF CHANGE MODALITIES

This is a partial listing of effective belief change modalities. Please check the Web for a full listing and description of these and other belief change processes.

PSYCH-K
www.psych-k.com
Your subconscious beliefs establish the limits of what you can achieve! Learn to rewrite the software of your subconscious mind and change your life! From Bruce Lipton: "I teach with Rob Williams the originator of PSYCH-K. This is the modality that we use personally and with which we are most familiar."

THE HENDRICKS INSTITUTE
www.hendricks.com
Resources for conscious living and loving. An International Learning Center that teaches core skills for conscious living. Assisting people in opening to more creativity, love, and vitality through the power of conscious relationship and whole-person learning.

CORE HEALTH
www.corehealth.us
Advancing from studying disease to understanding Health, this innovative process moves beyond treating symptoms to Truly Freeing each individual by internal energetic decisions.

BODYTALK SYSTEMS
www.thebodytalkcenter.com
BodyTalk is an astonishingly simple and effective form of therapy that allows the body's energy systems to be resynchronized so that they can operate as Nature intended.

HOLOGRAPHIC REPATTERNING
www.repatterning.org
Quantum Change made easy. The Resonance Repatterning System is an energy process which can help identify and clear the patterns of energy underlying any issue, problem, or pain you are experiencing.

CLINICAL HYPNOSIS
www.asch.net
www.bsch.org.uk
Hypnotherapy is a valuable therapy with which to release past trauma and decondition established habits. The Websites listed above for the American and British professional societies aim to promote and assure high standards in the practice of hypnotherapy.

INNER RESONANCE TECHNOLOGIES
www.innerresonance.com
IRT has 7 brief steps that facilitate you in making certain inner agreements that set the conditions to allow your own automatic system to rebalance and harmonize itself physically, emotionally, mentally, and spiritually, transforming all parts of your life.

INSTANT EMOTIONAL HEALING
www.instantemotionalhealing.com
Instant Emotional Healing: Acupressure for the Emotions, by Peter T. Lambrou, Ph.D., and George J. Pratt, Ph.D. Drs. Pratt and Lambrou have created a book that explains the foundations of a new branch of therapy call energy psychology.

NEUROLINK'S NEUROLOGICAL INTEGRATION SYSTEM (NIS)
www.neurolinkglobal.com
NIS is based upon the neurophysiology principle that the brain governs optimal function of all the body systems. Learn to leverage the brain's profound ability to restore the body and all its systems to full potential.

SILVA ULTRAMIND SYSTEM
www.silvaultramindsystems.com
Learn how to identify your mission in life and to use the power of your creative mind, to propel you toward this goal.

EMOTIONAL FREEDOM TECHNIQUE
www.emofree.com
Based on discoveries regarding the body's subtle energies, Emotional Freedom Techniques (EFT) have proven successful in thousands of clinical cases.

THE HEALING CODES
www.thehealingcode.com
Discover how to: supercharge your immune system; help your body heal itself; and turn on your natural healing systems to heal your pain, stress, fear, depression, and disease.

ABOUT THE COVER ART

In the creation of the *Vitruvian Man* (late 1400s), Leonardo da Vinci attempted to illustrate humanity's link to the cosmos and the divine using geometry, symmetry, and proportion. He used *Euclidean geometry*, the highest mathematics available to him at the time. Da Vinci based his iconic drawing on the writings of Vitruvius (27 B.C.E.), a Roman architect and engineer who was greatly influenced by Pythagoras (580–500 B.C.E.).

Over the centuries, *Vitruvian Man* has become unarguably one of the most powerful symbols of humanity as a whole—male and female alike (even though the image is overtly male). What's more impressive is that to this day it immediately and effortlessly conveys to the viewer the sense that there is more going on "behind the scenes" than meets the eye!

What I like is taking that centuries-old iconic image and adding imaginative wings to it—because the visual metaphor so readily implies a natural metamorphosis of all of humanity, as well as a positive, *beautiful* future for us all. Moreover, I like to think that da Vinci himself might even appreciate the use of *fractal geometry* to "extend" his creation in this way, since his vision embraced mathematics as a clue to our divine origin, and this modern-day branch of mathematics was not available to him.

Finally, the addition of the two flowing symmetrical *golden mean* (phi) spirals emanating from Vitruvian Man's navel and gracing the tips of his evolutionary "wings" not only bridges the two mathematics, but supplies a visual metaphor for time and evolution itself. The golden mean ratio was an enigmatic and "divine" geometric concept in Leonardo's time. Today we recognize that the Fibonacci sequence upon which the golden mean spiral was based is actually an iterative fractal equation.

As a fractal, this "divinely proportioned" self-similar spiral extends forward and backwards *without end*. Trace the spirals back through humanity's navel and you find we were born of the cosmos itself . . . and the white light of creation. Trace them forwards, out beyond our now-sprouting evolutionary wings and you will find . . . blue skies. And yes, you can call me optimistic.

bOB September, 2009

ENDNOTES

Preamble: Spontaneous Remission

1. Lord Martin Rees, "Martin Rees comment on doomsday clock," *The Royal Society Science News* (17 January 2007): press release.

2. Margaret Mead, International Earth Day speech delivered at the United Nations March 20, 1977, reprinted in *Earth Trustees Program Newsletter*, 1978, 1.

Part I: What If Everything You Know Is Wrong!

1. Robert Watson, A.H. Zakri, (eds), *Ecosystems and Human Well-Being: Current State and Trends, Findings of the Condition and Trends Working Group, Millennium Ecosystem Assessment*, 1st edition (Washington DC: Island Press, 2005).

Chapter 1: Believing Is Seeing

1. Matthew 17:2, Bible: New International Version.

2. W. A. Brown, "The placebo effect: should doctors be prescribing sugar pills?" *Scientific American*, no. 278 (1998): 90–95; Discovery Channel Production, "Placebo: Mind Over Medicine?" Medical Mysteries Series, *Discovery Health Channel*, 2003, Silver Spring, MD; Maj-Britt Niemi, "Placebo Effect: A Cure in the Mind," *Scientific American Mind* (Feb-March 2009): 42–49.

3. Alfred Lord Tennyson, *In Memoriam*, (London, UK: E. Moxon, 1850), Canto 56.

4. Kevin Crush, "Hotfoot It: Walking on red-hot coals is all about the energy", *Grande Prairie Daily Herald Tribune*, June 17, 2005, 4. Article can be read online for free at http://www.firewalks.ca/Press_Release.html (accessed March 17, 2009).

5. Cecil Adams, "SuperMom: Could a mother actually lift a car to save her child?" Interview and news story about Angela Cavallo, The Straight Dope, January 20, 2006, http://www.straightdope.com/columns/read/2636/supermom (accessed March 2, 2009).

6. V. J. DiRita, "Genomics Happens," *Science*, no. 289 (2000): 1488–1489.

7. B. E. Schwarz, "Ordeal by serpents, fire and strychnine," *Psychiatric Quarterly*, no. 34 (1960): 405–429.

8. Lewis Mehl-Madrona, *Coyote Wisdom: The Power of Story in Healing,* (Rochester, VT: Inner Traditions/Bear & Company, 2005), 37.

9. Michael Talbot, *The Holographic Universe,* (New York, NY: Harper Perennial, 1992), 72–78.

10. Suzanne C. Segerstrom, Gregory E. Miller, "Psychological stress and the human immune system: A meta-analytic Study of 30 years of inquiry," *Psychological Bulletin* 130, no. 4 (2004): 601–30.

11. E. Pennisi, "Gene Counters Struggle to Get the Right Answer," *Science,* no. 301 (2003): 1040–1041; M. Blaxter, "Two worms are better than one," *Nature,* no. 426 (2003): 395–396.

12. B. H. Lipton, *The Biology of Belief: Unleashing the Power of Consciousness, Matter and Miracles,* (Santa Rosa, CA: Elite Books, 2005), 161.

13. E. B. Harvey, "A comparison of the development of nucleate and non-nucleate eggs of Arbacia punctulata," *Biology Bulletin,* no. 79 (1940): 166–187; M.K. Kojima, "Effects of D_2O on Parthenogenetic Activation and Cleavage in the Sea Urchin Egg," *Development, Growth and Differentiation* 1, no. 26 (1984): 61–71; B. H Lipton, K. G. Bensch and M. A. Karasek, "Microvessel Endothelial Cell Transdifferentiation: Phenotypic Characterization," *Differentiation,* no. 46 (1991): 117–133.

14. Lipton, *The Biology of Belief: Unleashing the Power of Consciousness, Matter and Miracles,* 87.

15. W. C. Willett, "Balancing Life-Style and Genomics Research for Disease Prevention," *Science,* no. 296 (2002): 695–698.

16. Y. Ikemi, S. Nakagawa, "A psychosomatic study of contagious dermatitis," *Kyoshu Journal of Medical Science* 13, (1962): 335–350.

17. Daniel Goleman, Gregg Braden and others, *Measuring the Immeasurable: The Scientific Case for Spirituality,* (Boulder, CO: Sounds True, 2008), 196.

18. P. D. Gluckman, M. A. Hanson, "Living with the Past: Evolution, Development, and Patterns of Disease," *Science,* no. 305 (2004): 1733–1736; Lipton, *The Biology of Belief: Unleashing the Power of Consciousness, Matter and Miracles,* 177.

Chapter 2: Act Locally . . . Evolve Globally

1. E. Watters, "DNA is Not Destiny," *Discover* (November 2006): 32.

2. D. Schmucker, J. C. Clemens, et al, "Drosophila DSCAM Is an Axon Guidance Receptor Exhibiting Extraordinary Molecular Diversity," *Cell,* no. 101 (2000): 671–684.

3. R. A. Waterland, R. L. Jirtle, "Transposable Elements: Targets for Early Nutritional Effects on Epigenetic Gene Regulation," *Molecular and Cell Biology* 15, no. 23 (2003): 5293–5300.

4. Mario F. Fraga, et al, "Epigenetic differences arise during the lifetime of

monozygotic twins," *Proceedings of the National Academy of Sciences* 102, no. 30 (July 26, 2005): 1064–1069.

5. Lipton, *The Biology of Belief: Unleashing the Power of Consciousness, Matter and Miracles,* 178.

6. Gordon G. Gallup Jr., "Chimpanzees: Self-Recognition," *Science* 167, no. 3914 (2 January 1970): 86–87.

7. T. Nørretranders, *The User Illusion: Cutting Consciousness Down to Size,* (New York: Penguin Books, 1998), 126, 161.

8. Marianne Szegedy-Maszak, "Mysteries of the Mind: Your unconscious is making your everyday decisions," *U.S. News & World Report,* February 28, 2005, http://health.usnews.com/usnews/health/articles/050228/28think.htm (accessed March 13, 2009).

9. Sue Gerhardt, *Why Love Matters: How Affection Shapes a Baby's Brain,* (London, UK: Brunner-Routledge, 2004), 32–55.

10. R. Laibow, "Clinical Applications: Medical applications of neurofeedback," In J. R. Evans, A. Abarbanel, *Introduction to Quantitative EEG and Neurofeedback,* (Burlington, MA: Academic Press Elsevier, 1999).

11. Dr. Fred Luskin, *Forgive For Good: A Proven Prescription for Health and Happiness* (New York: HarperSanFrancisco, 2002), p viii.

12. Colin C. Tipping, *Radical Forgiveness: Making Room for the Miracle,* (Marietta, GA: Global Thirteen, 2002), 123–27.

Chapter 3: A New Look at the Old Story

1. "Radio Listeners in Panic, Taking War Drama as Fact," *The New York Times,* October 31, 1938, 1–2.

2. Joseph Campbell, *Thou Art That: Transforming Religious Metaphor,* (Novato, CA: New World Library, 2001), 49-54; Laura Westra, T.M. Robinson, *The Greeks And The Environment,* (Lanham, MD: Rowman & Littlefield, 1997), 11.

3. Susan Jane Gilman, "Five Star Mystic," *Washington City Paper* (Aug. 2–8, 1996), http://www.washingtoncitypaper.com/display.php?id=10843 (accessed March 12, 2009).

4. P. H. Silverman, "Rethinking Genetic Determinism: With only 30,000 genes, what is it that makes humans human?" *The Scientist* (2004): 32–33.

Chapter 4: Rediscovering America

1. Thom Hartmann, *Screwed: The Undeclared War Against the Middle Class–And What We Can Do About It,* (San Francisco, CA: Berrett-Koehler, 2006), 74–75.

2. Thom Hartmann, *What Would Jefferson Do? A Return to Democracy,* (New York: Harmony Books, 2004), 53.

3. Ibid., 52.

4. Ibid., 53.

5. Ibid., 67.

6. Sharon A. Lloyd, Susanne Sreedhar (eds), "Hobbes's Moral and Political Philosophy," Stanford Encyclopedia of Philosophy, Stanford University, first published February 12, 2002, substantive revision August 23, 2008, http://plato.stanford.edu/entries/hobbes-moral/ (accessed March 19, 2009).

7. John Locke, "Two Treatises of Government (1680–1690)," Lonang Library, http://www.lonang.com/exlibris/locke/ (accessed March 19, 2009).

8. Robert Hieronimus, *America's Secret Destiny: Spiritual Vision & the Founding of a Nation,* (Rochester, VT: Destiny Books, 1989), 6–9.

9. Ibid., 8.

10. Carol Hiltner, "The Iroquois Confederacy: Our Forgotten National Heritage," Freedom and National Security 2, (May 2002), Spirit of Ma'at www.spiritofmaat.com/archive/may2/iroquois.htm (accessed March 12, 2009).

11. Hieronimous, *America's Secret Destiny: Spiritual Vision & the Founding of a Nation,* 9.

12. Hartmann, *What Would Jefferson Do? A Return to Democracy,* 25.

13. Nancy Shoemaker, ed., *American Indians,* (Malden, MA: Blackwell Publishers, Ltd., 2001), 112.

14. Hieronimus, *America's Secret Destiny: Spiritual Vision & the Founding of a Nation,* 12.

15. Ibid., 11.

16. Ibid., 11–12.

17. Ibid., 17.

18. Ibid., 18.

19. Ibid., 16.

20. Ibid., 29–36.

21. Ibid., 23.

22. Ibid., 26.

23. Ibid., 41–42.

24. Ibid., 42.

25. Ibid., 93–99.

26. Hiltner, "The Iroquois Confederacy: Our Forgotten National Heritage," Freedom and National Security 2.

27. Ibid.

28. Ibid.

29. Ibid.

30. Ibid.

31. Ibid.

32. Ibid.; Original Source for this reference in Hiltner article: Sally Roesch Wagner, *Sisters in Spirit: Iroquois Influence on Early Feminists*, (Summertown, TN: Native Voices, 2001).

33. Ibid.

34. Alverto Taxo, *Friendship with the Elements*, (LittleLight Publishing, 2005), 3.

35. Melissa McNamara, "Diet Industry is Big Business," CBS Evening News, Dec. 1, 2006, http://www.cbsnews.com/stories/2006/12/01/evening-news/main2222867.shtml, (Accessed March 12, 2009).

36. Aura Glaser, *A Call to Compassion: Bringing Buddhist Practices of the Heart into the Soul of Psychology*, (Berwick, ME: Nicholas-Hays, 2005), 116.

37. John Perkins, *Confessions of An Economic Hit Man*, (San Francisco, CA: Berrett-Koehler, 2004), 210.

Part II: The Four Myth-Perceptions of the Apocalypse

1. 1. Eckhart Tolle, *The Power of Now*, (Novato, CA: New World Library, 1999), 1–2.

Chapter 5: Myth-Perception One: Only Matter Matters

1. MSNBC.com, "What are mothers' rights during childbirth?" Debate revived over pregnant woman's choice of delivery, *The Associated Press*, May 19, 2004, http://www.msnbc.msn.com/id/5012918/ (accessed March 9, 2009).

2. Eric Weisstein's World of Scientific Biography, "Kelvin, Lord William Thomson (1824-1907)", 1996–2007, http://scienceworld.wolfram.com/biography/Kelvin.html (accessed March 5, 2009).

3. Faye Flam, "The Quest for a Theory of Everything Hits Some Snags," *Science*, no. 256 (1992): 1518–1519.

4. Adam Crane, Richard Soutar, *MindFitness Training: The Process of Enhancing Profound Attention Using Neurofeedback*, 1st edition, (Lincoln, NE: AuthorHouse, 2000), 354.

5. Milic Capek, *The Philosophical Impact of Contemporary Physics,* (New York, NY: Van Nostrand, 1961), 319.

6. Lynne McTaggart, *The Field: The Quest for the Secret Force of the Universe,* (New York: Harper Perennial, 2002), 23–24.

7. Ibid., xvi–xvii.

8. David Brown, Rupert Sheldrake, "Perceptive Pets: A Survey in North-West California," *Journal of the Society for Psychical Research* 62 (July 1998): 396–406.

9. Rupert Sheldrake, *Dogs That Know When Their Owners Are Coming Home: And Other Unexplained Powers of Animals,* (New York: Harper Perennial, 2002), 23–24.

10. McTaggart, *The Field: The Quest for the Secret Force of the Universe,* 54–63.

11. Gregg Braden, *The Divine Matrix: Bridging Time, Space, Miracles, and Belief,* (Carlsbad, CA: Hay House, 2007), 116-117.

Chapter 6: Myth-Perception Two: Survival of the Fittest

1. J. B. de Lamarck, *Philosophie zoologique, ou exposition des considerations relatives à l'histoire naturelle des animaux,* (Paris, France: J.B. Baillière, Libraire, 1809).

2. Thomas R. Malthus, *An Essay on the Principle of Population,* (Whitefish, MT: Kessinger, 2004), 44–45.

3. Doug Linder, "Bishop James Ussher Sets the Date for Creation," *University of Missouri-Kansas City School of Law,* 2004, http://www.law.umkc.edu/faculty/projects/ftrials/scopes/ussher.html (accessed March 10, 2009).

4. E. Bailey, *Charles Lyell,* (Garden City, NY: Doubleday,1963), 86.

5. Ibid., 117.

6. de Lamarck, *Philosophie zoologique, ou exposition des considerations relatives à l'histoire naturelle des animaux.*

7. Leonard Dalton Abbott, ed., *Masterworks of Economics—Digests of 10 Great Classics,* (Garden City, NY: Doubleday, 1946), 195.

8. Charles Darwin, *The Autobiography of Charles Darwin,* (New York: Barnes & Noble, 2005), 196.

9. Charles Darwin, "Letter 729–Darwin, C.R. to Hooker, J.," *Darwin Correspondence Project,* 11 January 1844, http://www.darwinproject.ac.uk/darwinletters/calendar/entry-729.html (accessed March 15, 2009).

10. Arnold Brackman, *The Strange Case of Charles Darwin and Alfred Russel Wallace,* (New York: Times Books; 1st edition, 1980), 22.

11. Bailey, *Charles Lyell,* (Garden City, NY: Doubleday, 1963), 61.

12. Brackman, *The Strange Case of Charles Darwin and Alfred Russel Wallace,* 64.

13. Ibid.

14. Francis Hitching, *The Neck of the Giraffe—Darwin, Evolution, and the New Biology*, (New York: Meridian, 1982), 172.

15. T. M. Lenton, "Gaia and natural selection." *Nature*, no. 394 (1998): 439–447.

16. James Greenberg, "Enron: The Smartest Guys in the Room," *The Hollywood Reporter*, April 20, 2005, http://www.hollywoodreporter.com/hr/search/article_display.jsp?vnu_content_id=1000789841 (accessed March 12, 2009).

17. Fritjof Capra, *The Turning Point: Science, Society and the Rising Culture* (New York: Bantam Books, 1982), 43.

Chapter 7: Myth-Perception Three: It's in Your Genes

1. O. T. Avery, C. M. MacLeod, M. McCarty, "Studies on the Chemical Nature of the Substance Inducing Transformation of Pneumococcal Types: Induction of Transformation by a Desoxyribonucleic Acid Fraction Isolated from Pneumococcus Type III," *The Journal of Experimental Medicine*, no. 79 (1944): 137–156.

2. Erwin Schrodinger, *What is Life?*, (Cambridge, UK: Cambridge University Press, 1945), 76–85.

3. F. H. C. Crick, "On Protein Synthesis," *Symposia of the Society for Experimental Biology: The Biological Replication of Macromolecules* 12, (Cambridge, UK: Cambridge University Press, 1958), 138–162.

4. Howard M. Temin, "Homology between RNA From Rous Sarcoma Virus and DNA from Rous Sarcoma Virus-infected Cells," *Proceedings of the National Academy of Sciences* 52, (1964): 323–329.

5. H. F. Nijhout, "Metaphors and the Role of Genes in Development," *BioEssays* 12, no. 9 (1990): 441–446.

6. Richard Dawkins, *The Selfish Gene*, (New York: Oxford University Press, 1976).

7. Ibid., 2–3.

8. Svante Pääbo, "Genomics and Society: The Human Genome and Our View of Ourselves," *Science* 291, no. 5507 (16 February 2001): 1219–1220.

9. E. Pennisi, "Gene Counters Struggle to Get the Right Answer," *Science*, no. 301 (2003): 1040–1041.

10. Silverman, "Rethinking Genetic Determinism: With only 30,000 genes, what is it that makes humans human?" 32–33.

11. Lipton, *The Biology of Belief: Unleashing the Power of Consciousness, Matter and Miracles*, (Santa Rosa, CA: Elite Books, 2005), 49; K. Powell, "Stem-cell niches: It's the ecology, stupid!," *Nature*, no. 435 (2005): 268–270.

12. Robert Sapolsky, "Emergence of a Peaceful Culture in Wild Baboons," *PloS Biology*, April 13, 2004, http://biology.plosjournals. org/perlserv/?request=get-document&doi=10.1371/journal. pbio.0020124&ct=1 (accessed March 12, 2009).

13. Ibid.

14. Frans B. M. de Waal, "Bonobo Sex and Society," *Scientific America* (March, 1995): 82–88.

15. Matt Kaplan, "Why Bonobos Make Love, Not War," *New Scientist* 192, no. 2580 (2 December 2006): 40–43.

16. American Cancer Society, *Cancer Prevention & Early Detection Facts & Figures 2005*, (Atlanta: American Cancer Society, 2005), 1, http://www. cancer.org/downloads/STT/CPED2005v5PWSecured.pdf (accessed March 10, 2009).

17. Capra, *The Turning Point: Science, Society and the Rising Culture* 146.

18. Ibid., 108; Ibid., 115.

19. Lipton, *The Biology of Belief: Unleashing the Power of Consciousness, Matter and Miracles*, (Santa Rosa, CA: Elite Books, 2005), 75–89.

20. Ibid., 123–124.

21. A. A. Mason, "A Case of Congenital Ichthyosiform Erythrodermia of Brocq Treated by Hypnosis," *British Medical Journal* 30, (1952): 442–443.

22. Discovery Channel Production, "Placebo: Mind Over Medicine?"

Chapter 8: Myth-Perception Four: Evolution Is Random

1. Ben Waggoner, "Jean-Baptiste Lamarck (1744–1829)," *University of California Museum of Paleontology*, Feb. 25, 1996, www.ucmp.berkeley.edu/ history/lamarck.html (accessed March 5, 2009).

2. Freeman G. Henry, "Rue Cuvier, rue Geoffroy-Saint-Hilaire, rue Lamarck: Politics and Science in the Streets of Paris," *Nineteenth Century French Studies* 35, no. 3&4 (2007), http://muse.jhu.edu/journals/nine teenth_century_french_studies/v035/35.3henry.html (accessed March 3, 2009).

3. H. Graham Cannon, *Lamarck and Modern Genetics*, (Westport, CT: Greenwood Press, 1975), 10–11.

4. Isaac Asimov, *Biographical Encyclopedia of Science and Technology,* (Garden City, NY: Doubleday, 1964), 328.

5. S. E. Luria, M. Delbrück, "Mutations of Bacteria from Virus Sensitivity to Virus Resistance," *Genetics* 28, no. 6 (1943): 491–511.

6. John Cairns, J. Overbaugh, S. Miller, "The Origin of Mutants," *Nature*, no. 335 (1988): 142–145.

7. R. Lewin, "A Heresy in Evolutionary Biology," *Science*, no. 241 (1988): 1431.

8. Pierre Simon Laplace, *Théorie Analytique des Probabilités*, 1st edition, (Paris, France: Mme. Ve Courcier, 1812).

9. Tim Appenzeller, "Evolution: Test Tube Evolution Catches Time in a Bottle," *Science* 284, no. 5423 (25 June 1999): 2108.

10. E. N. Lorenz, "Three Approaches to Atmospheric Predictability," *Bulletin of the American Meteriological Society* 50, no. 5 (1969): 345–351.

11. E. N. Lorenz, "Deterministic Nonperiodic Flow," *Journal of Atmospheric Sciences*, no. 20 (1963): 130–141.

12. T. Dantzig, J. Mazur, *Number: The Language of Science*, (New York, NY: Plume, 2007), 141.

13. Iain Couzin, Erica Klarreich, "The Mind of the Swarm," *Science News Online* 170, no. 22, November 25, 2006, 347-49, quoted in The Free Library, http://www.thefreelibrary.com/The+mind+of+the+swarm:+math+explains+how+group+behavior+is+more+than...-a0155569993 (accessed March 12, 2009).

14. Ibid.

Chapter 9: Dysfunction at the Junction

1. Donald L. Bartlett, James Steele, "Monsanto's Harvest of Fear," *Vanity Fair*, May 2008, http://www.vanityfair.com/politics/features/2008/05/monsanto200805 (accessed March 12, 2009).

2. Percy Schmeiser, "Monsanto vs Schmeiser," http://www.percyschmeiser.com/ (accessed March 19, 2009).

3. Bartlett, Steele, "Monsanto's Harvest of Fear," *Vanity Fair*, May 2008,

4. Jeffrey M. Smith, *Seeds of Deception: Exposing Industry and Government Lies About the Safety of the Genetically Engineered Foods You're Eating*, (Fairfield, IA: Yes! Books, 2003), 1.

5. Bartlett, Steele, "Monsanto's Harvest of Fear," *Vanity Fair*, May 2008.

6. Ibid.

7. Morgan Adams, "LaDuke Sows Seeds of Reclamation," *Berea College, BC Now*, March 21, 2007, http://www.berea.edu/BCNow/story.asp?ArticleID=981 (accessed March 15, 2009).

8. A. Andreades, *History of the Bank of England*, (London, UK: P.S. King & Son, 1909), 157, 177, 184. Read online at The Open Library, http://openlibrary.org/b/OL7098867M/History-of-the-Bank-of-England (accessed March 19, 2009).

9. Benjamin Franklin, Liberty-Tree.ca, http://quotes.liberty-tree.ca/quote/benjamin_franklin_quote_8fb0 (accessed March 10, 2009).

10. Stephen Zarlenga, *The Lost Science of Money,* (Chicago, IL: The American Monetary Institute, 2002). 372–375.

11. Hartmann, *Screwed: The Undeclared War Against the Middle Class – And What We Can Do About It,* 100-102.

12. Ibid., 101.

13. Ibid.

14. Ibid., 102.

15. Woodrow Wilson, *The New Freedom: A Call for the Emancipation of the Generous Energies of a People,* (New York: Doubleday, Page & Company, 1918), 201.

16. Michael Hodges, "America's Total Debt Report," *Grandfather Economic Reports,* March 2008, http://www.opednews.com/populum/linkframe. php?linkid=70454 (accessed March 12, 2009).

17. The New Economics Foundation, "Happy Planet Index," *The New Economics Foundation,* http://www.happyplanetindex.org/index.htm (accessed March 12, 2009).

18. Matthew White, "Source List and Detailed Death Tolls for the Twentieth Century Hemoclysm," 1999, http://users.erols.com/mwhite28/warstat1. htm (accessed March 12, 2009).

19. Riane Eisler, *The Chalice and the Blade: Our History, Our Future,* (New York, NY: Harper Collins, 1987, 1995), 17–18.

20. Ibid., 25.

21. Riane Eisler, *The Real Wealth of Nations: Creating a Caring Economics,* (San Francisco, CA: Berrett-Koehler, 2007), 73.

22. The Library of Congress, "The Pinkertons," Today in History: August 25, http://www.memory.loc.gov/ammem/today/aug25.html (accessed March 19, 2009); Charles Siringo, source for, "Telling Secrets Out of School: Siringo on the Pinkertons," *History Matters, City University of New York, George Mason University,* http://historymatters.gmu.edu/d/5312/ (accessed March 19, 2009).

23. Jeremy Brecher, *Strike!: Revised and Updated Edition,*(Cambridge, MA: South End Press, 1997), 22, 47–48, 71–75, 77.

24. Automobile in American Life and Society, "Harry Bennett," University of Michigan, Benson Ford Research Center, http://www.autolife.umd. umich.edu/Design/Gartman/D_Casestudy/Harry_Bennett.htm (accessed March 19, 2009).

25. Smedley D. Butler, *War Is a Racket,* (Los Angeles, CA: Feral House, 1935, 2003), 21.

26. Kevin Phillips, *American Dynasty: Aristocracy, Fortune and the Politics of Deceit in the House of Bush,* (New York, NY: Penguin Books, 2004), 38–39, 190–195.

27. Frank Kofsky, *Harry S. Truman and the War Scare of 1948*, (New York: St. Martin's Press, 1995).

28. Noam Chomsky, *Understanding Power: The Indispensable Chomsky*, (New York: The New Press, 2002), 74.

29. Central Intelligence Agency, "CIA's Analysis of the Soviet Union, 1947-1991," (Please note specific document 4 on possibility of direct Soviet military action in 1949.), https://www.cia.gov/library/center-for-the-study-of-intelligence/csi-publications/books-and-monographs/cias-analysis-of-the-soviet-union-1947-1991/ore_46_49.pdf (accessed March 14, 2009). ORE 46-49, May 1949, Possibility of Direct Soviet Military Action During 1949

30. David Callahan, *Dangerous Capabilities: Paul Nitze and the Cold War*, (New York, NY: Harper-Collins, 1990), 66–67.

31. Ibid., 106–107.

32. Joel Andreas, *Addicted to War: Why the U.S. Can't Kick Militarism*, (Oakland, CA: AK Press, 2004), 44.

33. Amy Goodman, "Confessions of an Economic Hit Man: How the U.S. Uses Globalization to Cheat Poor Countries Out of Trillions," *Democracy Now!*, November 9, 2004, http://www.democracynow.org/2004/11/9/confessions_of_an_economic_hit_man (accessed March 12, 2009).

34. Eckhart Tolle, *A New Earth: Awakening to Your Life's Purpose,*(New York: The Penguin Group U.S.A., 2005), 14.

35. Zlatica Hoke, "U.S. Health Care: World's Most Expensive," *Voice of America*, 28 February 2006, http://www.voanews.com/english/archive/2006-02/2006-02-28-voa59.cfm?CFID=139027910&CFTOKEN=45495346&jsessionid=de308335ce2d9fbab900353h1319746136?c (accessed March 13, 2009).

36. Barbara Starfield, "Is US Health Really the Best in the World?," *Journal of the American Medical Association* 284, no. 4 (July 26, 2000): 483–485.

37. Gary Null, et al, "Death by Medicine," *Life Extension Magazine*, August 1, 2006, http://www.lef.org/magazine/mag2006/aug2006_report_death_01.htm (accessed March 13, 2009).

38. Fritjof Capra, *The Turning Point: Science, Society and the Rising Culture*, (New York: Bantam Books, 1983) 137-38.

39. Jacky Law, *Big Pharma: Exposing the Global Healthcare Agenda*, (New York, NY: Carroll & Graf, 2006), 15

40. Ibid.

41. Catharine Paddock, "47 Million Without Health Insurance, Census Reports," *Medical News Today*, 29 August 2007, http://www.medicalnewstoday.com/articles/80897.php (accessed March 13, 2009).

42. Law, *Big Pharma: Exposing the Global Healthcare Agenda*, 169–175.

43. Melissa Ganz, "The Medicare Prescription Drug, Improvement, & Modernization Act of 2003: Are We Playing The Lottery With Healthcare Reform?," 10/1/2004, *Duke Law & Technology Review,* http://www.law.duke.edu/journals/dltr/articles/2004dltr0011.html (accessed March 19, 2009).

44. Ibid.

45. Marcia Angell, *The Truth About the Drug Companies: How They Deceive Us and What to Do About It by,* (New York, NY: Random House, 2005), 11.

46. Law, *Big Pharma: Exposing the Global Healthcare Agenda,* 14.

47. J Abramson, JM Wright, "Are lipid-lowering guidelines evidence-based?," *The Lancet,* no. 369 (2007): 168–169.

48. R. A. Hayward, et al, "Narrative review: lack of evidence for recommended low-density lipoprotein treatment targets: a solvable problem," *Annals of Internal Medicine,* no. 145 (2006): 520–530.

49. Dean Ornish, et al, "Intensive Lifestyle Changes for Reversal of Coronary Heart Disease," *Journal of the American Medical Association* 280 (1998): 2001–2007.

50. Stephen R. Daniels, Frank R. Greer and the Committee on Nutrition, "Lipid Screening and Cardiovascular Health," *Childhood Pediatrics,* no. 122 (July 2008): 198–208.

51. Law, *Big Pharma: Exposing the Global Healthcare Agenda,* 48.

52. Marilyn Ferguson, *The Aquarian Conspiracy: Personal and Social Transformation in the 1980s,* (Los Angeles, CA: J. P. Tarcher, 1980), 23–43.

53. David Edwards, *Burning All Illusions: A Guide to Personal and Political Freedom,* (Boston, MA: South End Press, 1996), 207.

54. Edward L. Bernays, *Propaganda: with an Introduction by Mark Crispin Miller,* (Brooklyn, NY: Ig Publishing, 2004), 9–15.

55. Ibid., 54

56. Ibid., 71.

57. Ibid., 25.

58. Larry Tye, *The Father of Spin: Edward L. Bernays and the Birth of Public Relations,* (New York, NY: Henry Holt and Company, 1998), 156–170.

59. Jerboa Kolinowski, "Edward L. Bernays," *Everything2,* July 3, 2002, http://everything2.com/title/Edward%2520L.%2520Bernays (accessed March 13, 2009).

60. Ron Chernow, "First Among Flacks, Edward L. Bernays created many a public relations image, starting with his own," August 16, 1998, *New York Times,* http://www.nytimes.com/books/98/08/16/reviews/980816.16chernot.html?_r=1 (accessed March 19, 2009); Tye, *The Father of Spin: Edward L. Bernays and the Birth of Public Relations,* 163–184.

61. Kolinowski, "Edward L. Bernays," *Everything2*, July 3, 2002.

62. Norman Solomon, *War Made Easy: How Presidents and Pundits Keep Spinning Us to Death*, (New Jersey: John Wiley & Sons, 2005), 177.

Chapter 10: Going Sane

1. Erich Fromm, *The Sane Society*, (New York, NY: Henry Holt and Company, 1955), 15.

2. David Edwards, *Burning All Illusions: A Guide to Personal and Political Freedom*, (Boston, MA: South End Press, 1996), 62.

3. Michael Lerner, *The Left Hand of God: Taking Back Our Country From the Religious Right*, (New York, NY: HarperCollins, 2006), 15–36, 41–75.

4. Alan Watts, *The Wisdom of Insecurity*, (New York, NY: Pantheon Books, 1951), 23.

5. Fritjof Capra, *The Tao of Physics: An Exploration of the Parallels between Modern Physics and Eastern Mysticism*, (Boston, MA: Shambhala, 1975), 141.

6. Steve Bhaerman, "Unquestioned Answers: Nonconspiracy Theorist Takes Aim at the Official 9–11 Story," *North Bay Bohemian*, June 14–20, 2006, http://www.bohemian.com/bohemian/06.14.06/david-ray-griffin-0624.html (accessed March 13, 2009).

7. Aura Glaser, *A Call to Compassion: Bringing Buddhist Practices of the Heart into the Soul of Psychology*, (Berwick, ME: Nicholas-Hays, 2005), 11.

8. Braden, *The Divine Matrix: Bridging Time, Space, Miracles, and Belief*, 84–85.

9. Ibid., 87.

10. Glaser, *A Call to Compassion: Bringing Buddhist Practices of the Heart into the Soul of Psychology*, 21.

Chapter 11: Fractal Evolution

1. Matthew R. Walsh, David N. Reznick, "Interactions between the direct and indirect effects of predators determine life history evolution in a killifish," *Proceedings of the National Academy of Sciences*, no. 105 (2008): 594–599.

2. Steven M. Vamosi, "The presence of other fish species affects speciation in threespine sticklebacks," *Evolutionary Ecology Research*, no. 5 (2003): 717–730.

3. Appenzeller, "EVOLUTION: Test Tube Evolution Catches Time in a Bottle," *Science*, Vol. 284, no. 5423 (25 June 1999): 2108.

4. Lipton, *The Biology of Belief: Unleashing the Power of Consciousness, Matter and Miracles*, (Santa Rosa, CA: Elite Books, 2005), 65.

5. Ibid., 197.

6. William Allman, "The Mathematics of Human Life ," *U.S. News & World Report* 114, 1993, 84–85.

7. Eldredge, S.J. Gould, "Punctuated Equilibria: an Alternative to Phyletic Gradualism," In T.M. Schopf, (ed.), *Models in Palaeobiology*, (San Francisco, CA: Freeman Cooper, 1972), 82–115.

8. Christiane Galus, "La sixième extinction des espèces peut encore être évitée," *Le Monde*, 14 August 2008, http://www.lemonde.fr/cgi-bin/ACHATS/acheter.cgi?offre=ARCHIVES&type_item=ART_ARCH_30J&objet_id=1047018&clef=ARC-TRK-D_01, English version, http://www.truthout.org/article/sixth-species-extinction-can-still-be-avoided (accessed March 1, 2009).

9. J. W. Costerton, Philip S. Stewart, E. P. Greenberg, "Bacterial Biofilms: A Common Cause of Persistent Infections," *Science* 284, no. 5418 (21 May 1999): 1318–1322.

10. L. Margulis, *Symbiosis in Cell Evolution*, (New York, NY: W.H. Freeman, 1993).

11. L. Margulis, D. Sagan, *Microcosmos*, (New York, NY: Summit Books, 1986), 14.

12. Buckminster Fuller, *Operating Manual for Spaceship Earth*, (Illinois: Southern Illinois University Press, Reprint of 1969 edition, 1976).

Chapter 12: Time to See a Good Shrink

1. Albert Einstein, quote, to Margot Einstein, after his sister Maja's death, 1951, from Hanna Loewy in A&E Television Einstein Biography, VPI International, 1991, http://www.asl-associates.com/einsteinquotes.htm (accessed March 4, 2009).

2. Arnold J. Toynbee, David C. Somervell, *A Study of History*, (New York: Oxford Press, 1946, 1974), 575–577.

3. Lipton, *The Biology of Belief: Unleashing the Power of Consciousness, Matter and Miracles*, (Santa Rosa, CA: Elite Books, 2005), 146.

4. Ibid., 148-153.

5. Eisler, *The Chalice and the Blade: Our History, Our Future,* (New York, NY: Harper Collins, 1987, 1995), 43.

ENDNOTES

Chapter 13: The One Suggestion

1. R. C. Henry, "The mental Universe," *Nature*, no. 436 (2005): 29.

2. Ibid.

3. Ibid.

4. G. GrinbergZylberbaum, M. Delaflor, L. Attie, A. Goswami, "The EinsteinPodolskyRosen paradox in the brain: the transferred potential," *Physics Essays*, no. 7 (1994): 422–428.

5. Dean Radin, *Entangled Minds: Extrasensory Experiences In a Quantum Reality,* (New York, NY: Paraview Pocket Books, 2006), 164-170.

6. Ibid., 195–202.

7. Ibid., 203.

8. McTaggart, *The Field: The Quest for the Secret Force of the Universe*, 101–109.

9. Russell Targ, Jane Katra, *Miracles of Mind: Exploring Nonlocal Consciousness and Spiritual Healing,* (Novato, CA: New World Library, 1998), 40–44.

10. McTaggart. *The Field: The Quest for the Secret Force of the Universe*, 181–196.

11. Larry Dossey, M.D., *Prayer is Good Medicine,* (New York, NY: HarperCollins, 1996), 55.

12. Braden, *The Divine Matrix: Bridging Time, Space, Miracles, and Belief,* 84.

13. Gregg Braden, *Secrets of the Lost Mode of Prayer: The Hidden Power of Beauty, Blessing, Wisdom and Hurt,* 13–18.

14. Ibid., 167–69.

15. Dossey, M.D., *Prayer is Good Medicine,* 55.

16. Braden, *Secrets of the Lost Mode of Prayer: The Hidden Power of Beauty, Blessing, Wisdom and Hurt,* 168.

17. Doc Childre, Howard Martin, *The HeartMath Solution* (New York, NY: HarperCollins, 1999), 6.

18. Ibid., 10–11.

19. Ibid., 11.

20. Ibid., 13–16.

21. Global Coherence Initiative. To learn more about the Global Coherence Initiative, go here http://www.glcoherence.org/about-us/about.html (accessed March 12, 2009).

22. Braden, *Secrets of the Lost Mode of Prayer: The Hidden Power of Beauty, Blessing, Wisdom and Hurt,* 115–16.

23. "Science, Spirituality and Peace," CommonPassion.org, http://www.commonpassion.org/index.php?option=com_content&task=view&id=44&Itemid=58 (accessed March 13, 2009).

24. The Intention Experiment, http://www.theintentionexperiment.com/ (accessed March 13, 2009).

25. CommonPassion.org, http://www.commonpassion.org/ (accessed March 13, 2009).

26. Ibid.

27. Arjuna Ardagh, *Awakening Into Oneness: The Power of Blessing in the Evolution of Consciousness,* (Boulder, CO: Sounds True, 2007), 135–148.

28. McTaggart. *The Field: The Quest for the Secret Force of the Universe,* 184–85.

29. Targ, Katra, *Miracles of Mind: Exploring Nonlocal Consciousness and Spiritual Healing,* 110.

30. Leonard Laskow, *Healing With Love: A Breakthrough Mind/Body Program for Healing Yourself and Others,* (Mill Valley, CA: Wholeness Press, 1992), 20.

31. Ibid., 20–21.

32. Ibid., 303–307.

33. Ibid., 2.

34. Ibid., 4–10.

35. Ibid., 77.

36. Ibid., 65.

37. "The Universality of the Golden Rule in the World Religions," Teaching Values.com http://www.teachingvalues.com/goldenrule.html (accessed March 13, 2009)

38. Glaser, *A Call to Compassion: Bringing Buddhist Practices of the Heart into the Soul of Psychology,* xi.

39. Ibid.

Chapter 14: A Healthy Commonwealth

1. Chen, Shaohua, Martin, Ravallion, "The Developing World Is Poorer Than We Thought, But No Less Successful in the Fight against Poverty," *World Bank Policy Research Working Paper Series, Social Science Research Network,* August 1, 2008, http://ssrn.com/abstract=1259575 (accessed March 3, 2009).

2. Meg Howe, Graeme Young, "According to Survey Statistics Happiness of Wealthy People is No Greater!," *Small Farm Permaculture and Sustainable Living,* Jan. 5, 2009, http://www.small-farm-permaculture-and-sustain

able-living.com/statistics_happiness_of_wealthy_people.html (accessed March 5, 2009).

3. Charles Walters, *Unforgiven: The American Economic System Sold for Debt and War,* (Austin, TX: Acres, U.S.A., 1971, 2003), 37.

4. Ibid., ix.

5. Ibid., 31.

6. Robert Costanza, et al, "The value of the world's ecosystem services and natural capital," *Nature* 387, (15 May 1997): 253–260.

7. "Living Planet Report 2006 outlines scenarios for humanity's future," Global Footprint Network, http://www.footprintnetwork.org/ newsletters/gfn_blast_0610.html (accessed March 13, 2009).

8. Thomas Jefferson, "Thomas Jefferson on Politics and Government: Money and Banking," *The University of Virginia Archives,* http://etext. virginia.edu/jefferson/quotations/jeff1325.htm (accessed March 14, 2009).

9. Richard Kotlarz, personal interview with Steve Bhaerman, March 14, 2008.

10. Ibid.

11. Thomas Jefferson, quote, *The Quotations Page,* http://www.quotations page.com/quote/37700.html (accessed March 14, 2009).

12. Walters, *Unforgiven: The American Economic System Sold for Debt and War,* 239.

13. David C. Korten, *Agenda for a New Economy: From Phantom Wealth to Real Wealth,* (San Francisco, CA: Berrett-Koehler, 2009), 26.

14. Ibid., 49–50.

15. Ibid., 50.

16. Ibid., 51.

17. Ibid., 53.

18. Stephen Zarlenga, "The 1930s Chicago Plan and the American Monetary Act," *AMI Reform Conference,* October 2005, http://www.monetary. org/chicagoplan.html (accessed March 14, 2009).

19. Ravi Dykema, "An Interview with Bernard Lietaer: Money, Community and Social Change," *Nexus,* July–August, 2003.

20. Ibid.

21. Ibid.

22. James Taris, *Global Quest for Local LETS,* (E-book, 2002), http://www. jamestaris.com/TTW-Contents.htm (accessed March 14, 2009).

23. Civic Economics, "The San Francisco Retail Diversity Study," *Civic Economics,* May, 2007, 1-28, http://www.civiceconomics.com/SF/ (accessed March 14, 2009).

24. Civic Economics, *Economic Impact Analysis: A Case Study, Local Merchants vs. Chain Retailers,* (Austin, TX: Civic Economics, 2002), 1–16. http://www.bigboxtoolkit.com/index.php/Economic-Impact-of-Local-Businesses-vs.-Chains.html (accessed April 15, 2009).

25. "The San Francisco Retail Diversity Study," Studies in Economics, Sonoma County GoLocal Coop, April 2007, http://sonomacounty.golocal.coop/?page_id=61 (accessed March 14, 2009).

26. Kencho Wandi, "Bhutan - where happiness outranks wealth," *Developments,* http://www.developments.org.uk/articles/bhutan-where-happiness-outranks-wealth/ (accessed March 14, 2009).

Chapter 15: Healing the Body Politic

1. Jim Rough, *Society's Breakthrough: Releasing Essential Wisdom and Virtue in All the People,* (Port Townsend, WA: Jim Rough, 2002), 55–56.

2. Solomon, *War Made Easy: How Presidents and Pundits Keep Spinning Us to Death,* 281.

3. Richard Sanders, "Regime Change: How the CIA put Saddam's Party in Power," Coalition to Oppose the Arms Trade Quarterly, Press for Conversion!, 24 October 2002.

4. Malcolm Byrne, "The Secret History of the Iran Coup, 1953," National Security Archive Electronic Briefing Book 28, http://www.gwu.edu/~nsarchiv/NSAEBB/NSAEBB28/ (accessed March 19, 2009).

5. James Surowiecki, *The Wisdom of Crowds,* (New York, NY: Doubleday, 2004), xi–xii.

6. Ibid., xiv.

7. Ibid., 7–11.

8. Ibid., 28.

9. Don Tapscott, Anthony Williams, *Wikinomics: How Mass-Collaboration Changes Everything,* (New York, NY: Penguin Books, 2006), 67.

10. Ibid., 7–10.

11. Surowiecki, *The Wisdom of Crowds,* 140–145.

12. Tom Atlee, *The Tao of Democracy: Using Co-Intelligence to Create a World That Works for All,* (Eugene, OR: World Works Press, 2003), 55.

13. Ibid., 5.

14. Ibid., 107.

15. Ibid., 1.

16. Ibid., 85., Original Source for this reference in Atlee book: Roger Fisher and William Ury, *Getting to Yes: Negotiating Agreements without Giving In* (Boston: Houghton Mifflin Co. 1981)

17. Ibid., 9.

18. Alice Gavin, "Conflict Transformation in the Middle East: Dr. Johan Galtung on Confederation in Iraq and a Middle East Community for Israel/Palestine," Peace Power 2, no. 1, Winter 2006, http://www.calpeace power.org/0201/galtung_transcend.htm (accessed March 14, 2009).

19. Atlee, *The Tao of Democracy: Using Co-Intelligence to Create a World That Works for All,* 182.

20. Aldous Huxley, *Time Must Have A Stop,* (Illinois: Dalkey Archive Press, 1998), 45.

21. Rough, *Society's Breakthrough: Releasing Essential Wisdom and Virtue in All the People,* 11–12.

22. Ibid., 19–38.

23. Atlee, *The Tao of Democracy: Using Co-Intelligence to Create a World That Works for All,* v.

24. Ibid., 24–28.

25. Ibid., 25.

26. Ibid., 28.

27. Ibid., 128–129.

28. Ibid., 233.

29. Ibid., 130–143, 156–157.

30. Anodea Judith, *Waking the Global Heart: Humanity's Rite of Passage From the Love of Power to the Power of Love,* (Santa Rosa, CA: Elite Books, 2006), 18.

31. Richard Flyer, personal interviews by Steve Bhaerman, January 3, 2008 and February 5, 2009; For more information see: Richard Flyer, "Interview With Richard Flyer," The Conscious Media Network, Network, http://www.consciousmedianetwork.com/members/rflyer.htm (accessed March 12, 2009).

32. Ibid.; For more information see: Conscious Community Campaign, http://www.itstimereno.org/ (accessed March 12, 2009).

33. Ibid.

Chapter 16: A Whole New Story

1. Joseph Chilton Pearce, *The Biology of Transcendence: A Blueprint of the Human Spirit,* (Rochester, VT: Park Street Press, 2002), 119.

2. Hermann Goering, quote, ThinkExist.com, http://thinkexist.com/ quota tion/naturally_the_common_people_don-t_want_war/339098. html (accessed March 14, 2009).

3. M. K. Asante, Y. Miike, J. Yin, editors, *The Global Intercultural Communication Reader*, (New York, NY: Routledge, 2007), 114–117.

4. Nelson Mandela, "1993 Address to the Nation," *Black Past.Org*,http://www.blackpast.org/?q=1993-nelson-mandela-address-nation (accessed March 19, 2009).

5. Luskin, *Forgive For Good: A Proven Prescription for Health and Happiness*, 89–101.

6. Kathryn Watterson, *Not by the Sword: How a Cantor and His Wife Transformed a Klansman*, (Boston, MA: Northeastern University, 2001).

7. Ervin Laszlo, Jude Currivan, *CosMos: A Co-Creator's Guide to the Whole World*, (Carlsbad, CA: Hay House, 2008), 93.

8. Marci Shimoff, *Happy for No Reason: 7 Steps to Being Happy From the Inside Out*, (New York, NY: Simon & Schuster, 2008), 40.

9. Ibid., 21.

10. Ibid., 151.

11. Kiyoshi Nakahara and Yasushi Miyashita, "Understanding Intentions: Through the Looking Glass," *Science* 308, (2005): 644–645.

12. Martin Seligman, *Learned Optimism: How to Change Your Mind and Your Life*, (New York, NY: Pocketbooks, 1998).

13. Shimoff, *Happy for No Reason: 7 Steps to Being Happy From the Inside Out*, 125.

14. Glynda-Lee Hoffman, *The Secret Dowry of Eve: Women's Role in the Development of Consciousness*, (Rochester, VT: Park Street Press, 2003), 16.

15. Alexander S. Kochkin, Patricia M. Van Camp, *A New America: An Awakened Future on Our Horizon* (Stevensville, MT: Global Awakening Press, 2000-2005), 7–11.

INDEX

ABOUT THE AUTHORS

Bruce H. Lipton, Ph.D., is an internationally recognized authority in bridging science and spirit and a leading voice in new biology. A cell biologist by training, he taught at the University of Wisconsin's School of Medicine, and later performed pioneering studies at Stanford University. Author of *The Biology of Belief*, he has been a guest speaker on hundreds of TV and radio shows, as well as keynote presenter for national and international conferences.

Steve Bhaerman is an author, humorist, and political and cultural commentator, who's been writing and performing enlightening comedy as Swami Beyondananda for over 20 years. A pioneer in alternative education and holistic publications, Steve is active in transpartisan politics and the practical application of Spontaneous Evolution.

HAY HOUSE TITLES OF RELATED INTEREST

***YOU CAN HEAL YOUR LIFE*, the movie,**
starring Louise L. Hay & Friends
(available as a 1-DVD program and an expanded 2-DVD set)
Watch the trailer at: **www.LouiseHayMovie.com**

***THE SHIFT*, the movie,**
starring Dr. Wayne W. Dyer
(available as a 1-DVD program and an expanded 2-DVD set)
Watch the trailer at: **www.DyerMovie.com**

CHANGE YOUR THOUGHTS—CHANGE YOUR LIFE:
Living the Wisdom of the Tao
by Dr. Wayne W. Dyer

THE DIVINE MATRIX: Bridging Time,
Space, Miracles, and Belief
by Gregg Braden

THE SPONTANEOUS HEALING OF BELIEF:
Shattering the Paradigm of False Limits
by Gregg Braden

VIRUS OF THE MIND: The New Science of the Meme
by Richard Brodie

All of the above are available at your local bookstore,
or may be ordered by contacting Hay House (see next page).

We hope you enjoyed this Hay House book.
If you'd like to receive our online catalog featuring
additional information on Hay House books and products, or
if you'd like to find out more about the
Hay Foundation, please contact:

Hay House, Inc.
P.O. Box 5100
Carlsbad, CA 92018-5100

(760) 431-7695 or **(800) 654-5126**
(760) 431-6948 (fax) or **(800) 650-5115 (fax)**
www.hayhouse.com® • **www.hayfoundation.org**

Published and distributed in Australia by:
Hay House Australia Pty. Ltd., 18/36 Ralph St., Alexandria NSW 2015
Phone: 612-9669-4299 • *Fax:* 612-9669-4144 • www.hayhouse.com.au

Published and distributed in the United Kingdom by:
Hay House UK, Ltd., 292B Kensal Rd., London W10 5BE
Phone: 44-20-8962-1230 • *Fax:* 44-20-8962-1239 • www.hayhouse.co.uk

Published and distributed in the Republic of South Africa by:
Hay House SA (Pty), Ltd., P.O. Box 990, Witkoppen 2068
Phone/Fax: 27-11-467-8904 • info@hayhouse.co.za • www.hayhouse.co.za

Published in India by: Hay House Publishers India, Muskaan Complex,
Plot No. 3, B-2, Vasant Kunj, New Delhi 110 070 • *Phone:* 91-11-4176-1620
Fax: 91-11-4176-1630 • www.hayhouse.co.in

Distributed in Canada by: Raincoast, 9050 Shaughnessy St., Vancouver, B.C.
V6P 6E5 • *Phone:* (604) 323-7100 • *Fax:* (604) 323-2600 • www.raincoast.com

Take Your Soul on a Vacation

Visit **www.HealYourLife.com®** to regroup, recharge, and
reconnect with your own magnificence. Featuring blogs, mind-body-spirit
news, and life-changing wisdom from Louise Hay and friends.

Visit **www.HealYourLife.com** today!